DATE DUE

DEMCO 38-296

D1603972

A Nationality of Her Own

R

A Nationality of Her Own

Women, Marriage, and the Law of Citizenship

Candice Lewis Bredbenner

UNIVERSITY OF CALIFORNIA PRESS

Berkeley / Los Angeles / London

University of California Press
Berkeley and Los Angeles, California

University of California Press, Ltd.
London, England

© 1998 by
The Regents of the University of California

Library of Congress Cataloging-in-Publication Data

Bredbenner, Candice Lewis, 1955–
    A nationality of her own : women, marriage, and the law of
citizenship / Candice Lewis Bredbenner.
       p.   cm.
    Includes bibliographical references and index.
    ISBN 0-520-20650-9 (cloth : alk. paper)
       1. Married women—United States—Nationality—History.
    2. Citizenship—United States—History.   I. Title.
KF4720.W6B74   1998
342.73′083—dc21

97-20734
CIP

Printed in the United States of America
9 8 7 6 5 4 3 2 1

The paper used in this publication is both acid-free and totally
chlorine-free. It meets the minimum requirements of American
Standards for Information Sciences—Permanence of Paper for
Printed Library Materials, ANSI Z39.48–1984.

In memory of Irene Howard Watson
1911–1991

I have my stars in the sky
But Oh the unlit lamps in my house!

—Rabindranath Tagore

Contents

Acknowledgments

When people ask me how long I have worked on this project, I need only mention that my research notes are on 3x5 file cards, not computer disks. The history of this project is a long one, and an important element of that history is the valued contributions I am pleased to acknowledge here. First, I wish to thank William Harbaugh for his willingness to assume the direction of this project in its earlier form as dissertation. I relied on his firm guidance, forbearance, supreme professionalism, and good humor then, and subsequent experience has ripened my appreciation of his skillful mentoring. I wish to thank others who heroically read all or part of one of the much lengthier versions of this manuscript. The friendly criticism of Charles McCurdy, Cindy Aron, David A. Martin, Sara Piccini, Wayne Terwilliger, Dottie Broaddus, Emily Cutrer, and Phil Merkel inspired several improvements in the substance and organization of this book.

The generous assistance of the research consultants and reference staffs at the various libraries and archives I visited was invaluable. Peggy Holly of Alderman Library at the University of Virginia and John Spencer, Elizabeth Smith, and Dennis Isbell of Fletcher Library at Arizona State University West all cheerfully accepted my seemingly endless requests for interlibrary loan materials, even when it meant searching for the obscure. And Walter Newsome, Government Documents' librarian at Alderman, generously provided long-distance assistance. The archivists at the Judicial and Fiscal Records Branch of the National Archives offered their expertise in plotting the course of my investigations. The staffs of the YIVO Institute for Jewish Research, California State Archives, and Bentley Library at the University of Michigan ensured the success of brief research trips that placed high demands on my use of time. I also wish to thank Rabbi Moshe Kolodny at the Agudath Israel Archives for allowing me to look at the papers of Bella Roiter-Nyclich. I particularly wish to express my gratitude to the Schlesinger Library for its contribution to this project and for staff members who made my weeks there one of the highlights of my travels. I am also very grateful to Arizona State University and my department for a grant and travel funds to support the final stage of my research.

Special thanks to my editor at the University of California Press, Monica McCormick, for her interest in this project, her professionalism, and her willingness to expedite the publication process at a critical stage. I also wish to thank Rose Anne White and Pamela Fischer for their editorial support and patient consideration of my inquiries and concerns. The assistance of Laurie Goldberg, Michael I. Smith, and Kathy Franklin freed me from certain of the more tedious aspects of research and manuscript preparation. Their diligence, meticulousness, and amiability regardless of the task made working with them a pleasure.

Several friends and colleagues also assisted with the completion of this project in ways that they might not fully realize or that I cannot express adequately here, but their encouragement and enthusiasm are deeply appreciated. Thanks to Manny Avalos, Sara Gutierres, Cindy Kierner, Richard Hamm, Ellen Litwicki, and Rich Fiesta, who have always been ready to congratulate, commiserate, cajole, and advise.

My family always afforded a respite from academic life that reenergized me. My parents, who have provided examples of unwavering faith and compassion, have always attached to my endeavors a measure of confidence and optimism that I sometimes have not equaled. Those readers who share with me the blessings of sisters know that those siblings who as teenagers managed to distinguish themselves as your most candid critics often stand as adults among your most enthusiastic supporters. And so, Melody and Tami, in overdue recognition of your displays of sisterly devotion, I declare that I will hereafter refrain from any further accusing references to the mysterious disappearance of certain Girl Scout cookies twenty-odd years ago.

And, finally, I dedicate this book to the memory of Irene Watson, who offered me the opportunity to discover the unanticipated richness of a friendship that links generations.

I am grateful to the editor of *Cañon* for permission to use in revised form portions of "Defining the Woman Citizen: Marriage as a Measure of Feminine Patriotism," *Cañon* 1 (Spring 1994): 29–39, copyright 1994, American Studies Program, Arizona State University West; and to Harvard University Press for permission to reprint the quotation from Judith Shklar, *American Citizenship*, copyright 1991 by the President and Fellows of Harvard College.

Introduction

There is no notion more central in politics than citizenship, and none more variable in history, or contested in theory. In America it has in principle always been democratic, but only in principle.

—Judith Shklar, *American Citizenship*

The year 1931 marked another wrenching upheaval in Lillian Larch's already disordered life. Her latest crisis had begun to unfold when the unskilled, unemployed, and recently widowed Larch sought public assistance for her family of five. Her application for aid from the Detroit Department of Public Welfare did not produce the desired lifeline; instead, Larch's plea for help earmarked her and three of her children as deportable aliens. The federal government gave Lillian Larch only one day to prepare for her family's removal to Ontario, where she could claim no friends, relatives, or job. The deportation of immigrants as public charges certainly was not an uncommon occurrence, particularly during the Depression years, and Larch's expulsion from the United States as an undesirable alien might have remained unpublicized if a rather singular fact about the case had not seized the attention of woman's rights groups. Lillian Larch had been, by birth, a citizen of the United States.

Ethel Coope's marriage to the popular Scottish tenor Mackenzie Gordon (a.k.a. Gordon Mackenzie) had added the gilt of novelty to her place within the fashionable circles of San Francisco. Socially, Ethel

Mackenzie was well placed in her community; but in political terms she was impoverished. Mackenzie had earned a reputation as one of California's model club women, and as a member of the Club Woman's Franchise League she had participated actively in her native state's voter-registration drive. But when California women finally received the ballot in 1911, Mackenzie was unable to vote. Four years later the suffragist was fighting her disfranchisement in the U.S. Supreme Court.

Ethel Mackenzie and Lillian Larch occupied dramatically different worlds. Yet, despite the social chasm separating their lives, the two women shared a personal predicament of national consequence. When Mackenzie's legal counsel went before the country's highest court, he represented a woman who had been denied more than a ballot. The federal government had shorn Ethel Mackenzie of her citizenship. If Mackenzie had won the case against her involuntary expatriation, the decision would also have saved Lillian Larch from deportation fifteen years later. Larch and Mackenzie's link to one another—and to many other women in the United States—was their commission of an act that the federal government had transformed into a politically costly one. Larch and Mackenzie had married foreigners, and the penalty for that decision was forfeiture of their American citizenship.

This book is about the Lillian Larchs and the Ethel Mackenzies, as well as the countless immigrant women who were involuntarily divested of their citizenship by laws that demanded that a married woman assume her husband's nationality. It is also about the women and men who worked diligently for decades to abolish these rules and similar discriminatory policies threaded through the country's immigration and nationality laws. At every step, nationality-rights reformers encountered stiff resistance to their proposed changes in the law—changes that challenged the traditional distribution of power and privilege within marriage and among citizens and threatened to disrupt the operation of more recently minted policies relating to immigration and naturalization control.

The barriers to equal nationality rights eventually collapsed one by one under the weight of public opinion and the hammering assaults of feminists, and historians' recovery of the story of the crusade for women's nationality rights has also been slow and piecemeal. The history of married women's loss and restoration of their ability to hold an independent citizenship has been sparely noted in the last half of the twentieth century, an unfortunate pattern of neglect initially established by the omission of the subject from most studies of the country's woman suffrage movement. Scholars' subsequent interest in the struggle over an equal rights amendment and in interwar feminist politics generally, however, finally began to yield some fragments of the story.[1] J. Stanley Lemons first rescued the subject of women's nationality rights from three decades of obscurity with his exploration of the events leading to the passage of the Married Women's Independent Citizenship Act (Cable Act) in 1922. About ten years later, Virginia Sapiro offered valuable insights on the critical years of the crusade in an article that has since served many scholars as the standard reference work on the Cable Act.[2] This study builds on that small but solid foundation of scholarship in order to restore the issue of independent and voluntary citizenship to its original visibility and prominence in the interwar reform record of female activists.

For organized women of the pre-World War II era the phrase *independent citizenship* held meanings both general and specific. It could refer broadly to the comprehensive achievement of equal citizenship rights for women, but by the 1920s and 1930s female activists usually assigned this expression to a particular reform objective: the abolition of marital expatriation and naturalization. The women who participated in a large or small way in this reform movement became involved for various reasons. For some participants, the commitment sprang from strictly personal concerns about the loss of their premarital citizenship or the immigration status of a noncitizen spouse or child; but for the majority of women most visible in the campaign, the dedication to independent citizenship was more self-consciously ideological. Lemons's assumption that the campaign's postsuffrage participants acknowledged this cause to be "an unambiguous feminist issue" can be broadly applied—but only to the "ideological" group, which was composed largely of women who were not political novices but veterans of the suffrage campaign. Yet, even this collection of seasoned activists, many of whom would dedicate decades to the achievement of inde-

1. Susan D. Becker, *The Origins of the Equal Rights Amendment: American Feminism between the Wars* (Westport, Conn.: Greenwood Press, 1981); Christine Lunardini, *From Equal Suffrage to Equal Rights: Alice Paul and the National Woman's Party, 1913–1928* (New York: New York University Press, 1986); Nancy F. Cott, *The Grounding of Modern Feminism* (New Haven, Conn.: Yale University Press, 1987).

2. J. Stanley Lemons, *The Woman Citizen. Social Feminism in the 1920s* (Urbana: University of Illinois Press, 1973); Virginia Sapiro, "Women, Citizenship, and Nationality: Immigration and Naturalization Policies in the United States," *Politics and Society* 13, no. 1 (1984): 1–26.

pendent citizenship for women, never reached a shared understanding of the ideological frame of their work. The well-orchestrated drive for married women's independent citizenship provided an excellent theater for viewing both the common concerns that held woman's rights advocates together, however loosely, and the entrenched conceptual differences that fueled their rivalries.

The crusade for equal nationality rights began in the spring of 1907, induced by an unanticipated legislative development that woman's rights proponents viewed as more ominous and destructive than their exclusion from the polls. Congress had declared that "any American woman who marries a foreigner shall take the nationality of her husband," and on March 2 the federal government summarily denationalized and denaturalized thousands of American women for marrying foreign citizens. There were no exceptions to this rule. Choice of a spouse was the overriding legislative determinant of a married woman's citizenship, and assuming her husband's nationality was an unwritten part of a woman's nuptial contract.[3]

Although the 1907 statute provided the political spark necessary to ignite American feminists' interest in challenging derivative citizenship for women, this law did not mark the statutory introduction of the practice. The story of women's loss of nationality rights began in the 1850s, when the woman's rights movement was in its infancy, anti-immigrant oratory could boost the popularity of a politician running in Congressional elections, and the Know-Nothing Party attained short-lived prominence on a platform endorsing the restriction of voting privileges and office holding to the native-born. Yet in 1855, members of Congress appeared to check their distrust of aliens long enough to present foreign women with the gift of citizenship if they married American men. This naturalization policy operated quietly until the 1907 expatriation law awakened woman's rights advocates to some of

---

3. Birth statistics can provide some evidence of the level of intermarriage between citizen women and noncitizen men. The proportion of white children born in 1920 to a native-born mother and a foreign father was almost eighty-nine per thousand. All those mothers, of course, had lost their citizenship under the 1907 Expatriation Act. The number of white children born to native-born fathers and foreign-born mothers was significantly higher, almost 140 per thousand. See Table 106 in U.S. Department of Commerce, Bureau of the Census, Niles Carpenter, *Immigrants and Their Children. 1920. A Study Based on Census Statistics Relative to the Foreign Born and the Native White of Foreign or Mixed Parentage.* Census Monograph 7 (Washington, D.C.: G.P.O., 1927).

the harsher implications of dependent citizenship.[4] Thereafter, these two complementary and equally discriminatory nationality laws became the targets of numerous repeal bills carrying the endorsement of major women's political organizations.

Section 3 of the Expatriation Act of 1907 represented a stunning setback in women's progression toward full citizenship rights. The federal government had sent a deeply unsettling message to woman's rights reformers then struggling to secure voting privileges for their sex. One of the most basic of pro-suffrage arguments was that American women deserved the vote because they were citizens—independent citizens; but the Expatriation Act of 1907 seriously undercut the validity of that assumption by proclaiming that married American women derived their status as citizens from other Americans—that is, from the men they wed. The loss of an independent nationality within marriage deprived women's achievement of suffrage of some of its symbolic promise. Despite this extension of their political power and the vitality of their public activities, federal nationality law still denied a majority of women recognition as autonomous citizens.

The common law doctrine of coverture had begun its slow demise in the states decades earlier, but the laws forbidding a married woman to maintain an independent nationality appeared to be a statutory reassertion of the single-identity theory of marriage. The 1907 law was incompatible with prevailing trends in the legislating of woman's rights, but its timing had been determined by another, more powerful legal current—one in which individual rights were more often lost than gained. Each year of the new century had seen a rise in the level of immigration to the United States, and in 1907 the number of immigrants entering the country peaked at the unprecedented high of 1,285,349. Government statistics also revealed that an increasing percentage of these new arrivals were so-called new immigrants from eastern and southern Europe. This situation, which many private citizens and members of Congress declared a fearsome threat to the country's cultural and economic well-being, produced a series of statutes de-

---

4. The public antagonism toward foreigners only emphasized lawmakers' dismissal of immigrant women's potential as a political force. The Act of Feb. 10, 1855, declared that "any woman who is now or may hereafter be married to a citizen of the United States, and who might herself be lawfully naturalized, shall be deemed a citizen." Sect. 1994, Revised Statutes of the U.S. (1878).

signed to reduce not only the volume of arriving immigrants but the number of foreign-born residents who could become and remain U.S. citizens. The Expatriation Act of 1907 was one of these legislative responses to anxiety about immigration.

The 1907 statute that marked the citizen woman with a foreign spouse as a discardable American was situated within a small cluster of nationality statutes enacted in the early decades of the twentieth century to denaturalize or denationalize individuals whom the federal government judged had voluntarily forsaken their allegiance to the United States. In this political culture, coarsened by the nativist-tinged rhetoric of "100 percent Americanism," a citizen woman's marriage to a foreigner became vulnerable to interpretation as a brazenly un-American act and to the apposite punishment of expatriation. The federal government casually but emphatically declared that this "prodigal daughter" had voluntarily forfeited her citizenship.

"This law is in direct conflict with the Constitution," one legal expert had exclaimed in protest. "It is in direct conflict with the judgements of the Supreme Court." But, he added assuringly, "should it come up for review . . . [it] will undoubtedly be so held."[5] Eight years later the Supreme Court did deliver its opinion on the matter, unanimously affirming the constitutionality of marital expatriation. The women directly affected by the new expatriation rules were not, however, bereft of influential defenders. Woman's rights groups quickly rallied to restore the marital expatriate's legal status as citizen and her civic standing as loyal American. Determined to regain the political ground on which their argument for voting rights and full citizenship had once securely rested, woman's rights organizations repeatedly urged Congress to repeal its declaration of married women's political dependence before the ratification of the Anthony (Nineteenth) Amendment.

The woman suffrage campaign had easily accommodated the cause of independent citizenship, but the tandem achievement of these two major reform goals proved much more difficult to direct. Woman's rights activists believed that women's recovery of equal nationality rights was critical to full legitimation of their impending enfranchisement, but suffragists were unsuccessful in their attempts to repeal the country's marital expatriation and naturalization laws. After the ratification of the Anthony Amendment in 1920, however, equal national-

5. [C. A. Hereshoff Bartlett], "Women's Expatriation by Marriage," *Albany Law Journal* 70 (1908): 176–181.

ity rights survived as an independent cause robust enough to preserve the broad base of support it had inherited from the suffrage campaign. At the same time Congress proved more willing to consider revising the country's nationality laws once citizen women were constitutionally enfranchised nationwide, and the Supreme Court seemed promisingly acquiescent to the legislature's judgment in immigration and nationality matters.

In 1922 the federal government finally began a laborious retreat from derivative citizenship with the passage of the Cable Act, a law that would thereafter serve as the centerpiece of the national debate over a married woman's nationality rights. The Cable Act's preamble guaranteed that a woman's right to become a naturalized citizen would not be abridged because of her sex or marital status, but the specifics of the law betrayed this promise. Over the course of the next fifteen years, women's organizations lobbied ceaselessly and successfully for the repeal or revision of every discriminatory provision in the original law, but their task rarely seemed to grow easier. Each new proposed alteration in policy was often more controversial than the one preceding.

The forcefulness of organized women's domestic challenge to marital expatriation, as well as reform pressures abroad, would eventually convince the federal government to abolish all gender-based double standards in the country's nationality laws, and in 1934 the United States signed a Pan-American Union treaty committed to that goal. The contest for this final achievement, however, split the domestic nationality-reform coalition irreparably. The treaty appeared to be an expeditious solution to the persistent problem of women's dependent citizenship, but its introduction triggered a serious internal upheaval in the nationality-rights movement. The leaders of the National Woman's Party (NWP) and other equalitarian feminists promoted the treaty with an enthusiasm rivaled in intensity only by the protests from a large faction within the independent-citizenship campaign that deeply resented the proposal.

Predictably, the organizational and philosophical divisions that emerged within the nationality-rights crusade in the 1930s seemed to trace the fault lines defined earlier by the debate over an equal rights amendment. Yet, even though the lines drawn between the participating women's organizations were familiar ones, the reasons for and circumstances of their formation were not entirely identical. In both cases, conflict highlighted a struggle between different philosophies of reform. While one side urged a sweeping rights-based solution to sex discrimination, the other protested that such efforts sometimes generated proposals offering only hollow assurances of economic security and disturbing social consequences. However, unlike those advocating for an equal rights amendment, nationality-rights reformers never disagreed over the necessity of abolishing any policy that discriminated against women's maintenance of U.S. citizenship.

The crusade for equal nationality rights flourished despite the fact that some of the most powerful and dedicated contributors to this reform work were antagonists in the bitter confrontation over an equal rights amendment. The leaders of the National League of Women Voters (NLWV) and the National Woman's Party jointly directed an impressive assemblage of national women's organizations determined to restore independent citizenship to American women, but on another front they and their allies were battling one another fiercely over the merits of a Constitutional amendment mandating absolute legal equality between the sexes.[6] Until its closing years, the nationality-rights crusade appeared unencumbered by the debate over the equal rights amendment. Inevitably, that detachment ended, but nevertheless the years marking the fragmentation of the nationality-rights coalition yielded some of the reformers' most impressive triumphs.

Tracing the origins and development of the nationality-rights crusade requires an examination of its interplay with other reform enterprises: the woman suffrage movement, the quest for an equal rights amendment in the 1920s and 1930s, and the drive for restrictive immigration and naturalization legislation. Feminists' efforts to secure the vote and an equal rights amendment influenced the progress and personality of the nationality-rights campaign, but the significance of that highly organized effort to end derivative citizenship has been obscured rather than enhanced by its proximity to these other causes.[7] Such neglect has encouraged the retrospective judgment that, given organized women's rather slim record of federal legislative victories beyond the

6. The National League of Women Voters was the official name of the organization until 1946, when it dropped "National."

7. In 1978, Ellen Carol DuBois made a similar critical observation about the woman suffrage movement. "Suffragism," she wrote, "has not been accorded the historic recognition it deserves, largely because woman suffrage has too frequently been regarded as an isolated institutional reform. Its character as a social movement, reflecting women's aspirations for and progress toward radical change in their lives, has been overlooked." *Feminism and Suffrage. The Emergence of an Independent Women's Movement in America, 1848–1869* (Ithaca, N.Y.: Cornell University Press, 1978), 17.

Sheppard-Towner Act of 1921, the value of studying the interwar period rests primarily with its intellectual contributions to modern feminism. This study does not dispute but reaffirms the value of that ideological offering. At the same time, drawing the campaign for women's nationality rights in much fuller detail urges some upward adjustment in the marks historians have generally assigned to interwar feminists' reform record.

As noted earlier, the passage of the Expatriation Act of 1907 was, in part, fueled by growing public apprehension over the cultural, political, and economic consequences of rising immigration numbers. As gaining permanent entry into the United States became more complex and constrained, so did the process of becoming and remaining an American citizen. After the ratification of the Nineteenth Amendment the concerns that had produced new controls on immigration and naturalization now induced Congress to retreat from its unqualified support of derivative citizenship for immigrant women. Although the constitutional enfranchisement of women did not immediately erase resentment toward American women with foreign spouses, it did prompt Congressional deliberations on the wisdom of automatically naturalizing foreign women upon their marriage to Americans.

For decades the federal government had touted the derivative naturalization of married women as a policy that promoted "family unity" and the assimilation of female immigrants; but now the immigrant wife who had been naturalized by marriage could vote. Her acquisition of citizenship had become a more overtly political and verifiable achievement, and this new reality prompted Congress to abruptly retreat from the practice of marital naturalization in 1922. The foreign-born woman, the woman Congress had been wont to treat dismissively as a political cipher and to nonchalantly naturalize through marriage, had now gained a formal political voice—one the federal government did not wish to hear unless assured that the speaker was sufficiently "Americanized." Marital naturalization, then, was not simply a casualty of veteran suffragists' efforts to end derivative citizenship for women. It was a reform idea fed by a multitude of diatribes on the perils of immigration and the tepid loyalty of naturalized Americans. And as this study reveals, the connection between nationality law and woman's rights did not end with the Cable Act's abolition of marital naturalization.

The history of women's pursuit of independent citizenship is woven intricately into the chronicles of immigration reform. Although scholars have carefully scrutinized the development of immigration policies that ranked and rejected immigrants based on their race or national origin, the recognition that gender was also a very well-developed category of legal discrimination has been largely absent for decades from historical studies of interwar immigration policies. Yet, a married woman's ability to enter and remain in the United States relied heavily on her husband's prospects for citizenship and residency. Demonstrating the broad impact of this feature of immigration policy here will I hope generate increased interest in studying the experiences of foreign-born women as they negotiated the transition from nonresident alien to immigrant and, finally, to citizen.

An examination of the nationality-rights crusade also adds symmetrically to scholars' analysis of feminist politics in the interwar period. While the interwar debate over an equal rights amendment has allowed historians to study female reformers locked in intense debate, the pre-1930s nationality-rights campaign provides an opportunity to examine this corps of organized women in profitable collaboration. At the same time, the closing years of the campaign for equal nationality rights did bring into sharp focus some fundamental divergences in thought among that generation of politicized women. Studying the pursuit of woman's rights in the context of the independent-citizenship campaign presents an opportunity for us to expand our awareness of these differences beyond those placed in the foreground by the conflict over an equal rights amendment. The demands of the nationality-rights campaign contributed to that less forcefully tendered yet nonetheless critical exploration by female reformers of the integration of their identities as postsuffrage feminists and citizens and the impact of that fusion of responsibilities and convictions on their public lives.

In its advanced stages the woman suffrage movement might have presented such a receptive environment for women's articulation of a philosophy of reform faithful to that duplex identity, but in reality the final years of the national campaign for the ballot demanded less rather than more from its participants intellectually. But after devoting much of their last decade as suffragists promoting arguments designed to convince the American public that woman suffrage was not only a respectable middle-class reform but a patriotic imperative, the veterans of the crusade were able to turn more of their attention inward to contemplate the ideological fundamentals of their activism. And once the Anthony Amendment was a reality, the lingering problem of married women's derivative citizenship could emerge from suffrage's shadow as a shaping force in American feminists' interwar deliberations over what constituted for them a purposive public life.

As Nancy Cott observed, "What historians have seen as the demise of feminism in the 1920s was, more accurately, the end of the suffrage movement and the early struggle of modern feminism."[8] Certainly one aspect of this postsuffrage encounter was the search for answers to the now less avoidable question of how the demands of feminism and citizenship interacted to define the reform commitments of the feminist citizen. The resulting debates over the precepts of feminism and American citizenship highlighted a fundamental tension between the ideals of liberalism and republicanism as adapted and expounded by reform women. On one side of the divide stood equalitarian feminists—the promoters of an equal rights amendment, an equal-nationality treaty, and a boldly individualistic paradigm of citizenship. For these women citizenship was, fundamentally, defined by the rights it conferred. American citizenship was most valuable not because it secured membership in a superior cultural or political order (as Americanizers of the era would arrogantly argue) but because it secured the means to demand the fullest enjoyment of the rights and privileges one's country granted.

Other activist women in the nationality-rights campaign, many of whom considered themselves feminists, could not subscribe fully to this view and the reform philosophy assigned to it. They were more self-consciously American and believed passionately that the status of American citizen presumed membership in, and thus public obligations to, a unique national community. Their perspective on citizenship was more nationalistic in spirit and more society-centered than individual-focused.[9] For these women, disinterest rather than self-interest ideally defined the model citizen's activism. They emphatically agreed with equalitarians that the woman citizen must be politically independent and influential, but the reason for securing her autonomy was not only

8. Cott, *The Grounding of Modern Feminism*, 10.

9. Some scholars have described classical republicanism as more "feminine" in perspective than liberalism, with its emphasis on individualism. See, for example, Suzanna Sherry, "Civic Virtue and the Feminine Voice in Constitutional Adjudication," *Virginia Law Review* 72 (Apr. 1986), 543–616. Rogers M. Smith does not attempt to draw such a distinction but rather explores the contributions of both discourses to the subordination of women in " 'One United People': Second-Class Female Citizenship and the American Quest for Community," *Yale Journal of Law & the Humanities* 1 (May 1989): 229–293.

the expansion of her individual rights but the enhancement of her civic contributions.[10]

Those reformers within the nationality-rights movement who adopted a more communitarian perspective when articulating their views on the relationship between feminism and citizenship accused the NWP of promoting a feminist vision unanchored to the tenets of responsible citizenship. The crusade for equal nationality rights was for these women an unmistakably feminist effort to unburden the laws of nationality and immigration of their gender bias, but it was also a determined struggle for the recognition and security of women's public value and responsibilities as American citizens. The Expatriation Act of 1907 had been a sobering reminder to organized women that the federal government considered women disposable citizens. And in an era when being an alien in the United States was becoming an increasingly vulnerable status and expatriation and naturalization laws gauged a woman's character by her choice of a spouse, the need to secure the citizen woman's public recognition as a political and cultural asset to her country became critical.

The enactment of the Expatriation Act of 1907 also finally forced the advocates of woman's rights to confront the perils of privatizing female citizenship. By the early national period the ideology of "republican motherhood" had already linked a woman's value as an American citizen to her familial responsibilities—specifically the civic education of her children. Although the notion of a truly public woman was foreign to the political culture, the woman citizen could carve out alternative niches of influence by endowing her private duties with public significance. Thus, her commitment to her family's welfare and her patriotism could be conflated. The republican mother was the private mother cast as public servant, a role that required no real expansion of her formal political rights.[11]

When women began to organize for the vote, they were able to adapt the ideology of republican motherhood to promote their cause. Never-

10. As Sherry has noted (in a different context), "Individualists and communitarians may be expected to protest infringement of individual rights that protect against diminution or exclusion from community membership." "Civic Virtue and the Feminine Voice in Constitutional Adjudication," 592–593. The observation certainly applies to the movement for the recovery of women's independent citizenship.

11. Linda Kerber illuminated this concept of female citizenship in *Women of the Republic. Intellect and Ideology in Revolutionary America* (Chapel Hill: University of North Carolina Press, for the Institute of Early American History and Culture, 1980).

theless, the domestication of female citizenship eventually revealed its risks—and most dramatically in a federal law based squarely on the premise that a woman's personal loyalties fully and exclusively informed her political allegiances. The crisis created by that 1907 statute induced the participants in the postsuffrage nationality-rights crusade to deemphasize the traditional significance of the woman citizen's duties as wife and mother in order to stress convincingly her possession of a political character defined by interests and obligations formed independently from those domestic roles. In this respect, the pursuit of independent citizenship seems something of an anomaly when compared with organized women's previous reform endeavors. Rather than demonstrating women's engagement in public action to address social problems affecting their homes, the legislative case for women's independent citizenship required deemphasizing the confluence of the personal and the political. Instead of drawing attention to the connection between a woman's public activism and private devotion, there was a compelling circumstantial reason to do the opposite. Yet, the nature of such of a connection could remain isolated only temporarily from female reformers' discussions of the components of citizenship.

Commenting on the tension between individualism and other values or concepts that have shaped Americans' understanding of citizenship, H. Mark Roelofs observed that the citizen has been understood to be "both a public and a private person, to be both in and also out of society."[12] Roelofs's thoughts did not extend to an examination of the gender bias imbedded in Western political traditions, but his words certainly assume increased complexity and meaning when approached with this explicative intent.[13] This complexity was not lost on those inter-

---

12. H. Mark Roelofs, *The Tension of Citizenship. Private Man and Public Duty* (New York: Rinehart, 1957), 155.

13. Other critiques of liberal individualism have, of course, emphasized this point. For a sampling of discussions of individualism's historically gendered application, see the chapter "Feminist Critiques of the Public-Private Dichotomy," in Carole Pateman, *The Disorder of Women. Democracy, Feminism and Political Theory* (Cambridge, U.K.: Polity Press, 1989), 118–140; Linda K. Kerber, "Women and Individualism in American History," *Massachusetts Review* 30 (Winter 1989): 589–609; Mark E. Kann, "Individualism, Civic Virtue, and Gender in America," in *Studies in American Political Development. An Annual,* vol. 4, ed. Karen Orren and Stephen Skowronek (New Haven, Conn.: Yale University Press, 1990), 46–81; Anne Phillips, "Citizenship and Feminist Theory," in *Citizenship,* ed. Geoff Andrews (London: Lawrence & Wishart, 1991), 76–88; Susan James, "The Good-Enough Citizen: Female Citizenship and Independence," in *Beyond Equality and Difference. Citizenship, Feminist Politics and Female Subjectivity,* ed. Gisela Bock and Susan James (London and New York: Routledge, 1992), 48–65.

war feminists who tentatively and sometimes disputatiously sought to heighten their understanding of the relationship between the public and the private and of how that relationship shaped the practices of citizenship and the challenges of feminism. In theory and in practice the private and public lives of citizen women still stood distinct from those of men, and legal recognition of the free, decision-making individual remained weighted in favor one sex.

In the first of three two-chapter sections we will now explore the political motivations behind the enactments of the naturalization legislation of 1855 and the expatriation statute of 1907, laws that together deprived millions of women of voluntary citizenship. These first two chapters also detail the rise of organized protest against both marital expatriation and marital naturalization and the elaboration of reform arguments that drew inspiration from the Americanization and suffrage movements. Indeed, the latter stages of the woman suffrage movement cannot be understood fully without reflection on the ways in which the Expatriation Act of 1907 shaped American suffragists' attitudes toward and representations of the immigrant woman.

The subject of Chapters 3 and 4 is the various legislative proposals introduced between 1907 and 1922 to ameliorate the multiform discriminations that faced married women who fell under the jurisdiction of the country's immigration and nationality laws. The first victory, the Cable Act in 1922, signaled the beginning rather than the end of the most critical, if not most complex, phase of the reform crusade because the law's passage coincided with the addition of the NWP to the cohort of nationality-rights reformers. The last section of the book, Chapters 5 and 6, provides an analysis of the impact of the NWP's rapid movement to the forefront of the reform campaign. In part, this organization's transnational perspectives on both citizenship and feminism forced pointed discussion among nationality rights reformers over the problematic relationship between the tenets of individualist feminism and the civic obligations of American citizenship.

CHAPTER I

Conscripted Allegiance

Marital Naturalization and the
Immigrant Woman

The intimate relation, the mutual affection, the common
sympathies, the family, the education of the children in
allegiance, fidelity, and love to the government, the common
pecuniary interests, the obligation to live with each other as long
as life lasts, and the tranquility and harmony of domestic life,
all require that the husband and wife should be of the same
nationality.

—Excerpt from the case record of Elise
Lebret, in John Bassett Moore, *History and*
Digest of the International Arbitrations to
Which the United States Has Been a Party

"Any woman who is now or may hereafter be married to
a citizen of the United States, and who might herself be lawfully naturalized shall be deemed a citizen."[1] Section 2 of the Naturalization Act
of February 10, 1855, thus bestowed on the foreign wives of Americans
the ambiguous distinction of being the first and only group of adults
to receive United States citizenship derivatively. At the time of its enactment, the automatic naturalization of citizens' wives did not draw
any apparent puzzlement or alarm. Viewed from an international perspective, the policy was not remarkable; in fact, a British statute had
served as its model. The American public greeted the new naturaliza-

---

1. Act of Feb. 10, 1855, 10 Stat. 604, as reenacted in Revised Statutes of the U.S. (1878),
sect. 1994.

tion statute with indifference, while Congress commended itself for chivalrously sparing a group of female immigrants the rigors of naturalization. For half a century legal scholars, legislators, woman's rights reformers, and the general public barely reflected on the fact that the introduction of this statute marked a significant decline in the nationality rights of women living in the United States.

Organized efforts to rescind this denial of a married woman's right to choose her citizenship did not materialize until the next century. Even female reformers then failed to ponder the ominous implications of this naturalization policy; the leaders of the woman's rights movement, most of whom were U.S. citizens by birth, viewed naturalization policies as an issue outside their sphere of concern. But this era of neglect ended abruptly in 1907, when Congress revoked citizen women's ability to remain citizens after marriage to an alien.[2] Shocked by the government's punitive proceedings against women with noncitizen husbands, woman's rights activists promptly declared derivative citizenship an unwarranted political assault on women. The 1855 and 1907 statutes had revoked all married women's claims to an independent nationality. After 1907, the vast majority of married women in the United States no longer held the status of citizen or noncitizen as a consequence of birthplace, parentage, or independent naturalization. The citizenship of their spouse was the single factor ruling their nationalities.

The automatic naturalization of citizens' wives remained federal policy until 1922, but not every woman who married an American became a naturalized citizen. Affirming the customary understanding that automatic naturalization was the country's gift to the worthy wife of a valued American, the few exceptions to marital naturalization identified by the courts or Congress did not distinguish the exempted wife as a woman of privileged independence but rather as a person singularly unfit to receive American citizenship. The two factors that could independently disqualify an immigrant woman from assuming American citizenship through marriage were race and a record of immoral sexual behavior.

When the federal government first imposed derivative citizenship on foreign-born women, only free white persons could become U.S. citi-

---

2. Sect. 3, Act of Mar. 2, 1907, 34 Stat. 1228. Sect. 4, Act of June 29, 1906, 34 Stat. 596 at 598, provided that the widow and minor children of a declarant alien could be naturalized without making a declaration of intention.

zens through naturalization. After the ratifications of the Thirteenth and Fourteenth Amendments, Congress expanded the category of naturalization candidates accordingly to include people of African descent or nativity, but all other racial hurdles to adoptive citizenship remained firmly in place.[3] Then, almost fifty years later, the federal government amended the 1855 law to deny derivative citizenship to alien women of "sexually immoral classes."[4] The imposition of this second exception to the rule was part of a larger governmental initiative to curb the immigration of foreign prostitutes.

Throughout the second half of the nineteenth century, the practice of marital naturalization generated only sporadic legal commentary, in contrast to the policy granting citizenship derivatively to children born abroad. In 1855, the woman citizen's solitary protected political right was the ability to petition her government; and if married she held very limited civil rights. Clothing citizens' foreign wives with U.S. citizenship thus seemed to offer these women few tangible gains beyond the power to claim dower rights as citizens. But when the Expatriation Act of 1907 went into effect fifty-two years later, coverture doctrine had relaxed its grip on women's lives, and in the realm of political rights citizen women had the achievement of national woman suffrage in their sights. By the closing months of 1920, two legal developments had sharply enhanced the political significance of marital naturalization and expatriation. Congress had begun to move decisively toward implementing comprehensive and restrictive policies on naturalization and immigration, and the automatic naturalization of married women stood squarely in the path of that larger objective. At the same time, the woman suffrage campaign had concluded successfully. Once the Anthony (Nineteenth) Amendment became law, women naturalized by marriage could register to vote nationwide. Federal legislators could no longer describe the purposes of Section 2 of the 1855 law in nonpolitical terms because the enfranchisement of women had given marital naturalization a new and conspicuously political design.

Within the federal government, Congress was not the sole initiator of the debate over marital naturalization. By 1920, federal judges, the

---

3. Act of Mar. 26, 1790, 1 Stat. 103; Act of July 14, 1870, 16 Stat. 255–256. See *Broadis v. Broadis et al.,* 86 F. 951 (1898), declaring that African American women could be naturalized by marriage. This rule was extended to Native American women, except members of the "Five Civilized Tribes" (Cherokee, Creek, Seminole, Chickasaw, Choctaw) in Indian Territory, by the Act of Aug. 9, 1888, 25 Stat. 392.

4. Act of Feb. 5, 1917, 39 Stat. 874 at 889.

State Department, and the Department of Labor's Bureau of Immigration and Naturalization had already established a history of disagreement over the interpretation of Section 2 of the 1855 Naturalization Act. This series of conflicts had not begun to erupt until the 1900s, but the U.S. Supreme Court had sown the seeds of this intragovernmental quarrel decades earlier in the case of *Kelly v. Owen et al.*[5]

Although the recent ratification of the Fourteenth Amendment had finally provided a basic definition of U.S. citizenship, nationality law stood in a relatively rudimentary state in 1868, when the Supreme Court rendered its decision in this case.[6] Two distinct principles defined the acquisition of citizenship at birth: *jus sanguinis* and *jus soli*. The Fourteenth Amendment honored the rule of *jus soli* with the declaration that persons born within the territorial boundaries of the United States were its citizens.[7] When parentage defined nationality, however, an individual received citizenship by application of the rule of *jus sanguinis* (by right of blood). A series of nationality statutes introduced in the eighteenth and nineteenth centuries provided for this method of acquiring citizenship.[8]

As for naturalization, early nationality statutes made no explicit distinction between a mother's or father's ability to transfer American citizenship upon their naturalization to their children living in the United States. Thus, a naturalized woman's power to clothe her children with her citizenship (whether these minors were living in the United States or abroad) was neither explicitly denied nor recognized.[9] The drafters of the Naturalization Act of 1855, however, removed this ambiguity by substituting references to "parents" in an 1802 statute with the less inclusive "fathers," thus eliminating any claim by mothers to control over

---

5. *Kelly v. Owen et al.*, 74 U.S. 496 (1868).

6. Peter H. Schuck and Rogers M. Smith provide a chapter on the law of citizenship prior to the ratification of the Fourteenth Amendment in *Citizenship without Consent. Illegal Aliens in the American Polity* (New Haven, Conn.: Yale University Press, 1985), 42–71. A good reference volume is Prentiss Webster's *Law of Naturalization in the United States of America and Other Countries* (Boston: Little, Brown, 1895).

7. For general discussion of these rules, see John Bassett Moore, *A Digest of International Law*, vol. 3 (Washington, D.C.: G.P.O., 1906), 276–289.

8. 1 Stat. 103; Act of Jan. 29, 1795, 1 Stat. 414; Act of Apr. 14, 1802, 2 Stat. 153, as reenacted in Revised Statutes of the U.S. (1878), sect. 1993.

9. Richard W. Flournoy, Jr., and Manley O. Hudson, eds., *A Collection of Nationality Laws of Various Countries as Contained in Constitutions, Statutes and Treaties* (New York: Oxford University Press, 1929), is a useful reference work for comparative studies of nationality laws in the early twentieth century. On children's nationality, see Horace Binney, "The Alienigenae of the United States," *American Law Register* 2 (Feb. 1854): 207–209.

their "legitimate" children's citizenship. Having established the male citizen's exclusive control over his children's nationality, Congress then extended the compass of his authority even further to include governance of his foreign-born wife's citizenship.

These mid-nineteenth century changes in legal dependents' naturalization gave American men almost exclusive determination of the citizenship of their foreign-born wives and children and drew the United States into closer alignment with several countries whose laws similarly ensured the undivided nationality of the family. Together, common and statutory law turned marriage into a legal compact that denied many foreign-born women in the United States independent civil and political identities. Prior to the introduction of these revisions in naturalization policy, the country's courts generally recognized a married woman's ability to pursue naturalization or to maintain her premarital citizenship regardless of her spouse's nationality. Until abruptly withdrawn, this aspect of women's political autonomy had contrasted sharply with the common law doctrine of coverture, which effectively suspended a wife's civil identity for the duration of her marriage. Requiring a woman to assume her spouse's nationality harmonized well with the single-identity theory of marriage expressed through the doctrine of coverture, but until 1855 it was not an element of individual sovereignty a woman had to sacrifice as *feme covert*.

By 1855, coverture had begun its slow and fitful demise, a decline already signaled by the passage of married women's property laws in some states. When in force, this doctrine had dictated that a married woman generally could not sue or be sued, sign contracts or wills, or possess property (including her wages and children). Coverture ruled over the realm of civil rights, but citizenship was a political matter and thus fell outside its purview. This distinction between political and civil rights and the lingering concept of perpetual allegiance may explain the late arrival of marital expatriation and naturalization in the United States.[10]

Perpetual allegiance, a notion English colonists had carried to North America, gave national governments paramount control over an individual's acquisition and alteration of citizenship. In countries embracing that understanding of the relationship between a citizen and her political society, citizens could not formally renounce their birth alle-

---

10. *Shanks v. Dupont*, 3 Peters 242 at 246 (U.S. 1830); *Beck v. McGillis*, 9 Barb. 35 (N.Y. 1850), after *Shanks*.

giances without the consent of their government. In fact, the rule of indelible allegiance suggested that a person was more subject than voluntary citizen. Although the revolutionary ideology of the young country clashed with the notion that citizens lacked the power to choose their allegiances freely and independently, the U.S. government withheld statutory recognition of a citizen's power to renounce a birth allegiance for almost a century after the American Revolution. When Congress did act in 1868, the declaration was a forceful one, defining expatriation as nothing less than a "natural and inherent right of all people."[11] Yet, despite the use of the all-inclusive "people," foreign-born women married to Americans were still denied volitional citizenship. This inconsistency in the law would remain unchallenged, however, as long as Congress and the courts chose to maintain the fiction that a woman's marriage vows represented a voluntary oath of naturalization or declaration of expatriation.

The provisions of the 1855 statute testified to the mercurial nature of this "right" to expatriation, a right manifest either as a personal right voluntarily exercised or as a punishment meted out at governmental discretion. The Naturalization Act of 1855, working in coordination with the marital-expatriation laws in many foreign countries, robbed a large number of foreign-born women of a right that U.S. law had ostensibly ensured to all persons within its jurisdiction, regardless of sex or marital status—the right to consensual citizenship. At the same time, the 1855 law could offer some significant forms of protection. The United States' immediate conveyance of American citizenship to citizens' wives rescued many women from the hazards of statelessness; and as the federal government became increasingly aggressive in its efforts to expel or bar aliens from the country, marital naturalization provided immigrant

11. Act of July 27, 1868, 15 Stat. 223, as reenacted in Revised Statutes of the U.S. (1878), sect. 1999. As the provisions of the 1868 law indicated, its message was not directed primarily at American citizens who wished to renounce their allegiance to the United States but rather at those naturalized Americans whose native countries had refused to recognize the loss of these citizens and their services. For disagreement with British authorities over the nature of allegiance, see letter of Lord Grenville to Mr. King, American minister, Mar. 27, 1797, U.S. Department of State, *Papers Relating to the Foreign Relations of the United States* [title varies], vol. 2 (Washington, D.C.: G.P.O., 1832), 148–149. These papers, a record of diplomatic correspondence, will hereafter be cited as *For. Rel.*

For a detailed discussion of the competing principles of volitional and indelible allegiance, see James Kettner, *The Development of American Citizenship, 1608–1870* (Chapel Hill: University of North Carolina Press, 1978), 44–61, 173–209.

women with immunity from deportation or exclusion. In the nineteenth century, naturalization could also furnish the means of inheriting property in the United States. As a noncitizen, an immigrant woman would have been barred by common law tradition from owning, transferring title to, or inheriting land in most states.

Despite these valuable protections against statelessness and the loss of inheritance (including dower) rights, not all women welcomed the loss of one citizenship and the imposition of another without their express consent. Nevertheless, the federal government remained unsympathetic if not bewildered by some women's protests against their involuntary expatriation and naturalization because of their marriage to an American. As one federal agent explained bluntly: "The United States statute stands upon the ground of *public policy, not* on the ground of the *wife's consent*. . . . She may object to this naturalization and protest ever so formally that she will not become an American citizen; . . . it makes no difference. The law, founded on a wise public policy, requires her nationality to be the same as her husband's, and she becomes by operation of law an American citizen."[12] After noting that about a half million foreign-born women had likely become citizens by marriage, he reasoned that it would now be "a great wrong" to treat these women as aliens. And acknowledging women's right to consent to naturalization could serve no real purpose. "Men exercise political powers and privileges, and can vote and hold office, and are liable for military service. Women have no such powers and liabilities. By naturalization they get little or nothing."[13] This common defense of marital naturalization carried an obvious internal contradiction. If citizenship offered women "little or nothing," why must citizens' wives be naturalized automatically? And why deny these women the right to refuse to become Americans if their naturalization carried so little significance? But these inconsistencies were inconsequential to policymakers because the woman's citizenship was of little consequence. Marital naturalization was not about empowering immigrant wives through citizenship, it was about reaffirming the privileges of their citizen husbands. Indeed,

---

12. From the case of Elise Lebret, John Bassett Moore, *History and Digest of the International Arbitrations to Which the United States Has Been a Party,* vol. 3 (Washington, D.C.: G.P.O., 1898), 2499. See similar case of Jane L. Brand, in Moore, *History and Digest,* 2487–2488.

13. Ibid.

once marital naturalization gave women access to significant political privileges, Congress abolished the practice.

When organized women finally launched a campaign against dependent citizenship, they immediately faced resistant members of Congress, who viewed the 1855 rule as a benignant policy that protected women from the disabilities of alienage, properly rewarded wifely devotion to American men with the bestowal of U.S. citizenship, and assured the assimilation of immigrant mothers and their children. Until the ratification of the Anthony Amendment seemed imminent, Congress continued to treat marital naturalization as both a welcome gift to Americans' foreign wives and a vital national cultural investment. These defenses of women's automatic acquisition of citizenship highlighted different aspects of the relationship between the individual and her adoptive government, yet both suggested women's powerlessness and insignificance in the creation of that relationship.

In the 1910s Congress continued to resist woman's rights advocates' protests against derivative citizenship, but not all agencies of the federal government agreed this form of naturalization was beneficial to all the involved parties. In the preceding decade, the practice had provoked rumblings of dissent from the Bureau of Immigration and Naturalization, then housed in the Department of Commerce and Labor. The Bureau's officials were convinced that federal courts were encouraging widespread abuse of the privilege by immigrant female prostitutes and their procurers. And the major instigator of this predicament was the 1868 Supreme Court ruling in *Kelly v. Owen et al.* In this case, the Supreme Court had declared that the only persons who could not be naturalized upon marriage to American men were women racially ineligible for naturalization.[14] Thus, a woman's country of residence and time of her marriage—other factors that could plausibly affect a foreign wife's claim on U.S. citizenship—were apparently irrelevant. It should be noted, however, that neither race nor residence were factors

14. A North Carolina case decided the next year helped fix a broad interpretation of the 1855 statute that courts followed into the next century. *Kane v. McCarthy*, 63 N.C. 299 (1869), esp. at 302.

See also, 14 Op. Atty. Gen. 402 (1874), in which *Kelly* and *Kane* are accepted as setting the parameters of the 1855 law's reach. Also, "Naturalization of Women," *Century Law Journal* 3 (Aug. 4, 1876): 506. Other relevant cases of this era: *Headman v. Rose et al.*, 63 Ga. 458 (1879); *Luhrs v. Eimer*, 80 N.Y. 171 (1880); *United States v. Kellar*, 13 F. 82 at 83 (1882); *Halsey v. Beer*, 5 N.Y. Supp. 334 (1889); *Dorsey v. Brigham*, 177 Ill. 250 (1898).

in *Kelly.* The Court's statement on racial eligibility was *dictum,* not binding.

The case involved a widow's quarrel with her two sisters-in-law over the division of her husband's property. The Supreme Court declared the widow eligible to inherit, rejecting the sisters' claim that their naturalized brother was not a citizen at the time of the marriage and thus had been unable to make his wife a citizen. According to the Court, the language in the 1855 law, "who might lawfully be naturalized under the existing laws," was a reference only to the racial qualifications of the wife.[15] Justice Stephen Field, delivering the Court's opinion, failed to note explicitly, however, that identification as a "free white person" was not the only standard individuals had to meet before becoming naturalized citizens. They also had to be at least twenty-one years of age and a resident of the United States for a minimum of five years— requirements the Supreme Court may have assumed were set aside by the woman's status as a *feme covert* and by the intent of the framers of the 1855 statute.[16] The justices may also have neglected to mention residence as a factor in naturalization simply because it was irrelevant in this case, but the opinion's limited engagement of this and other questions raised by marital naturalization would complicate the disposition of subsequent cases involving governmental challenges to women's claims of citizenship. Many judges thereafter assumed that the Court's failure to mention other basic qualifications for naturalization signified something other than judicial restraint. Indeed, what the Court did not think to utter in this opinion quickly assumed greater significance than what it did say.

By the first decade of the twentieth century, Congress had begun to moved determinedly to selectively limit both immigration and naturalization. One result, among others, was the expansion of *Kelly*'s historical

15. 74 U.S. at 498. But see *Renner v. Muller,* 57 How. Pr. 229 (N.Y. 1880), exempting the wife of a citizen from the age requirement.

16. A case decided four years earlier had raised the question of residency. *Burton v. Burton,* 1 Keyes 359 (N.Y. 1864). The court concluded from the Congressional debates over Section 2 of the 1855 act that this provision naturalized alien white women, both resident and nonresident, whose husbands were citizens at the time of marriage. One judge contended that granting citizenship to persons "who know nothing of [our] institutions, who have never felt any of the responsibility which a permanent resident of a country must feel, would be an act of madness or folly of which sane men could not be guilty" (363). Curiously, the *Kelly* opinion cited this case as providing Section 2 with "the widest extension of its provisions" (74 U.S. at 499).

significance both as precedent and as the source of interpretational conflicts between federal judges and the Bureau of Immigration and Naturalization. If the framers of the 1855 statute had intended citizens' foreign wives to remain exempt from all general naturalization requirements except racial eligibility, prevailing interpretation of *Kelly* assured the success of that design. Many legal experts interpreted Justice Field's words as judicial affirmation that citizenship's door was open to any woman who married an American and was racially eligible for naturalization. As one judge cautioned, if an American man's spouse had to satisfy more than the racial requirement for naturalization, "the whole intent of the [1855] law would be nullified"; but immigration officials trying to deport or exclude certain citizens' wives from the United States disagreed vehemently with that opinion.[17]

Kelly had initially been introduced into a political atmosphere relatively unstirred by debates over the automatic naturalization of the *feme covert*. With the outstanding exception of exclusionary racial policies, immigration and naturalization standards remained relatively unexacting for the remainder of the nineteenth century. Although this situation changed dramatically in the first half of the twentieth century, most judges' recorded views on the 1868 decision's purpose did not. As the legislative and executive branches of the federal government sought to make the attainment of permanent residency and citizenship increasingly difficult for aliens, federal judges' assertion of an exceptionally liberal naturalization policy for citizens' wives stood in defiance of those objectives. While executive officials and Congress collaborated to construct increasingly restrictive general immigration and naturalization laws, federal judges shielded foreign-born white women married to Americans from exclusion or deportation by declaring them citizens by marriage. Inevitably, immigration officials accused the courts of furnishing foreign-born women with a simple and particularly offensive means of thwarting legitimate attempts to deport or exclude them.

The State Department also had a significant interest in the progression of this debate. Until the early twentieth century the State Depart-

---

17. *Halsey v. Beer*. The effect the misrepresentation of the *Kelly* case would have on immigration and naturalization policies was apparent in this case.

Other opinions waiving the residency requirement for wives of citizens: 14 Op. Atty. Gen. 402 (1874); *Ware v. Wisner*, 50 F. 310 (1883); *Headman v. Rose; United States v. Kellar; For. Rel.* (1891), 508.

ment ruled on cases involving the status of naturalized Americans living abroad without the benefit of statutes clearly delineating residency requirements for maintaining U.S. citizenship. As the dispensers of passports, State officials had to determine whether their department's policies regarding expatriation by foreign residence should also apply to foreign-born women who married Americans but still lived in foreign countries. Were nonresident, naturalized women protected from expatriation as long as their husbands remained U.S. citizens, or did these women forfeit their status as Americans—as did other naturalized citizens—if they continued to live abroad?

In the several decades before enactment of the Expatriation Act of 1907, the State Department had consistently assumed that a naturalized American's prolonged absence from the country signified abandonment of U.S. citizenship. Several treaties between the United States and other nations ratified before 1907 also provided for the loss of naturalized citizenship on these grounds. By the time Congress furnished statutory grounds for the application of this policy in 1907, U.S. courts and Secretaries of State had recognized nonresidence as one form of expatriation for more than a century.

As Secretary of State Hamilton Fish had explained in 1873, if a naturalized citizen permanently removed himself and his property from the United States, the federal government could assume that "he has so far expatriated himself as to relieve this Government from the obligation of interference for his protection."[18] The absence, however, had to be permanent; a return to the United States automatically swept away the presumption of expatriation. Thus, the individual's citizenship could more accurately be described as suspended rather than revoked during this period of absence.[19]

Prevailing interpretation of *Kelly* notwithstanding, the State Department had also assumed that women who received citizenship deri-

18. Hamilton Fish to Mr. Washburne, June 28, 1873, *For. Rel.* (1873), 256–261. Quoted in Moore, *Digest of International Law,* 763. Moore amply illustrated the operation of this policy, 757–795 and 554–565. For a list of naturalization conventions transacted between the United States and other countries, consult Frederick Van Dyne, *Citizenship of the United States* (Rochester, N.Y.: Lawyers' Cooperative,1904), 327–362.. See also *Treaties, Conventions, International Acts, Protocols, and Agreements between the United States of America and Other Powers, 1776–1909,* 61st Cong., 2d sess., 1910, S. Doc. 357.

19. Prior to 1907, the only means of expatriation described by statute was desertion from the military, sect. 1998 of the Revised Statutes of the U.S.; (1878).

vatively through marriage could forfeit their claim to American citizenship if they lived abroad, but whether the American's wife who never
lived in the United States could receive citizenship derivatively was another question to which federal statutes provided no clear answer. As
immigration regulations became increasingly restrictive, however, the
need for legislative clarification grew urgent. The significance of Congress's response was plain: if an alien woman did not become an American by marriage while living abroad, then she could not demand automatic entry into the United States as a citizen.[20]

In individual cases involving noncitizen women married to citizen
men, the State Department deferred to the nationality policies of the
woman's country in order to avoid conflicts of law. Following prevailing international practice, the Department treated the nonresident
woman married to an American as an alien if her country of origin still
claimed her as its citizen. From the Department's perspective, one of
the merits of this policy was its insurance against the woman's acquisition of two nationalities.[21] And if her country's law mandated her expatriation for an alien marriage, the United States adopted her as an
American, saving her from statelessness. (This home-law rule also applied to naturalized widows.) In some cases a woman naturalized by
marriage but separated permanently from her husband by death or divorce could reassume her premarital citizenship by simply returning to
her native country. This particular policy, observed in the United States
until 1922, suggested strongly that a woman's premarital citizenship

20. Prior to deliberations on *Kelly*, Secretary of State William Seward had raised this
particular issue and concluded that it was still "open to question whether the act of Congress of February 10, 1855, . . . can be deemed to have operated upon a woman who has
never been within the jurisdiction of this Government." Seward to Mr. Tinelli, Apr. 1,
1868, quoted in Moore, *Digest of International Law*, 486. For a broader understanding
of the workings of this policy, consult 464–488.

Federal law did not allow minors to assume U.S. citizenship after the naturalization of
their fathers until the children had established residence in the United States, but no statute explicitly demanded that citizens' foreign-born wives had to move to the United States
to claim American citizenship.

21. Edwin Borchard, *The Diplomatic Protection of Citizens Abroad* (New York: Banks
Law, 1927), 595. Secretary John W. Foster to David P. Thompson on Mrs. Michaelian's
case, Feb. 9, 1893, *For. Rel.* (1893), 599. As Secretary Foster explained, "This Department
prudently refrains from asserting its application to the case of an alien wife continuing
within her original allegiance at the time of her husband's naturalization in the United
States, inasmuch as the citizenship of the wife might not be effectively asserted as against
any converse claim of the sovereignty within which she has remained. The result would
naturally be a conflict of private international law."

was only suspended rather than eliminated by a foreign marriage and residence.[22]

The State Department described dual citizenship as a national affliction that undermined the integrity of U.S. citizenship, but its officials viewed the hardships of statelessness as the individual's misfortune. Governmental interest in developing naturalization and expatriation guidelines that harmonized with prevailing global practices did not always protect a woman from entering the limbo of statelessness when she married. In some instances both the woman's native country and her husband's nation declined to claim her as a citizen, and State Department correspondence records contain some tragic notations on the lives of women whose marriages cost them not only an independent citizenship but citizenship itself.

The case of Elisabeth Abeldt-Fricker highlighted the political jockeying and legal confusion transnational marriages could generate. Abeldt-Fricker had married an American citizen in 1892, divorced him in 1905, and then returned to her native Switzerland. Within a year, she was a resident in a Swiss insane asylum. Unwilling to bear the expenses of her care, the Swiss government declared that Abeldt-Fricker was still an American citizen despite her divorce and residence and called on U.S. officials to assume the costs of her medical treatment. The U.S. State Department, however, was equally unwilling to concede responsibility for a public charge.

Secretary of State Elihu Root informed Swiss authorities that Abeldt-Fricker had forfeited her American citizenship and reassumed her former nationality when she left the United States to resettle permanently in her native country.[23] Still unpersuaded of its responsibilities, the Swiss legation countered that Abeldt-Fricker was *non compos* when she left the United States and was thus unable to comprehend that her departure was an act of voluntary expatriation. The U.S. State Department held its ground and replied firmly and finally that its government would refuse to receive an insane, and thus inadmissible, alien.[24] In the end, the U.S. government prevailed, perhaps only be-

22. Fish to the minister to Russia, June 9, 1874, published in 51st Cong., 1st sess., 1890, H. Exec. Doc. 470, 24.

23. *For. Rel.* (1906), pt. 2, 1364–1368.

24. The Department's rule weighed heavily on those widows and divorcees who could only avoid denaturalization by living in the United States. Asked in 1879 whether the widow of a former government official, Marced de la Rodia, merited government protection abroad, Secretary of State William Evarts responded that "something more than a

cause it had the ability to block Abeldt-Fricker's reentry into the country.

For five years, and despite acute physical infirmities, Louisa Lassonne appealed directly but unsuccessfully to the U.S. government for recognition as a citizen by marriage. Lassonne, also a Swiss native, had married a naturalized American in Russia in 1874, but she and her deceased husband had never returned to the United States. Lassonne asked the State Department to renew her passport in 1897:

I am an old woman, weak and sickly, a widow; I earn my bread by teaching; in the winter I give lessons, in the summer I travel about with families at whom I engage as governess.

I never was in America, and can not go there if I wished, having no means; and what should I do there, I being a stranger, rather to say, foreign to the country; in which way could I get my existence; and should I say it frankly, I thought that I had a right to the aid and protection from the country I became a citizen by legal rights, and instead of that I am refused a passport.[25]

The U.S. legation in Russia was uncertain whether Lassonne was an American citizen but received instructions from Secretary of State John Sherman to deny her request. "[B]y the usual rules of continental private international law a woman marrying an alien shares his status, certainly during his life," he wrote; but once widowed the woman "reverts to her original status unless she abandons the country of her origin and returns to that of her late husband."[26]

Chronic arteriosclerosis had left Lassonne severely debilitated, and her doctors feared that a journey to Switzerland or the United States to reestablish residence and citizenship would prove fatal. In 1901 she penned what appears to be her last and most desperate plea to the U.S. government: "Sir, I am an old woman, a great invalid. . . . I can not undertake such a voyage, and if I were to break my home, my connec-

---

mere marriage solemnization is required to establish good citizenship, such, for instance, as a domicil of some considerable duration in this country." Evarts to Mrs. Marced de la Rodia, June 21, 1879, *For. Rel.* (1888), 1532. If a woman remained in the United States after her husband's death, she preserved her American citizenship. Second Assistant Secretary of State Adee to Mr. Kagenhjelm, Aug. 21, 1895, cited in Moore, *Digest of International Law,* 458.

25. Louisa Lassonne to Clifton Breckinridge at U.S. Legation in St. Petersburg, n.d., *For. Rel.* (1901), 442.

26. John Sherman to Breckinridge, Mar. 15, 1897, ibid., 443.

tions, my livelihood to start a new life, should I land there to go the workhouse? I have said all; now remains me to ask you, sir, to take my state into consideration, to grant me that paper, as it is the only means of living quiet the few days that are left to me."[27]

John Hay, who inherited the Lassonne case as the succeeding Secretary of State, told the U.S. ambassador that he must decline her request. "While the Department's sympathies are with Mrs. Lassonne," Hay replied, "it thinks that she is not entitled to a passport as an American citizen."[28] In the eyes of federal officials, the dissolution of their marriages to Americans had rendered Abeldt-Fricker and Lassonne aliens, and the women's absences from the United States and deteriorating health only reinforced the government's inclination to repudiate their claims to U.S. citizenship. These women's access to citizenship had one source: their American husbands. Once death or divorce had dissolved that connection, the obligation of the United States to assist these non-residents also ceased.

The Bureau of Immigration and Naturalization (transferred to the new Labor Department in 1913) was one of Section 2's most vocal critics. The Bureau urged imposing new restrictions on the naturalization of citizens' wives, but its laments over the impact of marital naturalization on immigration control were fruitless until the publication of the famous Dillingham Commission reports in 1911. This Commission, charged with the task of surveying immigrant life in the United States, offered corroboration of the Bureau of Immigration and Naturalization's assertion that immigrant prostitutes routinely used marriage to Americans to ward off expulsion or exclusion from the United States.

For decades immigration officials had submitted scattered accounts of fraudulent marriages between Americans and foreign citizens, but not all of these reports in the late nineteenth century highlighted abuses of marital naturalization. Indeed, the main target of the earliest investigations were women who could not receive citizenship through marriage. Immigration officials generally assumed that Chinese women immigrating as the wives of citizens were commodities in the international prostitution trade; but, unlike most citizens' foreign-born wives, these women were racially ineligible for naturalization even if they married Americans.[29]

27. Lassonne to Charlemagne Tower, U.S. Embassy, Oct. 21, 1901, ibid., 445.
28. John Hay to Tower, Dec. 6, 1901, ibid., 446.
29. *Chy Lung v. Freeman et al.,* 92 U.S. 275 (1875).

In his annual report for 1906 the commissioner general of immigration described a prostitution racket flourishing along the Mexican border involving Chinese women who would appear at an immigration inspection station in El Paso with an American husband they had just
acquired in Mexico. Once across the border, the brides traveled directly
to brothels. These women could not become citizens, but this did not
temper the commissioner general's outrage over the complicity of
American men of Chinese ancestry in this deception. Here was shocking evidence, he argued, that American citizenship had been "carelessly
and inconsiderately conferred" on persons of Chinese heritage and then
"prostituted to the accomplishment of results so utterly at variance with
American civilization and so repugnant to every moral sensibility of
our Christian nation."[30]

The following year, in his report to Congress on the operation of
the Chinese exclusion laws, the Secretary of Commerce and Labor alluded to reports that Chinese Americans routinely abused their right
to bring wives and children into the country. Claiming that the number of fraudulent wives had now reached "alarming proportions," he
seemed convinced that the vast majority of Chinese women who came
to the United States as the wives of Americans had married for illicit
purposes: "There are, doubtless, cases of a bona fide character—that is,
cases in which a real Chinese American citizen brings a real wife to this
country, but it is not believed that the files of the Bureau of Immigration contain a record of a case of the importation of a 'wife' of a native
that is free from at least a strong suspicion that such 'wife,' if married
to the American Chinaman at all, was made a party to such marriage
solely for the purpose of evading the exclusion laws and entering this
country."[31] Section 5 of the Immigration Act of March 3, 1875, had

30. U.S. Department of Commerce and Labor, *Annual Report of the Department of
Commerce and Labor* (Washington, D.C.: G.P.O., 1906), 568.
31. H. of Rep., Compilation fron the Records of the Bureau of Immigration of Facts
Concerning the Enforcement of the Chinese-Exclusion Laws, 59th. Cong., 1st. Sess.
(1906), H. Doc. 847, p. 110.
In *Low Wah Suey v. Backus*, 225 U.S. 460 (1912), the U.S. Supreme Court supported
the commissioner general of immigration's decision to deport the Chinese wife of a citizen
for engaging in prostitution. See also the related case of *Tsoi Sim v. United States*, 116 F.
920 (1902). Until the law was revised in 1930, Asian wives of Americans were unable to
join their husbands permanently in the United States. The Act of June 13, 1930, 46 Stat.
581, did not make these women eligible for naturalization but did permit their admission
to the United States.

made the admission of women "imported for the purposes of prostitution" unlawful, and over the course of the first decade of the next century Congress added further legislative barriers to the admission or residence of foreign-born prostitutes.[32] Whether a prostitute's marriage to a citizen could carry absolute immunity from expulsion, however, remained a debated issue.[33]

The Dillingham Commission contributed to this discussion with an investigation of immigrant women who married Americans either to gain permanent entry into the country or to beat deportation orders. Gathering its information in New York City, the Commission provided documentation of white women's resort to fraudulent marriages to avoid deportation. Although its report was primarily anecdotal, the Commission's accounts of this activity convinced Congress that the 1855 law had indeed provided a convenient means of bringing prostitutes into the country.[34] In one case a police detective in Manhattan assigned to vice work reported that he arrested foreign-born "Mary Doe" in 1908 for prostitution, a crime that carried the penalty of deportation for noncitizens. Although she was convicted, immigration officials delayed her expulsion so she could serve as a witness in another prostitution case. During that opportune postponement of her departure, "Richard Roe," an American, applied successfully to the Department of Commerce and Labor for permission to marry Doe.

A vice detective reported to the Commission that he had subsequently run into the woman on the street, just days after her marriage.

32. Act of Mar. 3, 1875, 18 Stat. 477.
33. The Immigration Act of 1903 also failed to authorize immigration officials' deportation of prostitutes. Act of Mar. 3, 1903, 32 Stat. 1213. In 1907, however, Congress finally authorized the expulsion of an alien prostitute "at any time within three years after she shall have entered the United States." Sect. 3 of the Act of Feb. 20, 1907, 34 Stat. 898. Supporters of this law were forced back to the drawing board when the U.S. Supreme Court virtually gutted the statute in *Keller v. United States,* 213 U.S. 138 (1909).
Congress, undeterred by the reprimand, produced another law authorizing the expulsion of an alien prostitute any time after her entry into the United States. A residence of three years or more was no longer a shield against deportation. Sect. 3 of Act of Mar. 26, 1910, 36 Stat. 263.
34. See the Dillingham Commission's report, *Importing Women for Immoral Purposes,* 61st Cong., 2d sess., 1910, S. Doc. 196. For an analysis of public and private efforts to shut down the "white slave trade," see Mark Thomas Connelly, *The Response to Prostitution in the Progressive Era* (Chapel Hill: University of North Carolina Press, 1980).

According to his account, she cheerily offered a full confession of her deception:

Don't you know what he wanted from me, that fellow Roe? Don't you know that he had another girl in his house at——street, and when we got there he introduced me to her (an old prostitute named Laura) and told me she was his wife, but that I would stay with them and that we both would make good money by both hustling from his house? . . . I now make $5 or $6 a day, which I keep for myself and Roe stays with his affinity, Laura. Of course, you know, John, that if I married that fellow Roe, it was only to beat deportation and be safe forever, as I am now an American citizen.[35]

The officer added that since this encounter he had espied "Mrs. Roe" taking men back to her house.

Another anonymous member of a Manhattan detective bureau reported a case to the Dillingham Commission that must have acutely embarrassed the immigration commissioner at Ellis Island. The city detective had arrested "Jane Doe" shortly after her arrival in the United States. Although the government detained Doe to serve as a witness in a prostitution case, the detective assumed she was eventually deported. A short time later, however, while patrolling Broadway and Twenty-eighth Street, the officer ran into the woman. He claimed she voluntarily approached him to relate her tale of deceit:

Hello; how are you? You didn't expect to see me back in New York, did you? Well, I am going to tell you the whole thing. An immigration official down on Ellis Island got "dead stuck" on me, because I appeared to be a nice girl when I was down there. I know how to behave, when necessary. This man hired a lawyer for me, who got me out of there on writ of habeas corpus. Some immigration officials got "wise" to the attention that he was paying me, and he was immediately transferred to Texas. But he came to New York a week ago, and he married me in New Jersey. Here is my marriage certificate. . . . I couldn't live with that man, he isn't making enough money. I don't want to go into the dressmaking business and earn $8 or $9 a week when I can make that every day on Broadway.

The detective added that "almost every night I see the said Jane Doe (now Mrs. Doe) soliciting on Broadway and taking men to hotels in

35. S. Doc. 196, 45.

that vicinity."[36] Congress apparently accepted these reconstructed conversations as sufficient corroboration of the Department of Commerce and Labor's reports that fraudulent marriages between American men and immigrant women were growing too common. These "Jane Does" could speak frankly about the circumstances of their marriages because a marriage certificate ensured them against further entanglements with immigration officials. Even if they divorced, these women did not lose their U.S. citizenship unless they committed some act of expatriation after that separation.

Although it was the Dillingham Commission's report that finally spurred Congress to narrow the application of Section 2 of the 1855 act, Secretary of Commerce and Labor Charles Nagel had already raised the issue of fraudulent marriages with Attorney General George Wickersham. Nagel and Wickersham, however, had disagreed over the disposition of such cases—a disagreement subsequently reenacted by members of Congress debating the virtues and vices of dependent citizenship.

The Secretary and Attorney General's argument involved a "Jane Doe" who had entered the United States in 1907 under an assumed name. After working less than a year as a domestic, she had turned to the more lucrative profession of prostitution. Doe was eventually arrested, and deportation proceedings against her were pending when she was released on bond. Doe did not squander her hours of freedom. She hastily married an American soldier and then challenged the government's authority to deport her. Secretary Nagel argued that any woman who had been a resident of the United States less than three years could not break free of the deportation net simply because she married an American.[37] The Attorney General disagreed with Wickersham, who, inclined to frame the case in more personal terms, was convinced that Doe wanted to remain with her husband. The Attorney General clearly preferred to accept her decision to marry as sufficient evidence of complete redemption from an illicit past. Referring to *Kelly v. Owen* and the intent of the framers of the 1855 statute, Wickersham informed Secretary Nagel that "Congress considered the fact that a woman was married to a citizen of the United States as indicative of her good character, whatever she may have been previous to her marriage. . . . Character is not immutable, and while acts of prostitution are indicative of bad

36. Ibid., 45–46.
37. 27 Op. Atty. Gen. at 507, 508 (1909).

character, the entering of a prostitute into the lawful state of matrimony indicates a reformation and present good character, which it is the duty of society to encourage."[38] Nagel considered this a rather naive appraisal of the virtues of Doe's marriage and submitted further evidence that Doe had not adopted the lifestyle of a respectable wife. Apparently, her soldier-husband had been paid for his services as groom and voiced no protest when his bride returned to her illegal pursuits. Immigration officials had rearrested Doe for soliciting less than a month after her wedding.

This new information prompted another and somewhat modified response from the Attorney General's office, this time from the Acting Attorney General Wade H. Ellis. Ellis assured Nagel he could act on his suspicions if the couple did not live as if bound by their marriage vows. Under those circumstances, the Department could declare the marriage fraudulent and deport Doe. Ellis urged Nagel to remain steadfast in his commitment to expose such "fraud of the grossest nature" but cautioned that immigration authorities had to honor the marriage if the parties remained together as husband and wife, even if evidence suggested they were united merely to stay the wife's deportation.[39]

An immigration law enacted in 1903 had given the Commerce and Labor Secretary the final word in deportation cases—unless, of course, the individual claimed she was a citizen. Consequently, women asserting citizenship could request judicial arbitration of their fate.[40] It is likely that the Secretary's decision to consult the Justice Department before submitting his ruling in this case stemmed from a desire to avoid judicial nullification of yet another deportation order. Although his exchange with the Justice Department on this matter left him unsatisfied, he soon received further direction from federal judges on how to proceed in these difficult cases.[41]

As Secretary Nagel's inquiries suggested, the Commerce and Labor Department was not confident that federal judges would support the expulsion or exclusion of citizens' wives. The 1907 Expatriation Act, silent on the status of citizens' nonresident, foreign-born wives, had left this critical issue in the hands of the judiciary, but some federal judges,

38. Ibid., at 516, 519.
39. Ibid., at 579–583.
40. Sect. 25 of Act of Mar. 3, 1903, 32 Stat. 1213.
41. *United States ex. rel. Nicola v. Williams* and *United States ex. rel. Gendering v. Williams,* 173 F. 626 (1909).

such as George Holt and Learned Hand, had already shown they could be more combative than cooperative when dealing with immigration officials. It also was unclear how the Supreme Court might rule on this particular issue.[42] Overall, the federal courts had not been stalwart opponents of the Bureau's efforts to exclude family members who lacked admission qualifications, but prior to passage of the Immigration Act of February 5, 1917, cases involving the exclusion or deportation of citizens' wives had revealed some significant divisions in opinions between the two major arbiters of these women's fates.[43] Between 1907 and 1911 the federal courts issued five major opinions relating to the arrival status of immigrant wives, but the decisions failed to produce a clear set of standards for the disposition of future cases. Insufficient legislative guidance partially explains the elusiveness of judicial consensus in cases involving citizens' wives, but inconsistencies in judicial outcome were also symptomatic of the courts' struggle to reconcile competing policy concerns.[44]

When Egsha Rustigian arrived at Ellis Island from Turkey in 1908 with plans to join her husband in Rhode Island, she was detained for trachoma at the Immigrants' Hospital in New York City. Rustigian's husband, still a subject of the sultan of Turkey, had filed his declaration of intention to become a U.S. citizen in 1906. A "first-paper" (declarant) immigrant, he had not yet submitted a final petition for naturalization when Egsha arrived in New York. Her husband tried to complete his naturalization but ran into resistance when the federal government

42. See, for example, George Holt's comments in *United States ex. rel. Bosny et al. v. Williams,* 185 F. at 599 (1911), condemning a hearing that allows the immigration inspector to act as "informer, arresting officer, inquisitor, and judge." In his annual report for 1911, the commissioner general of immigration and naturalization defended Williams's administration and criticized the judge, who "seems impatient at the power Congress has seen fit to confer upon the executive authorities rather than upon the courts." U.S. Department of Commerce and Labor, *Annual Report of the Department of Commerce and Labor* (1909), 305.

43. The expulsion of resident aliens was a controversial practice. See Clement L. Bouvé, "The Immigration Act and Returning Resident Aliens," *University of Pennsylvania Law Review* 59 (Mar. 1911): 359–372; Howard Bevis, "The Deportation of Aliens," *University of Pennsylvania Law Review* 68 (Jan. 1920): 97–119; Jane Perry Clark, *Deportation of Aliens from the United States to Europe* (New York: Columbia University Press, 1931); Sigfried Hesse, "The Constitutional Status of the Lawfully Admitted Permanent Resident Alien: The Pre-1917 Cases," *Yale Law Journal* 68 (July 1959): 1578–1625.

44. Derivative citizenship remained available to minors, but now these children could not assume citizenship until they resided permanently in the United States. Sect. 5 of the Act of Mar. 2, 1907, 34 Stat. 1228.

discovered that naturalizing him likely meant naturalizing and admitting his ill wife.

District Court Judge Arthur L. Brown supported the government's decision to exclude the woman, agreeing that it was "more consistent with the welfare of the citizens of the United States to deny both than to admit both [to citizenship]."[45] But Brown ventured further, questioning whether a nonresident woman could ever become a citizen by marriage. He cited an earlier case involving the exclusion of a citizen's ill child, which he believed contained "expressions which seem to indicate that the political status of the alien wife cannot be changed until she comes within the territorial limits of the United States."[46] Therefore, until she gained legal entry, Egsha Rustigian could not claim U.S. citizenship even if her husband became an American.[47]

Legal scholars' reactions to *Rustigian* testified to the importance of the growing debate over the automatic naturalization and the open admission of citizens' immigrating wives. The *Harvard Law Review* carried a somewhat perfunctory note on the decision, suggesting that such cases required little deliberation. "That the act [of 1855] should be so construed as to admit persons otherwise excluded by the immigration laws seems unreasonable," declared the editors flatly.[48] The author of an article in another leading law review noted that racial disqualifications had customarily been the only bar to marital naturalization, but the judge's suggestion in this case that it was in the country's best interests to deny both the wife and husband naturalization was unmistakable proof that the United States was now closing its once "open door."[49]

45. *In re Rustigian*, 165 F. 980 at 982, 983 (1909).

46. Ibid. The following classes of aliens were deportable when Rustigian was in court: those who committed a crime of moral turpitude (1875); prostitutes (1875); the mentally retarded (1882); those likely to become a public charge (1882); the insane (1891); those having a dangerous contagious disease (1891); paupers, professional beggars, vagrants (1891); subversives (1903); those accompanying an excluded alien (1903); those with a disease affecting their ability to earn a living (1907).

47. The case ended inconclusively, but the Labor Department hoped it could combine the influence of *Rustigian*, other cases, and the Expatriation Act of 1907 to break the *Kelly* doctrine's hold on the judiciary. Attorney General Wickersham accurately predicted that the Bureau still lacked a judicial precedent compelling enough to accomplish this break. 27 Op. Atty. Gen. at 518.

48. "Aliens—Necessity of Residence for Naturalization by Marriage," *Harvard Law Review* 22 (May 1909): 533.

49. "Naturalization—Status of the Wife of a Naturalized Citizen," *Columbia Law Review* 9 (1909): 452.

Subsequent decisions would soon undermine *Rustigian*'s precedential influence, but the Department of Commerce and Labor was heartened by one judge's willingness to question the relevance of *Kelly v. Owen*. In 1868, a person immigrating to the United States or seeking naturalization had faced fewer obstacles than her twentieth century counterpart; it was no longer sufficient to merely prove that the applicant for admission was a free white person, Judge Brown had insisted. "She must also be a person not within the classes excluded by the [current] immigration laws."[50]

The following year another judge upheld the exclusion of a woman whose husband was a naturalized citizen. In *Ex parte Kaprielian* the court (citing *Rustigian*) declared that Congress had not intended the 1855 rule "to annul or override the immigration laws so as to authorize the admission into the country of the wife of a naturalized alien not otherwise entitled to enter."[51] A nonresident woman with a citizen spouse did not possess a legal right to enter the United States as a citizen. As long as she remained outside the United States, she remained a foreign citizen.

Rustigian and *Kaprielian* temporarily provided a more secure foundation on which to rest the argument that the Bureau of Immigration and Naturalization could exclude citizens' wives who by general entry standards were ineligible for admission. But two other cases of citizens' wives that ended more favorably for the women involved soon overshadowed the Bureau's victories. Thakla Nicola had married an American citizen in Syria and had remained in that country for years until her husband wished to bring her into the United States. She was detained upon arrival for medical reasons. Bertha Gendering had married by proxy in the Netherlands and had stayed with her American husband seven years before he deserted her. Gendering was living in the United States with another man, whom she said she intended to marry when she obtained a divorce from her American husband, but immigration officials sought to expel her for entering the United States for "immoral purposes."

Judge Learned Hand might have dismissed the women's appeals by declaring them both inadmissible or deportable aliens, but he ignored Judge Brown's suggestions in *Rustigian* and focused instead on the two

50. *In re Rustigian*, 165 F. at 982, 983.
51. *Ex parte Kaprielian*, 188 F. 694 (1910). This policy was also upheld in *Chung Fook v. White*, 264 U.S. 443 (1924).

foreign statutes that had governed these women's postmarital citizenship. Under Turkish nationality law, Nicola had lost her native citizenship on marrying an alien; a similar law governing Dutch citizenship had denationalized Gendering. Judge Hand argued that once these countries dissolved their ties with Nicola and Gendering, the women became U.S. citizens. In view of the State Department's earlier rulings in such cases, the distinguished judge's decision seemed sound. The 1855 statute granted citizenship to a woman who "may herself be lawfully naturalized" at the time of her marriage. The law did not say, observed Hand, that the woman had to be capable of being lawfully "admitted and naturalized."[52]

The decision in Nicola's case once again cast doubt on the Bureau of Immigration and Naturalization's power to classify citizens' immigrating wives as incoming aliens. The Bureau, which thought Hand's opinion in these two cases was too critical to leave unchallenged, appealed but lost. The appellate judges, commenting on the prostitution charge against Gendering, concluded that at the time of her marriage there was "not a breath of suspicion against her moral character." On their wedding days both Gendering and Nicola could have been lawfully naturalized. "If at the time [of their marriages] they gained American citizenship, how did they lose it?" asked Judge Alfred C. Coxe. "What law deprives a citizen of his citizenship because he is so unfortunate as to have contracted a contagious disease? . . . [A] woman does not lose her citizenship because her health is bad or her moral character open to criticism." The court was undoubtedly also impressed by the fact that if the United States did not accept Nicola and Gendering as its citizens, the women would be stateless.[53]

Although Judge Coxe defended the women's personal qualifications for citizenship, his decision was based on his faith in the societal benefits of women's dependent citizenship. The court's judgment, he advised, was "only important as it asserts the importance of maintaining an undivided allegiance in the family relation."[54] For Judge Coxe, Nicola's

---

52. *United States ex. rel. Nicola v. Williams,* 173 F. at 627 (1909); affirmed 184 F. 322 (1911). *United States ex. rel. Gendering v. Williams,* 173 F. 626 (1909); affirmed 184 F. 322 (1911). In 1910 Attorney General Wickersham held that the alien-born wife of a naturalized citizen must be admitted, although she had trachoma. 28 Op. Atty. Gen. 504 (1910). See also *Hopkins v. Fachant,* 130 F.839 (1904), admitting a citizen's wife.

53. 184 F. 322 at 323.

54. Ibid.

and Gendering's fates hinged ultimately on their preembarkation status as Americans' wives rather than on their personal fitness or desire for citizenship.

Attorney General Wise, the commissioner general of immigration, and Ellis Island's Immigration Commissioner William Williams were all dismayed by this affirmation of Hand's decisions. Williams, the one most vexed by these decisions, urged seeking vindication in the Supreme Court, but the Attorney General declined to appeal.[55]

Until the practice of marital naturalization ceased in 1922, the foreign-born wives of Americans remained the only foreign citizens able to acquire U.S. citizenship without ever stepping foot in the United States. Minor children could be naturalized through their fathers' acquisition of citizenship, but they still had to enter the United States as legal immigrants to claim the rights and privileges of that status.[56] In contrast, by 1911 the federal courts had moved most citizens' wives beyond the reach of immigration law. The Bureau of Immigration and Naturalization reluctantly adjusted to this situation but did not cease to press for legislation that would give it authority to regulate the entry of Americans' immigrating wives.

In his annual report to Congress for 1909, Commissioner General of Immigration Daniel Keefe presented his blueprint for a new immigra-

55. Williams to the commissioner general of immigration and naturalization, Feb. 9, 1911. Internal correspondence surrounding these cases revealed lingering disagreement within the Labor Department over the admission privileges of citizens' wives. Assistant Commissioner General Frank H. Larned had to retreat from the policy set out in a letter of Dec. 21, 1909, that nonresident wives were to be treated as incoming aliens. In 1910 the commissioner notified the Acting Secretary of Commerce and Labor of the policy change necessitated by Judge Hand's decision in *Nicola* but emphasized that the status of minor children had not been affected by this case. Letter from Larned to Acting Secretary, July 11, 1910. This correspondence is in the files of the Bureau of Immigration and Naturalization, U.S. Department of Labor, RG 85, National Archives, 52730/77. (These papers will hereafter be cited as *BIN*.)

Commissioner Williams had been the subject of a House investigation in 1911. Hearings before the House Committee on Rules, *Hearings on House Resolution No. 166 Authorizing the Committee on Immigration and Naturalization to Investigate the Office of Immigration Commissioner at the Port of New York and Other Places*, 62d Cong., 1st sess., May 29, July 10 and 11, 1911. Critics described Williams's administration as a "star chamber" and "a stench in the nostrils of the Nation." The Commissioner presented a lengthy defense of his actions.

56. Acting commissioner general to Acting Secretary of Commerce and Labor, July 11, 1910, *BIN*, 52730/77.

tion bill that would amend the 1855 statute to allow the naturalization only of citizens' wives who possessed "the qualifications of race and character required by law of an alien applying for naturalization."[57] Five years later, in a letter to the Senate, the Secretary of Labor voiced concern over the practice of allowing citizens' wives who had never lived in the United States to enter the country as Americans. "In no other one respect are the provisions of law regarding alien immoral women and the trafficking in such women evaded so extensively as by the marriage of such women to American citizens," the Secretary argued.[58] The solution to the problem was to prohibit women of this class from acquiring citizenship by marriage.[59]

Congress did produce a major immigration statute the next session—and overrode a presidential veto in the process.[60] When enacted, the Immigration Act of 1917 was the country's most significant piece of immigration legislation. One historian described its appearance as marking "a turning point in American immigration policy, a definite move from regulation to attempted restriction."[61] The 1917 law, whose provisions were shaped in part by the Dillingham Commission's recommendations, has attracted historians' notice most often for both its reaffirmation of racism's prominence in immigration policy and its introduction of a controversial and long-sought literacy requirement. As a House bill, it had originally included the Labor Secretary's suggested limitation on marital naturalization, but the introduction of this point had aroused fatal opposition on the floor of the House.

The debate over the Labor Secretary's proposal drew out the disparate views held by lawmakers and administrators over what constituted a violation of the spirit and integrity of the 1855 law. Representative James R. Mann of Illinois suspected that denying naturalization to certain citizens' wives violated the constitutional command to establish uniform naturalization standards. (He did not, however, then venture

57. U.S. Department of Commerce and Labor, "Draft of Proposed New Immigration Law," app. 1 of *Annual Report of the Department of Commerce and Labor* (1909), 216, 249–270.

58. *Comments of Labor Department on Bill to Regulate Immigration,* 63d Cong., 2d sess., 1913–1914, S. Doc. 451, 10.

59. Ibid., 6, 10.

60. Act of Feb. 5, 1917, 39 Stat. 874.

61. E. P. Hutchinson, *Legislative History of American Immigration Policy 1798–1965* (Philadelphia: University of Pennsylvania Press, 1981), 167. Note general discussion of the debates and amendments of H. R. 6060 and H. R. 10384 on pp. 160–167.

to question the gender-based standards for expatriation and naturalization as similarly untenable.) "When we say . . . that a person becomes an American citizen, that person is an American citizen for all purposes," Mann argued. William Bennet of New York also opposed the measure but on other grounds, protesting that such a disqualification for naturalization was "putting under the chance of blackmail every alien woman who hereafter marries an American citizen, although she may be chaste as the driven snow."[62]

Most of the early discussions of the benefits and liabilities of marital naturalization had been confined to the correspondence or reports of executive departments and to professional legal journals, but at times such as this, when Congress engaged more directly than usual in discussions about marital naturalization's future, the exchanges were more spirited, confrontational, and, of course, accessible to public view. Although some participants in the discussions about this particular amendment to the law considered the alteration a necessity, the Labor Secretary's suggestion clearly disturbed many members of Congress who held strong views about the sacredness of marriage and the immunity of that relation from government inspection. Many immigration officials cast a jaundiced eye on some immigrant women's marital arrangements, but seeking Congressional assistance to expose their fraudulence meant contending with legislators' unfaltering faith in the redemptive power and sanctity of marriage to an American.

In the end, the new law contained a compromise version of the Secretary's proposal: the new restriction on marital naturalization would apply only to women of "sexually immoral classes" who had committed deportable acts or had been arrested before their marriages to citizens. Postmarital misconduct was not grounds for denaturalization, and in these cases immigration officials could not interfere with the husband's claim on his wife's citizenship. As long as she shared his status as an American, the federal government could not challenge her naturalization. This policy would remain unaltered but was rather short-lived. Five years later, Congress repealed Section 2 of the Naturalization Act of 1855.

---

62. *Congressional Record* 53 (Mar. 30, 1916), 5173. (*Congressional Record* hereafter cited as *CR.*) See *Dorsey v. Brigham,* 177 Ill. 250 (1898), involving the constitutionality of Section 2 as a possible violation of Article I, Section 8's provision for creating uniform naturalization rules. The judge defended the 1855 law on the grounds that it "extends to all of that class who are in the same situation or circumstances" 258.

Few of the country's lawmakers could imagine that the foreign-born woman naturalized by marriage suffered from the incontestable forfeiture of her premarital citizenship. She had become, after all, a compatriot—an American. The prevailing attitude in Congress from 1855 to 1920 was that the conveyance of citizenship to the citizen's wife cost the giver and receiver little, if anything—a view that persisted until the ratification of the Nineteenth Amendment forced a reassessment of the accuracy of that equation. Refusing to concede that marital naturalization was fundamentally a policy of coercion rather than choice, the country's legislators long praised the automatic naturalization of foreign wives as a generous bestowal of citizenship on immigrant women. In reality, it was a nod to male prerogative, the power of the federal government, and the principles of international comity. As a policy incentive, the importance of securing women's political rights simply could not compete against these forces.

The woman naturalized by marriage to an American did not receive a certificate of citizenship from the federal government—the government's reminder to her that a marriage certificate was the only document supporting her claim to U.S. citizenship. Immigrant women sustained another major assault on their already impaired "natural and inherent" right to determine their citizenship when the U.S. government guaranteed that no married woman in the country would be able to initiate her naturalization. If an immigrant wife wanted to become an American, she would have to wait until her husband held the rank of citizen.[63]

By 1907, federal law had reduced the immigrant wife's citizenship to a mere reflection of her spouse's status. If she was naturalized, the government did not have to treat her as an individual possessing an independent claim to U.S. citizenship; rather, her assumption of citizenship best confirmed her husband's and the federal government's ability to manipulate that status. Certainly, as federal legislators generally assumed, many resident, foreign-born women did welcome the protections that U.S. citizenship granted, but lawmakers' presumption that the unsolicited claim of the United States on these women's loyalty

63. In the pre-1855 case *Sutliff v. Forgey,* 1 Cowen 89 (N.Y. 1821), a court rejected the argument that a *feme covert* could not apply for American citizenship separately because her nationality must follow her husband's.

conformed to the ideal of consensual citizenship bared the insidiousness of marital naturalization.

The true substance of legislators' commitment to marital naturalization became apparent after ratification of the woman suffrage amendment. Although in the 1910s support for dependent citizenship finally began to show some sign of yielding to reformers, the 1920s heralded its collapse. In guaranteeing an independent vote to the woman naturalized by marriage, the new Nineteenth Amendment gave her citizenship an independence and energy the framers of the 1855 law had never imagined. Rapidly draining away many of the rhetorical resources long held by the Congressional champions of dependent citizenship, women's enfranchisement proved fatal for marital naturalization. Derivative citizenship could no longer function exclusively as the agent of marital solidarity and patriarchal power if it also served as married women's pathway to achieving an autonomous political voice.

From 1907 until 1922, woman's rights activists' commitment to independent citizenship consisted of a two-pronged assault against marital expatriation and marital naturalization; but until 1920 the majority of Congress's members felt reform in these areas was not politically imperative. Legislators' staid indifference to the plight of expatriate women and their fear that citizens' foreign wives would not seek citizenship independently stalled reform during those years, as did the realization that the alteration or repeal of the rule of derivative citizenship would precipitate conflicts in international law. Finally, the powerful ideal of marital unity continued to shield derivative naturalization from mortal challenge. This roseate view of family relations long obscured the political transgression of binding a woman to her husband's country without her explicit consent. By romanticizing domestic life, equating a woman's relinquishment of basic elements of personal identity with marital fidelity, and presenting what was legally mandated as merely Congress's recognition of a natural shift in allegiance, this forced passage from one citizenship to another could easily be represented as a voluntary act of wifely devotion but never as a grievous loss of civil and political rights. This view of marital harmony long sustained the public's toleration of derivative citizenship, and legislators' ever-ready appeals to family unity allowed them to dodge tough questions about derivative citizenship's legitimacy. Ultimately, however, changing political realities did force most federal lawmakers to choose between voluntarily abandoning their defenses of derivative citizenship or enduring the dethroning of their views. Faced with increasing demands to curb immigration, to raise the standards for naturalization, and to attend more assiduously than in the past to the expressed interests of its newly enfranchised female constituents, Congress eventually had little choice but to respond decisively to growing dissatisfaction with marital naturalization.

CHAPTER 2

America's Prodigal Daughters and Dutiful Wives

Debating the Expatriation Act of 1907

---

*Every woman who leaves the duty and decorum of her native
land and prostitutes her American name to the scandals, the
vices, the social immoralities and moral impurities of foreign
cities not only compasses her own shame, but mars the fair fame
of the republic.*

—James Blaine, *Columbus and Columbia*

Naturalization proceedings in Justice Adelbert P. Rich's
court had moved ahead rather mundanely that day—until interrupted
by the unscheduled appearance of fourteen young women attired in
academic regalia. An attentive audience commonly gathered to watch
relatives become U.S. citizens, but it was unlikely that the gowned spec-
tators sporting the yellow and white ribbons of the woman suffrage
movement belonged to this group. The women stood in sentinel-like
silence at the rear of the courtroom until Justice Rich requested that
they be escorted to the seats, where they then silently observed the proceedings. A knot of reporters and curious bystanders formed outside
the courthouse to gain an interview with the women as they exited,
but the protesters refused to break their silence. The local woman suffrage organization issued a formal statement revealing the symbolic
purpose of the event: "This demonstration is intended as a silent protest against a system of government which gives the ballot to men who
scarcely understand our language and institutions and denies it to
women, born, reared, and educated in this country. It is in no wise

intended as a slur upon the men being naturalized. . . . We do not ask that any privileges be taken from these men, but that the same privileges be accorded us women."[1] The protest, staged in 1919 in Susan B. Anthony's hometown of Rochester, New York, might have been unusual, but the demonstrators' grievances repeated a familiar suffragist lament. The political status of the foreign-born voter was not of incidental interest to many woman suffragists. While suffragists were either willing or constrained to speak favorably of the character of the foreign-born woman, many viewed the voting male immigrant voter as an affront to the patriotism of the American-born, yet disfranchised, woman. The native-born suffragist protested that she should outrank the average foreign-born man in political power by virtue of her native birth, education, and loyalty. The rights and privileges of American citizenship were her birthright, not his; yet, she was the one forced to plead for the political voice he might possess.

Some prominent suffrage leaders publicly vilified the alien male voter as a usurper of citizenship's privileges and a confirmed adversary of woman's rights. Forced to appeal to enfranchised alien or naturalized men for political recognition, some suffragist leaders developed a competitive and antagonistic attitude toward the male immigrant voter.[2] Lashing out at the immigrant voter was not always a successful political strategy, but as the country grew increasingly wary of the impact of immigration on social and political institutions, woman suffragists found this xenophobic trend advantageous to their cause. By the final decade of the woman suffrage movement, federal and state laws had turning alienage into a stigma, and assimilationists were emphatically proclaiming that "Americanization" was the immigrant's true and certain path to moral and cultural enrichment, financial success, and, of course, American citizenship. The Americanization movement's exaltation of the virtues of the "100 percent American" appealed to both native-born and foreign-born residents, and many woman suffragists

1. It was not uncommon for woman suffragists to march publicly in academic gowns. Account taken from typescript of excerpted article in the Rochester *Union and Advertiser*, Mar. 30, 1919. *The Papers of the National Woman's Party, 1913–1972*, ser. 1 (Glen Rock, N.J.: Microfilming Corporation of America, 1972), hereafter cited as *NWPP*.

2. The authors of the famous 1848 Seneca Falls manifesto hinted at this sensitivity to citizen women's political subordination to foreign-born men when they accused the government of withholding from American women rights that it bestowed on "the most ignorant and degraded men—both natives and foreigners." "Declaration of Sentiments," in *Report of the Woman's Rights Convention* (Rochester, N.Y.: Printed by John Dick, 1848).

embraced this celebration of cultural homogeneity as validation of their cause.

In such a political atmosphere, native-born women should have been able to claim unimpeachable possession of loyalty to the United States, but the federal government had challenged that presumption of allegiance with the passage of the Expatriation Act of 1907. American nativity and education, civic virtue—indeed, all the factors women had historically cited to underscore the justice of their demands for equal citizenship rights—were rendered almost meaningless by the country's new expatriation law. When the federal government declared that "any American woman who marries a foreigner shall take the nationality of her husband," citizen women lost a political right more fundamental than their ability to cast a ballot.[3] For the next fifteen years, that legislative command denationalized or denaturalized every woman who married an alien.

Meanwhile, federal law continued to grant citizenship to most alien women who married American men. Not surprisingly, then, woman's rights activists' responses to the female immigrant in the early 1900s were ambivalent—at times charitable, sometimes insensitive, but rarely indifferent.[4] When suffragists expressed their reservations about immigrant voting, those immigrants were generally understood to be male.[5] The *Woman's Journal*, a prominent suffrage paper, decried political parties' practice of paying men's naturalization fees in exchange for the assurance of their vote—a routine that turned "dirty, ignorant, illiterate men . . . into citizens in a single week." The *Journal* often directed this message at American men, admonishing them to "cease to make their

3. Sect. 3, Act of March 2, 1907 (34 Stat. 1228).
4. On the racial and ethnic biases exhibited by leaders of the woman suffrage movement, see Aileen S. Kraditor, *The Ideas of the Woman Suffrage Movement, 1890–1920* (New York: Columbia University Press, 1965; New York: Norton, 1981), 123–218; Ellen Carol DuBois, *Feminism and Suffrage. The Emergence of an Independent Women's Movement in America 1848–1869* (Ithaca, N.Y.: Cornell University Press, 1978), 174–178; Rosalyn Terborg-Penn, "Discontented Black Feminists: Prelude and Postscript to the Passage of the Nineteenth Amendment," in *Decades of Discontent: The Women's Movement, 1920–1940*, ed. Lois Scharf and Joan M. Jensen (Westport, Conn.: Greenwood Press, 1983), 261–278.
5. There is an interesting exchange about the need for an "educated vote" in the *Woman's Journal* 25 (1894). (The *Woman's Journal* is hereafter cited as *WJ*.) E. C. Stanton, "Educated Suffrage Justified," *WJ*, Nov. 3, 1894, 385; "Educated Suffrage Our Hope," *WJ*, Dec. 8, 1894, 385; comments by Henry B. Blackwell, *WJ*, Oct. 27, 1894, 340; Louise Cary Smith, "California Plea for Educated Suffrage," *WJ*, Dec.1, 1894, 378; letters from Anna Gardner and William Lloyd Garrison, *WJ*, Dec. 22, 1894, 401, 332; H. S. Blatch, "An Open Letter to Mrs. Stanton," *WJ*, Dec. 22, 1894, 402.

own educated mothers, sisters, wives, and daughters the political inferiors of the most ignorant and degraded male human being."[6]

Carrie Chapman Catt, who would later become president of the National American Woman Suffrage Association (NAWSA), likewise warned that the nation was "menaced with great danger . . . in the votes possessed by the males in the slums of the cities and the ignorant foreign vote." Her simple solution to this problem: "cut off the vote of the slums and give it to woman."[7] Catt's comment revealed her interest in cultivating the "educated vote." The "woman" she desired to enfranchise was not an unschooled slum dweller. The core of NAWSA's membership shared Catt's preference for stricter voter qualifications for both the citizen and noncitizen, and citizen women's loss of independent citizenship only intensified the organization's commitment to this goal. In 1920 NAWSA approved a nine-point voting-standards plan endorsing direct citizenship for women, which included the independent naturalization of foreign wives. In addition, the plan's framers suggested that immigrants (regardless of sex) should earn a certificate from a "school of citizenship" to qualify for naturalization and enfranchisement.[8]

Excluding the foreign-born woman from the polls was not one of NAWSA's goals, but its members had no desire to let anyone vote—male or female, native-born or naturalized—unless that individual exhibited an understanding of and appreciation for the country's customs, government, and language. Some suffragists did express reservations about the voting fitness of foreign-born women whose loyalty remained untested by the naturalization process, but the sharpness of their comments was often blunted by references to the domestic virtues of foreign women as wives and mothers. Instituting citizenship-training programs for immigrant women was one method NAWSA proposed for remedy-

6. "Editorial Notes," *WJ*, May 12, 1894. Antisuffragists could also manipulate the country's anti-immigrant temperament, but in such cases they exchanged places with suffragists by refusing to distinguish between the voting readiness of the sexes, arguing that both were equally unfit. See Kraditor, *The Ideas of the Woman Suffrage Movement*, 30, 31n.

7. "Iowa Annual Meeting," *WJ*, Dec. 15, 1894, 394.

8. Carrie Chapman Catt, "The Nation Calls," *Woman Citizen* 3 (Mar. 29, 1919): 921; Carrie Chapman Catt and Jane Brooks, "The League of Women Voters," *Woman Citizen* 3 (May 3, 1919): 1044. (*Woman Citizen* is hereafter cited as *WC*.) NAWSA was urging further education and screening of naturalization applicants, not the general curtailment of immigration into the United States. See also the presidential address of Julian Mack for the League for the Protection of Immigrants, *Annual Report* (n.p., 1910–1911), 4–7.

ing immigrant women's lack of formal training for citizenship; the other was the abolition of marital naturalization.[9]

Suffragists, of course, were not the only critics of first-paper aliens' voting, but they were participants in a larger movement that resulted in new state restrictions on declarants' political privileges. One indicator of the country's nativist drift was state voting laws. In the nineteenth century, the number of states granting aliens the franchise had risen as high as twenty-two; by 1900, that number had been halved. The fear of alien dissidents, intensified by labor unrest and World War I, nearly wiped out voting privileges for first-paper male aliens.[10] Nevertheless, as suffragists pointed out, at the end of World War I nine states still allowed noncitizen men to participate in as many or more elections than citizen women.[11]

During the war suffragists tapped public uncertainty over the loyalty of the resident foreign population to generate additional support for their cause. Suffragists warned that when American men left for war, aliens of dubious character would rush in to fill the political void. But if citizen women had the power to vote, they could guard against alien assaults on Americans' government. Suffragists explained that deepseated loyalty to country compelled them to speak out with renewed urgency for the political weapons to challenge those who would undermine American unity and democratic values. "Not only a burning patriotism has aroused the women of these states as never before to work for their right to voice their own principles of government, but a real desire to protect the interest of their sons and husbands at the front from possible domination by a hostile spirit at home," declared Catt.[12] Suffragists insisted, and polls suggested, that the majority of American soldiers did favor women's enfranchisement.[13] Although negative propaganda questioning the allegiances of the foreign-born probably

9. For a description of equal rights for women as an "American notion," see "The Foreign Vote," *WJ*, Jan. 10, 1903.

10. Leon E. Aylsworth, "The Passing of Alien Suffrage," *American Political Science Review* 25 (Feb. 1931): 114–16. See comments on the possible security threat posed by the foreign-born during war in *Immigrants In America Review*, reprinted in Julius Drachsler, *Democracy and Assimilation: The Blending of Immigrant Heritages in America.* (New York: Macmillan, 1920), 4.

11. Mary Sumner Boyd, *The Woman Citizen: A General Handbook of Civics, with Special Consideration of Women's Citizenship* (New York: Frederick A. Stokes, 1918), 50–61.

12. C. C. Catt, "Introduction" to Boyd, *The Woman Citizen*, 8.

13. Carrie Chapman Catt in *WJ*, June 29, 1918.

did promote the short-term goals of suffragists, it also confirmed the presence of an antiforeign bias within the suffrage movement. Such sentiments had deep roots, nurtured by the conviction that most alien men were opposed to women's enfranchisement and that too many foreign men had perverted a political privilege that native-born women would treat reverently.

Prior to 1920, most declarant alien voters were men, but propaganda against foreign voters circulated by suffragists and the opponents of derivative naturalization inevitably cast doubt on the immigrant woman's fitness as well. By 1907, a married immigrant woman could gain citizenship only through her husband, a circumstance that made it even more difficult than before for suffragists to argue that citizen women were as prepared as citizen men to cast an informed and independent vote. Suffragists realized that the automatic naturalization annually of thousands of immigrant women married to Americans was fuel for the antisuffrage charge that women's enfranchisement would swell the number of foreign-born, foreign-thinking voters. Immigrant women who became Americans by marriage did not take a naturalization examination or even the standard oath of allegiance, and these facts provoked criticism of the government's naturalization policies from both sides of the suffrage debate.

Suffragists argued forcefully for an end to marital naturalization. At the same time they offered the immigrant woman a nod of respect they steadfastly withheld from the alien man. J. Maud Campbell, lecturing to the Boston chapter of NAWSA on the competence of the foreign-born woman as voter, assured her listeners that the foreign-born woman was more reliable than her male counterpart. A woman's vote could not be purchased, she argued; and, as a mother and voter, this immigrant would support the child-welfare legislation NAWSA endorsed.[14]

As Campbell's comments suggest, suffragists were willing to adjust the image of the female citizen as a community-oriented mother and conscientious voter to fit both the native-born and the naturalized woman. In 1917 the *Woman Citizen* (successor to the *Woman's Journal*)

---

14. "Bostonian Woman Makes Citizens of Immigrants," *WJ*, Mar. 31, 1917. See also Grace H. Bagley, "Americanization as War Service" and "Program of Suffrage Americanization Committee," *WC* 1 (June 30, 1917): 84–86. Bagley was head of NAWSA's Americanization Committee. For opinions on Americanization within the Daughters of the American Revolution, see Elizabeth Ellicott Poe, "America's Greatest Problem," *Daughters of the American Revolution Magazine* 54 (Jan. 1920): 29–33.

printed a reassuring message on this particular subject for its predominantly native-born readers entitled "Why Worry?" "To suffragists," observed the author, "the foreign-born are a hope and a promise. . . .
Seeking the vote, suffragists have come to know what and how much
the foreign-born have to offer America. They have come to know it
through coming to know foreign-born women, their habits of thrift,
their intensive neighborliness, the pathetic yet inspirational quality of
their concern in their children's advancement."[15]

While suffragists denounced the political practices of the male alien,
they spoke more confidently of the foreign-born woman's potential as
conscientious citizen, and their urban-based suffrage organizations established voting-preparatory programs to ensure that immigrant
women fulfilled that promise. Some states' enfranchisement of women
naturally intensified interest in providing this training for immigrant
women. Mary Dreier, a member of the New York voter-education committee, noted that more that two hundred thousand women in New
York City alone had already been naturalized through marriage. When
the state adopted woman suffrage in 1917, these women could register
to vote, but Dreier feared their voting preparedness had never been truly
tested. "They alone have remained in the backwater," she declared.[16]

Other suffragists shared the suspicion that the world of the immigrant mother was too often defined by the narrow boundaries of her
ethnic neighborhood, and they criticized the federal government's
method of naturalizing foreign wives for perpetuating that isolation.
For immigrant women, they insisted, practicing good citizenship required not only receiving citizenship training but gaining citizenship
independently. With proper instruction, the foreign-born woman could

15. "Why Worry?" WC 2 (Nov. 17, 1917): 470.
16. "Will Americanize Immigrant Women," New York Times, 23 Dec. 1917. When New
York granted woman suffrage in 1917, its suffrage amendment required foreign-born wives
of citizens to reside in the state for at least five years before receiving voting privileges.
On Nov. 6, 1917, the Naturalization Bureau in New York City was deluged with married
women seeking citizenship. The women were informed at that time that they must await
their husband's naturalization. Suffragists wanted to regulate, not exclude, foreign-born
women's appearance at the polls. As Esther Lape of the New York State Woman Suffrage
Party argued, "No group needs the vote more than these women." "Americanizing Our
New Women Citizens," Life and Labor 7 (May 1918): 97. Compare this attitude with an
earlier comment by Henry Blackwell that, given the backwardness of New York's Italian-
born women, "no one need wonder at the slow progress of equal suffrage for women in
our Atlantic States." "Italian Women in New York Tenements," WJ, July 23, 1904, 236.

learn to take full advantage of the benefits of living in a democratic and modern society, but her independent naturalization was an essential step in that civic education.

Perhaps no group of private citizens expressed more concern for the fitness of the foreign-born wife in this respect than suffragists. Undeniably, NAWSA's and other suffragist-sponsored citizenship-training programs for immigrants were self-serving as well as philanthropic. Equal-suffrage proponents needed to reduce public wariness that passage of a national woman suffrage amendment would invite a host of ignorant female voters to the polls.[17] And NAWSA's commitment to civic training for the immigrant woman certainly did not lead to a moderation of its demands for selective voting standards or dispel members' deeply ingrained conviction about the superiority of American values and citizenship. Many of the organization's members had embraced the ethnocentric rationale for "Americanizing" the immigrant, and a belief in the unique assets of both their sex and their country's "100 percent" citizenry fed their interest in civics classes for the foreign-born woman.[18]

"The proper education of a man decides the welfare of an individual," Catharine Beecher had observed, "but educate a woman and the interests of a whole family are secured."[19] Americanizers reflected a similar faith in the impact of the foreign-born mother's assimilation. Indeed, argued one, "her family's chance to become a social unit in the new world depends on it."[20] The advocates of the immigrant mother's

17. For comments by suffragists on the immigrant community, see Hearings before the House Committee on the Judiciary, *Woman Suffrage*, 62d Cong., 2d sess., serial 2, Mar. 13, 1912.

18. NAWSA's educational work among foreign-born women did draw mild praise from at least one historian of the suffrage movement. William L. O'Neill concluded that the organization's Americanization program "probably did not further demoralize the overburdened immigrant population, and it reflected creditably on the good will and good sense of the suffrage movement." *Everyone Was Brave: A History of Feminism in America* (Chicago: Quadrangle Press, 1974), 205–206. See also Kraditor, *The Ideas of the Woman Suffrage Movement*, 138–144. Kraditor credited the influence of women such as Jane Addams for improving NAWSA's understanding of immigrant issues. For evidence of a heightened sensitivity among native reformers, see Grace Abbott and Frances Wetmore, "The Carrie Chapman Catt Citizenship Course: What Do We Mean by Americanization?" *WC* 5 (Sept. 4, 1920): 378–379, 384.

19. Catharine Beecher, *Treatise on Domestic Economy for the Use of Young Ladies at Home and at School* (New York: Harper and Brothers, 1859), 37.

20. Vira Boarman Whitehouse, "The Immigrant Woman and the Vote," *Immigrants in America Review* 1 (Sept. 1915): 68. See, for example, the comments by Lucy B.

Americanization could be found on either side of the debate over marital naturalization. The defenders of marital naturalization insisted that the foreign-born wife's immediate assumption of her husband's nationality ensured her family's internal stability, while the critics of marital naturalization argued that derivative citizenship allowed women to achieve citizenship effortlessly and thus discouraged their assimilation. The practice did nothing to promote family unity, they complained, but rather fostered tense relations between the un-Americanized mother and her assimilated child.[21]

Just as the ideology of republican motherhood designated the citizen mother the purveyor of cultural values, Americanizers represented the immigrant mother as the key to her family's successful absorption into the dominant culture. Assimilationists praised the immigrant woman for her devotion to her family but wished to draw her into a larger world where American customs prevailed. Her stubborn adherence to the conventions of her native country, they warned, would eventually disrupt her family. As the unassimilated immigrant wife and mother gradually lost touch with the ways of her Americanized husband and children, her authority within the home would deteriorate: "The child comes home from school in her American clothes; the husband and brother come home in American uniforms or store clothes, but the mother still wears her shawl on her head or goes bareheaded and clings to her old country clothes. And picturesque though she is, pretty soon the daughter and husband go out without her. She loses her hold and the family morale is gone. America will become Americanized just in proportion as American life finds its place at the fireside."[22] "The immigrant

Johnstone that "almost every foreign woman's vote in [Kansas] represents a *home*." She was confident that foreign-born women's votes for community improvements would mirror those of native women because they shared the same concerns for their children.

Elizabeth A. Woodward, a New York State supervisor for citizenship classes, agreed, adding that "we have not yet come to realize the power of these foreign-born women for community reform." "Language and Home Links," *Survey* 45 (Feb. 12, 1921): 697.

21. Two significant studies of Americanization efforts are Edward George Hartmann, *The Movement to Americanize the Immigrant* (New York: Columbia University Press, 1948), and John Higham, *Strangers in the Land: Patterns of American Nativism, 1860–1925* (New York: Atheneum, 1963, 1971). Drachsler, *Democracy and Assimilation,* provides a contemporary's critique of Americanization. For a retrospective examination of social reformers' views on cultural pluralism, see Rivka Shpak Lissak, *Pluralism & Progressives. Hull House and the New Immigrants, 1890–1919* (Chicago: University of Chicago Press, 1989).

22. Frances A. Kellor, *Americanization of Women: A Discussion of an Emergency Cre-*

woman is the last member of her family to be reached by American influence," cautioned one social worker.[23] Yet, added another, the English-speaking woman was "one of the strongest bulwarks against social unrest." Mothers unfamiliar with that language lost control of their children.[24] In short, when mothers remained unassimilated, "one of the great conservative forces of the community becomes inoperative."[25]

Home teaching for the immigrant mother was the favored preventive for these domestic tragedies. As one director of citizenship training classes for the foreign-born explained: "It is not alone in the physical realm that the mother is the controlling factor. She has the responsibility, also, of maintaining discipline in the home and of determining what kind of citizens her children will become. . . . General and specific education of the mother is the only effective way to enable her to take her full responsibility in the home and in the community."[26] Home teachers sent by the government or private organizations could assist the family by providing the foreign-born mother with the cultural tools to retain proper command of her children. Once brought into the fold of the assimilated, "Mother once more will stand at the head of the household."[27]

Organizations involved in the civic training of immigrant women could not rely on one of the principal reasons men enrolled in citizenship-training classes. Federal law barred a wife from initiating her own naturalization, so taking citizenship classes did nothing to improve her chances of becoming a naturalized American. And if her husband was naturalized, she automatically acquired the status of American citizen without attending the training. Conceding that federal law did create these educational disincentives, the Citizenship Training Division of the Bureau of Naturalization made an effort to encourage the wife of the naturalization petitioner to attend citizenship classes with her

---

ated by Granting the Vote to Women in New York State (New York: n.p., c. 1918), 5. Kellor was a major figure in the Americanization movement.

23. U.S. Dept. of the Interior, Bureau of Education, Americanization Division, "Connecticut's Plans for Women," *Americanization Bulletin* (Oct. 1, 1919), 9.

24. "Teaching English to Adult Women, " *Survey* 42 (Apr. 26, 1919): 156.

25. "Standard of Living," *Immigrants in America Review* 1 (Mar. 1915): 53. See also Thomas Burgess, *Foreign-Born Americans and Their Children* (New York: Department of Missions and Church Extensions of the Episcopal Church, n.d.), 19.

26. Elizabeth A. Woodward, *Educational Opportunities for Women from Other Lands,* Bulletin 718 (Albany: University of the State of New York, 1920), 3.

27. Dan Feeks, "Putting Mother in Her Right Place," *World Outlook* 4 (Oct. 1918), 10.

spouse. One Bureau form letter sent to these women assured the recipient that "the United States government is especially interested in you. . . . America is to be your home, and the Government knows you desire to be an American in every respect." After reminding the reader that her husband and children were being schooled in the language and customs of the country, the government encouraged her to follow that lead.[28]

According to the 1910 census, over five million immigrant women twenty-one years of age or older were living in the United States. The Naturalization Act of 1855 guaranteed that the great majority of these women could be naturalized immediately if they married American citizens. This fact prompted the editors of *Immigrants in America Review* to ask how the United States could rely on naturalized mothers to inculcate American values "when their understanding is largely acquired through the husband or father receiving his naturalization papers?"[29] The *Woman's Home Companion* likewise complained that few women attended their husbands' naturalization ceremonies: "How can they vote intelligently if they lack proper understanding and then again, how can they have proper understanding if they so utterly lack interest and desire for knowledge, even on such a day, when they should go and take the Oath with their husbands?"[30]

The head of the Bureau of Naturalization's Citizenship Training Division also questioned whether naturalized citizenship, acquired effortlessly created "100 percent" Americans. According to Bureau Chief Raymond Crist, immigrant women married to citizens were not credible Americans. "Their utter isolation from America and American contacts in the distinctly foreign atmosphere of their homes leaves them in a position to gain an entirely false notion of America," he warned. Yet, states were handing them "the reins of Government" through the gradual advancement of woman suffrage.[31] Many woman suffragists agreed with Crist, but they had other reasons for rejecting the notion that mar-

28. Letter from Raymond Crist, *BIN* E1990, pt. 1. The Labor Department praised women's organizations for "carrying the message of America" to foreign-born women. U.S. Department of Labor, *Annual Report of the Secretary of Labor* (Washington, D.C.: G.P.O., 1912), 34.

29. "Citizenship for Women," *Immigrants in America Review* 1 (Sept. 1915): 12.

30. Anna Steese Richardson, "The Good Citizenship Bureau," *Woman's Home Companion* 49 (Sept. 1922): 28.

31. Hearings before the House Committee on Immigration and Naturalization, *Proposed Changes in Naturalization Laws: Education and Americanization*, pt. 6, 66th Cong., 1st sess., Oct. 16, 1919, 12–13.

riage to a citizen was sufficient preparation for the franchise. Derivative citizenship sustained the belief that husbands invariably dictated their wives' interests, opinions, and actions—a myth equal rights advocates had to banish in order to win independent citizenship and votes for women. NAWSA maintained that it acted in the best interests of all women when the organization urged Congress to abandon the practice of derivative naturalization before the ratification of the Anthony Amendment—a move that would inevitably end or delay thousands of women's chances to become naturalized voters. Nevertheless, the advocates of independent citizenship insisted that their proposed revisions in the nationality laws benefited foreign-born women. Retiring the rule of derivative citizenship would give women the option and distinction of becoming naturalized Americans on their own merits. The immigrant woman's progression toward citizenship would become an invaluable personal experience, one which drew her out of the home, exposed her to superior patterns of thought and conduct, cultivated her appreciation of her new country, bolstered her self-esteem, and preserved her status in the household as the trustee of cultural values. Native-born feminists assured skeptical federal legislators that independent naturalization would not create tension within the immigrant family but would instead promote the wife's and mother's role as the primary assimilating force in the home.

In 1855, the limited scope of married women's civil and political rights seemed to invite the introduction of marital naturalization. In contrast, the appearance of marital expatriation in 1907 seemed untimely; its declaration of women's political dependence was better suited to that earlier era when the common law doctrine of coverture ruled and a woman suffered civil death upon marriage.[32] However, Congress did not pass the Expatriation Act of 1907 to revive the dying legal concept of coverture, although lingering presumptions about female dependence certainly informed the statute's provisions. A variety of impulses inspired this legislation—some rooted in domestic and in-

32. See Tapping Reeve's treatise *The Law of Baron and Femme,* 2d ed. (Burlington, Vt.: Chauncey Goodrich, 1846), for a description of married women's civil death under the common law. For historical examinations of the subject, consult Norma Basch, *In the Eyes of the Law. Women, Marriage, and Property in Nineteenth-Century New York* (Ithaca, N.Y.: Cornell University Press, 1982); Marylynne Salmon, *Women and the Law of Property in Early America* (Chapel Hill: University of North Carolina Press, 1986); Joan Hoff, *Law, Gender, and Injustice. A Legal History of U.S. Women* (New York: New York University Press, 1991).

ternational policy objectives, others in patriotism or prejudice. Viewing Section 3's marital expatriation rule in isolation might lead to the assumption that the drafters of such a drastic policy were reacting to strong public pressure to divest American women of their citizenship for entering into marriages with aliens. This was not the case; rather, as the law's other provisions make clear, Congress was responding to a general demand from inside and outside the government to enact restrictive nationality and immigration laws.

The motives behind the introduction of this expatriation act were diverse, encompassing policy concerns relating to immigration control, dual citizenship, and naturalization, as well as the more nebulous matter of women's patriotism. The basic objective of the Expatriation Act of 1907 was a reduction in the number of Americans who, in the eyes of the federal government, had compromised their citizenship status by maintaining or establishing foreign ties of some type. The expatriation of women with alien spouses was only one strategy adopted by the government in pursuit of that goal.

The expatriation statute was Congress's initial response to a series of policy proposals submitted the previous year by a presidential commission appointed to recommend general changes in the country's nationality laws. In 1906, the small group of international-law experts commissioned by President Theodore Roosevelt completed their study of the country's nationality laws, and their report heavily influenced the design of the 1907 law.[33] The commission had emphasized the importance of incorporating a residency requirement into the laws governing the status of naturalized adults and minors, and Congress responded readily to this cue by imposing new limitations on naturalized Americans' ability to remain abroad and preserve their citizenship. Section 2 of the 1907 law denaturalized citizens who lived in their native country for two years or in any other foreign nation for five years and revoked the naturalization papers of those with prolonged absences from the United States. The law also required a minor child to establish residence in the United States before assuming American citizenship through a naturalized father. Standing in striking contrast to this set

---

33. *Citizenship of the United States, Expatriation, and Protection Abroad,* 59th Cong., 2d sess., 1906, H. Doc. 326. The three members of the commission were James Brown Scott, then solicitor for the State Department; David Jayne Hill, minister to the Netherlands; Gaillard Hunt, chief of the Passport Bureau. Scott and Hunt later opposed marital expatriation.

of suggestions from the commissioners was their proposal to ignore the significance of residence entirely in cases involving American women married to aliens. These women, they suggested, should be expatriated, whether residents or nonresidents.[34] Congress worked this advice into Section 3 of the law. An American woman who married an alien automatically assumed her husband's nationality even if she never left the United States.

These policies reflected the government's effort to avoid cases of dual nationality as well as other difficulties commonly arising from conflicts with other nations' laws governing transnational marriages. However, the new statutory rules marked a departure from the State Department's customary treatment of citizen women who married aliens. Admittedly, the status of American women in transnational marriages had remained unsettled until 1907, but a few basic rules had emerged from cases on the question. The State Department and the courts generally agreed that a citizen woman married to an alien resident did not endanger her American citizenship unless she also moved permanently to her husband's country. Although no ironclad policy evolved from the State Department's various decisions relating to nonresident women, in most instances the Department ruled that these absentees were not entitled to passports if they remained domiciled within foreign jurisdictions. The Department did not go so far as to declare these women expatriates, however, for as Secretary Hamilton Fish noted in 1876, it had never been "incontrovertibly established" that an American woman lost her citizenship by marriage.[35] Nonresident women did forfeit some of the privileges of U.S. citizenship, such as a passport or government protection abroad, but marriage to a foreigner and absence from the country at most meant the suspension of a woman's citizenship and not its revocation.[36]

This State Department policy received recognition from federal judges in a string of cases reaching back to the late eighteenth century.[37] Indeed, the residency factor never lost its relevance in such judg-

---

34. Ibid., 33.

35. Moore, *Digest of International Law*, 453, quoting Hamilton Fish to Mr. Rublee, April 11, 1876.

36. Secretary of State James Blaine to Phelps, minister to Germany, *For. Rel.* (1890), 301. For a related discussion of residency requirements for the foreign-born wife of a citizen, see Chapter 1.

37. *Talbot v. Jansen*, 3 Dall. 133 (U.S. 1795); *Comitis v. Parkerson et al.*, 56 F. 556 at 561 (1893); *Wallenburg v. Missouri Pacific Railway Co.*, 159 F. 217 at 219 (1908), where the

ments until the passage of the 1907 Expatriation Act. In a case decided only seven years before the passage of that statute, a federal court had ruled that a nonresident, native-born woman married to an alien was an expatriate, but the court emphasized that removal from the United States or a similar express act had to follow the marriage or a woman remained an American citizen.[38]

Prior to 1907, the majority of executive and judicial decisions did not recognize a citizen woman's marriage to an alien as an act of expatriation. However, some judges did not follow these guidelines, and the Roosevelt commission chose to argue the merits of their rulings.[39] If customary practices failed to provide adequate justification for adopting marital expatriation (and the commission admitted they did), pragmatic considerations did support the commission's advice. Internationally, marital expatriation had become a common consequence of citizen women's marriages to aliens. If the United States followed this trend, the federal government could prevent an American woman from retaining both her U.S. citizenship and her husband's nationality when she married—an outcome the State Department strongly supported. The

---

judge declared that "I am clearly of the opinion that a woman, a citizen of the United States, does not lose that citizenship by marriage to an alien, at least so long as she continues to reside in the United States."

38. *Ruckgaber v. Moore*, 104 F. 947 (1900).Other expatriation cases involving wives' removal from the United States: 12 Op. Atty. Gen. 7 (1866); *Trimbles v. Harrison et al.*, 1 B. Mon. 140 (Ky. 1840). For contemporaries' views on the status of American women living abroad, see William Beach Lawrence, *Disabilities of American Women Abroad: Foreign Treaties of the United States in Conflict with State Laws Relative to the Transmission of Real Estate to Aliens* (New York: Baker, Voorhis, 1871); Robert Sewell, "The Status of American Women Married Abroad," *American Law Review* 26 (May-June 1892): 362–363; Clifford S. Walton, "Status of a Wife in International Marriages," *American Law Review* 31 (Nov.-Dec. 1897): 870–875; M. W. Jacobs, "The Requisites of a Change of National Domicile," *American Law Review* 13 (Jan. 1879): 261–279; Binney, "Alienigenae of the United States." For historical analyses of early expatriation policy in the United States, see Edwin M. Borchard, "The Citizenship of Native-Born Women Who Married Foreigners before March 2, 1907, and Acquired a Foreign Domicile," *American Journal of International Law* 29 (July 1935): 396–422; John P. Roche, "Loss of American Nationality: The Years of Confusion," *Western Political Quarterly* 4 (June 1951): 268–294.

39. The commission singled out *Pequignot v. Detroit*, 16 F. 211 (1883). The fact that Pequignot was not a native-born citizen may have influenced the court's decision, but, if so, the opinion offered no evidence of such bias. For comment on the confused state of married women's nationality by the end of the nineteenth century, see opinion in *Ryder et al. v. Bateman*, 93 F. 16 (1898). *Moore v. Tisdale*, 5 B. Mon. 352 (Ky. 1845), presented an interesting exception to the general rule that residence jeopardized the woman's citizenship. See also 30 Op. Atty. Gen. 412 (1915), in which Attorney General T. W. Gregory declared that an American woman did not lose her citizenship although her husband had expatriated himself *after* the marriage by joining the Canadian expeditionary force.

provisions of the new law satisfied the Department's interests in stemming absenteeism among American citizens as well as dual citizenship. If, as the Department asserted, too many naturalized citizens were leaving the United States shortly after receiving naturalization papers and then requesting the assistance and protection of the federal government while abroad, the law could curtail this exploitation of citizenship's privileges. In light of these objectives, the practice of denaturalizing or denationalizing American women because of foreign marriages seemed highly profitable: it not only eliminated a potential group of dual citizens but also rid the body of citizenry of another set of disloyal Americans.

Throughout their collaboration on the drafting of these new expatriation policies, the executive and legislative branches disregarded the interests of thousands of resident women who would immediately lose their U.S. citizenship upon the enactment of such a law. Some federal legislators mistakenly assumed that Section 3 of the new law was simply an affirmation of current State Department policy, but the new policy actually erased the critical distinction the State Department had long maintained between resident women and those residing outside the United States. The new law expatriated both groups.

Congress designed the 1907 statute to single out Americans it presumed had forsaken their allegiance to the United States through the assumption of either a foreign residence or a foreign husband. Before and after the passage of this law, maintaining a foreign domicile was the most common reason for expatriation—a fact that rendered the expatriation of resident female citizens for mere marriage even more exceptional. A woman's wedding vows now served as a renunciation of her premarital citizenship and allegiance. Her right to remain a citizen or become one, to vote or exercise other political perquisites of American citizenship, to reside in the United States without threat of deportation or expatriation, to enter certain occupations, to re-enter the country after an absence abroad, to enjoy the protection of the U.S. government while traveling outside the country, and to secure American citizenship for her children was now wholly dependent on the citizenship of the man she wed.

The policy arguments employed to justify the imposition of these uniquely burdensome citizenship standards were closely linked to the government's interest in restricting immigration. Not only the State Department's claim that an increasing number of Americans were abusing the privileges of their adopted citizenship but also native-born

Americans' anxiety over the expanding population of immigrants fueled discussion about what was often dubbed the "immigrant problem." Annual reports revealing proportional changes in the ethnic composition of recent immigrants had produced noisy demands for new laws that would allow officials to survey the pool of arrivals with a more discriminating (and discriminatory) eye. Not coincidentally, Congress passed the Expatriation Act of 1907 the year immigration from southern and eastern Europe peaked.

Congress did not undertake the construction of a comprehensive plan for reducing immigration until the first few decades of the twentieth century. The law of nationality, which had remained virtually unrevised since the 1870s, simultaneously underwent intense review. Although the timing of marital expatriation's statutory debut seems peculiar when contrasted with the era's general trend toward the improvement of married women's legal status, its appearance in 1907 is much more comprehensible once it is placed on the time line marking major legislative trends in the country's nationality and immigration policies.

Surprisingly little ink was spent defending the new policy of marital expatriation prior to its implementation. Magazines and newspapers occasionally reported outbursts of public indignation over American women's marriages to foreigners, but such scattered eruptions had never coalesced into organized protest. What did emerge from the public's otherwise dimly formed views on transnational marriages was a highly unflattering stereotype of the American woman who wed an alien. By popular report this woman was a young heiress, and not only did her rich American parents have the bad taste to mimic the ostentatious and insipid lifestyle of Europe's nobility, but they crassly pursued foreign aristocrats for sons-in-law.[40]

The great majority of transnational marriages involving American women did not fit that socioeconomic profile, but marriages involving socially prominent families naturally attracted the most public interest and ire. Although the editors of the society pages seemed delighted to report on the foreign social engagements of the New York City–bred Duchesses of Manchester and Marlborough, these women attracted

40. In her monograph on transnational marriages, Maureen Montgomery lists eighty-five marriages between American women and British peers between 1870 and 1914. *"Gilded Prostitution": Status, Money, and Transatlantic Marriages, 1870–1914* (London and New York: Routledge, 1989), 249–253.

something less than admiration in other quarters. For some Americans, a titled American was an affront to American ideals, a blatant repudiation of democratic tradition.

American society had acquired a class of families of unprecedented wealth whose opulent lifestyles stirred both popular awe and resentment. For some Americans of more modest financial means this spectacular wealth reflected the country's economic prosperity and power; for others, the extravagant materialism and aristocratic pretensions of the extraordinarily wealthy seemed downright un-American. For an American heiress, marriage to a well-settled European nobleman did often require leaving the United States, a circumstance the woman's public critics cited as further proof of her indifference toward, if not contempt for, the virtues of democratic society. Even some of the most enthusiastic supporters of American women's independence and character apparently thought the danger of this corruption real enough to warrant issuing some sobering words of caution. In 1904, the *Woman's Journal* carried a "Warning to American Heiresses" who might be contemplating such foreign liaisons. "Think of the suicidal folly of abandoning the cheerful freedom and rational simplicity of our democratic social life for such a fate!" the editor entreated. "Let us hope that the higher education of women may gradually wean the daughters of our millionaires from the worship of titles and aristocracy, and bring them to an intelligent appreciation of the nobility and value of American citizenship."[41]

If the sublime "New World" represented Europe democratized and purified, then the citizen woman who decided to leave its salutary environs for life in the "Old World" revealed some serious deficiencies of character.[42] Transatlantic marriages of the country's social elite were often deprecated as purely mammonistic arrangements, a characterization designed to affirm the moral bankruptcy of such unions. According to President Theodore Roosevelt, a voluble critic of foreign marriages, the American citizen who deserved the least respect was the man "whose son is a fool and his daughter a foreign Princess."[43] Such marriages were "a matter of sale and purchase," the Rev. Dr. R. S. Mac-

41. *WJ,* July 23, 1904, 236. Henry B. Blackwell was the editor of the *Journal* at that time.

42. James Blaine, J. W. Buel, John Clark Redpath, and Benj. Butterworth, *Columbus and Columbia* (Philadelphia: Historical Publishing, 1892), 64.

43. "Roosevelt Censures Foreign Marriages," *New York Times* 3 May 1908, pt. 2, 18.

Arthur scornfully reported to his listeners at the Calvary Baptist Church in New York City. "American girls have sold their womanhood, their country, their language, and their religion for husbands who are peculiarly contemptible cads."[44]

Representative Charles McGavin of Illinois was also moved to denounce these marriages publicly and took his convictions to the floor of the House. These women were guilty of "sacrific[ing] their souls and honor upon the altar of snobbery and vice," he declared, and their existence was offensive to the memory of the virtuous pioneers who had built the country. But McGavin did not fail to honor the woman who chose not to squander her virtue in pursuit of a debauched foreigner: "While I have engaged in some criticism of those particular women who have made a mockery of the most sacred relations of life—of those not satisfied with any other name than Countess Spaghetti or Macaroni,—I want to say one word in tribute to those true American women who spurned the wiles of earls, lords, and counts for the love of His Majesty, an American citizen."[45]

The assignment of moralistic and nationalistic dimensions to women's transnational marriages, the increasing anxiety about the visibility and loyalties of the immigrant population in the United States, the government's concern over the rising number of foreign-domiciled and dual citizens, and, perhaps most immediately, the executive commission on nationality's 1906 report to Congress were all factors helping to set in motion the extension of derivative citizenship to citizen women.

Congress did not engage in a struggle with woman's rights groups over marital expatriation before the passage of the 1907 statute. In fact, virtually no substantive public debate about this took place prior to its imposition. The nationality commission submitted its findings and recommendations, and in less than a year the country had a new law declaring that marriage to an alien man was an act of expatriation.

---

44. "Says Our Women Influence Europe. Rev. Dr. MacArthur Talks on Good and Bad Features of International Marriages," *New York Times,* 20 Jan. 1908, 6.

45. "American Women of Title Scorned," *New York Times,* 29 Jan. 1908, 3. McGavin was promoting a bill to tax the property of expatriate women. For some more humorous and pictorial representations of this young American wife, see the cartoons depicting these "Dollar Princesses" leading their rich husbands about on leashes or pulling them by strings in William Cole and Florett Robinson, eds., *Women Are Wonderful. A History of Cartoons of a Hundred Years with America's Most Controversial Figure* (Cambridge, Mass.: Riverside Press, 1956), 50, 51, 146.

Woman's rights groups were uncharacteristically unprepared to thwart this major legislative move by their national government. Perhaps they did not try to shield titled women from these blasts of opprobrium because they silently condoned the women's indictment. In fairness to this group of politically astute and organized women, although they failed to register their complaints before the policy's placement in the statute books, there was also no evidence of a popular drive to introduce marital expatriation. The scattered denunciations of American women's European marriages never amassed enough political heft to force specific legislative remedies, a fact that probably contributed significantly to rights reformers' apparent complacency. Furthermore, woman suffrage groups, which did contribute much to the debate over derivative citizenship after 1907, might have assumed their allies in Congress would apprise them of impending legislative action affecting their campaign for citizenship rights. Yet, it appears that women's groups were not consulted.

Woman suffragists had appeared heedless of the injustices of dependent citizenship until its rules began to prey on the rights of native-born women. Women's disfranchisement and marital expatriation were kindred problems. Both issues highlighted the legal impediments standing between the woman citizen and her achievement of an independent political identity. As the two gravest political disabilities suffered by citizen women, these two barriers to equal citizenship rapidly attracted broad-based and intense opposition from woman's rights advocates after 1907.

The strong link between independent citizenship and woman suffrage, now apparent to the two causes' defenders, gained public confirmation when marital expatriation's impact on women's voting rights in suffrage states became more explicit. In states where women had gained the vote, foreign-born women naturalized by marriage were able to register to vote while native-born women with alien husbands were turned away. Leaders of the woman suffrage movement protested that the government had once again invited a group of foreign-born residents to exercise a fundamental political right still denied most native-born women, but support for the repeal of Section 3 of the new expatriation law was unlikely to collapse under this attack. Marital naturalization and expatriation were the prevailing international policies governing transnational marriages and, from the federal government's perspective, were highly practical measures that ensured unity of nationality within the family and a decline of dual citizenship and statelessness.

In 1915, a case before the Supreme Court involving a California woman expatriated and disfranchised by marriage did prompt some legislators to offer mild acknowledgments of marital expatriation's inequitable effect. Ethel Mackenzie, a resident of San Francisco, had begun her fight against Section 3 in the California Supreme Court.[46] She had lost her American citizenship when she married a noncitizen and then her right to vote when California women gained that privilege. Mackenzie was a member of the Club Woman's Franchise League and had been an active participant in her state's voter-registration drive. When her state's highest court declined to challenge the constitutionality of the law that had transformed her into an alien, Mackenzie sought relief in the country's highest court. She could have avoided a long and costly court battle by allowing her British husband to apply for naturalization (which he was willing to do), but Mackenzie possessed both the financial means to challenge the law and the conviction that she should fight for the political rights due her sex. Regaining her citizenship through marital naturalization, she realized, "would still avail nothing to other women."[47]

In their appeal to the U.S. Supreme Court, Mackenzie's counsel contended that Section 3 had deprived her of U.S. citizenship without her express consent, thus violating her constitutional guarantee of due process. Ethel Mackenzie had never physically or willingly placed herself under the jurisdiction of the British government.[48] Furthermore, argued her lawyers, Congress's power to make uniform laws governing naturalization did not furnish that body with the power to *denational-*

46. *Mackenzie v. Hare,* 165 Cal. 776 (1913); 239 U.S. 299 (1915.)

47. "Becomes Citizen for Wife's Vote," *WJ,* Dec. 20, 1913, 401. The *Journal* had scattered earlier reports on the 1907 statute, but the Mackenzie case sharpened its attention. In 1910, the editors noted that many alien men had relied on their American wives' testimony in naturalization court, but these women were now disqualified as witnesses because they were aliens. "Women and Citizenship," *WJ,* Dec. 24, 1910, 247. Alice L. Park, "Women Naturalized by Marriage," *WJ,* July 15, 1911, 224, commented on derivative naturalization for alien women.

48. *Mackenzie v. Hare,* Brief for Plaintiff in Error (Englewood, Colo.: Microcard Editions, Information Handling Services, 1979), microfilm. See H. Doc. 326 (1906), 1, 27, 50; 14 Op. Atty. Gen. 295 (1873). Mackenzie's argument that the 1907 law was intended to apply exclusively to nonresident women was also suggested indirectly by a member of the executive commission that provided a blueprint for the statute. Gaillard Hunt, "The New Citizenship Law," *North American Review* 185 (July 5, 1907): 530–539.

ize citizens.[49] Decades later, when constitutional understandings of due process and civil liberties could provide more comfortable accommodations for such arguments, some Supreme Court justices would question the integrity of legislative expatriation; but in 1915 the Court refused to declare Section 3 an undelegated exercise of federal power. Rather, declared the Court unanimously, "as a government, the United States is invested with all the attributes of sovereignty, and has the character and powers of nationality, especially those concerning relations and intercourse with foreign powers."[50] Justice Joseph McKenna, speaking for the Court, also dismissed the suggestion that derivative citizenship was a decrepit principle due for burial in coverture's graveyard. "The identity of husband and wife is an ancient principle of our jurisprudence," he wrote. "It was neither accidental nor arbitrary, and worked in many instances for her protection. . . . It has purpose, if not necessity, in purely domestic policy; it has greater purpose, and it may be, necessity, in international policy."[51]

Ethel Mackenzie had married a couple years after the passage of the 1907 act, a fact that allowed the Supreme Court to avoid examining one of the more controversial aspects of the expatriation law's operation—the denationalization of women married to aliens prior to 1907. The argument that American women's marriages to noncitizens were voluntary acts of expatriation seemed logically insupportable when applied retrospectively to pre-1907 marriages. Federal officials' explanation for this seemingly indefensible policy—that Section 3 was simply a belated legislative acknowledgment of a marrying woman's obvious intentions—was unpersuasive and inaccurate.[52]

49. Brief for Plaintiff in Error, 26–38. In the landmark decision, *United States v. Wong Kim Ark*, 169 U.S. 649 at 703 (1898), the Supreme Court declared that "the power of naturalization, vested in the Constitution, is a power to confer citizenship, not to take it away." It was an important case but of limited value to Mackenzie because it did not involve expatriation. Other cases cited in the *Mackenzie* brief on Congressional power over citizenship included: *Burkett v. McCarty*, 73 Ky. 758 (1866); *Ainslie v. Martin*, 9 Mass. 454 (1813); *Dred Scott v. Sandford*, 19 How. 393 (U.S. 1857); *In re Look Tin Sing*, 21 F. 905 (1884).

50. 239 U.S. 299 at 300.

51. 239 U.S. at 311.

52. Upon enactment of the Expatriation Act of 1907, the State Department also began to treat women married before 1907 as aliens and reject their requests for passports. The practice continued until 1925, when a federal court declared that resident women married to aliens before 1907 had not lost their American citizenship. *In re Fitzroy*, 4 F.2d 541 (1925). However, the policy remained unsettled as federal courts continued to issue inconsistent rulings on this question. See *In re Page*, 12 F.2d 135 (1926); *In re Lazarus*, 24

Legal scholars speculated about the limits of legislative expatriation in the wake of the Mackenzie decision, but most concluded that the Supreme Court had not veered off course while navigating in some poorly charted waters. Meanwhile, women's organizations supportive of Mackenzie's causes seemed to abandon hope that the judiciary would force significant changes in the application of Section 3. Congress thereafter was almost the exclusive object of their appeals for independent citizenship.[53]

Nationality rights advocates heartily concurred with the *Virginia Law Register*'s post-Mackenzie admonition that woman suffragists should "see to it that this new 'restraint upon marriage' is changed before they obtain the vote." It was far more difficult to convince Congress of the wisdom of this observation.[54] Too many legislators still thought repealing Section 3 prior to the ratification of the suffrage amendment was, to use an old saw, placing the cart before the horse. As their colleague N. E. Kendall of Iowa bluntly put it, women had "waited several thousand years for the suffrage privilege," so surely they could "wait a little longer."[55]

F.2d 243 (1928); *In re Krausmann*, 28 F.2d 1004 (1928). In these three cases, the court mistakenly presumed that the 1907 statute was simply a restatement of prevailing common law rules.

53. *Mackenzie v. Hare* seemed to discourage further test cases as a reform strategy. In 1920 Mrs. John O. Miller rounded up twenty-five other Philadelphia women affected by the Expatriation Act of 1907 to challenge their expatriation for marriages to foreigners. The distinguished lawyer George Wharton Pepper, however, advised against the plan and suggested that the women continue to fight for Congressional repeal of Section 3. Indeed, women did not fare well when challenging the constitutionality of the law in the federal courts. *United States v. Cohen*, 179 F. 834 (1910), upheld the denial of separate naturalization for married women.

54. "Expatriation by Marriage," editorial, *Virginia Law Register*, n.s., 1 (Mar. 1916): 867. Other articles on the Mackenzie case and the suffrage question: H.E.A., "Citizenship, Expatriation, Suffrage," *California Law Review* 4 (Mar. 1916): 239; "Loss of Citizenship by Marriage," *Iowa Law Bulletin* 2 (May 1916): 137–140; W.W.S., "Expatriation Resulting from Marriage to Alien Husband," *Michigan Law Review* 14 (Jan. 1916): 233–235; "Woman Loses Citizenship on Marriage to Alien," *Chicago Legal News* 46 (Apr. 11, 1914): 285.

55. House Hearings, 1912, *Woman Suffrage*, 4. For further discussion of the issues raised by the Mackenzie case, see *CR* 51 (Dec. 21, 1914), 450–452; *CR* 51 (July 20, 1914), 12389–12390; Ernest J. Schuster, "The Effect of Marriage on Nationality," in *Report of the Thirty-Second Conference of the International Law Association* (London, 1924), 9–44; John Wesley McWilliams, "Dual Nationality," *American Bar Association Journal* 6 (1920): 204–217; Catheryn Seckler-Hudson, *Statelessness: With Special Reference to the United States: A Study in Nationality and Conflict of Laws* (Washington, D.C.: Digest Press, 1934), 11–99.

Federal legislators rarely acknowledged the full impact of the losses a resident woman incurred because of marital expatriation. Immigration laws were turning alienage into an increasingly precarious status. In addition to being denied a voice at the polls, women married to aliens could be excluded or expelled from the United States, denied access to or fired from certain occupations (including female-dominated professions such as public school teaching), and exempted from many public-assistance programs. The situation only worsened during World War I, when the government classified women as "alien enemies" if their spouses were citizens of the Central Powers. These women received a shocking lesson in the perils of alienage when the Alien Property Custodian confiscated their property.[56]

Although pitted against powerful governmental forces, women organized to ensure that independent-nationality bills appeared at every Congressional session between 1913 and 1922. Most of these proposals died in committee. Media treatment of Mackenzie's case matched Congress's myopic approach to derivative citizenship. The California newspapers appeared generally sympathetic to Mackenzie's plight and faithfully reported on her losses in the courts. The state press's coverage, however, did not extend the discussion of Mackenzie's expatriation beyond her loss of voting privileges and thus failed to explore fully the penalties incurred by a resident's involuntary expatriation. Readers with no or limited knowledge of the relevant law would have assumed from newspapers reports that the 1907 statute fell with greatest force on well-to-do, native-born women who had married foreign men of social distinction.[57] Some months after Mackenzie's defeat in the U.S. Supreme Court, the *San Francisco Chronicle* revisited the subject but continued to obscure the fundamental nature of the case with the following headline: "S.F. Women Are Hit by Court Ruling. Many Socially Prominent Who Are Wed to Aliens Must Relinquish Voting Right." Ethel Mackenzie's picture appeared adjacent to the article, decoratively surrounded

56. Hearings before the House Committee on Immigration and Naturalization, *Relative to Citizenship of American Women Married to Foreigners,* 65th Cong., 2d sess., Dec. 13, 1917; Hearings before the House Committee on Immigration and Naturalization, *Readmission of Augusta Louise De Haven-Alten to the Status and Privileges of a Citizen of the United States,* 66th Cong., 2d sess., Jan. 29, Feb. 3, 1920; *Hughes v. Techt,* 188 N.Y. App. Div. 743 (1919), and *Techt v. Hughes,* 229 N.Y. 222 (1920); "Privilege of Alien Enemies to Inherit under Treaty," *Yale Law Journal* 30 (Dec. 1920): 176–180.

57. One San Francisco newspaper alerted its readers to Mackenzie's dilemma with the headline "Wife of Scotch Tenor Trying to Recover Her Vote, Lost by Marriage to an Alien," *San Francisco Chronicle,* 7 Apr. 1915, 1.

by photographs of marital expatriates Baroness Van Eck, Countess von Faulkenstein, and Baroness von Brincken—all "socially prominent" San Franciscans.[58] The local newspapers' preoccupation with Ethel Mackenzie's and her husband's social pedigrees came dangerously close to conjuring up that troublesome stereotype of the American heiress.

"If Mackenzie Gordon, member of the Bohemian and Family clubs, and gifted singer, was not blessed with an artistic temperament, which disapproved of contact with prosaic immigrants, this story never would have been written," observed the editors of the *San Francisco Call.*[59] Too often newspaper reporters proved more adept at displaying their class biases than communicating the chief merits of Mackenzie's case. Californians who read the society pages for news of their social peers may have sympathized with the baronesses and duchesses of American birth who lost their citizenship, but elsewhere such stories risked arousing contempt rather than pity.

Newspapers' miscasting of the controversy as a suffrage issue dogging the country's social elite and Congress's determination to postpone serious discussion of marital expatriation until after ratification of the woman suffrage amendment both reflected a general weakness in the country's comprehension of this issue. The preoccupation with disfranchisement in the 1910s suggested the difficulties of altering public sensibilities. As long as a woman was unable to exercise the same citizenship rights as a man, it was difficult to convince federal legislators and many of their constituents that her denationalization had profound and damaging personal consequences.

When women were denied the right to vote regardless of their nationality, they could not argue that a loss of U.S. citizenship was responsible for their political disabilities. However, in this respect Ethel Mackenzie's case was genuinely distinctive, and this fact probably gained her some public sympathy. Federal law had authorized her expatriation because she was a woman married to an alien, but the state of California had denied her the vote because she was no longer a citizen. Mackenzie had indeed lost a key political right she would have exercised if she had not married—and this fact furnished her denationalization with a loss tangible enough for Congress and the public to perceive.

58. "S.F. Women Are Hit by Court Ruling," *San Francisco Chronicle,* 7 Dec. 1915, 3.
59. "Has Committed No Crime; Mrs. Mackenzie Gordon Would Vote," *San Francisco Call,* 4 Feb. 1913, 1.

Much of the public discussion surrounding *Mackenzie v. Hare* had provided only a superficial glance at the problem of dependent citizenship. Yet, the media's tendency to highlight the expatriate's loss of voting rights did have some benefits. Woman suffrage, an issue that already enjoyed broad popular recognition, provided a familiar context in which to introduce the more complex and less understood issue of marital expatriation. And the public recognized that once woman suffrage became Constitutional law, many more women would share Mackenzie's loss.

Predictably, negative reaction to *Mackenzie* was strongest among woman's rights supporters. Ethel Mackenzie as suffragist and citizen had belonged to a national congregation of female activists committed to achieving equal citizenship, and her demotion from the rank of citizen deeply incensed her sisters in the cause of woman's rights. From their perspective, Mackenzie's disownment represented the federal government's lack of regard for even its most respectable and active female citizens. When one of their number, Jeanette Rankin of Montana, became a member of the House of Representatives, her presence held more than symbolic significance for woman's rights advocates. Rankin, a supporter of equal nationality rights, introduced a bill in 1917 to amend the offending Section 3 of the 1907 Expatriation Act, and her proposal netted women's organizations their first formal audience before the House Committee on Immigration and Naturalization to discuss the issue of marital naturalization.[60]

By the time this inaugural hearing on independent citizenship was held, however, World War I had agitated the country's antiforeign anxieties. The war had intensified public demands on the woman citizen to reaffirm her patriotism and provoked insistent demands from suffragists for the enfranchisement of American women, who had faithfully kept the home fires burning. Although the U.S. involvement in World War I may have given the suffrage movement a boost, it initially had the opposite effect on the campaign to abolish derivative citizenship. As the 1917 House hearing on the Rankin bill revealed, the Con-

60. H.R. 4049, 65th Cong., 2d sess. (1917). The bill was known as the Rankin-Sheppard bill in Congress. Crystal Eastman, who was about to marry an Englishman, had urged Rankin to present the proposal in the House. See "Cupid Championed by Miss Rankin in Talk to Congress," *Washington Times,* 8 Dec. 1917, and "Miss Rankin Urges Repatriation for American Women," *New York Herald,* 14 Dec. 1917. Rankin is probably best known for her vote against the U.S. entry into World War I in 1917.

gress that was calling on all citizens to demonstrate the full measure of their loyalty had little patience with sympathetic pleas on behalf of women suspected of forsaking their citizenship for a foreign husband.

Although the Rankin bill was the first to prompt a hearing on marital expatriation before the House Committee on Immigration and Naturalization, it ultimately suffered the same fate as preceding bills concerning married women's nationality. The hearing on the bill revealed Congressmen's less than cordial feelings about the proposed amendments as well as the women they would assist.[61] When some Committee members began verbally attacking American women with foreign husbands, the supporters of the Rankin bill recklessly retaliated by questioning the loyalty of certain groups of foreign-born women. The interests of both foreign and native-born women suffered in the debacle. Indeed, the most vivid message reformers conveyed to the Committee on Immigration and Naturalization was that they were willing to exploit the native-born American's wariness of the immigrant to advance their cause. At the hearing, this communication found no friendly listeners on the Committee.

Ellen Spencer Mussey, one of the founders of the Washington College of Law, was also the author of the Rankin bill.[62] Then dean of her law school and an active member of the Daughters of the American Revolution, Mussey hoped to convince Committee members that the restoration of women's nationality rights met a patriotic objective. Native-born women married to aliens wanted to fulfill the responsibilities of American citizenship, but the Expatriation Act of 1907 blocked their advance. This emphasis on the duties rather than the privileges of citi-

---

61. House Hearings, *Relative to Citizenship of American Women Married to Foreigners*, 33. For a newspaper report on this problem, read "Your American Citizenship Is Yours until You Marry the Handsome Foreigner," *New York Evening Sun*, 28 Aug. 1917.

The National Women's Trade Union League did support the bill, although no representative from that organization appeared at the hearing. "The Woman Citizen," *Life and Labor* 9 (May 1919): 115. It should also be noted that the National Association Opposed to Woman Suffrage was a member of the National Council of Women until the Council announced its support of the Rankin bill. "Women Miffed at Suff Bill Quit Council," *Washington Herald*, 27 Dec. 1917; "Quits Women's Council," *New York Times*, 28 Dec. 1917.

62. Mussey had established the Washington College of Law (now American University School of Law) in response to the exclusion of women from many of the country's law schools. Her life is recounted by Grace Hathaway in *Fate Rides a Tortoise; A Biography of Ellen Spencer Mussey* (Philadelphia: John C. Winston, 1937).

zenship certainly had served the cause of woman suffrage well, and in an environment friendlier than this hearing Mussey might have had more success employing it. In an attempt to draw sympathy for expatriated women, she noted that although the federal government did not classify a German-born woman married to an American as an alien enemy, it did consider a resident, native-born woman an alien enemy if she had married a citizen of one of the Central Powers before the war.[63] Acting on the assumption that a woman's political loyalties inevitably followed her spouse's, the federal government had confiscated property worth over $25 million from former citizen women with alien enemy husbands.[64] Members of the House Committee appeared unmoved by Mussey's facts. Instead, Harold Knutson of Minnesota used the moment to reflect on the dear price the country might pay for the marriage of a German spy and a wealthy American heiress. Couldn't this wife "secretly and quietly furnish these millions to her husband to assist in destroying the boys of our country?" he asked.[65]

Generous in its criticism of citizen women who married aliens, the Committee reserved its sympathy and respect for the woman who married an American man. The women testifying at the hearing were baffled and distressed by this blatant display of bias, but Representative John Raker of California had a simple explanation for his and his colleagues' partiality. The immigrant wife of an American was hardly capable of disloyalty, he announced confidently, because "under the tutelage of her kind American citizen husband she has become an American and patriot at heart."[66] Mary Wood of the General Federation of Women's Clubs, however, wanted the Committee to understand that she was there to champion the interests of the native-born woman. She

63. House Hearings, 1917, *Relative to Citizenship of American Women Married to Foreigners,* 6. In 1918, the House recommended revising the Alien Enemy Act by striking the word *male* from its text. The statute made no explicit reference to females, so women technically could not be interned as "alien enemies" and could be apprehended only through ordinary judicial processes. *To Amend Section 4067, Revised Statutes,* 65th Cong., 2d sess., 1918, H. Rept. 285. Women in other countries experienced similar hardships under nationality laws that cast them as alien enemies by marriage.

64. By the end of the war, the Alien Property Custodian held property valued at approximately $56 million dollars. A postwar report noted the frequency of requests for legislation to return this property, especially to women married to alien enemies prior to Apr. 6, 1917. House Committee on Interstate and Foreign Commerce, *To Amend Trading with the Enemy Act,* 66th Cong., 2d sess., 1920, H. Rept. 1089.

65. House Hearing, 1917, *Relative to Citizenship of American Women Married to Foreigners,* 5.

66. Ibid., 8.

did not come to plead for "the Claudias, the Consuellos, and the Imogenes" but for the wronged "plain Janes and plain Marys" who had married loyal immigrant laborers.[67] And Kate Waller Barrett proudly made a similar confession when she reassured the Committee that "whatever laws you pass restricting naturalization will have the support of the united intelligent womanhood of this country."[68]

The Committee members, however, preferred to direct their anger rather than praise at the American woman who married a foreign man. "She becomes 'Countess So-and-So' and is an American citizen; that is not my conception of democracy," fumed Knutson.[69] Mussey pointed out vainly that only a small percentage of those American women with foreign husbands actually received titles by marriage, but this information provoked no sympathetic responses from the Committee.[70] Even Raker, an ally in the woman suffrage cause, revealed no compassion for the expatriated woman. In his view, it was a "clear, open, broad daylight, voluntary surrender of citizenship" when a native-born woman married a foreigner. But Kate Devereaux Blake refused to let the California Congressman's remark go into the record unrebuked. "Every question you asked this morning has been from . . . the standpoint of the man who is safe in his citizenship," Blake declared indignantly. "You have your citizenship; we love ours."[71]

From the perspective of the women testifying, the hearing was a failure. No point they raised proved capable of eliciting a constructive exchange of views with the Committee members. The Rankin bill would have saved many resident women from the dilemma of having to choose between husband and country, but its detractors insisted that allowing women to retain American citizenship and foreign spouses only encouraged "mixed" marriages and drained financial resources away from the

67. Ibid., 20–21.
68. Ibid., 16–17.
69. Ibid., 14.
70. Ibid., 14. For statistics on marriages between citizens and noncitizens, consult Julius Drachsler's *Intermarriage in New York City. A Statistical Study of the Amalgamation of European Peoples*, vol. 94 of *Studies in History, Economics and Public Law* (New York: Columbia University, 1921). Another useful investigation of intermarriage is E. P. Hutchinson's *Immigrants and Their Children, 1850–1950*, Census Monograph Series (New York: Wiley, 1956). Niles Carpenter completed an earlier study for the Bureau of the Census. U.S. Department of Commerce, Bureau of the Census, *Immigrants and Their Children*.
71. House Hearing, 1917, *Relative to Citizenship of American Women Married to Foreigners*, 19.

United States. And there was the crucial question of national loyalty. Snubbing that national icon, the citizen man, was a serious transgression. As one Committee member remarked, the hazards of such marriages were "a good lesson to our American girls to marry American boys."[72]

The battles at the hearing belied the fact that the Rankin bill did not propose to alter the rules for naturalizing alien women; its provisions would have affected only resident, American-born women. But the defenders of the bill failed to remind their audience of this fact and, in general, fumbled their way through their first formal hearing before the House Committee on Immigration and Naturalization. They seemed unprepared to confront a barrage of criticism and too often responded recklessly with recriminations against foreign-born women. Judging from the tenor of the hearing and the subsequent fate of the Rankin bill, the supporters of independent nationality gained little satisfaction or no converts from this audience with the House Committee on Immigration and Naturalization. Nevertheless, the Rankin bill hearing was a historically significant confrontation. It was a benchmark event, organized women's first opportunity to present their case for independent citizenship before a Congressional committee. In many hearings over the next fifteen years, defenders of independent citizenship would never again appear unprepared or unnerved by the reactions to their requests. Indeed, later hearings allowed women committed to the cause to demonstrate, and sometimes embarrass their hosts with, their expertise in the area of nationality law.

The House Committee tabled the Rankin bill, despite the impressive list of supporters, which included the National American Woman Suffrage Association, National Federation of College Women, Daughters of the American Revolution, General Federation of Women's Clubs, Woman's Relief Corps, and the International Council of Women.[73] The NWP was not oblivious to the commitments other women's groups had made to the abolition of marital expatriation and naturalization, but its most prominent leaders appeared almost unaware of this issue until it vaulted onto the reform platform in 1922.

Outside the United States, there was strong evidence of a growing interest in nationality-law reform. Some countries that expatriated citi-

---

72. Ibid., 33.
73. "A Woman's Citizenship Is Her Husband's," editorial, *Chicago Tribune,* 28 May 1922.

zen women because of foreign marriages, including Great Britain, Canada, Sweden, Switzerland, the Netherlands, New Zealand, South Africa, and France, were considering legislation similar to the Rankin bill. Other voices within the United States also contributed to the publicizing of the domestic situation. The Bureau of Immigration and Naturalization, long dissatisfied with the courts' handling of immigration cases involving citizens' wives, supported ending or modifying derivative citizenship for women (albeit not with feminist convictions). Americanizers praising the virtues of "100 percent Americans" also added their voices to the debate.[74]

Interested women's organizations criticized both the defeat of the Rankin bill and the current mode of naturalizing foreign-born wives. The editors of the National Women's Trade Union League's publication, *Life and Labor,* called on members to promote the assimilation of those women who had been handed a ballot "on a silver platter without working for it." These women had American husbands but still knew "no more about the American Constitution than they know about the Egyptian Book of the Dead."[75] The *Woman's Journal* displayed a similar strain of resentment toward the naturalized immigrant wife: "Down the gangplank with the daughter of a United States President who has to pay her alien tax if she has married a foreigner may walk a foreign born woman coming to this country for the first time, who pays no alien fee because her naturalized husband awaits her on the wharf, and the moment she steps on our shores she enjoys the privileges of citizenship and the protection of our flag, because 'a married woman follows the nationality of her husband.' "[76]

According to Mary Sumner Boyd, 62 percent of foreign-born wives were able to "take their right to vote as a gift from their husbands." But, she added, "the law does not help the loyal American wife of an enemy alien husband—it only holds out to her the hope of widowhood."[77] In her book, *The Woman Citizen,* published a year after the

74. For an editorial favoring the independent naturalization of women, see "Citizenship for Women," *Immigrants in America Review* 1 (Sept. 1915): 13.

75. "I Am a Citizen, Too," *Life and Labor* 7 (May 1918): 95.

76. House Hearings, *Relative to Citizenship of American Women Married to Foreigners,* 49. The article, read aloud to the House committee, was entitled "When Are American Women Not American Women" and appeared in the Aug. 19, 1916, issue of the *Woman's Journal.* The President's daughter mentioned did exist. Nellie Grant Sartoris, the child of U. S. Grant, lost her citizenship. It was restored by special act of May 18, 1898, 30 Stat. 1496.

77. Mary Sumner Boyd, "Have You Been Enfranchised Lately? Naturalization," *WC* 2 (Jan. 5, 1918): 114.

Rankin bill hearing, Boyd proposed adopting a restrictive interpretation of the 1855 statute. The courts, she urged, should recognize the marital naturalization of only those citizens' wives who had fulfilled other criteria for assuming citizenship. Boyd, unlike the Bureau of Immigration and Naturalization, supported this change in policy largely as a means of combating the criticism that woman suffrage would enfranchise unprepared immigrant women.[78] Although not acknowledged in her book, she also had a strong personal interest in dispelling the notion that marriage to a foreign citizen compromised a woman's loyalty to her country. Boyd had lost her citizenship when she married a British subject, and the consequences of her forced expatriation dogged her at home and abroad.[79]

Criticism of marital naturalization varied in source and argument, but the volume of this somewhat eclectic protest increased steadily. The general public's awareness of the existence and implications of the Expatriation Act of 1907 improved in the wake of the Supreme Court's decision in *Mackenzie v. Hare* and when major newspapers began publicizing the plight of former American women treated as enemy aliens by the federal government because their husbands were citizens of the Central Powers. Opposition within the federal government to independent citizenship, however, remained active. The *New York Times* offered the sparest yet most candid explanation for the Rankin bill's failure to win sufficient converts. To proclaim that marriage to an alien left a woman's allegiance to the United States untouched was still "asking a good deal."[80]

Even some advocates of independent citizenship for women were dissatisfied with the bill and expressed concern that its easy rules for expatriation encouraged women to adopt their husbands' nationalities. In their view, the Rankin bill did too little to dispel the notion that women were more expendable, and inherently less reliable, citizens. And the proposal had other limitations. Recouping or holding onto one's status as an American after marriage remained problematical under the plan. A resident woman who had already lost her American citizenship by marriage retrieved it by filing a declaration of intention in a natu-

78. Boyd, *The Woman Citizen,* 17.
79. Boyd's problems were related in Catt, "The Nation Calls," 921; Catt and Brooks, "The League of Women Voters," 1044.
80. "Endeavoring to End Inequality," *New York Times,* 28 Dec. 1917.

ralization court, but there was no comparable provision for repatriating the nonresident woman who had already lost her citizenship under the 1907 act. Furthermore, the Rankin bill offered no assistance to women already living abroad with alien spouses—the women most vulnerable to accusations that they had abandoned the United States and their loyalties to it.

In subsequent years the women's coalition for independent citizenship would continue to find sponsors for its nationality bills, but their proposals made no significant headway in Congress prior to the ratification of the Nineteenth Amendment. Congressional discussions often focused narrowly on the disfranchisement of resident, expatriate women rather than on the more fundamental problem of denationalization. Lawmakers consistently underestimated the value of American citizenship for women by consistently subordinating the issue of independent citizenship to that of suffrage. Congress and the media's relatively shallow comprehension of the implications of marital expatriation was perhaps most evident in their initial reactions to Ethel Mackenzie's dilemma. When the House of Representatives discussed Mackenzie's fate, members often treated expatriation as incidental to her disfranchisement. Some legislators suggested that the states could remedy the situation by selectively enfranchising these denationalized Americans. National women's organizations, however, refused to promote what they considered to be a rather feeble if not evasive response to their demands for independent citizenship.

Until 1920, the suffrage issue continued to dominate the debate over equal nationality rights and thus temporarily limited the extent and gravity of that discussion. When federal legislators thought about female citizenship, they focused first (and too often exclusively) on the most publicized and politicized "woman's question" of the day—voting rights. So, in 1907, when Congress discussed placing stricter controls on the adoption and retention of U.S. citizenship, legislators were not inclined to make a thorough assessment of the implications of marital denationalization for the woman citizen. Ten years later, as the 1917 hearing on the Rankin bill revealed, that situation had not altered significantly enough to support reform legislation. Some members of Congress displayed their feeble grasp of the relevant issues in bombastic speeches lambasting titled American heiresses, while other legislators declared with unabashed ignorance that the loss of American citizenship could signify little to those who did not yet possess political rights.

With the restoration of peace, the diatribes against transnational marriages grew less impassioned; and the fascination with "ducal degenerates," which some social and political commentators claimed had afflicted the country's young heiresses, was reportedly fading. The federal government's postwar response to the Alien Property Custodian's treatment of resident, expatriate women was almost penitent; and with a victorious end to the war and the ratification of the woman suffrage amendment in 1920, Congress finally seemed willing to adopt a more sympathetic view than it had in the past of the female expatriate's tribulations. Most legislators who cared about their political futures became more attentive to women's issues once their female constituents were enfranchised.

In this postwar, postsuffrage environment, the stereotype of the American heiress began to look somewhat passé, and its decline coincided with the emergence of a much more positive and powerful representation of the American woman. The Nineteenth Amendment had furnished the defenders of equal nationality rights with the political capital to build a new image of the woman citizen—a citizen whose devotion to country was not only equal in value but identical in nature to that of her male counterpart. The titled heiress had represented a betrayal of American values. The new female voter was, in contrast, a glorious symbol of American democracy. Nowhere was this affirmation of democracy's virtues linked so closely to woman suffrage and independent citizenship as in the image of the voting immigrant woman fashioned by the advocates of women's nationality rights, that woman for whom arrival in America promised a journey toward cultural enlightenment and political empowerment—but only if the federal government consented to abolish derivative citizenship and enfranchise its female citizens.

The women's organizations that continued to lobby for equal nationality rights after 1920 also had to confront the limitations of their popular, presuffrage representation of the model citizen woman—a woman for whom devotion to family was the truest test of her civic virtue. As long as the woman citizen had limited access to those traditionally male activities that identified an individual as a good citizen (voting, holding public office, military service), necessity had required that she claim alternative sources of public influence and credibility as a citizen. The public commitments and private responsibilities of the woman citizen had consequently remained largely undifferentiated, and women's citizenship appeared complementary rather than identical to the male model.

This image of the woman citizen could destroy as well as advance her good standing in the public eye. If her civic obligations were so tightly bound to familial duty, it was not unreasonable to suggest that a woman's selection of a spouse could be a reflection of the strength of her loyalty to country. Giving this suggestion the force of law, the Expatriation Act of 1907 revealed the punishing side of a gendered construction of American citizenship that had long assured a measure of respect to the married woman citizen.

After the war, the iniquitous Countess No-Account also found herself increasingly challenged by a strikingly different but also clichéd version of the marital expatriate. The creation of woman's rights proponents, this postsuffrage female expatriate had not abandoned her country; indeed, she always preferred the superior company of Americans. She was native-born, educated, active in civic affairs, supportive of the Americanization movement, and devoutly patriotic. In sum, she was the era's model citizen even though an absurd legal technicality labeled her an alien and denied her a political voice. This was the image of the female expatriate reformers most often paraded before House Committees throughout the 1920s. As a response to the opponents of independent citizenship, her appearance attested to the growing presence of woman's rights groups in the debates over marital expatriation; but her creation did not immediately ensure her credibility. It took more than a decade to convince legislators that in all her various forms this former American was worth reclaiming.

CHAPTER 3

The Cable Act

Solutions and Problems

Feminism today demands patient research rather than
eloquence, and brains even more than devotion.
—Crystal Eastman, "Suffragists
Ten Years After"

By the closing decades of the woman suffrage movement, the ballot had become the leading symbol of women's civic aspirations. Ratified in an era when voting was well on its way to becoming the exclusive privilege of the citizen, the Nineteenth Amendment was heralded as women's ticket out of second-class citizenship. But for the women shorn of their U.S. citizenship by marriage, the nationwide extension of suffrage to American women magnified the gravity of that expatriation. For some, the most unsettling reminder of their dilemma was no longer the first-paper male voter but the foreign-born woman naturalized and enfranchised by marriage. Helen Papanastasion, who had lost her citizenship when she married a Greek, expressed her frustration in a letter to the NWP. "A few days ago in my social work I visited a Greek woman, a 'picture bride,' married to a Greek, who is naturalized. She knows not one word of English and probably never will, for most of my Greek women . . . have no intercourse with Americans. . . . Well, when I left this particular woman her husband followed me out in the street and wanted to know how soon his wife can vote.

Presently, she will be voting and I who have read our literature, imbibed our standards, thrilled with our ideals, am an alien !"[1]

Congress, too, had grasped the implications of the Nineteenth Amendment's ratification, and this recognition had immediately infused the debates over marital expatriation and naturalization with a new intensity and urgency. Federal lawmakers were finally ready to negotiate the terms of reform. Once the country's female citizens acquired the Constitutional prerogative to vote, more members of Congress acknowledged that marital expatriation imposed hardships on married women, and they began to question whether national interests were still best served by a naturalization practice that now also enfranchised female immigrants. Marital expatriates' involuntary forfeiture of the right to vote and naturalized women's simultaneous acquisition of the vote made the political consequences of derivative citizenship concrete.

Federal lawmakers, sensing the existence of wide support for independent citizenship among the newly enfranchised female population, did not wish to alienate these new and numerous voters. The month the Nineteenth Amendment was ratified, female citizens gained not only the Constitutional right to vote but also pledges from both major political parties to support independent citizenship for resident women.[2] As one member of the House Committee on Immigration and Naturalization declared, the ratification of the national woman suffrage amendment had rendered the concept of derivative citizenship "as archaic as the doctrine of ordeal by fire."[3]

Women's organizations had initially introduced independent-nationality rights as a corollary to woman suffrage, and the two goals shared broad support within women's reform organizations. Although

---

1. Papanastasion, a Bryn Mawr graduate, had been employed previously at the American consulate in Greece and had married a Greek lawyer during that assignment in 1917. Food had become scarce during the war, but her superiors informed Papanastasion that she could not buy the bread made for the U.S. legation because she was no longer an American. The government then refused to promote her and placed a ceiling on her salary. She eventually lost her job when federal regulations made American citizenship requisite for employment in the consular service. Helen Papanastasion to Eleanor Brannon, Sept. 7, 1922; to Elsie Hill, April 4, 1921, *NWPP*.

2. Both Democrats and Republicans skirted the controversy over the expatriation of nonresident women. Donald Bruce Johnson, comp., *National Party Platforms*, vol. 1: *1840–1956* (Urbana: University of Illinois Press, 1978), 219, 236. The NLWV had asked for statements favoring an end to derivative citizenship for alien and American women. Only the Prohibition Party endorsed the League's request without revisions. See "Note," *WC* 4 (May 15, 1920), 1254.

3. John Jacob Rogers, *CR* 62 (June 20, 1922), 9047.

the national achievement of woman suffrage did add considerable ballast to demands to repeal or revise the laws proscribing women's independent citizenship, the struggle to end sex discrimination in the country's nationality laws continued long after the Nineteenth Amendment's ratification and the passage of the first women's nationality-rights reform act in 1922. During those reform years the federal government's attitude toward equal nationality rights remained unpredictable, guaranteeing that women's full recovery of their nationality rights would remain throughout a story of piecemeal reconstruction.

Despite conscientious efforts by suffragists, none of the women's nationality bills introduced in the few years before or after ratification of the Nineteenth Amendment survived. Each failure seemed to spotlight another facet of the political culture of the interwar years and, more particularly, the various forces obstructing reform. Congressional Republicans and Democrats hesitated to expunge all gender-based double standards from the country's nationality laws; the State Department grew increasingly uneasy about American feminists' involvement in the international expansion of the nationality-rights campaign; and although the Americanization movement had already peaked and waned, public concerns over the sociopolitical impact of the country's growing cultural diversity continued to impede the advancement of women's nationality rights.

When the ratification process of the Nineteenth Amendment had entered its final six months, Representative John Jacob Rogers unveiled a reform bill that allowed American women with foreign husbands to retain their citizenship as long as they remained residents of the United States—the same proposal that shortly found its way into the party platforms of both major political parties. But Rogers's bill was doomed because it required husbands and wives to work through the same set of naturalization procedures.[4]

Asking a foreign-born wife to apply for citizenship independently provoked few complaints from legislators at a House hearing on the Rogers bill, but requiring that she then meet all the standard naturalization requirements—including proof of five years' residence in the United States—met stiff resistance. John Raker, whose uncurbed sarcasm had earlier enlivened debates over the Rankin bill, spoke for many of his colleagues when he objected to this fundamental change in the government's treatment of citizens' foreign-born wives. "We have been trying to give [these] women an opportunity to participate in the elec-

4. H.R. 12749, 66th Cong., 2d sess. (1920).

torate," he reminded his colleagues. "Why should we jump around now and deprive these good women who marry American citizens, and who are rearing American citizens, from the right to vote?"[5]

Advocates of the bill tried to shift attention to the injustices dependent citizenship dealt married women.[6] One witness cited the high incidence of desertion among alien husbands to illustrate the difficulties facing some women forced to remain noncitizens. These abandoned wives did not qualify for public assistance, might be dismissed from their jobs and face deportation because they were aliens. Federal law denied them the means of avoiding these crises by prohibiting them from pursuing naturalization.

Florence Bain Gual knew such hardship. After fifteen years as a public school teacher in New York City she faced dismissal from her job because she had lost her citizenship when she married a Cuban. And she had poor prospects for becoming an American again. The husband for whom she had forfeited her citizenship had deserted her and their baby and had not followed up on his declaration of intention to become an American citizen. As the distraught woman told a correspondent, "I am the daughter of an American citizen and the mother of an American citizen, yet I am to be deprived of my livelihood in my own country because of the citizenship of a man."[7] Rogers's bill would have extended the option of naturalization to Gual and others similarly situated, even if their spouses had disappeared, were not qualified for naturalization, or declined to seek citizenship.

Nevertheless, the Rogers bill offered only a partial remedy for the harsh effects of marital expatriation. Even if the proposed suffrage amendment and the Rogers bill had both become law in 1920, a married woman with a foreign spouse would have been forced to remain in the country to take advantage of the new rules. The American who left the United States with her foreign husband was still forced to relinquish her citizenship at the border. Gauging a female's allegiance by her choice of a marital partner still retained some credibility in 1920. Even

5. Hearings before the Committee on Immigration and Naturalization, *Proposed Changes in Naturalization Laws,* 66th Cong., 2d sess., Feb. 28, 1920, 10. In further hearings on naturalization reform, the House Committee heard testimonies conveying related concerns. See Hearings before the Committee on Immigration and Naturalization, *Progress and Processes of Naturalization,* 67th Cong., 1st sess., Oct. 19–22, Nov. 22, 1921, 1024–1025, 1073–1074, 1084.

6. House Hearings, Feb. 28, 1920, *Proposed Changes in Naturalization Laws.*.

7. Florence Bain Gual to Harriot Stanton Blatch, Apr. 5, 1921, *NWPP.*

Rogers acknowledged that he had no desire to protect the interests of nonresident women—women who, in his words, were mere "title-hunters."[8] The *Chicago Tribune* offered this conventional appraisal of the merits of the policy: "Women sentimentally adopt the land of their husbands when they marry abroad. That is the land of their children. Generally they marry because of social ambition and they take a great deal of American money abroad in doing so. A law which regarded them as American citizens in spite of their transfer of allegiance would be a harmful fiction."[9]

The Rogers bill was just one of an ample handful of women's nationality bills introduced before the ratification of the Anthony Amendment.[10] The most radical provisions surfaced in a bill sponsored by Representative Daniel R. Anthony of Kansas. Anthony proposed giving American mothers the ability to transmit their citizenship to their foreign-born minor children, an innovation requiring a significant alteration in the country's customary understanding and application of the rule of *jus sanguinis*.[11]

A family's shared nationality, like its common surname, was more a tribute to paternal authority than to family unity, and patriarchal notions about familial headship deterred the adoption of this reform in the United States. Indeed, transferring U.S. citizenship to their children would be the last major advance by married women in the realm of nationality rights.[12] Only a minority of countries allowed the rule of *jus sanguinis* to include maternal rights in the conveyance of nationality from parent to child.

The Anthony bill suggested another controversial departure from the rules governing marital domicile in order to preserve the citizenship of a nonresident American woman with a noncitizen spouse. Unless a woman married to an alien submitted a declaration of renunciation of her citizenship to a naturalization court or an American consul, she

---

8. House Hearings, Feb. 28, 1920, *Proposed Changes in Naturalization Laws*, 16.

9. "A Woman's Citizenship Is Her Husband's," editorial, *Chicago Tribune*, 28 May 1922.

10. H.R. 10374, 66th Cong., 2d sess. (1920); H.R. 10435, 66th Cong., 2d sess. (1920).

11. Federal law finally granted married mothers the ability to transfer U.S. citizenship to their children in 1934. See sect. 1 of Act of May 24, 1934, 48 Stat. 797, revising sect. 1993 of the Revised Statutes.

12. See Albert Levitt, "The Domicile of a Married Woman," *Central Law Journal* 91 (July 2–9, 1920): 4ff. By 1920 some states had eased this common law rule of matrimonial domicile by granting citizen wives limited opportunities to establish a separate domicile for divorce or voting purposes.

could not be denationalized. This provision implied that, in addition to receiving an independent and personal nationality, wives could claim a legal domicile other than their husbands' for citizenship purposes. Congress's rather cynical view of the nonresident woman's attachment to the United States made this provision unpopular.

The reactions to this spate of reform proposals varied widely outside Congress. The National League of Women Voters (NLWV), which formed shortly after the suffrage victory, publicly applauded the Anthony bill but privately dismissed its provisions as unrealistic.[13] Instead, the League seemed satisfied with the comparatively modest Rogers plan, which aided only resident women seeking to gain or retain American citizenship. Undoubtedly, the League's cautious leaders favored the more conservative bill because it had the best chance for survival. At its first annual convention, held shortly before the Congressional hearing on these nationality bills, NLWV members had agreed to press for nationality-reform legislation that would produce only minimal international complications. This decision by the most prominent organization in the women's independent-citizenship campaign silenced any endorsement of nonresidents' repatriation until after the passage of legislation granting independent citizenship to women living in the United States. The NLWV had not discussed the Rogers bill at its annual convention, but when asked for an opinion on this legislative proposal, NLWV president Maud Wood Park pronounced the bill a promising candidate for League endorsement and compatible with her views. "Realizing that if the woman were to go abroad there might be complications, I personally am very glad to see that this bill . . . applied . . . to circumstances when women remain in the country," she responded.[14]

John M. Maguire, a legal scholar, was one of the decidedly unfriendly

13. The League actually first appeared in March 1919, prior to ratification of the Anthony Amendment, as a department within NAWSA. Its American Citizenship Committee proposed establishing English as the language of instruction in public schools, the creation of citizenship schools that would issue certificates required for naturalization, educational qualifications for the vote, and direct citizenship for women. *Program for Work of the National League of Women Voters. Reports of the Standing Committees* [c. 1920], 14; copy in papers of Maud Wood Park, Women's Rights Collection, Schlesinger Library, Cambridge, Mass. (papers hereafter referred to as *MWPWRC*). For public reaction to the announcement of the League's formation, see Louise M. Young, *In the Public Interest. The League of Women Voters, 1920–1970* (Westport, Conn.: Greenwood Press, 1989), 35–40.

14. House Hearings, Feb. 28, 1920, *Proposed Changes in Naturalization Laws,* 7.

commentators on the debate over women's naturalization and expatriation. In his article for the *American Law Review*, which appeared a few months after ratification of the Nineteenth Amendment, Maguire noted that recent nationality bills did not clarify whether a married woman could establish an independent domicile. This was a serious oversight, he argued, because an American woman departing from the country with her alien husband could leave behind a host of unanswered questions regarding the circumstances of her removal, her future plans, and the taxation of her property. However, Maguire's major objection to these independent-nationality bills was their reactivation or retention of an expatriated woman's premarital citizenship, even if her husband was classified as an alien enemy. This policy, he warned, could seriously compromise national security interests: "Just as we have for more than sixty years acted upon the reasonable hope that the average foreign-born wife of an American would herself be a loyal citizen, so we must recognize that this country is likely to forfeit some of an American-born woman's original loyalty after her foreign marriage. . . . A woman torn by double allegiance and with her affections pledged to a man in the enemy camp may easily be a very bad citizen indeed. Often it will be necessary to restrain her activities as we restrained those of alien enemies during the war."[15] Former American women married to these aliens always had the option of divorce, Maguire reasoned. As long as a wife remained with her foreign husband, she compromised her devotion to the United States. The wisdom of allowing her to petition for naturalization while still married was, concluded the cautious Maguire, "doubtful to say the least."[16]

The vigorous struggle for women's independent citizenship would continue unabated until the mid-1930s. In the early 1920s, members of the fledgling Women's Joint Congressional Committee (WJCC) dominated the campaign; and standing at the forefront of that coalition was the NLWV. The WJCC was a confederation of independent women's groups, self-defined as "a clearinghouse for organizations engaged in promoting in Congress legislation of especial interest to women." Respectfully dubbed by outsiders as "the Women's Lobby on Capitol

---

15. John M. Maguire, "Suffrage and Married Women's Nationality," *American Law Review* 54 (Sept.-Oct. 1920): 654–655.

16. Ibid., 655. Maguire should have noted, however, that federal law prohibited changing one's citizenship during time of war.

Hill," the WJCC represented twelve organizations in 1921, when it created its subcommittee on independent citizenship.[17]

The original citizenship subcommittee included some of the most influential organizations within the WJCC: the NLWV, National Women's Trade Union League, American Association of University Women, National Council of Jewish Women, National Woman's Christian Temperance Union, and General Federation of Women's Clubs. Maud Wood Park coordinated the subcommittee's efforts. Having served as a president of both the NLWV and the WJCC and highly respected by federal legislators, Park was amply qualified for this leadership role. Over the decade, Park and her associates would successfully cultivate key allies within the House Committee on Immigration and Naturalization, including John Raker, John Cable, and its chairperson, Albert Johnson. The National Federation of Business and Professional Women was not a member of the subcommittee, but it also endorsed federal legislation for independent citizenship at its July 1922 convention.[18] The NWP was conspicuously absent from both the WJCC's membership list and, until 1922, from the nationality-rights crusade, but that absence was not lamented by the network of WJCC members orchestrating lobbying efforts from 1920 to 1922. The WJCC subcommittee preferred a gradualist approach to legal equality, a tactical style the NWP found inhibiting and inefficient as a way to reach its ambitious goals.

Nationality-reform bills for women appeared then disappeared regularly in the two years immediately following achievement of woman suffrage, and the absence of any legislative triumph during these few years belied the fact that the Nineteenth Amendment had begun to work a significant alteration in lawmakers' attitudes toward derivative citizenship. Despite evidence of a favorable shift in attitude within Congress toward nationality reform, the women had to direct their ap-

17. "Minutes of the Meeting of the Women's Joint Congressional Committee, March 31, 1921," *Women's Joint Congressional Committee Records, 1920–1970* (Washington, D.C.: Library of Congress, 1983), microfilm; hereafter cited as *WJCC*. Sophonisba P. Breckinridge, *Women in the Twentieth Century: A Study of Their Political, Social, and Economic Activities* (New York and London: McGraw-Hill,, 1933), 260. The WJCC began with ten organizational members in 1920 and doubled its size within five years. It should not be confused with the Women's Joint Legislative Committee, formed later as a coalition of pro–Equal Rights Amendment organizations.

18. Nettie Ottenberg, "In the Beginning", undated draft, *WJCC*.

peals to a federal government charged with establishing more effective (that is, more stringent) immigration and naturalization practices. Many of the consequences of granting independent citizenship to women conflicted with this objective.

Proposals to redeem women's autonomous citizenship appeared at every session of the Sixty-sixth and Sixty-seventh Congresses, but an outpouring of omnibus nationality-reform bills during these years created new difficulties for independent-citizenship activists. Many of these proposals lumped together several other reforms—some of which were highly controversial—with independent citizenship for resident women.[19] For example, one omnibus naturalization bill presented before the Sixty-sixth Congress required derivative citizens (wives and children) to take an oath of allegiance—a provision based on the notion that women who voted should offer an explicit expression of their national loyalty.[20] This requirement would have marked a modest step away from the assumption that vows of marital fidelity constituted an indisputable oath of political allegiance, but it was placed in a bill that also dealt with subjects unrelated to gender such as the elimination of first-paper voting in the states and the introduction of an English-literacy test for naturalization.

As a result, women's nationality rights proponents spent a frustrating two years trying to save their cause from being consumed in the debates on these other proposals, but Congress resisted isolating independent citizenship for married women from other legislative concerns relating to immigration and naturalization. The members of the WJCC subcommittee found they could not easily harness the growing interest in immigration and naturalization reform to work in their favor. Lawmakers' attentiveness to immigration and nationality policies generated brisk debate and a multitude of reform bills but not rapid progress in the expansion of married women's nationality rights. Legislation proposing comprehensive and controversial alterations in naturalization procedures repeatedly swamped proposals backed by the WJCC subcommittee. Although the women's coalition could continue to rely on

19. For discussion of an omnibus bill (H.R. 13646) produced by blending fifteen separate bills, see *Naturalization and Citizenship*, 66th Cong., 2d sess., 1920, H. Rept. 846. See also House Hearings, Oct. 19–22 and Nov. 21, 1921, *Progress and Processes of Naturalization.*.

20. *Naturalization and Citizenship*, 66th Cong., 3d sess., 1921, H. Rept. 1185, 2.

their supporters in Congress to champion independent citizenship, omnibus bills routinely sidelined their legislative proposals and dimmed their hopes of gaining even the smallest victory for equal nationality rights.[21]

The WJCC's subcommittee believed a separate nationality bill could at least progress to a floor vote if it was not absorbed or pushed aside by a package bill freighted with provocative provisions. That opportunity finally materialized when Albert Johnson, chairperson of the House Committee on Immigration and Naturalization, agreed to heed the subcommittee's demands for a separate bill.[22] In early summer of 1922, a major House hearing reopened discussion on naturalization reform for women, focusing particularly on one bill from the previous session that proposed to equalize naturalization standards and opportunities for immigrant women and men.[23] The House Committee on Immigration and Naturalization also discussed a new bill authored by one of its members, John L. Cable of Ohio. Strictly a women's nationality-rights bill, it quickly secured the endorsement of the NLWV, General Federation of Women's Clubs, American Association of University Women, National Council of Jewish Women, National Woman's Christian Temperance Union, and National Women's Trade Union League—all members of the WJCC's independent-citizenship subcommittee.[24]

Cable's bill differed somewhat from its predecessors; it abbreviated the repatriation process for resident, American-born women who had lost their citizenship through marriage by waiving the five-year resi-

21. At one point the subcommittee managed to have a separate nationality bill for women introduced in the Senate, but it succumbed to the same fate as their House proposals. S. 3403, 67th Cong., 2d sess. (1922). Secretary of Labor James Davis supported this bill. *CR* 62 (May 5, 1922), 6372–6373.

22. For preliminary negotiations between the WJCC and Albert Johnson, chair of the House Immigration and Naturalization Committee, see "Cable Act. Introductory Notes," folder 764, *MWPWRC.*

23. This Rogers bill was H.R. 15, 67th Cong., 1st sess. (1921). For discussion, see Hearings before the House Committee on Immigration and Naturalization, *Naturalization and Citizenship of Married Women,* 67th Cong., 2d sess., June 8, 1922.

John Raker's bill, also introduced the previous session and supported by the women's coalition, mirrored Rogers's in this particular respect. Obviously Raker had undergone an abrupt reversal in opinion by the time he advocated that citizens' wives meet all the standard prerequisites for U.S. citizenship. Raker's bill was H.R. 5525, 67th Cong., 1st sess. (1921).

24. H.R. 11773, 67th Cong., 2d sess. (1922), was a hybrid of H.R. 15 and H.R. 5525 (introduced the previous session) and Johnson's H.R. 10860.

dency requirement for naturalization. Yet, in other critical respects the plan did not represent an improvement over earlier proposals. The non-resident American who married an alien still lost her citizenship, and women who married aliens in the United States but subsequently established a residence abroad remained expatriates. The WJCC subcommittee still endorsed the bill, despite the restrictions it maintained on women's control of their citizenship.[25] It was apparent to the reform coalition that a viable bill would have to deny independent citizenship to some nonresident women in order to obtain relief for other women.

Cable's bill offered no shortcuts to naturalization for the foreign-born wife of a citizen and thus assured its failure. Subsequent developments suggested that this bill could have passed if it had distinguished itself from preceding bills on this particular issue. The majority in Congress still resisted the notion that American men's foreign wives should have to jump through all the conventional hoops leading to naturalization. Many legislators still viewed automatic naturalization as protective legislation for an especially deserving class of foreign-born women. Convinced that American citizenship carried unrivaled distinction and privilege, most members of Congress had never viewed automatic naturalization as an oppressive rule that robbed foreign women of something valuable. Alien women presumably welcomed the advantages of becoming "a citizen in a minute." Although immigrant women as a group were not customary recipients of Congressmen's solicitude, those who purportedly demonstrated their love for America by wedding an American enjoyed uncommon favor. If the advocates of independent naturalization expected to argue persuasively for the legislative abolition of marital naturalization, they would have to exhibit more compassion for the welfare of the citizen's immigrant wife.[26]

By 1922 the members of the House Committee on Immigration and Naturalization were prepared to discard the practice of automatically naturalizing wives in favor of a modified independent-naturalization process. Many of their colleagues also appeared more receptive than they had been in the past to this modification in the law, but the sort

25. Maud Wood Park, when asked about H.R. 11773, replied, "Of course on the basis of the absolute principle of the thing a good many of us women would prefer to see the law exactly the same for men and women. But we are willing to waive that point if the provision for residence in this country will help to discount any further international complications." House Hearings, June 8, 1922, *Naturalization and Citizenship of Married Women*, 572.
26. On H.R. 11773, see "Cable Act. Introductory Notes," folder 764, *MWPWRC*.

and number of naturalization requirements to be placed on the American citizen's wife was still a matter of debate.[27]

A new Cable bill offered an acceptable compromise: abolish marital naturalization but offer some special naturalization privileges to citizens' wives. Although marriage to an American would no longer immediately naturalize women, they could follow a simplified and speedier naturalization process that allowed them to bypass the declaration of intention and fulfill the residency requirement for naturalization after one year rather than five. Shoring up arguments against the abolition of marital naturalization was the underlying presumption that foreign-born women suffered from a kind of cultural affliction that made them less independent-minded than their American counterparts.[28] In the context of the debate over women's citizenship, these assumptions were rarely articulated so baldly but were nevertheless discernible in legislators' comments on the social implications and political consequences of transnational marriages. An American woman's marriage to an alien was, as one Congressman described it, "a clear, open, broad daylight, voluntary surrender of citizenship." Her act was defiant and deliberate and, ironically, was evidence of her singularly American spirit of independence. Indeed, the most devastating personal loss self-inflicted by her marriage was her submission to a man who could not appreciate or perhaps even tolerate the sense of autonomy that had distinguished her as an American woman.[29]

If the American woman was celebrated for her self-possession, the immigrant woman's unhappy distinction was her presumed lack of it. Given this conventional stereotype of the immigrant woman, it was no stretch of faith to assume that such a woman would readily submit to "the kind tutelage of her American husband" and embrace his country with an undivided heart.

Both supporters and critics of derivative citizenship believed Ameri-

27. *Naturalization and Citizenship of Married Women*, 67th Cong., 2d sess., 1922, H. Rept. 1110.

28. See, for example, comments by the Department of Labor's director of citizenship training attributing younger women's participation in citizenship classes to their being "more or less free from the conventions of their native land." He also praised the "nearly 5,000 foreign-born women who have reached the years of middle life, broke through the shackles of home duties and Old World customs and exercised their rights as prospective American citizens." Report of the commissioner of naturalization in U.S. Department of Labor, *Annual Report of the Secretary of Labor* (1920), 857.

29. John Raker in House Hearing, 1917, *Relative to Citizenship of American Women Married to Foreigners*, 19.

canization would boost an immigrant woman's self-esteem—but by what means she would truly become a "100 percent American" was debatable. The proponents of marital naturalization confidently entrusted that job to her citizen husband, while opponents insisted that citizenship training should precede rather than follow naturalization. Furthermore, the reformers asserted, marital naturalization robbed immigrant women of the opportunity to move independently through the process of achieving U.S. citizenship. It was this denied opportunity, not simply living with an American man, that would develop an immigrant woman's civic consciousness.

Park, the major spokesperson for the WJCC's subcommittee on nationality, expressed her impatience with the stock argument that independent naturalization posed an unscalable barrier to immigrant women's acquisition of citizenship. "If citizenship is a valuable thing to that woman, she will . . . find few obstacles in her way," she retorted. "If she does not pursue citizenship, then she will not suffer at its lack because it simply is not important to her." However, if perseverance led to success—and Park seemed assured that it would—achieving citizenship would give the immigrant woman "new standing in her family and in the community" because she alone had labored for the prize.[30]

After the NLWV successfully completed its first major postsuffrage campaign, the passage of the Sheppard-Towner Infancy and Maternity bill, independent citizenship for married women became the major federal measure on the League's agenda.[31] Its presuffrage predecessor, NAWSA, had been drawn to nationality-rights reform by American women's denationalization and disfranchisement under the 1907 act—not foreign women's loss of independent citizenship. The League had inherited many of NAWSA's members as well as its perspective on the securing of women's citizenship rights. It represented primarily, although not exclusively, the interests of native-born women, and League leaders spoke most earnestly when addressing the need to safeguard the citizenship of native-born women.[32]

30. House Hearings, June 8, 1922, *Naturalization and Citizenship of Married Women*, 589.

31. "Women Citizens at Work: The Next Campaign," *WC* 6 (Dec. 31, 1921): 18; Maud Wood Park, "No Sex in Citizenship," *WC* 6 (Jan. 14, 1922): 15–16.

32. Some feminists did more openly suggest that automatic naturalization produced citizens unworthy or unprepared to assume the responsibilities of their new status. See "Can the Wife and Daughter Vote?" letter to the editor, *WC* 4 (April 24, 1920): 1167;

The League's work among the foreign-born never persuaded its leadership to support the derivative naturalization of alien women; rather, it invigorated their interest in naturalization reform. When urging an end to marital naturalization, the NLWV refrained from arguing that automatic naturalization would produce generations of ignorant female voters. Instead, the organization approached the issue more diplomatically by emphasizing the personal disadvantages of marital naturalization. All women merited the freedom to chose their own citizenship, which was denied to them by both marital expatriation and marital naturalization. And, League spokespersons argued further, if the law enabled immigrant wives to seek naturalization on their own, it would enhance their status as citizens and the quality of their personal and political lives.

The NLWV promoted both the cultural assimilation and political education of foreign women. Indeed, its clear political objective made the League's work with immigrant women distinctive. The primary purpose of the NLWV's work with immigrant women was the production of responsible, *voting* female citizens. Any alien woman residing in the United States, the League enjoined, must be given the opportunity to assume the responsibility of pursuing American citizenship independently, regardless of whom she married.

The picture of the married immigrant woman carefully sketched by feminists during the course of the debates over marital naturalization was that of an independent individual. This representation provided little hint of her roles as wife or mother. Discussions about wifely devotion and maternal responsibilities had too often worked against the reformers' objectives. But members of Congress found the more familiar, family-focused image of the foreign-born woman far more appealing. Indeed, in the House debates over the revised Cable bill, the image of the immigrant woman as mother overwhelmed all others.

House and Senate opponents and supporters of the Cable bill both relied heavily on this domestic image of the immigrant wife, but the Congressional advocates of reform proved most skillful at using it to their advantage. One of the standard arguments raised against independent naturalization was that the woman who claimed a different nationality than her husband and children undermined her family's

---

Ellen Spencer Mussey, "International Marriages," *Daughters of the American Revolution Magazine* 54 (Feb. 1920): 92.

sense of unity. The Congressional advocates of the Cable plan had to arrest this argument quickly or risk losing major support for their bill. They responded by not only placing themselves under the family-unity banner raised by their opponents but also declaring that their opponents were marching under false colors. Pro-Cable legislators vowed that they, not their challengers, wished to reinforce the ties that bound family members together. Their argument was as simplistic and no less nationalistic than their rivals': the stable immigrant home was the home in which every member had earned U.S. citizenship by the distinction of birth or the discipline of training.

Although both sides in the Congressional debate shared an interest in Americanizing the citizen's foreign wife, they disagreed hotly over the means to that end. House members resistant to wives' separate naturalization argued that most immigrant women with families lacked the will or the time to prepare for the rigors of a naturalization examination. Consequently, the number of fully assimilated immigrant families would decline if married alien women were forced to satisfy all criteria for citizenship.[33] Raker, a supporter of the Cable bill, disagreed passionately: "[Immigrant wives] will be given an opportunity to be naturalized under this law and . . . become American citizens, irrespective of the sluggish, un-American, lazy husbands, who do not want to take the time and opportunity to give their wives American citizenship. We will eliminate that class, and they will wake up when mother begins to take an active part. . . . Father will wake up and take a bath and put on decent clothes and go with mother and become naturalized."[34]

Raker had a weakness for melodrama, but judging from the House record of the Cable debates, many of his colleagues were equally indulgent. Legislators' most vivid image of the immigrant woman was as a mother raising the country's budding citizens. Raker's message of redemption through naturalization capitalized on that image, enabling the Cable bill's advocates to subdue Congressional fears that independent citizenship threatened cherished models of marriage, motherhood, and family. But if this woman was not properly schooled for citizenship and the vote, it followed that her children and the country would suffer from her ignorance. Cable exploited this concern when extolling the virtues of his bill: "The true process of naturalization should include the education of the mother of this immigrant family.

---

33. House Hearings, June 8, 1922, *Naturalization and Citizenship of Married Women*.
34. *CR* 62 (June 20, 1922), 9056–9057.

The mother's influence and guidance would be lost to the family without the education that naturalization proceedings provide and require. My bill is intended to permit this wife and mother to learn something about the country. She is the one who should guide these children and ought to have the same privileges of an education as the father."[35]

This particular image of motherhood was far from new. The "republican mother" whose greatest civic duty was training her children to be virtuous Americans could be traced back to the early national period. The earliest calls for improving the education of American women had linked that reform to the maternal responsibilities of child rearing. In 1922 the association between maternalism and citizenship remained strong. Legislators respected the traditional division of parental responsibilities, which gave the mother principal responsibility for her children's moral and civic instruction. And when promoters of independent naturalization warned that dependent citizenship not only limited immigrant women's opportunities for self-improvement but stunted their ability to transmit American concepts to their children, their Congressional audience listened.

When one Congressman dared then to ask whether it was reasonable to "throw the same burden, the same mental requirement upon that wife when she is busy with her family and her household duties from morning until night," Cable quickly censured him. "We seek to give these foreign-born women a chance to be educated, and we are opposed to keeping the mother and wife in ignorance of our language and laws, as you do in many cases under the present naturalization law," he proclaimed.[36] Likewise, Raker accused the opposition of preferring to see the immigrant woman remain "a beast of burden . . . without any opportunity to see God's sunlight, or to get some of the benefits of civilization."[37]

Once assimilated, the immigrant woman presumably made that critical conversion from quaint "Old World" relic to proselyte of Americanization. The key transformative factor was, of course, her power to become a citizen on her own. Thus, the independent naturalization of alien wives, earlier condemned as a threat to family stability, was superbly marketed by the legislative supporters of the Cable bill as the most promising means of accelerating the Americanization of families

35. Ibid., 9045.
36. Ibid., 9045–9046.
37. Ibid., 9056.

and elevating the status of the immigrant woman within her home and her community. How could their opponents question the merits of such goals?

These arguments in support of independent naturalization for women carried a subtle warning to immigrant women. Acceptance of the Cable bill appeared to herald legislators' recognition of married women's right to autonomous citizenship and self-directed lives. Yet, in building a case for the independent naturalization of alien women, legislators emphasized not only the need for but the responsibility of foreign-born mothers to be educated, Americanized, and naturalized—all for the welfare of others. Thus a paramount obligation of those mothers of Americans was to assimilate and seek U.S. citizenship for the sake of their children. Resistance to Americanization betokened two of motherhood's deadly sins: ignorance and selfishness.

And despite all the rhetoric about a woman's influence over her children's citizenship, no member of Congress ventured to suggest that this influence should assume a more tangible form, such as the transmission of nationality from mother to child. Legislators seemed more comfortable continuing to assess maternal authority as an invisible tangle of moral and affective forces rather than something concrete enough to command the force of law.

•   •   •

Picture the scene described by a reporter for the *Woman Citizen* moments after the revised Cable bill's decisive victory in the House on June 20, 1922: "The women in the gallery stood up and smiled; the men on the floor looked up and smiled and one of them waved a hand to the group of women who have worked so hard for the bill. A man and a brother and a fellow-citizen, he made use of a sentence which from time immemorial has been held to be the inalienable property of women. 'I told you so,' he called out. 'Ladies, I told you so.' "[38]

The President would sign the bill three months later. Christened the Married Women's Independent Citizenship Act and nicknamed the Cable Act, the new law was initially hailed by both the enthusiastic and the disgruntled as a highly significant reform measure. The Cable Act would soon reveal its conservative reach, but at the moment of victory those who had labored so long for the law were not inclined to be apolo-

38. "The New Law," *WC* 7 (Oct. 7, 1922): 18.

getic or to be disheartened by the law's imperfections. The Cable Act was the best deal the reformers could negotiate in 1922.

The editors of the *Christian Science Monitor* shared feminists' initial satisfaction with the statute, proclaiming that the United States had "freed a legion of women from an archaic law which took no cognizance of political and moral progress."[39] Within a year of its enactment, however, sobering analyses had subdued praise for the Cable Act. The law had handed new freedoms to some women but removed legal protections from others. Even the law's supporters had initially underestimated the range of obstacles left intact or newly erected by the Cable Act. Its erstwhile boosters agreed that the statute served women inadequately, and bills to amend the law soon followed. Within a dozen years of its passage, all major provisions of the original statute would be amended or repealed.

The ratification of the Anthony Amendment had nudged Congress to consider the reasonableness, if not justness, of making some alterations in the laws prescribing marital expatriation and naturalization. Some legislators acknowledged that woman suffrage made derivative citizenship an archaic practice. Others declined to repudiate the rule so decisively but feared that the United States did risk dulling its recently burnished postwar image as a champion of democracy if the federal government continued to withhold independent citizenship and votes from thousands of resident women. But the most widely shared concern of federal legislators on the eve of the Cable bill's passage was the reaction of newly enfranchised women to Congress's resistance to reform. At a time when American women were still expected to form a bloc vote, Democrats and Republicans in Congress judged it politically hazardous to refuse to support some improvement in the nationality rights of women.

The Cable Act affected both alien and citizen-born women—women who had already married men of a different nationality as well as those who would wed noncitizens in the future. The new law granted most resident wives the option of maintaining their premarital citizenship or, in the case of aliens, pursuing naturalization independently. Nevertheless, without the protection of an American spouse, married women could still face exclusion from U.S. citizenship and in some cases from the country. A woman's ability to pursue naturalization or maintain

39. "Women No Longer Forfeit Nationality by Marriage," *Christian Science Monitor,* 23 Sept. 1922.

U.S. citizenship remained contingent on her spouse's eligibility for naturalization.[40] If he could not be naturalized for any reason, she could not; and if she was a citizen, she was denationalized for wedding a man ineligible for citizenship and could not seek repatriation until the termination of the marriage.

Under the Cable Act, race remained a central factor in the determination of a married woman's naturalization privileges. Indeed, as other barriers to women's independent citizenship gradually fell away, this criterion for naturalization emerged as one of the greatest threats to married women's citizenship—rivaled perhaps only by the equally durable residency requirement. If an alien woman was racially ineligible for citizenship, she could not be naturalized under any circumstances.

One of the most shocking consequences of the country's race-based naturalization policies was the permanent denationalization of native-born women of color. The American-born woman not identified as Caucasian or of African descent who married an alien ineligible for naturalization lost her U.S. citizenship permanently. Unlike other women who married men barred from naturalization, her situation could not be reversed by a subsequent divorce or widowhood. She assumed the ineffaceable and highly precarious status of an alien ineligible for naturalization. And in 1924, new immigration rules made her ability to retain residency in the United States even more problematical. If she left the country, immigration officials could deny her reentry into the United States, her country by birth.

As for the fate of other American women who married foreigners and resided abroad, the Cable Act made them "subject to the same presumption as a naturalized citizen," which meant they would lose their U.S. citizenship if they lived for two years in their husband's country or five years in any foreign territory.[41] Section 15 of the Expatriation Act of 1906 allowed the federal government to cancel citizens' naturalization papers if they established a permanent residence in another country within five years of receiving American citizenship.[42] Section

40. H.R. 12022, 67th Cong., 2d sess. (1922).

41. This particular provision would eventually draw the Cable Act into a major debate over expatriation policy in the interwar years. Cable may not have realized the full implications of incorporating this policy into his bill. He was surprised to discover that the State Department denied passports to nonresident women who married aliens after 1922. Cable to Burnita Shelton Matthews, NWPP, Jan. 7, 1931.

42. Act of June 29, 1906, 34 Stat. 596 at 601.

2 of the 1907 Expatriation Act, which also only applied to naturalized citizens, provided specific guidelines for the withdrawal of government protection once a naturalized citizen left the United States.

Federal law provided for the loss of United States citizenship if a naturalized citizen resided in his or her native country for two years or in any other country for at least five years. However, this absence did not necessarily result in the unrebuttable loss of citizenship—*unless* the individual had an alien husband. The act of returning to the country in all but these exceptional cases lifted the presumption of expatriation imposed by Section 2 of the Expatriation Act of 1907.

The relevant provisions in the 1906 and 1907 statutes generally only suspended or revoked the citizenship of absentee naturalized Americans.[43] The Cable bill not only extended this expatriation-through-residence policy to a group of native-born citizens, but after its passage American women who married foreigners and left the country had to seek reentry into the country as aliens not citizens. Rather than creating greater uniformity in the naturalization laws' treatment of the sexes, this particular provision actually increased the disparities. As the country's immigration laws grew increasingly restrictive, it became increasingly difficult and sometimes impossible for marital expatriates to return to the United States. The provisions of the Cable Act, working in conjunction with new immigration policies introduced in 1921 and 1924, barred some foreign-born and U.S.-born women from naturalization and repatriation and virtually excluded others from the United States.

43. By 1922 the question of expatriation by residence was still not settled, as the courts offered inconsistent interpretations of the 1907 statute. Not all judges followed the Attorney General's opinion in the Nazara Gossin case, 28 Op. Atty. Gen. 504 (1910), which had recognized that citizenship could be preserved after a lengthy residence abroad if the American returned to the United States. See also *Banning v. Penrose*, 255 F. 159 (1919), and *United States v. Eliasen*, 11 F.2d 785 (1926). Contra, *United States ex. rel. Anderson v. Howe*, 231 F. 546 (1916), and *Rojak v. Marshall*, 34 F.2d 219 (1929). Secretary of State Elihu Root's guidelines to diplomatic and consular officers on implementation of the Expatriation Act of 1907 are in a letter dated Apr. 19, 1907, *For. Rel.* (1907, pt. 1), 3.

In cases involving women married after 1922, the federal government skirted debate about the ambiguous status of returning citizens by revoking a woman's citizenship if she lived abroad with her foreign husband. For further discussion of this subject, see Borchard, *Diplomatic Protection of Citizens Abroad;* Margaret Lambie, "Presumption of Cessation of Citizenship: Its Effect on International Claims," *American Journal of International Law* 24 (1930): 264–278.

The Cable Act carried both enumerated and hidden disadvantages for expatriate women with foreign spouses or domiciles. Indeed, some of the law's provisions meted out penalties harsher than those imposed on any other group of citizens, native or naturalized. For example, married women seeking repatriation had to demonstrate that they would live in the United States permanently. In most cases their repatriation involved requesting permanent entry into the country as a quota immigrant, establishing permanent residency, and then submitting to naturalization proceedings to regain American citizenship. If naturalization examiners or courts did not believe the applicant would remain in the United States, they could refuse to grant naturalization papers.

Marriage to a noncitizen man clearly remained a serious liability under the Cable Act. Even if a married woman successfully navigated through the various stages of the naturalization process, her citizenship remained endangered. If she left the country, the Bureau of Naturalization could revoke her naturalization certificate on the grounds that it was procured fraudulently.[44] If Congress had not carefully classified all women who resumed U.S. citizenship under the Cable plan as naturalized Americans, the reach of the Bureau's supervision over marital expatriates would have ended at the point of repatriation. But, technically, a native-born American woman was not repatriated but naturalized under the Cable Act rules. The new law allowed the government to disavow any knowledge of this woman's former status as a U.S. citizen. By refusing to restore her former status as a birth citizen, the federal government retained its control over her future status as a citizen.

The Cable Act's provisions did not apply exclusively to married women, and the restrictions they placed on the repatriation of women previously married to aliens exceeded those imposed by previous rules. If these women were still living abroad after the termination of the marriages, they would have to follow the same "repatriation" guidelines set out for other female expatriates living abroad. Prior to 1922, the rules governing the repatriation of widowed or divorced women had been more lenient: a woman simply returned to the United States or registered as an American citizen with a consul. The Cable Act discarded this simple repatriation procedure and replaced it with a more

---

44. *United States v. Martin*, 10 F.2d 585 (1925). Emily Martin had not left the country, but the federal government revoked her naturalization papers on the grounds that she had not proven her intent to reside in the United States permanently.

complicated naturalization process. All nonresident, expatriate women followed the same set of procedures applicable to the foreign-born wives of citizens. They had to affirm their allegiance to the United States by returning to the country, establish residency, *and* petition for naturalization. This particular policy also governed the restoration of a resident woman's citizenship. Even if she had never left the country while married to a noncitizen, she had to petition for naturalization. Prior to the passage of the Cable bill, she would have automatically reassumed her premarital citizenship when her marriage ended. Although the proposed new set of repatriation and naturalization procedures simplified the administration of the law, it complicated the lives of many married foreign-born and native-born women who sought U.S. citizenship after 1922.

Under the Cable plan it was possible for a resident American woman married to an alien to hold two nationalities—a situation that provoked some protest from the State Department. The more serious dilemma posed by the new statute, however, was the rise in cases of statelessness resulting inevitably from the abolition of automatic naturalization by marriage. For example, British law expatriated a citizen woman who married an alien. If her husband was an American, she became stateless because she did not automatically become a U.S. citizen. This dilemma confronted any foreign woman who married an American and who was a citizen of one of the many countries that continued to enforce the rule of marital expatriation.[45]

The reduced residency requirement built into the Cable Act was designed to provide some relief to *heimatlos* (stateless) women married to Americans by allowing them to become U.S. citizens after living one year in the country. The House Committee on Immigration and Naturalization had anticipated this problem but reasoned that women could escape from statelessness quickly. "In the first place, [the married alien woman] will have every incentive to qualify herself as rapidly as possible," noted the Committee, "and, in the second place, if she can qualify, it is desirable to relieve her of the embarrassment of being without a

45. British opinion on the Cable Act is found in "Women without a Country Are in Straits from the New American Nationality Law," *New York Times,* 18 Oct. 1922. The largest group of noncitizen women rendered stateless by the Cable Act were Canadian. Any Canadian woman who married an American between Sept. 22, 1922, and Jan. 15, 1932, remained stateless until she was naturalized separately under U.S. law. (Canada revised its nationality law in this respect in 1932.)

country as soon as may be consistent with the welfare of the United States."[46] Regardless of these assurances, the law put many women's ability to hold any citizenship at risk. If a U.S. citizen's wife could not satisfy other basic naturalization standards established by federal law, she would remain trapped in the limbo of statelessness. Her other means of escape were divorce or the death of her husband.

When the Cable bill had reached the Senate Committee on Immigration, several members had hesitated to approve it, citing the State Department's objections to some provisions. Lebaron Cott, the chair of the Senate Committee, warned that a bill producing significant international complications "should not be passed in the absence of very weighty reasons."[47] Cott was echoing the views of Secretary of State Charles Evans Hughes, who had worried that the bill's expatriation-by-residence rule would create new problems for his Department. The federal courts were still wrestling with the original expatriation rules related to foreign domiciles because they contained no clear agreement on the definition of "residence." "These provisions have never been construed by the court of last resort," Hughes told Cott. "I believe unfortunate and vexatious questions would arise should the bill under consideration become law."[48]

The State Department was also alarmed by the prospect of a rise in the number of dual citizens, a trend that would surely develop if the bill passed. This was a concern that proved far more durable as an influence on future policymaking than the purported lack of virtue of expatriate heiresses. An increasing number of Americans moved and settled abroad after World War I, and an estimated 435,000 natives and 62,000 naturalized citizens left the United States between 1918 and

46. *Naturalization and Citizenship of Married Women,* H. Rept. 1110, 2.

47. *Citizenship and Naturalization of Married Women. Letter from the Secretary of State to the Chairman of the Committee on Immigration Transmitting Views Relative to the Curtis Bill, and Other Memoranda Bearing on the Curtis and Cable Bills,* 67th Cong., 2d sess., 1922, unpublished S. Doc. 3.

48. Charles Evans Hughes to Lebaron Cott, ibid., 4. The State Department's representative at the Cable bill's hearing had offered a favorable personal report. Fred K. Nielsen, solicitor for the State Department, testified that he objected to the Cable bill's expatriation of women for foreign residence. Nielsen pointed out correctly that this innovation represented a serious break from precedent by proposing to denationalize native-born Americans for moving abroad—something even the Expatriation Act of 1907 did not do explicitly. House Hearings, June 8, 1922, *Naturalization and Citizenship of Married Women,* 575–579. See also Nielsen's article, "Some Vexatious Questions Relating to Nationality," *Columbia Law Review* 20 (1920): 840–861.

1929 for extended, sometimes permanent "visits" to other countries.[49] As the size of this absentee citizen population increased, so did protests from State Department officials responsible for protecting citizens abroad.

The State Department had not been a highly visible contributor to the debates over the Cable bill, but subsequent efforts by proponents of equal nationality rights to amend this policy would face stiff opposition from State Department officials. Eventually reformers would find themselves standing at odds with the Department not only over this particular policy but over others relating to the transference of nationality from citizen women to their foreign-born children.[50]

The Labor Department's internal discussions of the Cable bill had revealed considerable concern over the uncertain impact of some key provisions. Secretary of Labor James Davis accurately predicted the "practical difficulties" that would face the Cable bill if it became law, and his correspondence with other Labor officials and President Warren Harding revealed that Davis initially planned to derail what he considered a highly imperfect piece of legislation. Davis sent the President a lengthy list of suggested alterations to the Cable bill compiled by his Bureau of Naturalization. Then, in a letter dated a few days before the bill moved successfully through Congress, Davis suggested that Harding should, if it arrived on his desk, send the bill back to the House with the Naturalization Bureau's amendments attached. Davis's correspondence suggests some ambivalence toward the bill. He berated Cable's plan as nothing less than "a radical departure from the fundamental principles of society upon which the Anglo-Saxon governments have been founded" but then conceded that it was "widely endorsed by women's organizations all over the country, and for that reason, perhaps, . . . should become a law."[51]

Davis wanted to see a more precise blueprint for reform, one that

49. The total number of Americans departing between 1918 and 1931 was an estimated 539,619. Table 80 in U.S. Department of Labor, Bureau of Immigration, *Annual Report of the Commissioner General of Immigration* (Washington, D.C.: G.P.O., 1931), 215.

50. *Nationality Laws of the United States. Message from the President of the United States Transmitting a Report Proposing a Revision and Codification of the Nationality Law of the United States.* Pt. 1: *Proposed Code with Explanatory Comments* (Washington, D.C.: G.P.O., 1939).

51. James Davis to Warren Harding, 15 Sept. 1922, Chief Clerk's Files, U.S. Department of Labor, RG 174, National Archives, 155/22. (These papers will hereafter be cited as *CC*.) See also "Reasons for Changes Suggested in HR 12022," undated, *CC,* 155/22.

painstakingly detailed the benefits and losses dispensed by the law. His concern was legitimate. The Naturalization Bureau's proposed alterations would have provided needed clarifications in the bill without altering its framers' intent. However, this list of amendments probably never reached the House Committee because Davis abruptly rescinded his advice to the President. Consultations with his advisors had convinced the Secretary that meddling with the bill after it passed both houses of Congress could have unpleasant political repercussions. Theodore Risley, solicitor for the Department of Labor, had agreed with Davis that the changes suggested by the Bureau of Naturalization would put the legislation "in better form." But "at best," he added, "it would be impossible to reframe the act in language which would give a positive assurance that it was tight in every respect." The Solicitor's Office advised letting the bill proceed without interference; the bill's effect on the Immigration Quota Act of 1921, an issue that naturally concerned the Labor Department, could be adjusted later through an amendment to the immigration laws.[52]

Davis had received similar warnings from other Department members. His secretary, reacting to Risley's comments, pointed out that if Harding returned the bill to Congress, his action would be "of no appreciable benefit and might be the source of embarrassment to Congressman Cable."[53] Harriet Taylor Upton, vice chairman of the Republican National Committee's Executive Committee, also cautioned against instigating any stalling maneuvers. "Several Congressmen whom I know feel that their seats depend on the passing of this bill," she warned. "Mr. Cable . . . is perfectly sure that he cannot be elected if it does not pass." Upton also believed that the bill would succeed despite Harding's objections, and the Republicans would have sacrificed "every advantage we hope to gain by its passage." However, if the Cable bill passed before the November elections, "the Republican Party will take unto itself a group of bi-partisans, non-partisans, neutrals or whatever you want to call them, women."[54]

Davis then sent a letter to Harding advising acceptance of the Cable bill. Perhaps to dispel any doubts he may have planted earlier in Harding's mind (or to justify his reversal), Davis noted that Cable had

52. Memo from Theodore Risley to Davis, Sept. 15, 1922, CC, 155/22.

53. Memo from Davis's private secretary, Sept. 15, 1922, CC, 155/22.

54. Harriet Taylor Upton to Davis, Sept. 13, 1922, CC, 155/22. Upton was the vice-chair of the Republican National Committee's Executive Committee.

agreed to support the Labor Department's amendments once the bill passed.[55]

Despite Secretaries Davis's and Hughes's doubts, Park and a few other lobbyists managed to persuade a quorum to file a favorable Senate Committee report in early September.[56] On September 9, 1922, the Cable bill passed in the Senate without a roll call, and on the September 22 it became law. When the President signed the bill, he presented the signatory pen to Park in recognition of her distinguished efforts in behalf of women's nationality rights.[57]

The WJCC subcommittee on citizenship had agreed to let the bill's residence restriction on repatriation pass unchallenged. Park did acknowledge that she and her colleagues eventually hoped to rout all double standards from the country's nationality laws, but she confessed that for the moment "we are willing to waive that point if the provision for residence in this country will help to discount any further international complications."[58]

The strong Congressional support for the Cable Act confirmed that many members of Congress still believed that American women's foreign liaisons carried cultural and political liabilities that American men's marriages to foreigners simply could not. While women's marriages to aliens still struggled for respect, American men's marriages to noncitizens drew praise as pro-American rather than anti-American acts. The ratification of the Nineteenth Amendment alone could not banish all the arguments arrayed against women's demands for equal political rights, and deeply ingrained notions about male dominance and female passivity had knit a gendered contradiction into the law of nationality that was not easily unraveled. Marrying an alien could be either an act of disloyalty or one of patriotism, depending on the sex and nationality of the actor. As one American woman disowned by her country lamented, "If for men it is even a patriotic deed to extend by marriage the influence and partnership of their country in foreign lands, why should it not be the same when it is an American girl who marries a foreigner?"[59]

55. Davis to Harding, Sept. 19, 1922, *CC*, 155/22.

56. R. H., "Unfinished Business," *MWPWRC*, folder 764.

57. Congratulatory letter from Cable to Park, July 21, 1922, *MWPWRC*, folder 765.

58. House Hearings, June 8, 1922, *Naturalization and Citizenship of Married Women*, 572.

59. Letter of Linda E. Hardesty de Reyes-Guerra to NWP headquarters, May 1922, *NWPP*.

The Cable Act did not explain this legal conundrum, and the government's ability to sidestep this question had been part of the bargain struck by reformers in 1922 to reap key votes in Congress. Realizing that legislators' distrust of women who had left the United States to marry foreigners could not then be dispelled by lobbying alone, the reform coalition and its allies in Congress temporarily set aside the interests of these so-called prodigal daughters living abroad in order to build legislative support for an independent citizenship bill.[60]

The Cable Act drew mixed responses from the distinguished members of the American Society for International Law.[61] Some influential participants attacked the law as a breach of international comity; and one highly placed member, who held a position in the State Department's Solicitor's Office, openly criticized the Cable Act. While participating in a discussion at a meeting of the Society, Richard Flournoy, Jr., was asked why the State Department had not pressed President Harding to reject the Cable bill. "I cannot answer that question," he declared flatly. "I had nothing to do with it myself. I would have vetoed it."[62] Flournoy was dissatisfied not only with the provisions of the law but the reason for its passage. Speculating that a group of aggressive female lobbyists forced the law on Congress, he thought it "questionable whether the majority of women of this country really wanted the new law." "Probably most of them knew nothing about it," he added.[63]

Flournoy was one of the more prominent critics of the Cable Act in the 1920s, but another well-known member of that circle of interna-

---

60. Cable presented this provision in his bill as one of its strengths. *CR* 62 (June 20, 1922), 9046.

61. James Brown Scott, one of the former members of the executive commission that provided the guidelines for the Expatriation Act of 1907, had strongly supported the membership of Emma Wold and Doris Stevens in the American Society for International Law. Scott was a close friend of Stevens, whom he met at an international conference in the 1920s. There is some interesting correspondence between Stevens and Scott in Stevens's papers at the Schlesinger Library, Radcliffe College, Cambridge, Mass., 76–246, folders 161 and 162; 78-M196, folder 13. (Stevens's papers hereafter referred to as *DS.*)

62. *Proceedings of the American Society for International Law at Its Twentieth Annual Meeting Held . . . April 22–24, 1926* (Washington, D.C., 1926), 98–99. Although Flournoy suggested he had no hand in the negotiations, Secretary Hughes had sent Park and Cable to him to work out the rough spots in the Cable bill.

63. Richard W. Flournoy, Jr., "The New Married Women's Citizenship Law," *Yale Law Journal* 33 (1923): 159–170. For another critical assessment of the Cable Act and the rising problem of statelessness, see Jesse S. Reeves, "Nationality of Married Women," *American Journal of International Law* 17 (1923): 97–100.

tional-law experts also withheld his applause for the new statute. Edwin Borchard, a law professor at Yale University, thought it most practical for the nationality of husband and wife to be identical, but he also believed women should have an opportunity to avoid expatriation. "The Cable Act, I think, would have created much less confusion than it has if it had been left . . . that the nationality of the wife shall follow that of the husband, provided she does not, by some affirmative act, indicate her desire to the contrary," concluded Borchard. "That would, I think, have preserved all the liberty that most of the women would like."[64] Borchard suggested presenting a more generous alternative to women but stopped short of questioning the application of unique expatriation rules to married women. Both he and Flournoy failed to address the principled argument for gender-blind expatriation policies forwarded by the WJCC subcommittee, choosing instead to place a higher value on the administrative expediencies afforded by pre-Cable policies.

Borchard and Flournoy were legal technicians, more concerned with avoiding legal conflicts between nations than with analyzing the merits of feminists' case for equal nationality rights. The individual's basic right to enjoy an independent personal nationality, overlooked by Flournoy and Borchard and too many others, was the heart of the coalition's argument. Yet, it is revealing that both the critics and the proponents of gender-blind nationality policies never challenged sex-based naturalization standards as a violation of Article I, Section 8, of the U.S. Constitution, which gave Congress the power and responsibility to establish uniform naturalization rules. Although such a Constitutional argument probably would not have fared well in the federal courts at that time, the absence of a serious attempt to present this position in any governmental forum reflects the limited tactical insight of the defenders of equal nationality rights.

Some legal scholars did defend the Cable Act. Gladys Harrison, responding directly to Borchard's critique of the Cable Act, challenged the persistent assumption that a woman's marriage vows represented her voluntary consent to expatriation. However, Harrison made it clear that although she welcomed the passage of the Cable Act, she believed the task of reform was far from complete. Most women in international marriages, she complained, still only received "a choice between penalties."[65]

64. *Proceedings of the American Society for International Law*, 91.
65. Gladys Harrison, "The Nationality of Married Women," *New York University Law Quarterly Review* 9 (June 1932): 449.

James Brown Scott and Cyril Hill, who had both served as members of the Roosevelt commission instrumental in the drafting of the Expatriation Act of 1907, also defended the Cable Act. Scott, a renowned expert in international law, would later support a gender-blind international code on nationality. His endorsement of the Cable Act in 1922, however, was not enthusiastic. He offered no generous praise of the Cable Act but welcomed the new law as a foundation for further reform.

Hill seemed more approving, presenting evidence of widespread support for the Cable Act among naturalization judges. A survey undertaken by the Carnegie Corporation of New York prior to the passage of the law had revealed that a majority of these judges supported the reforms the Cable Act instituted. When asked whether they favored women's separate naturalization regardless of the eligibility of their husbands as well as the preservation of an American woman's citizenship after marriage to an alien, two-thirds of the judges answered affirmatively.

Hill also questioned the reasonableness of the marital-unity argument that had once shielded derivative citizenship from harsh scrutiny. "The ties which unite husband and wife do not result from motives and desires of a political nature," counseled Hill. "Rarely does marriage result solely because the man is a member of a certain club, a certain church, a certain athletic organization, a certain political party, or a member of a certain political state. Marriage and citizenship are two institutions, separate and distinct. Never in the history of the world did they have less in common than they do today."[66]

The effectiveness of the Married Women's Independent Citizenship Act of 1922 remained a topic of debate throughout the 1920s and into the next decade. The voices for dependent citizenship grew fewer and fainter, and although a few bills to repeal the Cable Act appeared, they represented no real danger to the survival of law. Although the law never had to endure a battle for its repeal, it was the target of numerous reform bills. Before the statute was a year old, plans were underway for its reconstruction.

As predicted, the Cable Act did create some "vexatious" conflicts of law between the United States and those nations clinging to the tradi-

---

66. Cyril D. Hill, "Citizenship of Married Women," *American Journal of International Law* 18 (Oct. 1924): 723.

tional rules of matrimonial naturalization and expatriation; but the statute also reflected a new trend in nationality-law reform.[67] As its defenders noted, several countries were contemplating similar changes in their nationality laws, and other nations had already adopted them. Global uniformity in the laws dealing with women's transnational marriages was disintegrating, making conflicts of law inevitable whether or not the United States altered its rules.

Interest in women's nationality rights was quickening globally. With the enactment of the Cable Act, the U.S. government placed itself in the vanguard of a developing international movement that promised to grant women around the globe increased control over their citizenship. Nevertheless, top officials in the State Department and other experts in international relations continued to caution against the introduction of new nationality rules that could further disrupt the reciprocal practices the United States and most countries still followed to determine the citizenship of transnational couples.

Frustrated with the many limitations imposed by the so-called Married Women's Independent Citizenship Act, women in the United States continued to seek the freedom to hold a truly distinct political identity. If granted this status unconditionally, they could finally place themselves beyond the reach of punitive immigration laws: they would be able to travel outside the country without jeopardizing their citizenship, maintain their citizenship regardless of their spouse's eligibility for naturalization, bring family members to the United States as nonquota immigrants, and clothe their foreign-born children with American citizenship—all privileges or protections guaranteed to citizen men. Throughout the interwar years, a well-organized host of women would demand and secure these changes in federal law, moving women continuously closer to the goal of equal nationality rights. Their relentless reform efforts and the federal government's developing interest in creating an international code of nationality law would keep the issue of women's nationality rights within Congress's sights for many years. As before, attention to the issue did not mean easy work for reformers.

67. Most countries did provide for the automatic expatriation of their female citizens. France, Portugal, Italy, Switzerland, Bulgaria, China, Costa Rica, Mexico, and Nicaragua made expatriation dependent on the law of the husband's country in order to reduce cases of statelessness. If the wife could assume the husband's citizenship by marriage, she lost hers. The Soviet Union, Ecuador, and Salvador permitted a woman to retain her nationality after marriage to an alien.

They were asking the federal government to do nothing less than re-draw the boundaries between volitional and nonvolitional expatriation, between consensual and conscripted allegiance.[68] A successful struggle by women to achieve increased independence in matters of nationality meant granting citizen women a host of legal protections and privileges long enjoyed by citizen men. It also promised to infuse the concept of volitional citizenship with greater meaning than it had in the past by restraining Congress's ability to expatriate American citizens without their explicit consent.

When female reformers crusading under the banner of equal protection demanded a confrontation with their government on this ideological terrain, federal administrators repeatedly shrank from the challenge. Preoccupied with demands to restrict immigration and beginning to feel less intimidated by the demands of female voters, the federal government resisted acknowledging that independent citizenship was fundamentally a question of a woman's or even any individual's rights. Lawmakers certainly could not attempt the feeble argument that women and men enjoyed equal treatment under the country's immigration and nationality laws, and a dwindling number of legislators were willing to argue openly that citizen women deserved to be expatriated for marriages to aliens. But the inequities in the country's immigration and nationality laws lingered nevertheless because the policies in which they were embedded ably served the restrictionist goals of the era.

What evolved in the 1920s was a struggle between two reform objectives of irreconcilable parts. As the champions of citizens' rights, the advocates of independent citizenship believed their demands occupied a higher plane than those represented in other nationality-reform bills. Nevertheless, it proved impossible to broach the question of independent citizenship without becoming mired in the debates over containing the immigrant population and aliens' access to citizenship. Woman's rights reformers contended that these policy objectives, which focused on the status of the foreign-born, were irrelevant to discussions of the woman citizen's rights. The federal government, however, viewed all issues touching on immigration and expatriation as inter-

---

68. James Kettner describes the emergence and dominance of the principle of volitional citizenship in the United States in *The Development of American Citizenship*. For another analysis of the same development and its contemporary implications, see Schuck and Smith, *Citizenship without Consent*.

locking concerns facing a nation of immigrants. In the 1920s, the ideal of equal nationality rights for women simply was not powerful enough to remain untouched by the other public-policy matters that so engrossed Congress during these years of anxiety over immigration.

The *New York Times* spoke for many proponents of the Cable Act when it expressed both enthusiasm for the new statute and concern over its fate. "The principle of this [law] is excellent," the editors announced, "though it may encounter practical difficulties in execution."[69] As the decade progressed, making progress toward achieving equal nationality rights became increasingly difficult because the issue of dependent citizenship became even more entangled than it had been in the past in the elaborate net of federal legislation set to entrap undesirable aliens or absentee naturalized citizens. Most of the major laws passed to regulate immigration in the first half of the 1920s complicated rather than enhanced women's ability to control their citizenship and the fate of their families.

Initially, women had been able to capitalize on the Nineteenth Amendment's ratification. Emphasizing the interdependence of equal nationality rights and the citizen's right to vote, women's groups had argued that a country that accepted female suffrage could not deny a woman's entitlement to self-determined citizenship. Such arguments appeared to draw sympathy from crucial quarters: Congress agreed that, theoretically, a woman's determination of her citizenship should be represented by an uncoerced, unambiguous act; the Labor and State Departments claimed to accept the argument that a woman's marriage to an alien was not in itself a declaration of expatriation.

Yet, these concessions did not translate readily into new laws because pleas for independent citizenship filtered through a federal bureaucracy that was still more inclined to fortify than diminish the requisites for living and becoming a citizen in the United States. Liberalizing the standards governing married women's nationality meant undercutting a major policy goal many legislators thought vital to the nation's strength. Requiring women to provide detailed proof of their fitness for naturalization meshed with restrictionist aims; allowing American women to maintain their nationality despite foreign residences, to transfer their citizenship to foreign-born children, or to petition for the admission of their foreign spouses did not.

In the defense of its objectives, however, the women's coalition for

69. "Women Citizens," *New York Times*, 25 June 1922, sect. 2.

independent citizenship never abandoned the fundamental conviction that the nation's commitment to volitional citizenship did advance national interests and that one of those vital interests was aiding the emergence of one who had been too long shuttered from public view—the independent woman citizen.

CHAPTER 4

Entangled Nets

Immigration Control and the
Law of Naturalization

---

*The very best service we can render the world, and the largest
contribution we can possibly make to the sum and total of
human happiness, is to keep our country a land of improving
standards of living, of cleaner moral perceptions, of more robust
physical and mental health, and of finer ideals of government.
We cannot do this if we are careless and indifferent about the
elements which make up our composite citizenship.*

—Eugene Black, member of U.S. House of
Representatives, *Congressional Record* 65
(April 11, 1924)

*The immigration law of the future should be wholly American,
drawn by Americans, enforced by Americans for the benefit of
America to-day and in the future.*

—James J. Davis, *Annual Report of the
Secretary of Labor* (1923)

When the Cable Act went into effect in 1922, a new legislative plan to curtail foreign immigration had been in operation for
over a year.[1] Congress had designed the Immigration Act of 1921 (popularly known as the Quota Act) as a temporary measure and introduced
it as a more "scientific" and comprehensive approach to immigration

---

1. Immigration Act of May 19, 1921, 42 Stat. 5. See the Appendix in Kitty Calavita,
U.S. Immigration Law and the Control of Labor: 1820–1924 (London and Orlando, Fla.:
Academic Press, 1984), for immigration figures from 1820 to 1940.

control. The new law allowed Congress to spot-reduce immigration by placing greater restrictions on the annual admission of "new immigrants" from southern and eastern Europe than on "old immigrants" from western and northern Europe. By 1895, "new immigrants" constituted 57 percent of incoming aliens. By the first decade of the next century, that proportion had reached almost 72 percent.[2]

Legislation designed to stem immigration from certain countries had appeared in the last quarter of the 1800s with the construction of barriers to Chinese immigration. The addition of an Asiatic "barred zone" in 1917 had expanded the geographical compass of that restriction. At the same time, the addition of a long-debated literacy test to admissions requirements had entered the list of exclusionary factors, which already included race, criminality, moral turpitude, political radicalism, and medical infirmity.[3]

During its brief lifetime, the Quota Act of 1921 weathered harsh criticism for producing legal embarrassments for the Immigration Bureau, discriminating against certain ethnic groups, and inflicting hardship on thousands of families separated by its restrictive policies. The law also appeared to fuel the debate over the citizenship status of the American's nonresident wife. According to the statute, wives who were foreign citizens at the time of their marriage to Americans were "preference immigrants," a designation that suggested that the federal government did not recognize these women as derivative citizens *before* they resided in the United States. However, unless a woman's marriage

2. Under this new quota system, the total number of immigrants arriving from countries in northern or western Europe could reach 202,212. The ceiling on immigration from outside this area was 153,249. People applying for admission to the United States who were then living in a Western Hemisphere country and had resided there for at least five years were not affected by the quota system. See *Statistical Review of Immigration, 1820– 1910*, 61st Cong., 3d sess., 1911, S. Doc. 756, 8.

3. See sect. 3 of the Immigration Act of Feb. 5, 1917, 39 Stat. 874 at 875–878, for a list of excludable aliens. Many historians of U.S. immigration have noted the role of eugenical arguments in drawing this distinction between the "new" and the "old" from Europe. For some general discussions of the significance of nationality or national origin in the construction of immigration policy, consult Oscar Handlin, *Race and Nationality in American Life* (Garden City, N.Y.: Doubleday, Anchor Books, 1957), 74–110; Higham, *Strangers in the Land*, 1971 ed., 68–105, 300–330; Milton M. Gordon, *Assimilation in American Life. The Role of Race, Religion, and National Origins* (New York: Oxford University Press, 1964), 84–114; Leonard Dinnerstein and David M. Reimers, *Ethnic Americans. A History of Immigration and Assimilation* (New York: Dodd, Mead, 1975), 36–72; Roger Daniels, *Coming to America. A History of Immigration and Ethnicity in American Life* (New York: HarperCollins, 1990), 265–284.

to an American appeared fraudulent or she fell into one of the excludable classes, immigration officials generally allowed her to join her husband in the United States.[4]

Although the passage of the Cable Act did not affect the citizenship status of alien women who had married citizens before September 22, 1922, nonresident foreign women who married citizens after that date were subject to the quota restrictions imposed by the Quota Act of 1921. This immigration statute made special admission allowances for these Americans' wives, as well as other select family members; Section 2 explicitly directed officials to extend quota preference to the wives, parents, siblings, minor children, and fiancees of American citizens, declarant aliens, and aliens who served in the U.S. military during the recent war.[5] As preference immigrants these individuals could leapfrog over other immigrants to the top of the quota list, but the identification of American and resident alien men's wives and fiancees as preference immigrants provoked some querulous responses from women's groups angered by the government's persistent discrimination against citizen women's spouses and marital expatriates. The new law extended special privileges to the foreign spouses of men but made it more difficult than before for the immigrating husband of a citizen woman to gain admission to the country and virtually barred some expatriate women from entering the United States for permanent residence.

As preference immigrants, however, citizens' wives were still quota immigrants, and immigration officials could regulate their entry closely if economic or other circumstances prompted a general tightening of admissions. The citizen's wife's ability to take advantage of her special admission benefits depended on the strength of her ties to her American husband. If she emigrated with her citizen husband or followed him to the United States, her chances of entering the country improved; but if immigration officials suspected that a wife's plans to remain with her husband after entry seemed uncertain, the possibility of her exclusion increased, especially if she was requesting permanent resi-

---

4. The Immigration Act of 1917 also furnished evidence of the federal government's greater willingness to admit adult women than men. The statute's controversial literacy test did not apply to the alien's or citizen's immigrating wife, daughter, or grandmother. His father or grandfather also qualified for the exemption if over the age of fifty-five. Clearly the class of immigrants most heavily burdened by this test was the working-age man. Sect. 3, 39 Stat. 874 (1917).

5. Sect. 2(d), 42 Stat. 5 (1921).

dent status. And if she subsequently separated from her American husband, the government could expel her as an alien "likely to become a public charge."[6]

Post-Cable marriages to citizens could still offer some immigration and naturalization privileges to women, but their enjoyment of these perquisites rested on their continued status as the legal, loyal wives of Americans. This brief report appearing in the *New York Herald Tribune* was one reminder of the tenuous hold women had on these privileges:

BRIDE WIDOWED AT SEA; CITIZENSHIP IN DOUBT

A new problem was put to the immigration authorities yesterday when a woman twenty-five years of age who left Europe the bride of an American citizen reached here on the Ile de France the widow of the citizen. Vincente Pozarsky, fifty years of age of Milwaukee died at sea Sunday morning. As the wife of a citizen Mrs. Pozarsky was entitled to admission to the United States, but the inspectors on the ship were uncertain as to her status. They sent her to Ellis Island, where the case will be heard today. Her husband went abroad last month for no other purpose than to marry and bring his bride to America.[7]

With the introduction of the quota system, immigration policy assumed a more pronounced bias against not only certain nationalities and races but also family structures presumed less stable economically or in other respects less compatible with the cultural and material interests of American society. In the 1920s a household headed by an employed male citizen or declarant alien was the most highly preferred domestic arrangement, and policymakers made families in this category the most favored recipients of immigration privileges. The federal government assumed married women were economically dependent on their husbands, and, consequently, a husband's rather than a wife's merits as an immigrant generally determined the immediate family's

6. In contrast, if the citizen's wife requested only temporary admission as a visiting alien (to gain a divorce from her American husband, for instance), her chances of entering the country improved. Allan J. Eastman, "Australian Nationality Legislation: Nationality of Married Women," in *The British Year Book of International Law* (London: Oxford University Press, 1937), 181.

7. *New York Herald Tribune*, 18 Apr. 1929. See also *Ex parte Gorelick et al.*, 296 F. 572 (1924), in which a noncitizen woman's resident husband died while she was en route to the United States. The court responded that "it is settled policy of Congress not to separate a husband from his wife and minor children." Yet, "the husband and father having died, the reason for their admission ceases to exist" (573).

chances of entering the country, avoiding deportation, and bringing other relatives to the United States.

Married women were more likely to follow or accompany rather than precede their husbands to the United States. Not only could the husband generally find more gainful employment once he entered the labor force, but the chances of both husband and wife entering the United States improved if he arrived first or brought his spouse with him. A large percentage of men, married or single, arrived in the United States unaccompanied by family, and the government considered it sound social policy to foster the reunion of this resident man with his absentee family. Despite the restrictions imposed by the quota law, the government encouraged these men to reestablish a stable home life in the United States—*if* they intended to stay—by offering special admission and naturalization arrangements to the wives and children of male declarant aliens or citizens. Resident male laborers' wives and minor children were unlikely competitors for most American men's jobs, a reality that partially explained the government's willingness to assist the admission of citizens' or declarants' wives.[8]

Congress had provided a new system for regulating immigration and had revoked the practice of marital naturalization, but the tough task of detailing the admissions policy governing citizens' immigrant wives came to rest with the Labor Department. The Immigration Bureau worked to develop a stable policy applicable to these cases, but the difficulty of the task forced a rather fitful approach to the problem. Less than a week after the Cable Act went into effect, the Bureau's central office was fielding questions about the impact of the new law on immigration regulations. Commissioner General of Immigration W. W. Husband responded with a circular letter to all inspectors-in-charge, suggesting that they advise citizens' wives who could not obtain visas to procure an affidavit explaining why this endorsement had been withheld. Depending on the reason for the denial, the visa requirement might be waived. If wives faced delays simply because their country's quota was full, they could still be paroled.[9]

---

8. The laboring male immigrant who never intended to bring his family to the country—or to settle in the country—was often maligned as the greatest peril to American men's employment. For an example of the resentment toward these "birds of passage" on the part of leaders of organized American labor, see John Mitchell, "Protect the Workman," printed in *Restriction of Immigration*, 67th Cong., 2d sess., 1922, H. Rept. 710, 373. The Dillingham Commission recommended excluding temporary, unskilled male laborers unaccompanied by wives or children. Ibid., 47.

9. The wife who was paroled in, however, was not technically an *immigrant,* a term

Only months after promulgating this post-Cable policy, Assistant Commissioner General of Immigration I. F. Wixon notified immigration officials that the decision to admit quota wives who had been denied visas had robbed the Bureau of a measure of discretion it wished to preserve in cases involving citizens' relatives. The government would not assure American husbands that their wives would be able to rejoin them in the United States.[10] Nevertheless, the Immigration Bureau suffered some loss of control in its attempts to implement this revised policy when federal courts intervened on behalf of some excluded wives. These judicial reversals of its decisions sent the Bureau scrambling through another series of policy changes.[11]

A year after the Cable Act's enactment, the Labor Department and its agency were still struggling to establish a general admissions policy for citizens' wives. That spring the Labor Department had informed the Secretary of State that a citizen's foreign wife was indeed subject to the quota restrictions.[12] Yet when the commissioner general of immigration responded to an inquiry about citizens' wives later that year, he declared that "immediately upon an alien's receiving full citizenship, his wife may be admitted, after due inquiry, regardless of the Quota Law."[13] According to Acting Secretary of Labor Robe Carl White, his Department had felt pressured to breach the quota law in order to admit more citizens' wives: "As a matter of law, we may not admit her, but as a matter of fact, they all are admitted, because, thus far, no public

<hr>

applied to persons admitted for permanent residence. She was a visiting alien, and the difference between the two statuses was critical if the woman later attempted to petition for naturalization. "Circular letter to all Commissioners of Immigration and Inspectors-in-Charge," Oct. 27, 1922, *BIN*, 52903/43D.

10. "Memorandum for all employees engaged in the preparation of correspondence," Dec. 12, 1922. See also letter of Commissioner General W. W. Husband to royal counselor of emigration at the Italian Embassy, Dec. 16, 1922; letter from Husband to the Foreign Language Information Service, Dec. 28, 1922. *BIN*, 52903/43D.

11. Perhaps foreseeing the difficulties ahead, Second Assistant Secretary Robe Carl White observed a few months after the Cable Act's introduction that, regarding the admission of citizens' foreign wives, it was "inadvisable, at present, to state what that policy will be." White to Anson W. H. Taylor, Dec. 28, 1922, *BIN*, 52903/43D.

12. Letter of Second Assistant Secretary of Labor to the Secretary of State, Apr. 18, 1923. For an expression of concern over this policy's impact on families, see letter from the Society for Italian Immigrants to Secretary of Labor, Oct. 9, 1923. *BIN*, 52903/43D.

13. Letter of commissioner general to Erla Rodakiewicz of the YWCA, Oct. 17, 1923. See also correspondence of Acting Secretary of Labor White to Gaspare M. Cusumano of the Society for Italian Immigrants, Oct. 17, 1923; Assistant Commissioner General W. W. Sibray to commissioner of immigration at Boston, Oct. 26, 1923. *BIN*, 52903/43D.

officer has been found able to stand up under the everlasting hammering of hundreds of public officers and millions of American citizens who are shocked beyond expression at the thought that the wife of an American citizen should be denied admission. They care not that the law prohibits it. The truth of the matter is, cases of this kind almost wreck the machinery of the immigration service."[14]

After passage of the first quota law, Congress continued to debate the possibility of expanding the nonquota categories to promote family reunification.[15] A majority of the members of the House Committee on Immigration and Naturalization supported upgrading certain categories of relatives to nonquota status. As one bill's promoter explained, the Committee recognized that the American people favored reducing the flow of immigration but "not without sympathy for the interests of resident aliens and citizens struggling to bring dependent relatives to the United States."[16]

The persistent demand to lower immigration levels and the deepening concern over quota-divided families produced immigration-reform bills ranging in intent from the repeal of the literacy test to the suspension of immigration. What emerged from this tangle of bills was the Immigration Act of May 26, 1924, also known as the Johnson-Reed or National Origins Act.[17] By continuing to categorize and rank immigrants by nation of origin, the new statute reconfirmed Congress's preference for those ethnic groups popularly believed to produce the most assimilable, law-abiding, and civic-minded residents. Those individuals deigned least desirable as permanent residents—that is, persons ineligible for American citizenship—were now inadmissible.[18] The Johnson-

14. Memorandum from the Acting Secretary of Labor to the commissioner of naturalization, Feb. 2, 1924, reprinted in Harold Fields, "Shall We Naturalize Aliens Whose Wives Are Living Abroad?" *New American* 1 (Aug. 1925): 5.

15. For some discussion of these proposals, see *Admission of Certain Refugees from Near Eastern Countries and Restriction of Immigration into the United States, Including Revision of the Quota Act,* 67th Cong., 4th sess., 1923, H. Rept. 1621.

16. *Restriction of Immigration,* H. Rept. 710, 2.

17. For debates on the final bill, H.R. 7995, 68th Cong., 1st sess. (1924), see 65 *CR* (Apr. 11, 1924), 6110–6150, 6153–6177; on S. 2576, 68th Cong., 1st sess. (1924), see 65 *CR* (Apr. 18, 1924), 6608–6649. Immigration Act of May 26, 1924, 43 Stat. 153. Persons from Canada, Newfoundland, Mexico, Cuba, Haiti, the Dominican Republic, the Canal Zone, or any independent nation in Central or South America still did not have to submit to the quota head count. The 1952 McCarran-Walter Act repealed the 1924 Johnson-Reed (National Origins) Act.

18. The law did provide some exemptions from this exclusionary provision. See sect. 13, 43 Stat. at 162 (1924).

Reed Act did increase the number of relatives qualifying for nonquota entry but decreased the annual allotment of quota immigrants for several countries. Another now familiar pattern of discrimination also carried over to the new statute: the spouses of American women and American's wives did not receive equal consideration for admission. The Johnson-Reed Act advanced the resident citizen's immigrating wife to nonquota status. If her American husband was not yet a resident, however, she remained a preference immigrant—the government's subtle way of discouraging "new-seed" immigration. Congress did not entirely ignore the foreign husband of the American woman, but it did not grant him the nonquota status provided in the original draft of the bill. He could qualify as a preference immigrant, providing his petitioning resident wife was at least twenty-one years of age.[19] The new law offered nonresident expatriates married or once married to foreign men no protection from the quota snare. With the reduction in the size of the quotas and the ban on admitting persons ineligible for citizenship, many expatriate women found it more difficult than before or impossible to gain entry to the United States or permanent residence.

The new law reflected the federal government's unslackened commitment to immigration control and its concurrent desire to make admissions policies more responsive than they had been to the goal of family reunification. In negotiating a balance between these somewhat conflicting objectives, Congress devised preference quota and nonquota classifications that ranked immigrants not only by nationality and race but by family composition and circumstances. Immigrants' family connections to the United States increasingly affected their chances of gaining entry into the country. As immigration law became more restrictive, it exhibited a pronounced partiality not only for specific racial and ethnic groups but for particular family arrangements. Legislators presumed that certain factors contributed to a family's assimilation and economic stability, and those families possessing the highest sum of these factors had the best chances of uniting and remaining permanently in the United States. The family with a citizen or declarant hus-

19. Sect. 6(a) guaranteed preference in the issuance of quota visas to "a quota immigrant who is the unmarried child under 21 years of age, the father, the mother, the husband, or the wife, of a citizen of the United States who is 21 years of age or over." Sect. 4(a) provided nonquota status to "an immigrant who is the unmarried child under 18 years of age, or the wife, of a citizen of the United States who resides therein at the time of the filing of a petition under section 9."

band or father continued to enjoy most-favored-family status under the law, while households in which a wife or mother was the lone citizen or naturalization candidate received far less recognition. When grappling with the quota-related problems of immigrating families, the principal object of legislators' solicitude remained the married man forced to live without the comforts of family. As Representative Victor Berger of Wisconsin confidently announced, "All thinking people will agree that the wives and children of the immigrants we have permitted to come in will not be a disturbing element in our civilization." "On the contrary," he added, "if you do not encourage them to send for their families as soon as these immigrants have the necessary money, you help immorality; in fact you create it."[20] Secretary of Labor James Davis, an immigrant himself, agreed. "The man that can live in the bosom of his family is a better worker, a better citizen, [and] a better man."[21]

The Johnson-Reed Act of 1924 did not silence those critical of the immigration law's impact on families. The new statute did add flexibility to the quota system, but it still offered limited if any relief to the thousands who waited years for their names to rise to the top of the quota list.[22] "Is the quota more sacred than the family?" asked the editors of the *Interpreter,* published by of the Foreign Language Information Bureau: "So unbelievable is the [quota] barrier, that often a husband or wife cannot be convinced that it exists. Suspicion destroys their confidence in each other. He cannot believe that his wife cannot come to America when he sends for her. He thinks her unfaithful. He stops sending money. Perhaps he contracts a bigamous marriage. The wife hears that an American citizen can send for his wife outside the quota.

20. *CR* 65 (Apr. 11, 1924), 6135.
21. Reprint of speech by Davis in *CR* 63 (Apr. 11, 1924), 6174–7177. In his annual report for 1924 Davis offered a draft "selective-immigration" act designed to reduce further the number of families fractured by the new entry barriers. U.S. Department of Labor, *Annual Report of the Secretary of Labor* (1924), 87–97. Davis also urged altering the law to permit the husbands of Americans to enter as nonquota immigrants. See U.S. Department of Labor, *Annual Report of the Secretary of Labor* (1925), 111.
22. A study by Helen F. Eckerson in 1945 revealed that southern and eastern Europeans residing in the United States relied heavily on the nonquota provisions for relatives between 1925 and 1944. Eckerson noted that prior to 1910 northern and western European men were more likely to bring their families with them to the United States; in contrast, eastern and southern Europeans were more likely to send for their families later, a practice that obviously became more complicated in 1924. "Nonquota Immigration, Fiscal Years 1925–1944," U.S. *Immigration Naturalization Service Monthly Review* 3 (Aug. 1945): 187.

Why does her husband not become a citizen? He has ceased to care for her."[23]

Even if a resident husband did successfully petition for his wife's visa, the 1924 law left intact the government's power to exclude or detain her at entry point. Although changes in the quota system improved many citizen and declarant husbands' chances of hastening their families' arrival in the United States, the Bureau of Immigration's authority to exclude any "undesirable" member of his family remained substantial. Marriage to an American man provided no absolute guarantee against deportation or exclusion.[24]

One of the most controversial cases involving the exclusion of a citizen's wife began when the United States consul in Berlin denied a visa application to the wife of American millionaire and war veteran John Ulrich. Apparently Anna Minna Venzke Ulrich had a criminal record, which included convictions for moral turpitude, larceny, and forgery; but she had not troubled German authorities for several years and had been a minor when charged with the offenses. Her American husband sought a writ of mandamus to compel the U.S. State Department to issue the visa, but a federal district court rejected the petition. The Court of Appeals also declined to act, declaring that Section 2 of the Johnson-Reed Act clearly gave consular officers discretion over the issuance of nonquota and quota visas. The U.S. Supreme Court then rejected Ulrich's petition for a writ of certiorari.

John Ulrich spent thousands of dollars publicizing the federal government's refusal to allow his wife into the United States. He dispatched his lawyer to the halls of the Capitol to buttonhole legislators and to take advantage of any benefit he might gain from having the Republican House majority leader as his Congressional representative. The millionaire's money, persistence, and influence eventually paid off. Not coincidentally, the provisions of the Immigration Act

23. "Is the Quota More Sacred Than the Family?" *Interpreter* 6 (Oct. 1927): 4. For a description of general rules followed by residents when requesting visas for family members, see U.S. Dept. of Labor, Immigration and Naturalization Service, *Visa Petitions,* Lecture 5, Mar. 13, 1934.

24. *Gomez v. Nagle,* 6 F.2d 520 (1925). *Smith v. United States ex rel. Grisius,* 58 F.2d 1 (1932), is an example. In this case, the wife of a citizen was deported in 1932. After 1929, a deportee could not reenter the United States for permanent residency, so Grisius was effectively excluded from citizenship. Ten years earlier, the country's nationality law would have immediately granted her citizenship and thus saved her from either deportation or permanent exclusion.

of July 3, 1930, guaranteed Anna Ulrich's admission to the United States.[25]

If the letter of the law does not work in your favor, the spirit of the law might—or so Emilie Dorto, the wife of a naturalized American, discovered. She had arrived in the United States after the exhaustion of Italy's quota, but for reasons that are not clear from the court record immigration officials decided to release her on bail. Dorto was not married at the time, and her attorneys reportedly suggested that, under the circumstances, she should wed an American to shield herself from deportation. Following this advice, she found a man willing to come to her aid, but her impromptu marriage to a citizen was not speedy enough to free her from immigration officials. She had married one day after the Cable Act went into effect and thus remained a surplus quota immigrant.

The judges who heard Dorto's case preferred to focus on her husband's rights as a man and a citizen rather than on her deportable condition. Relying on *Mackenzie v. Hare* and *Tinker v. Colwell,* the latter a case in which the husband's right to his wife's companionship was described as a "property right," Judge Arthur Brown declared that the deportation of Emilie Dorto would violate her citizen husband's rights. Brown refused to use the Cable Act to justify her deportation, reasoning that Congress had not intended "to so enlarge the powers of administrative officers . . . as to deprive the American husband of the services of his lawful wife."[26] The federal government appealed the decision, but the judgment was affirmed. By the date of the appeal, Dorto's marriage had provided her with another buffer against deportation. Pregnant, she was now not only the wife of an American but the expectant mother of an American. The judges realized that she had

25. *United States ex rel. Ulrich v. Kellogg,* 30 F.2d 984 (1929). Act of July 3, 1930, 46 Stat. 849, revising sect. 8 of the Act of Sept. 22, 1922, 42 Stat. 1021, to read: "Provided, that no such wife shall be excluded because of offense committed during legal infancy, while a minor under the age of twenty-one years, and for which the sentences imposed were less than three months, and which were committed more than five years previous to the date of the passage of this amendment."

For debate on S. 3691, 71st Cong., 2d sess. (1930), see *CR* 72 (June 30, 1930), 12098–12103. Also, *Amending Cable Act to Permit the Wife of a Native-Born American Citizen and World War Veteran to Join Her Husband in the United States,* 71st Cong., 2d sess., 1930, S. Rept. 442 and H. Rept. 1697. Although other Cable Act amending bills did not become embroiled in partisan politics, this one did.

26. *Dorto v. Clark,* 300 F. at 571 (1924); *Mackenzie v. Hare,* 239 U.S. 299 (1915); *Tinker v. Colwell,* 193 U.S. 473 (1904).

married to avoid deportation but were persuaded that the couple planned to remain together in what had begun as a marriage of convenience. Noting that "love, mutual affection, and a child have resulted from a union thus primarily motived," the court refused to sunder this family.[27] Although Dorto's case was unusual in some respects, her treatment as an American's immigrant wife was less irregular. Whether Emilie Dorto was by law a deportable alien could have been the exclusive question in this case, but the courts chose to direct their attention elsewhere to consider the impact of her expulsion on her American husband and the citizen she carried. Standing before the bench *sans* family, Dorto would have lost her battle against deportation, but as both the wife and expectant mother of citizens she had acquired a social value she could never possess as an unmarried alien woman.

Legislators' sympathy for the pain and inconvenience caused by family separation produced a steady parade of bills and a handful of new laws to amend portions of the Johnson-Reed Act. By 1928, the foreign wives of both citizens and declarants had improved chances of securing residency in the United States, with the major exception of racially excludable wives. Prior to the passage of the Cable and Johnson-Reed Acts, the Labor and State Departments had permitted Chinese wives of American citizens into the country despite the Chinese exclusion laws. As an Acting Secretary of Labor had explained in a letter to the Secretary of State in 1914, "Even women of full Chinese blood who are married to American citizens are regarded as admissible to the United States . . . if admissible under the provisions of the general immigration act, upon the theory that the husband . . . has a right to have his wife with him in the country of his citizenship, whatever her race may be."[28] The Cable Act, however, invited immigration officials to challenge this privileging of husbands and their rights. Technically, the Cable Act had no effect on the admission status of Chinese wives; these women never had access to U.S. citizenship through marriage. Yet, the Bureau used the Cable Act as a strip of statutory ground from which to launch an assault on the notion that a husband's credentials for residence and citizenship transferred fully to his alien wife.

The Chinese wives of Americans were not on the Johnson-Reed list

27. *United States v. Dorto*, 5 F.2d 596 (1925).
28. Acting Secretary of Labor J. B. Densmore to Secretary of State, Jan. 28, 1914, *For. Rel.* (1914), 7. See also the leading pre-1924 case on the admissibility of Chinese wives of citizens, *Tsoi Sim v. United States*, 116 F. 920 (1902).

of nonquota immigrants, and it is unclear whether the law's architects anticipated the resulting exclusion of these women as persons ineligible for naturalization. Once again, it fell initially to the federal judiciary to grapple with the problem. In 1925, the Supreme Court heard two related cases involving the exclusion of Chinese wives whose husbands resided in the United States, but these judgments intensified rather than squelched criticism of the Johnson-Reed Act.

The steamship *President Lincoln* was en route from China to San Francisco when the Johnson-Reed Act went into effect on July 1, 1924. On board ship were thirty-five Chinese women married to either American citizens or Chinese merchants living in the United States. When the ship docked later that month, government officials informed the passengers that they were prohibited from landing by Section 13 of the new immigration statute, which excluded persons ineligible for citizenship. Apparently immigration officials were not certain they could exclude all thirty-five wives, and the women were detained at Angel Island to await word from the Secretary of Labor. Secretary James Davis then sustained the board of special inquiry's decision to exclude all the women.

At this time the Labor Department was smarting from a recent defeat in which a district judge in Massachusetts, James Arnold Lowell, had ordered the release of a citizen's Chinese wife who was being held for deportation. Lowell had concluded that the immigration commissioner's proceedings against the woman disturbed "settled law" permitting these women to live with their husbands in the United States.[29] The purpose of the Johnson-Reed Act was to regulate the movement of aliens in and out of the country, not reduce the rights of American citizens. The woman's ill-conceived deportation would only make her husband "discontented with his American citizenship" and "deprive him of the society of his wife, to which he is entitled by law."[30]

In the subsequent decision to admit the women of the *President Lin-*

29. *Ex parte Chiu Shee,* 1 F.2d 798 (1924). See also *Ex parte Goon Dip et al.,* 1 F.2d 811 (1924), in which a district judge asserted that the House Committee report on the 1924 statute and the act itself "clearly show the intent of Congress not to disturb the relations existing under the prior law and treaty"—that is, the Bureau of Immigration should not have assumed that sect. 13 of the 1924 law abrogated the policy allowing wives to enter as long as they were physically, morally, and mentally sound. For a useful summary of executive and judicial interpretations of the inadmissible-alien clauses of the Johnson-Reed Act, see A. Warner Parker, "The Ineligible to Citizenship Provisions of the Immigration Act of 1924," *American Journal of International Law* 19 (Jan. 1925): 23–47.

30. 1 F.2d at 799. Lowell had concluded that the legislators intended sect. 13 to apply only to aliens unrelated to citizens.

coln, Judge Frank H. Kerrigan echoed the convictions of his Massachusetts colleague. He acknowledged that the general purpose of the law was to restrict immigration but believed this objective was "not thwarted, or its attainment even menaced, by the admission of the wife and children ineligible to citizenship of an American citizen."[31] Judges Lowell and Kerrigan both suggested that the importance of preserving family bonds and men's traditional marital entitlements should ultimately guide the disposition of such cases. The Labor Department appealed, determined to fight this "doctrine of family unity," which threatened to unravel many of its cases involving the exclusion or expulsion of a citizen's close kin.

The Supreme Court considered the cases of the merchants' wives and citizens' wives separately. In *Cheung Sum Shee*, the case involving the Chinese merchants' wives on the *President Lincoln*, the Labor Department argued that the notion of marital unity had "lost much of its force" since the Cable Act's passage and could no longer be used to defend inadmissible aliens' entry as residents' wives.[32] While Labor Department officials contended that the admission of the women from the *President Lincoln* would impair the integrity and execution of immigration policies, the State Department worried that detaining the women violated the treaty rights of Chinese merchants. The Department's solicitor, Charles Cheney Hyde, argued that Chinese merchants' treaty rights naturally extended to their wives and minor children.[33] The law should treat a wife, in his words, as "an integral part of the husband's sphere of activity." The merchants' wives thus had no independent standing before the law.

As one observer reported, "The United States as appellee was in the rather amusing position of having one executive Department on one side of the question, another on the other, and a third presenting the case neutrally."[34] This interdepartmental disagreement was inevitable,

31. *Ex parte Cheung Sum Shee et al.* and *Ex parte Chan Shee et al.*, 2 F.2d 995 at 998 (1924). Prior to the passage of the Johnson-Reed Act, Chinese wives of citizens did run afoul of the Immigration Act of 1917. See *Ex parte Leong Shee*, 275 F. 364 (1921), and *Chung Fook v. White*, 264 U.S. 443 (1924). In these cases immigration authorities ruled for exclusion on medical, not racial, grounds.

32. *Cheung Sum Shee et al. v. Nagle*, 268 U.S. 336 at 339 (1925).

33. 268 U.S. at 342.

34. Philip C. Jessup, "Some Phases of the Administrative and Judicial Interpretation of the Immigration Act of 1924," *Yale Law Journal* 35 (Apr. 1926): 714. For remarks of House Committee Chairman Johnson and Senator Shortridge regarding this concern, see *CR* 65 (Apr. 5, 1924), 5661, 5741–5743.

given the contradictions knit into the country's immigration and nationality policies. One did not have to look beyond the conflicting provisions of the Cable Act for evidence of such inconsistency. The Cable Act declared that a woman's marital status would no longer interfere with her access to naturalization but then denied her citizenship because she had married a man ineligible for citizenship. In *Cheung Sum Shee*, the disagreement revolved around whether a Chinese wife was an independent immigrant or a satellite within her husband's "sphere of activity." Immigration law supported both conclusions, but the Supreme Court ruled that "by necessary implication" the wives of treaty merchants could be admitted with their husbands.[35]

The merchants' wives on the *President Lincoln* were able to move past vigilant immigration officials with the assistance of the law, the courts, and the State Department; but the Chinese wives of Americans who arrived on the same ship did not find equal support from either statute, judge, or other federal official. The State Department, which had intervened on behalf of the merchants' wives, had done so only because the Department believed the integrity of a treaty was at stake in that case. And, although Section 13 of the Johnson-Reed Act listed exceptions to the rule banning persons ineligible for naturalization from entering the country, the Chinese wife of a citizen was not one of them.[36] Counsel for the citizens' wives argued that their omission from Section 13's list of exceptions was "nothing but a slip," but the Supreme Court handily discarded this defense.[37] The Chinese wife of a citizen was simply "an alien departing from any place outside the United States destined for the United States," and as an alien she was ineligible for citizenship or permanent residency.[38]

Cheung Sum Shee and *Chang Chan*, the citizens' wives' cases, left critics of the Immigration Act of 1924 with much to feast on.[39] Ac-

35. The decision reaffirmed the ruling in *United States v. Mrs. Gue Lim et al.*, 176 U.S. 459 (1900).

36. Sect. 13, 43 Stat. 153 (1924).

37. *Chang Chan, Wong Hung Kay, Yee Sin Jung et al. v. Nagle*, 268 U.S. 346 at 349 (1925).

38. 268 U.S. at 353 (1925). The State Department then notified consular officers that alien wives of citizens ineligible for naturalization could not enter the United States as immigrants. U.S. Department of State, *Admission of Aliens into the United States* (Washington, D.C.: G.P.O., Sept. 30, 1925), 6.

39. Parker, "The Ineligible to Citizenship Provisions of the Immigration Act of 1924," 23–47. For an overview of the laws on this policy, see D. O. McGovney, "Race Discrimination in Naturalization," *Iowa Law Bulletin* 8 (Mar. 1923): 129–161.

cording to the Supreme Court, the law denied American citizens a spousal privilege granted to alien merchants and ministers. Although the Labor Department was relieved to see the Court set some limits on the arguments for family unity, as a public exhibition of the disjointed workings of the immigration laws the decision in *Chang Chan* was an embarrassment to the government.[40]

By upholding the Labor Secretary's exclusion order in this case the Supreme Court had implicitly acknowledged that immigration officials could treat a married woman as an independent immigrant unless the law instructed otherwise. There was no small irony in the Court's delivery of that message in this case. A married woman's legal status as dependent had often been the source of her subordination, but in this instance the Chinese women's status as citizens' wives was their remaining source of legal protection from the racist policies that demanded their permanent exclusion from the United States. The judicial declaration of their independence as immigrants destroyed that last defense.

In the few years preceding enactment of the 1924 act, the number of admissions of Chinese wives of American citizens had been rather insignificant numerically—fewer than four hundred annually. In fact, the thirty-five women who came to California on the *President Lincoln* in 1924 were still in the United States on bond when Congress produced a reform law six years later that annulled the Court's decision in *Chang Chan*.[41] The Secretary of Labor did not oppose the law's passage.[42] These facts suggest that the Labor Department's major concern in pursuing a court battle over the Chinese wives' admission was defending its discretionary authority over inadmissible aliens—a power that the above-mentioned Immigration Act of 1930 left virtually undisturbed. As the Labor Department's arguments in the cases of the Chinese wives illustrated, the Department was determined to contain the legal force of a doctrine that threatened to seriously interfere with its ability to exclude inadmissible aliens. Nothing in the Johnson-Reed Act could be identified as a "theory of unity of family doctrine," the De-

---

40. Sucheng Chan provides a useful overview of the federal government's efforts to limit the admissions of Chinese female immigrants in "The Exclusion of Chinese Women, 1870–1943," in *Entry Denied. Exclusion and the Chinese Community in America, 1882–1943*, ed. Sucheng Chan (Philadelphia: Temple University Press, 1991), 94–146.

41. U.S. Department of Labor, *Annual Report of the Secretary of Labor* (1927), 175.

42. *CR* 72 (May 12, 1930), 8760.

partment had insisted, despite that theory's warm reception in some courtrooms.[43]

Other resident aliens with absentee spouses did encounter difficulties when petitioning for naturalization as well as for the admission of their relatives. As it grew harder for some noncitizens to bring their relatives into the country, the advantages they acquired on their transition from alien to citizen became strong incentives for naturalization, as naturalization statistics in the 1920s revealed. According to the Secretary of Labor, in the five years following enactment of the Johnson-Reed Act of 1924, the number of men petitioning for citizenship increased markedly. Naturalization petitions in 1925 surged to an estimated twenty-nine thousand; two years later, the number exceeded thirty-four thousand. Moreover, 75 percent of the citizens seeking visas for relatives had been recently naturalized. According to the commissioner general of immigration, many of these new Americans were married men who hoped to bring their families to the United States as nonquota immigrants.[44]

The Secretary of Labor admitted that some naturalization courts concerned about this trend were rejecting naturalization applicants if bringing a man's family to the United States seemed to be his main motivation for acquiring citizenship. Secretary Davis conceded that reunion with close kin was an admirable goal, but he felt it was "a matter of regret when American citizenship is sought for that reason alone."[45] Assistant Secretary Robe Carl White thought the situation more than merely regrettable and gave a conspiratorial cast to the situation. "No doubt, many aliens ask for naturalization with honest purposes, so far as their family abroad is concerned," he remarked, "but the bulk of them ask for it under those circumstances for the sole purpose of putting the immigration forces of America over a barrel." He instructed officials to challenge the naturalization of applicants suspected of such a scheme.[46] Consequently, some petitioners for naturalization discov-

---

43. Quoting from the commissioner of immigration's brief in the case of Yee Jick Wo, *BIN*, 55466/603D.

44. U.S. Department of Labor, Bureau of Immigration, *Annual Report of the Commissioner General of Immigration* (1927), 13. Statistics on visa petitions for the years 1925–1929 are listed in U.S. Department of Labor, Bureau of Immigration, *Annual Report of the Commissioner General of Immigration* (1929), 23.

45. Quoted in "Why Men Become Naturalized," *Interpreter* 8 (Dec. 1929): 157.

46. Memorandum from the Assistant Secretary of Labor to the commissioner of immigration, Feb. 2, 1924, reprinted in Fields, "Shall We Naturalize Aliens Whose Wives Are Living Abroad?" 6.

ered that leaving their family behind, even for strictly economic reasons, could work against them in naturalization court.

Meanwhile, support for adding the husbands of American women to the class of nonquota immigrants showed signs of strengthening. While many members of Congress were eager to shield husband's rights against possible incursions by restrictive immigration laws, the legislative champions of wives' rights were fewer, but growing, in number. The lingering belief that a wife should not only be permitted to follow her husband but *should* follow her husband continued to make a married woman's establishment of a separate residence in the United States socially suspect; and her overlong estrangement from her spouse, unlike her male counterpart's separation from his wife, was presumed to be a self-inflicted predicament. Spousal reunification, as understood generally within the framework of immigration policy, meant that a wife moved to rejoin her husband, not the reverse. Finally, what was widely acknowledged to be one of men's basic rights—family companionship and the services of family members—seemed at best to be women's uninsured privilege.

Law and tradition still allowed the husband and father to determine his family's legal domicile, while economic realities and societal norms identified the husband as the family's primary breadwinner. Immigration officials were thus predisposed to assume that a man steadily employed in the United States would support his immigrating wife and children. The wage-earning wife, however, could not muster the same image of financial responsibility and stability. If a wife petitioned for her husband's admission, she had the difficult task of convincing immigration authorities that she could support a family single-handedly.

The sex-segregated job market guaranteed that the average wage-earning woman's income potential would be lower than that of her male counterpart, married or single. Immigration examiners had additional doubts about young wives' ability to maintain a steady income because the examiners assumed these women would soon become pregnant and retire, at least temporarily, from paid employment. Consequently, a woman petitioning for her spouse usually had to demonstrate that she would have access to other sources of income if she was unable to contribute to the household financially. Although the American consul or immigration official could demand similar proof from the male petitioner seeking his wife's admission, a married woman had to battle against the presumption that she was, and should properly be, economically dependent on her spouse. Law, custom, her comparatively weak wage-earning power, and the growing unpopularity of imported male labor all aligned against the American woman pleading for her foreign spouse's admission to the United States.

By granting special quota exemptions to certain wives and minor children, the federal government had been able to reduce the problem of separated families while continuing to limit the admission of those aliens considered to be the greatest threat to the welfare of the American laborer: working-age men.[47] The reappearance after the Cable Act's enactment of a group of women who were the American wives of nonresident aliens, however, posed a new challenge to the framers of immigration policy. Lawmakers now felt pressured to abandon patriarchal rights in favor of equal rights by granting to citizen women the petitioning privileges then enjoyed by citizen and declarant men; and proposals to extend nonquota status to Americans' husbands appeared among the several immigration-reform bills introduced during the Sixty-ninth Congress.[48] Although these legislative attempts were unsuccessful, the Secretary of Labor and the commissioner general of immigration both openly endorsed such an amendment to the Johnson-Reed Act.[49] Of the six bills introduced in the first session of the Sixty-ninth Congress to assist entry of Americans' relatives, two had promoted citizens' wives' admission, two aided aliens' wives and children, one offered the husbands of Americans quota-exempt status, and another made the same allowance for the admission of wives and children of noncitizen ministers and professors living in the United States prior to July 1, 1924. Only the last bill survived to become the Immigration Act of July 3, 1926.[50]

Equal rights proponents did secure a victory when President Calvin

47. For a more detailed discussion of the ambivalence toward immigrant male labor see Calavita, *U.S. Immigration Law and the Control of Labor,* 97–165.

48. H.R. 5, S. 2245, 69th Cong., 1st sess. (1926). For discussions of nonquota bills, see Hearings before the Senate Committee on Immigration, *Admission of Certain Relatives,* 69th Cong., 1st sess., Mar. 18, 1926; Hearings before the House Committee on Immigration and Naturalization, *Admission of Certain Relatives,* 69th Cong., 1st sess., Jan. 7, 1926; Hearings before the House Committee on Immigration and Naturalization, *Immigration of Relatives of Citizens,* 69th Cong., 1st sess., Jan. 26, 1926.

49. U.S. Department of Labor, Bureau of Immigration, *Annual Report of the Commissioner General of Immigration* (1926), 23.

50. Immigration Act of July 3, 1926, 44 Stat. 812. In addition, the Immigration Act of May 26, 1926, 44 Stat. 654, eased the admission of some relatives of alien veterans. It provided that "the unmarried children under eighteen . . . , the wife, or the *husband,* of an alien veteran shall . . . be considered as a non-quota immigrant when accompanying or following within six months to join him [or her]" (italics added).

Coolidge signed the Copeland-Jenkins bill on May 29, 1928.[51] This new statute provided that an unmarried woman who lost her citizenship by reason of marriage to an alien before the Cable Act's passage could apply for a nonquota visa. In addition, the noncitizen man who had married an American before June 1, 1928, entered the country as a non-quota immigrant.[52] Congress had once again acquiesced to reformers demands but moved ahead at a halting pace. The new law set clear limits on the scope of the relief granted to citizen women and their foreign husbands. Only single women expatriated through former marriages could apply for nonquota visas; and an American woman marrying an alien after June 1 still could not petition for her husband's quota-exempt admission to the country. As the Copeland-Jenkins Act demonstrated, Congress remained reluctant to admit a "chain" of relatives unless their strongest link to the United States was a resident man. From the government's perspective, resident women's immigrating family members were "new-seed" immigrants who had yet to establish firm roots in the United States.

Woman's rights groups were a major force behind this legislation. The members of the WJCC, especially the influential NLWV, now actively sought the erasure of legal limitations on married women's ability to return to the United States with citizenship intact after living abroad with a foreign husband. At the same time, the Legal Research Committee of the NWP, had rapidly gained an impressive knowledge of the various immigration and nationality rules and procedures affecting married women. By the end of the decade, constant lobbying by these women's groups had yielded lower admission barriers for the husbands of citizens.

51. The Copeland-Jenkins Act of May 29, 1928, 45 Stat. 1009, was one of five immigration bills passed during that session of Congress. It amended the Johnson-Reed Act by adding three categories of nonquota immigrants: minor (under twenty-one) unmarried children of citizens, men married to American citizens at the time of the law's enactment, and single women who had lost their American citizenship by marriage.

52. Commissioner General of Immigration Harry Hull and Secretary of Labor Davis had supported nonquota status for all husbands of American citizens meeting other immigration standards. Davis went on record as opposing the time restriction placed on this class, remarking that "there is no justice or reason in preferring one citizen to another. The wife is still a citizen whether the marriage was on May 31 or on June 1." U.S. Department of Labor, *Annual Report of the Secretary of Labor* (1928), 146. Emma Wold of the NWP recognized that the Labor Department was now friendlier than it had been to reform legislation benefiting expatriated women, noting that "we seem to have the interest and sympathy, if not the active support, of some officials in the Department of Labor." "Report of the Legislative Secretary as to Certain Bills before Congress," [Nov. 1928], *NWPP*.

Although interested women's organizations were committed to pressing ahead toward the achievement of equal nationality rights and immigration privileges for women, some members of Congress hoped the passage of the 1928 Copeland-Jenkins Act would mark a plateau in quota-immigration reform activity. According to Albert Johnson, chair of the House Committee on Immigration and Naturalization, this statute had finally "silenc[ed] the contentions of those who criticized the immigration act of 1924 on account of the division of alien families." And Johnson's admiration for the law only grew stouter. A year later he declared that the new immigration policies worked "splendidly" and relieved "innumerable cases of hardship." The virtue of the amended 1924 law was its ability to aid divided families without jeopardizing restrictionist goals.[53] It is doubtful, however, that the resident women still separated from their husbands by the country's immigration laws shared Johnson's enthusiasm for the efficacy of the law.

The Quota Act of 1921 and the Johnson-Reed Act of 1924 had also complicated marital expatriates' ability to return to the United States, establish permanent residence, and regain their citizenship. Aside from excepting those women no longer married to aliens, the Copeland-Jenkins Act left this situation unaltered. As the number of immigrants allowed into the country diminished, so did women's chances of returning to the United States to reclaim a citizenship lost by marriage. The Cable Act required American women married to noncitizens and foreign women married to citizens to live in the United States for one year before applying for naturalization papers, but many expatriate women seeking permanent admission to the country faced exclusion or long delays because their adopted nation's quota was exhausted. Because Congress had designed the Cable Act to benefit resident women, its naturalization provisions remained inaccessible to nonresident expatriates or citizens' alien wives until they gained entry to the United States.

The hearings and reports on the original Cable bill had suggested that Congress did not carefully weigh the impact of existing immigration laws and regulations on the bill's repatriation provisions. The Secretary of Labor had predicted the difficulties that would plague the law (and his Department) once it took effect, but he was circumspect in his criticism for partisan reasons.[54] Woman's rights groups also had reason

53. *CR* 70 (Mar. 2, 1929), 5134.
54. "Reasons for Changes Suggested in H.R. 12022," [Sept. 1922], *CC*, 155/22; letter

to stifle their concern about the bill's limitations until it became law; but shortly after the Cable Act's implementation, women's organizations began urging Congress to grant nonquota immigrant status to all marital expatriates and the husbands of American women.

Immigration regulations and the Cable Act worked together to thwart many nonresident women's repatriation. The Cable Act had repealed the provision in the Expatriation Act of 1907 that allowed nonresident marital expatriates to reclaim their U.S. citizenship at the termination of their marriages by simply registering with an American consul or returning to the United States. The Cable rules complicated this process by requiring these women to live in the country one year and to submit to a naturalization examination in order to restore their U.S. citizenship. Although some women tried to skirt the quota system by entering the country as visiting aliens and then applying for citizenship after living in the United States for a year, their efforts were futile. Only persons admitted for permanent entry could file naturalization petitions.[55]

The Cable Act held out the promise of restoring American citizenship to the thousands of women who had been expatriated for their "un-American" marriages, but immigration laws often frustrated attempts to recover that lost citizenship. The Cable Act's preamble boldly proclaimed that "the right of any woman to become a naturalized citizen of the United States shall not be denied or abridged because of her sex or because she is a married woman."[56] Yet, some of the law's most critical provisions blatantly contradicted that promise.

Even if marital expatriates cleared all the hurdles inhibiting their repatriation, they could not find real security in their status as citizens. All women repatriated under the Cable rules became naturalized citizens, regardless of their country of birth. A native-born woman did not recover her original legal status as a birth citizen because the federal government wanted to retain the opportunity to revoke her citizenship papers. Consequently, resident women who regained their citizenship under the Cable Act never fully escaped the threat of denaturalization or, worse, deportation. Section 3 of the Cable Act of 1922 also

---

of the Secretary of Labor to J. Cable, Dec. 26, 1922, *CC*, 155/22, urging nonquota status for husbands and wives of citizens.

55. Sect. 3, Act of March 2, 1907, 34 Stat. 1228; Sects. 2, 4, and 7, 42 Stat. 1021 (1922).
56. Sect. 1, 42 Stat. 1021 (1922).

declared that "any woman citizen who marries an alien ineligible to citizenship shall cease to be a citizen of the United States."[57] This restriction mocked the spirit and letter of the statute's preamble.[58] When the courts issued one of their desultory pronouncements on racial disqualifications for citizenship, immigration officials notified the naturalized Americans affected by the decision that their "fraudulent" citizenship papers were revoked. Immediate family members could also lose their citizenship in these cases. A child naturalized through a father lost her or his citizenship upon revocation of that parent's citizenship; and Section 3 declared that women married to men ineligible for naturalization could not become or remain U.S. citizens. In these cases, the women could not apply or reapply for citizenship for the duration of their marriages or, in some cases, ever. In declaring that these wives must assume their husbands' state of alienage, Section 3 lent a rather satiric tone to the law formally titled the Married Women's Independent Citizenship Act.

The case of Mary Das illustrated the plight of women denationalized or denaturalized by their husbands' loss of citizenship. Das, a native-born American, had married a naturalized citizen in 1914. Her husband subsequently lost his citizenship when the U.S. Supreme Court declared that Hindus were racially ineligible for citizenship. After denying her request for a passport, a State Department official advised Mary Das to divorce her husband in order to regain her citizenship; her only other option was to remain stateless until some other country was willing to receive her as a naturalized citizen. "Has the American Government fallen to such a state of degradation that to it the civil rights of its citizens have less value than property rights?" she wrote despairingly in 1926.[59] The Cable Act had not just taken away Mary Das's U.S. citizenship—it had made her a woman without a country. Her situation was

57. Sect. 3, 42 Stat. 1021 (1922).

58. The first naturalization act passed in the United States had limited naturalization to free white persons. After the ratification of the Fourteenth Amendment, the law was amended to include people of African descent, but thereafter Congress turned the task of identifying racially ineligible groups over to the judiciary. See *Takao Ozawa v. United States*, 260 U.S. 178 (1922), and *Takuji Yamashita v. Hinkle*, 260 U.S. 199 (1922). *United States v. Thind*, 261 U.S. 204 (1923).

59. Mary K. Das, "A Woman without a Country," *Nation* 123 (Aug. 4, 1926), 106. See also Emma Wold, "A Woman Bereft of Country," *Equal Rights* 12 (Aug. 15, 1925): 213–214, and "Some Problems of Wives' Nationality," *Equal Rights* 12 (Aug. 15, 1925): 214–215.

a troubling reminder of Cable's imperfections. As one contributor to the *Woman Citizen* bluntly declared, the only thing that law offered Mary Das was the "hope of widowhood."[60]

Das's situation was nightmarish, but it was not as desperate as the fate of some women expatriated by marriages to so-called ineligibles. As a white woman, Das could apply for naturalization if her marriage ended; for other women, their loss of citizenship was irreversible. For example, Fung Sing was a native-born American, but when she wed a Chinese man in 1920, she was unaware that she had irretrievably lost her citizenship. Five years later, when she attempted to return to the United States, the remaining provisions of Expatriation Act of 1907, the Cable Act, and the Johnson-Reed Act all worked against her reentry into her native country: the Expatriation Act stripped her of her citizenship; the Cable Act declared her an expatriate ineligible for repatriation; and the Johnson-Reed Act barred her from the United States as an alien racially ineligible for naturalization.[61]

Factors other than a spouse's race could cause the expatriation of a married woman, render her ineligible for naturalization, or both. If a man withdrew his declaration of intention to become an American citizen in order to avoid military service, for example, he could not later reapply for naturalization. Likewise, since 1865, desertion from the armed forces when the country was at war also brought permanent forfeiture of citizenship and naturalization privileges.[62] Cases involving a husband's postnuptial loss of citizenship provided a point of debate that the Cable Act reagitated. Could the government presume that a wife had consented to the forfeiture of her citizenship when her husband committed a unilateral act of expatriation? In the absence of any clear legislative declaration of married women's right to remain citizens if their husbands became ineligible for citizenship after marriage, the courts fell back on the pre-Cable rule that a wife's citizenship—for better or for worse—followed her husband's.

Rose Schar's husband had been permanently barred from U.S. citizenship after he withdrew his first papers to avoid military duty during World War I. (He was a citizen of a neutral country.) Schar had

60. Boyd, "Have You Been Enfranchised Lately?" 114.
61. *Ex parte (Ng) Fung Sing,* 6 F.2d 670 (1925).
62. Sects. 1996, 1998, Revised Statutes of the U.S. (1878); Act of Aug. 22, 1912, 37 Stat. 356. During World War I a large number of men had been charged with desertion, and although they were later pardoned by President Coolidge, it was never clear whether the men's temporary expatriations had affected the nationalities of their wives and children.

thus unexpectedly lost her citizenship after she married, but now sought repatriation under the new Cable Act rules. The government informed her, however, that her husband's actions had rendered her equally ineligible for naturalization. Anna Panoner found herself in similar straits. Her citizen husband had been convicted of espionage after their marriage. Although President Warren G. Harding had commuted his prison sentence, he did not receive a full pardon and lost his citizenship as a result of the conviction. Anna feared that Section 3 of the Cable Act had denaturalized her for her husband's conduct. In the absence of any court ruling or statute qualifying Section 3's mandate, Panoner's fears were well-founded.[63]

In 1926 some members of the NWP asked Senator Robert M. La-Follette, Jr., of Wisconsin and Representative Robert Bacon of New York to introduce bills allowing a woman to petition for naturalization despite her husband's ineligibility for citizenship.[64] Emma Wold of the NWP's Legislative Committee began to collect information on women denationalized for marriages to Chinese or Japanese men for presentation at House and Senate hearings on the bills. Wold chanced provoking some shrill commentary from Committee members, and even if calmer draughts prevailed, the bills could face dismissal as special legislation for a small group of women. There is some evidence that Wold found many of her cohorts in reform reluctant to contribute time or encouragement to her task.[65] The other provision in the bills, simplifying the

63. Schar's case is related in a letter from Elizabeth Black, executive secretary of the Griffin Bill Committee, to NWP headquarters, July 8, 1930, *NWPP*. See also the letter of Anna Panoner to A. Paul, Jan. 19, 1923, *NWPP*. Upon reviewing the Cable Act before its passage, Secretary of Labor Davis had specifically referred to cases of this kind and warned that the bill's reference to husbands "ineligible to citizenship" was too vague. "The question of proper construction . . . would be ever before the courts," he complained. "Reasons for Changes Suggested in H.R. 12022," [Sept. 1922], *CC*, 155/22.

64. Letter to Senator Robert M. LaFollette, Jr., unsigned, Dec. 30, 1925, *NWPP*. Letter to Evelyn Trent from E. Wold, Mar. 1, 1926, *NWPP*. See Hearings before a subcommittee of the Senate Committee on Immigration, *Naturalization and Citizenship of Married Women*, 69th Cong., 1st sess., Mar. 24, 1926; Hearings before the House Committee on Immigration and Naturalization, *Immigration and Citizenship of American-Born Women Married to Aliens*, 69th Cong., 1st sess., Mar. 23, 1926; *Granting Non-Quota Status to American-Born Women Married to Aliens Prior to the Passage of the Cable Act*, 69th Cong., 1st sess., 1926, H. Rept. 659. The Bureau of Immigration and the State Department both approved the Bacon bill. According to Emma Wold, Bacon had been hesitant to introduce this bill and had to be "brought along on this subject." Wold to Evelyn Trent, June 5, 1926, *NWPP*.

65. Letter from Wold to Alice K. Frazer, Mar. 8, 1926, *NWPP*. As another involved member of the NWP revealed, "I cannot understand the apathy of what we call 'intelligent

repatriation process for all marital expatriates, was then more appealing to the general body of nationality-rights reformers.

The Senate and House Committee hearings on the proposals were not substantially different, although Maud Wood Park's appearance before the House Committee suggested some degree of cooperation between the NWP and the NLWV on this piece of legislation. The House Committee's comments on the bill were often sharp-edged and delivered by a handful of vocal members who reserved little compassion for the woman who had made her match with a man ineligible for citizenship. When Wold pleaded for the women thus denationalized by marriage, Representative Arthur Free of California demanded to know whether the bill was really about "getting back these few women who married persons ineligible to citizenship." "Is that what the fuss is all about?" he sputtered.[66]

When Wold shifted attention to the less controversial yet critical problems still facing nonresident marital expatriates, her presentation was disrupted again, this time by sarcastic comments from Samuel Dickstein of New York. These women's difficulties were due punishment for foolish marriages, he retorted. After all, there had been "enough Americans for them to select from." Chairman Albert Johnson agreed with Dickstein: the decision to live in a foreign land with a foreign man was a declaration of expatriation.[67] Representative Adolph Sabath of Illinois dusted off the old image of the American-born heiresses who left the United States in delusional pursuit of "the little glory, the temporary glory that they attain by that sort of marriage."[68] Park's assurances that she personally supported a stricter naturalization process for some noncitizens was not enough to calm the tempest.[69]

Wold was disgusted by the proceedings and immediately conveyed her displeasure to Alva Belmont, the NWP's most generous but demanding benefactor. Her recent dealings with the "muddle-headed men" in Congress, Wold reported, had left her firmly convinced that an equal rights amendment to the Constitution was "all the more desir-

---

women' in regard to the amendment to the Cable Act which is so unjust to women married to 'aliens ineligible for American citizenship.' " Kate C. Havens to Burnita Shelton Matthews, letter dated Jan. 3, 1927, *NWPP*.

66. House Hearings, Mar. 23, 1926, *Immigration and Citizenship of American-Born Women Married to Aliens*, 13.

67. Ibid., 18.

68. Ibid., 20.

69. Ibid., 44.

able."[70] She then drafted a circular letter to all state chairs of the NWP
and its National Council, urging them to educate Congress about the
problems confronting women in transnational marriages. Her report
on the recent hearing appeared in the NWP's *Equal Rights:*

Before a committee, some of whom are of alien birth or of so recent foreign
ancestry that their speech betrays them, members of the National Woman's
Party asked for justice to American-born women who have lost their American citizenship by marriage, asking only that the character of women's citizenship shall be the same as men's. No red-blooded American woman present could smother every particle of indignation, however Christian and
tolerant her spirit. It was not only the markedly hostile attitude of the chairman of the Committee—one has come to expect that of a man whose bark
may be worse than his bite. The sneer with which Representative Free of
California inquired what all this "fuss" was about, . . . the insulting assumption that citizenship to a woman means no more than a garment to
be donned and doffed . . . —these coming from a committee, some of
whom, at least, scarcely know the law about which the "fuss" was made.[71]

Chairman Johnson conveyed his surprise at Wold's withering por-
trayal of his and his colleagues' conduct and suggested that she "mis-
took the strain under which the Committee has been working of late,
on account of pressure of time and multitudes of bills, for hostility."
The Committee's published report on the bill did offer some compen-
sation for its behavior; it contained a brief but unqualified endorsement of the bill's provisions. However, the proposals were not palatable
enough to pass unchecked through both houses of Congress.[72]

For most nonresident women seeking repatriation under the Cable
Act, their first and often greatest challenge in their journey back to citizenship was gaining admission to the United States. The quota laws
made compliance with the Cable Act's repatriation rules difficult if not
impossible for most nonresident women emigrating from quota countries.[73] They had to arrive as immigrants because, technically, only per-

70. Wold to Mrs. Belmont, Apr. 19, 1926, *NWPP*. Howard Thayer Kingsbury, of the
Executive Council of the American Society of International Law, also withheld praise for
the Committee members, calling both the House Committee and Senate Subcommittee
"equally ineffectual." Letter of Kingsbury to Wold, July 19, 1926, *NWPP*.
71. Emma Wold, "Hearings on Married Women's Citizenship," *Equal Rights* 13 (Apr.
3, 1926), 62–63. Wold was also foreign-born.
72. Letter from Johnson to Wold, Apr. 7, 1926, *NWPP*.
73. 46 Stat. at 854, adding Sect. 4(f) to the Johnson-Reed Act of 1924. 45 Stat. 1009

sons admitted for permanent entry were classified as immigrants, and, with few exceptions, naturalization officials rejected petitions from individuals who had entered the country on visitor's visas.

Renee Pezzi had forfeited her American citizenship when she married an Italian in 1920, but she hoped the Cable Act could help her regain it. Although the Italian quota was exhausted, she and her husband thought they could maneuver around that roadblock by entering the country as "temporary visitors." Pezzi planned to remain in the United States for at least a year, long enough to petition for naturalization under the Cable Act. But when her request for citizenship reached District Court Judge Edward J. Henning, a former Assistant Secretary of Labor, he declared her ineligible for citizenship.

Pezzi's visitor status made her pledge to remain in the United States meaningless, and Judge Henning dismissed her peremptorily from his court with the announcement that she was a woman with "no status in the United States other than being the wife of her husband."[74] Henning's remark was cruel but accurate. Under present law, Pezzi's status as the wife of a visiting alien completely eclipsed her premarital standing as a resident and citizen of the United States. If Pezzi's husband had been a citizen or a declarant alien, she could have entered the United States as a nonquota immigrant.

It was easier for the foreign-born wives of citizens to enter the country than for American-born women seeking repatriation—a discrepancy in treatment that did not go unnoticed by expatriates stranded abroad and nationality-law reformers at home. Loretta Guignet, a marital expatriate living in France, recalled that a *New York Herald* article announcing the quota-exempt arrival of fifteen Czechs as the fiancees of naturalized men had kindled her indignation. "That was the day I woke up from my Rip van Winkle sleep," Guignet recalled. "When I compared my children's and my own humiliation each time we enter my native land as aliens to the joy of those fifteen foreign born women about to enter the country as Americans, because the naturalized citizens who gave them the right to enter thus were men, and I was only a woman, I realized that it was high time that we American born 'aliens' bestirred ourselves."[75]

(1928) allowed only unmarried women who had lost their American citizenship through alien marriages to apply for nonquota visas.

74. *In re Pezzi*, 29 F.2d at 1002 (1928).

75. Letter of Loretta Guignet to E. Wold, Sept. 12, 1929, *NWPP*.

Meanwhile, *Equal Rights* publicized incidents such as the following to illustrate the immigration problems besetting marital expatriates:

Louise Riva, American-born, American-bred, even American-wed, since she married an Italian in this country, was held at Ellis Island for deportation. Deserted by her husband in Italy, where else could she go but to the land of her birth, of her parents' citizenship, of her nearest kin who are willing and able to help her? Even the visitor's visa with which she had been provided in Italy, could not get her past the immigration inspectors when she audaciously declared that she was going to stay here forever because this is her country. This could not happen to an American-born man unless he had voluntarily given up his citizenship here by taking an oath of allegiance to another government.[76]

Emily Martin's case also demonstrated the legalized prejudice dogging women in transnational marriages. As an American-born woman expatriated by her pre-Cable marriage to a German, Martin had petitioned successfully for naturalization in 1924. During the course of her interview with a naturalization examiner Martin had admitted that she would consider returning to Germany with her two children if her husband preferred to live there. Her candor later cost Martin her recently recovered citizenship. After issuing her citizenship certificate, the Bureau of Naturalization apparently had second thoughts about Martin's fitness. A federal district court supported the Bureau's decision to revoke her naturalization papers after concluding that Martin never intended to remain in the United States permanently. Despite the Cable Act, Martin's ties to the United States were still too weak to sustain a bid for citizenship.[77] Her inability to argue successfully for her repatriation once again highlighted the remaining disparities between American men's and women's power to assert and sustain an independent identity. Martin remained a disowned American because she remained the wife of an alien. As one native-born woman expatriated by marriage and facing deportation complained bitterly, "The government of the U.S.A. seeks to prove that I am not an asset to my country, but a chattel of my . . . husband."[78]

"If she was good enough to be a citizen before marriage, she is good

76. Emma Wold, "American Women and the Immigration Law," *Equal Rights* 14 (Mar. 26, 1927): 53.

77. *United States v. Martin*, 10 F.2d 585 (1925).

78. Letter of Blanche Bole-Singleton to Maud Younger, June 27, 1928, *NWPP*. She had managed to remain in the United States for eighteen months on a visitor's visa.

enough to be a citizen after marriage," argued Burnita Shelton Matthews of the NWP. Why, she asked, did a resident or nonresident marital expatriate have to satisfy special naturalization requirements before she could once again call herself an American?[79] The circumstances that had sabotaged the repatriation of Martin were not identical to those thwarting the revival of Pezzi's, Riva's, or Guignet's citizenship; but in each case a gender-based double standard had obstructed their repatriation. Claire de Montagut summed up the sentiments of many American-born women who, like she, had married foreign men, remained in the United States, but were now required by law to petition for naturalization: "How can a woman take out papers to assume citizenship in a country that is already hers by birth? It is not hers by adoption but her birthright. . . . My husband's citizenship papers would restore that right to me, but why shall women depend on another's papers. . . . I would far rather be given the National [sic] right to be what I was born to be—an American citizen."[80]

Native-born resident women like de Montagut had never stopped viewing themselves as Americans and their citizenship as their birthright. For these women, the law that expatriated them had defined them in almost incomprehensible terms, for nothing else about their lives suggested that they were no longer Americans. Contrary to a lingering popular myth, the American woman married to an alien could preserve intact her loyalty and affection for her native country. The emotion-filled letters these women wrote to newspapers, women's organizations, federal legislators, executive department officials, and one another record their pain, anger, and disbelief over their involuntary loss of citizenship. But federal law had placed barriers, some insurmountable, between these women and their native country. As one expatriated woman remarked contemptuously, "Other countries pass laws to keep their people who have migrated to other lands, whereas our own grand United States passes laws repudiating her own loyal native and adopted children for the dreadful crime of marrying."[81]

The provisions of the original Cable Act affirmed that the federal

---

79. Burnita Shelton Matthews, "The Woman without a Country," *Equal Rights* I (May 26, 1923): 118.

80. Letter of Claire de Montagut to Alice Paul, Oct. 27, 1922, *NWPP.* See also Marjorie P. Hoinko, "Naturalizing a Yankee. An American Woman Who Married an Alien before the Cable Act Became Law Measures the Red Tape That Restored Her Citizenship," *WJ,* Apr. 1928, 13, 38.

81. Letter of Mrs. Yaviournis [sic] to E. Wold, Apr. 26, 1929, *NWPP.*

government did not intend to treat the repatriation of these women as a mere formality. Although the government had taken a significant step toward releasing some married women from the state of dependent citizenship, that move had not signaled a full repudiation of the principal justification for marital expatriation: that women's marriages to foreigners were, as one Congressman put it, "open broad daylight" decisions to become aliens. Federal law defined expatriation as a voluntary act, but in Congress and the courtroom this question of consent rarely gained thoughtful consideration in cases of marital expatriation. In the 1920s, that decade celebrating the independence of the "new woman," wifely subservience still had a legislative foothold. In matters of nationality, marriage could yet thrust a woman into that perverse legal realm in which a wife's consent was always stressed but never really required. As the Supreme Court had intimated in *Mackenzie v. Hare*, although the act of expatriation had to be uncoerced, whether the woman *intended* to renounce her citizenship by that act was irrelevant.

The Cable Act's framers did raise the standard of consent a notch by making a foreign residence or a husband ineligible for citizenship necessary to expatriate, but they deliberately left untouched the losses incurred under the 1907 act. Rather than declare all marital expatriations automatically void, Congress told women they must appeal to the government for the restoration of their citizenship. Even women who had married noncitizens before the Expatriation Act of 1907 went into effect had to plead for citizenship in the country's courtrooms, and the inconsistent rulings in these cases only reconfirmed that, despite the Cable Act, women's access to citizenship was still capriciously granted or denied.[82] Legislators' continued adherence to gendered standards of volition, their lingering resentment toward women living abroad with

---

82. Cases in which courts declared expatriated those women married to aliens prior to 1907: *In re Page*, 12 F.2d at 135 (1926); *In re Lazarus*, 24 F.2d 243 (1928); *In re Kraus-mann*, 28 F.2d 1004 (1928); *In re Wohlgemuth*, 35 F.2d 1007 (1929). In the Krausmann case, the court overrode the Naturalization Bureau's opinion that she was an American. Cases in which women retained their citizenship: *In re Lynch*, 31 F.2d 762 (1929); *Petition of Zogbaum*, 32 F.2d 911 (1929). In 1925 the State Department moved toward a settlement of the issue by declaring that women who married aliens prior to 1907 could receive passports unless they had married a "treaty national," had lived in their husband's country, or had received another citizenship by marriage. The Labor Department eventually adopted the State Department rules. See U.S. Department of Labor, Immigration and Naturalization Service, Leigh L. Nettleton, *Loss of Citizenship (Expatriation) and Presumptive Loss of Citizenship*, Lecture 27, Dec. 17, 1924, 4; and Ernest J. Hover, "Citizenship of Women in the United States," *American Journal of International Law* 26 (1932): 700–719.

foreign spouses, and the persistent fear that too many naturalized Americans would weaken the constitution of the citizenry all worked against women's achievement of equal nationality rights in the 1920s.

But other policy concerns also stood between women and independent citizenship, not the least of which was the State Department's desire to limit the number of persons claiming U.S. citizenship but living permanently abroad. Congress heeded this request in 1906, 1907, and then again in 1922, when limiting the Cable Act's repatriation provisions to resident women.[83] For marital expatriates like Emily Martin, merely contemplating a departure from the country was reason enough for the government to stamp their naturalization papers "void."

The Supreme Court had declared that citizenship implied "a duty of allegiance on the part of the member and a duty of protection on the part of the society" to which she belonged.[84] As the country's naturalization policies increasing exhibited, residency in the United States had become an influential factor in determining whether a new citizen was, indeed, an American in fact as well as in name—one as willing to shoulder the duties and responsibilities of citizenship as demand its protections.

The residency requirement also worked against American women who married noncitizens after the Cable Act went into effect. They discovered that the law allowed a prolonged absence from the country to cause the revocation, not just suspension, of their citizenship. To recoup their citizenship, these women had to return to the United States on immigrant visas and then seek naturalization. These Cable rules represented a significant departure from the government's general policy on expatriating absentee citizens. As Dorothy Straus of the NLWV explained to a House Committee, the Cable Act had turned what traditionally had been "a presumption" into "a legislative enactment." The State Department now interpreted even a native-born woman's absence from the country "in the most rigid way," thus depriving those living outside the United States of their citizenship. "It would seem that Congress is showing its disapproval of the American daughter who

83. "So much of this instruction as relates to residence abroad is not applicable to natural-born citizens of the United States," wrote Secretary of State Elihu Root regarding sect. 2 of the Expatriation Act of 1907. Circular instructions to diplomatic and consular officers, "Expatriation," Apr. 19, 1907. Also, see correspondence of Acting Secretary Huntington Wilson to diplomatic and consular officers, "Protection of Native Americans Residing Abroad," July 26, 1910. *BIN*, 52903–52943.

84. *Luria v. United States*, 231 U.S. 9 at 10 (1913).

goes to a far country," concluded Wold. "When she wishes to return, she has not the welcome of the prodigal son. We shall have to continue to play the role of the importunate widow."[85]

State Department officials surveyed this situation from a different angle and continued to echo the view of the Secretary of Labor that the presumptive expatriation rule must apply to nonresident American women married to aliens. Otherwise, their exemption would cause "no end of problems."[86] American women with foreign residences and spouses still represented the kind of citizen the State Department increasingly sought permission to ignore—the citizen suspected to be more foreign than American. And the Cable Act had given the Department permission to indulge in that neglect.

The expatriation-by-residence rule was a troublesome one, not just for female expatriates seeking naturalization but for those who had to supervise its application. According to one legal expert, there was "a seemingly hopeless conflict" over its interpretation.[87] No statute adequately explained how a presumption of expatriation evolved into a state of expatriation and, consequently, the rule was inconsistently applied in cases involving absentee naturalized Americans requesting passports or personal protection from the federal government. Citing its ambiguity and diminishing effectiveness, many legal experts called for the rule's replacement with a more precise policy, while others argued

85. Quoting Straus from Hearings before the House Committee on Immigration and Naturalization, *Amendment to the Women's Citizenship Act of 1922,* 71st Cong., 2d sess., Mar. 6, 1930, 10. E. Wold to Howard Kingsbury, Apr. 17, 1926, *NWPP.* As a Labor Department publication later confessed, the Act of March 3, 1931, 46 Stat. 1511, revoking this objectionable policy appeared to be a "legislative recognition that presumptive termination constituted actual expatriation" in past cases involving the citizen wives of aliens. U.S. Department of Labor, Immigration and Naturalization Service, *Loss of Citizenship,* 7.

86. Copy of letter of Secretary of Labor James J. Davis to Senator Hiram Johnson, Mar. 13, 1926, *NWPP.* Davis was commenting on a bill that would have repealed sects. 3, 4, and 5 of the Cable Act. He reaffirmed his Department's view that sect. 3 should not be removed and that women seeking repatriation should continue to petition a naturalization court and take an oath of allegiance.

87. Henry B. Hazard, "International Problems in Respect to Nationality by Naturalization and of Married Women," in *Proceedings of the American Society for International Law . . . April 22–24, 1926* (Washington, D.C., 1926), 81. Another expert in the State Department echoed these sentiments: "There is not doubt whatsoever that hundreds of our naturalized citizens residing abroad deserve to have their citizenship terminated, but such a serious matter as final loss of citizenship should not be made to depend upon the ex parte decision of a clerk in a Government office." Richard W. Flournoy, Jr., "Naturalization and Expatriation, *Yale Law Journal* 31 (June 1922): 866.

that the confusion was best remedied by an international code on nationality matters.[88]

The Cable Act had only added to the confusion surrounding these expatriation rules. Two months before passage of the law, the assistant commissioner general of immigration had notified his commissioners of immigration as well as district inspectors that a naturalized citizen whose absence from the United States exceeded the two-or five-year limit could reenter the country as a citizen if he provided proof of his naturalization. The assistant commissioner general added that this policy reflected the views of the Attorney General, Labor Department solicitor, and Bureau of Naturalization.[89] A month after the introduction of the Cable Act, the Immigration Bureau began its retreat from this policy. In a vaguely worded annulment of the earlier memo, the acting commissioner general proposed that each absentee's case be decided on its own merits. If immigration agents always assumed that returning to the United States reinstated citizenship, "a considerable number of indigent, aged, diseased, disabled and otherwise undesirable persons will be admitted to become a menace to the health of the community and to become public charges within the states."[90] The announcement did not mention the situation of American women abroad, but the timing of the policy reversal strongly suggests that the introduction of the Cable Act had revived internal discussions about the Bureau's interpretation of the presumptive expatriation rules.[91]

88. As Charles Cheney Hyde, one of the members of the commission consulting on the design of the Expatriation Act of 1907, strongly advised, "It is of utmost importance that the Congress define its view with such clearness that the several branches of the government find little cause for divergent conclusions in applying and interpreting the law." "The Non-Recognition and Expatriation of Naturalized American Citizens, pt. 2, *American Journal of International Law* 19 (Oct. 1925): 744. See also Edwin M. Borchard, "Decadence of the American Doctrine of Voluntary Expatriation," *American Journal of International Law* 25 (Apr. 1931): 312–316; Margaret Lambie, "Presumption of Cessation of Citizenship," 264–278. Congress would not respond affirmatively to Hyde's advice until 1940.

89. Letter of assistant commissioner general of immigration, July 19, 1922, *BIN*, 52903/43C. In an earlier memo, dated Feb. 13, 1911, a predecessor had informed the Acting Secretary of Labor that foreign residence alone was not sufficient for expatriation. *BIN*, 52903/43(A)B.

90. Memorandum to Second Assistant Secretary of Labor from Acting Commissioner General I. F. Wixon, Oct. 31, 1922, *BIN*, 52903/43D. For the decision of the acting solicitor referenced by Wixon, see *BIN*, 54841/12.

91. Secretary of Labor Davis noted in his assessment of the original Cable bill in 1922 that "no change has been made in the working of section 3 . . . because it was understood that the section had been submitted to the Department of State and they were inclined

In 1923 the State Department issued a general letter to its diplomatic and consular officers stating that, in the absence of a court decision on this particular point, a citizen's reentry into the United States dispelled the presumption of expatriation. The State Department's interpretation of Section 2 of the 1907 Expatriation Act could have been employed to support the returning marital expatriate's claim to citizenship, but no test case ever materialized.[92] Some policymakers and legal experts interpreted this lack of litigation as evidence that most women did not care deeply about the loss of their citizenship through marriage. Lucius Crane, a man who apparently thought he knew as much about the workings of women's minds as he did about international law, offered this explanation: "For today it is sufficient to remember that, in the vast majority of families, the husband is the protector and the home-maker and carries the burden of the family responsibilities. That the vast majority of wives are more than content to so regard their husbands and to throw in their lot with them, whatever it be, irrespective of home or nationality, is undoubted. One cannot seriously contemplate the average young woman declining an otherwise pleasing proposal of marriage on the ground that she will change her citizenship thereby."[93]

Perhaps Crane could afford to blithely dismiss the hardships of marital expatriation because as a designated "protector" of his family he would never experience them directly, but the woman who married an

to approve it as drawn. It is not amiss, however, to refer to the fact that a woman coming within the terms of the section residing abroad . . . would still be a citizen of the United States under the statute as drawn, by her return to this country notwithstanding the fact that she might perhaps not be recognized as a citizen while abroad." "Reasons for Changes Suggested in H.R. 12022," [Sept. 1922], CC, 155/22. In 1926, Davis advised against repealing sect. 3 of the Cable Act, which would have allowed these nonresident women to claim American citizenship and the right to U.S. protection while abroad. Letter to Hiram Johnson, Mar. 13, 1926, NWPP.

92. See Hazard, "International Problems," 75–76, for State Department's rules. In the 1920s the Department had sought the enactment of a stricter statutory policy that would have provided generally for the loss, not just suspension, of American citizenship because of the establishment of a foreign domicile. The Nationality Act of 1940 would satisfy that objective, but the passage of the Cable Act had earlier signaled Congress's willingness to move in this direction. See Act of Oct. 14, 1940, 54 Stat. 1137. Sect. 317 (a) and (b) provided for the repatriation of women who lost their citizenship through marriage. Sect. 404 provided for the loss of U.S. citizenship because of foreign residence (applicable only to naturalized Americans). But the absentee citizen could avoid expatriation if she or her spouse lived abroad for one of the enumerated reasons permitted by the law.

93. Lucius F. Crane, "The Nationality of Married Women," Journal of Comparative Legislation and International Law, 3d ser., 7 (1925): 60.

alien and moved out of the country could testify that her actions incurred heavy personal losses. "Those of us who were married to foreigners before the Cable Act and the Immigration Acts little dreamed that one day the doors of our homeland might be shut to us and our children forever," lamented Loretta Guignet.[94] Unlike an American man married to a noncitizen, she did not possess the legal means to reenter the United States as a citizen or even as a nonquota immigrant, to assist her children's admission to the country, or to effect their naturalization as American citizens.[95]

For Guignet and other women in transnational marriages, the introduction of the quota system in 1921 and the Cable Act the following year dramatically revised the immigration and naturalization options available to them. Yet, these laws and the regulations they begot did not affect married women in a uniformly positive or negative way. Indeed, even the small number of cases profiled in this chapter should extinguish any assumption that all women enjoyed some measure of improvement in their access to or maintenance of American citizenship under the Cable Act.

The Cable Act and the other immigration acts had widely varying effects on former citizens who had lost their citizenship for marrying aliens. Those marital expatriates residing in the United States and married to resident men eligible for naturalization profited significantly from the Cable Act's provisions for repatriation. As Congress intended, these women were the principal beneficiaries of the law's modification of the rules of marital expatriation. In contrast, the woman of color, citizen or alien, who had married a man ineligible for citizenship could not even stand in that benefits' line. The Cable Act and immigration laws offered her nothing more than the irreversible loss of her citizenship if she had been an American before her marriage and permanent exclusion from citizenship if she had not been.

---

94. Letter from Guignet to Alva Belmont, May 19, 1929, *NWPP*. Alva Belmont's daughter, Consuelo Vanderbilt, was one of the original "Dollar Princesses," having married (with her mother's strong approval) the Duke of Marlborough in 1895.

95. Guignet and other alumnae of Vassar College living in Paris who shared her predicament or concern organized to publicize the impact of the immigration and nationality laws on their lives. For information on the group, see "Immigration Law Protested by Paris Group of Americans," *New York Herald*, Paris ed., 2 July 1929. The *New York Herald*, Paris ed., 9 Aug. 1929, published a letter from the Vassar Paris subcommittee, reprinted by the Paris *Chicago Tribune* on Aug. 12. For a report of a protest by American students at Oxford University, see "Students Demand Co-ordination of Law on Marriage," *Chicago Tribune*, Paris ed., 16 July 1929.

The Cable Act closed the short and easy route to citizenship that immigrant wives of citizens had once enjoyed, a development that satisfied many American feminists but not everyone interested in promoting the welfare of immigrants. The nationality law opened no path to U.S. citizenship to the foreign woman who belonged to a race ineligible for naturalization; and in 1924 the Johnson-Reed Act delivered the *coup de grace* by ending her prospects of either entering or reentering the country for permanent residence. For immigrant women with spouses eligible for naturalization, the law's advantages were less ambiguous. These women finally possessed the power to petition independently for naturalization.

Together, the Cable Act and the quota system placed unprecedented restrictions on the admission of marital expatriates and immigrant women married to American men. The Cable Act's abolition of marital naturalization provided a legal opportunity for the Immigration Bureau to challenge the automatic admission of citizens' foreign wives to the United States. Although the Bureau's efforts met with limited success, some women who once could have readily entered the country as citizens now lived subject to the rigorous rules imposed by the country's immigration laws until they became independently naturalized Americans.

The Cable Act of 1922 fell short of disinfesting the country's naturalization and immigration policies of gender discrimination. Naturalization law, and to a greater extent immigration law, still assumed a married woman's legal dependence when expedient. This assumption limited the ability of women in transnational marriages to claim and retain an independent citizenship. At the same time, it did yield significant benefits for some immigrating women with husbands in the United States. Despite the federal government's broad commitment to immigration and naturalization control in the 1920s, Congress was still willing to support special admission and naturalization privileges for the wives of citizens or resident aliens once marital naturalizations ceased. Legislators' consideration for the social wants of American men and their families improved many foreign-born women's chances of gaining permanent entry into the United States despite the quotas, and it abbreviated the length of time they waited before becoming citizens.

The unique status that wives gained by being certified through these special circumstances was equally capable of delivering unpleasant consequences. Although the political and economic situation of her husband could improve a woman's chances of gaining access to both the country and the ranks of citizenship, it was equally capable of effecting her denaturalization, exclusion, or deportation from the United States. Immigration and nationality law recognized a married woman's independent standing before the law insofar as that autonomy advanced key policy goals. A resident married woman could retain her U.S. citizenship despite marriage to an alien, but her independent citizenship immediately converted to a dependent one if she crossed the country's borders. Likewise, a woman's independent citizenship evaporated without a trace if the law declared her husband unsuitable for citizenship. Traditional notions about the structuring of marital identity and power still informed portions of the law, ensuring that a woman's ability to enter the United States, to reside in the country, and to remain a citizen or become a citizen might still depend ultimately on the federal government's assessment of her spouse's economic and social value to the country.

The advocates of equal nationality rights persisted well into the 1930s, seeking to replace some of the fundamental principles used to construct the country's immigration and naturalization policies with less discriminatory underpinnings. Eventually, the assumption of female dependence would be supplanted by a presumption of women's independence and the notion of patriarchal rights would be cleared away to make room for recognition of corresponding spousal rights. When the revolution was complete, marital expatriates and noncitizen women would pursue and possess U.S. citizenship unencumbered by their spouses' economic or political liabilities. Some married women would still enjoy admission privileges but not because their husbands held some ancient claim to their services; rather, it was wise and humane social policy to foster the reunion of spouses and their children. Wives would have equal petitioning power to request the admissions of their immigrant husbands and children, and American mothers would gain the ability to clothe their children with their citizenship.

These developments remained elusive in the 1920s, but never outside the realm of the imagination of nationality-rights reformers. The decade had brought some notable successes: the Cable Act; preference-quota status for Americans' husbands by 1924; and, within the next four years, nonquota status for some husbands and marital expatriates. In the 1920s, dismantling the fences barring married women from residency and citizenship was a task that had to be tackled post by post, but national and international developments of the next decade presented the possibility of employing a bolder strategy.

CHAPTER 5

Living with the Law

The 1930s

I am not a chattel. As a free human being, an individual unit of a sovereign people, the undisputed possessor of my own means of livelihood, I deny the right of Congress to legislate away my citizenship.

—Rebecca Shelley, marital expatriate, "Statement to the Naturalization Court before presenting my Petition for Repatriation" (1931), in *Papers of the National Woman's Party, 1913–1972*

The first decade of the 1900s was a frustrating one, offering few rewards to American woman suffragists who had hoped a new century would quicken the inauguration of a new era in the history of woman's rights. Across the Atlantic in Great Britain, however, suffragettes under the leadership of the magnetic Emmeline and Christabel Pankhurst had entered a vigorously militant phase in their struggle for a political voice. Lured by the verve of the Englishwomen, several spirited American suffragists embarked for England to work with the Women's Social and Political Union; among them were Alice Paul, Lucy Burns, Emma Wold, Alva Belmont, and Harriot Stanton Blatch. The American proselytes returned to the United States determined to revitalize the domestic suffrage movement, but their plan to reinvigorate the cause by duplicating the tactics of the Women's Social and Political Union found little favor with the leaders of the more conservative National American Woman Suffrage Association (NAWSA).[1]

Alice Paul and her cohorts never found NAWSA's activities an entirely satisfactory outlet for their energy and ideas, and NAWSA's leadership, in turn, grew wary of these upstarts. The promotion of the nationalization of the suffrage campaign annoyed those leaders within NAWSA who still favored a state-based approach; and the Paul faction's insistence that the political party in power should be held responsible for women's disfranchisement also seemed too partisan and uncompromising for the movement's moderates. After forming the Congressional Union (CU), Paul and her followers still desired to maintain their formal association with NAWSA, but the differences between mainstream NAWSA members and the Union proved too disquieting. When Paul submitted the CU's request for readmission as an auxiliary member of NAWSA, the National Executive Council rejected the application; by 1914, the CU was operating independently. Some CU members in suffrage states had formed the Woman's Party, and in 1917 the branch and trunk became the National Woman's Party.

Unlike the nineteenth-century split within the suffrage movement, the divide between NAWSA and the NWP grew increasingly difficult to span.[2] The publicity-seeking NWP earned both ardent admiration and fierce criticism for its confrontational tactics. Among suffragists, many feared that the NWP's actions would repel some tentative supporters of the cause, particularly crucial Congressional Democrats. The NWP's leaders were undaunted by unfriendly responses to their stratagems, which included picketing the White House, fueling "watch fires" with copies of President Woodrow Wilson's speeches, and staging highly publicized prison hunger strikes. After the achievement of

1. For details on the British-American connection, see Linda G. Ford, *Iron-Jawed Angels. The Suffrage Militancy of the National Woman's Party 1912–1920* (Lanham, Md.: University Press of America, 1991), 15–77.

2. For narratives of the suffrage campaign by participants, see Elizabeth Cady Stanton, Susan B. Anthony, and Matilda Joslyn Gage, *The History of Woman Suffrage*, 6 vols. (New York: Foster and Wells, 1881–1922); Carrie Chapman Catt and Nettie Rogers Shuler, *Woman Suffrage and Politics: The Inner Story of the Suffrage Movement* (New York: Scribner's, 1926); Doris Stevens, *Jailed for Freedom* (New York: Boni and Liveright, 1920); Maud Wood Park, *Front Door Lobby* (Boston: Beacon Press, 1960); Inez Haynes Irwin, *The Story of the Woman's Party* (New York: Harcourt, Brace, 1921). The contrasting visions of NAWSA and the CU are also described in Eleanor Flexner, *Century of Struggle: The Women's Rights Movement in the United States,* rev. ed. (Cambridge, Mass.: Belknap Press, 1975); Kraditor, *The Ideas of the Woman Suffrage Movement.*

woman suffrage and throughout the interwar years, the critics of the NWP remained plentiful, while the Party's numbers dwindled.

In August of 1920, the critical thirty-sixth state ratified the Anthony Amendment, but clashing strategies and principles still divided the women who had helped secure the national victory. Equipped with new political power, women's organizations began to debate new priorities, sorting and ranking those miscellaneous issues they believed should command the immediate attention of the woman voter. While the members of the new Women's Joint Congressional Committee (WJCC) preferred a steady but moderately paced agenda for securing equal citizenship rights for women, the NWP envisioned rapid and revolutionary progress. More immediatist in spirit and intrepid in action than the WJCC's members, the NWP soon fastened its postsuffrage hopes to a Constitutional amendment that would ensure legal equality between the sexes.

NAWSA had naturally dissolved with the appearance of the Nineteenth Amendment, and the new National League of Women Voters (NLWV) picked up many NAWSA veterans. The NLWV adopted a broad postsuffrage reform agenda that included (to name a handful of platform planks) the abolition of child labor, the elimination of discrimination against women in the civil service, compulsory civics classes in public schools, and independent citizenship for married women.[3] In contrast, within a year of the suffrage victory the NWP's Alice Paul hinted that her organization would pursue legal equality between the sexes through blanket legislation. As Nancy Cott observed, the pronouncement suggested that the NWP would operate much the same as it had during the suffrage campaign. "It remained," Cott notes, "an autocratically run, single-minded and single-issue pressure group."[4]

Paul, the NWP's dynamic and charismatic leader, hoped a new campaign would restore female reformers' ebbing sense of unity, but she mistakenly assumed that her organization's equal rights amendment could serve that purpose.[5] Ironically, the NWP's promotion of that amendment (sometimes referred to as the Lucretia Mott amendment)

---

3. The NLWV actually appeared in 1919 as a NAWSA auxiliary but became an independent organization the following year. Louise M. Young, *In the Public Interest*, 1–2.

4. Cott, *The Grounding of Modern Feminism*, 80.

5. Paul expressed great confidence in women's enthusiasm for a global movement for their legal emancipation. "Women are the same the world over," claimed Paul. "They want a world-wide movement—like a church. Something universal." "Alice Paul Returns," *Equal Rights* 27 (Apr. 1941): 31.

contributed to the philosophical stalemate that diminished communication and cooperation among feminists between the world wars. Instead, feminists' commitment to women's nationality rights proved better able than an equal rights amendment to fill the psychic void left by the ratification of the suffrage amendment.

The debate over protective legislation for women quickly provided a focal point for organized women's heated exchanges over the NWP's proposed blanket amendment, and the conflict threatened to polarize feminist politics between the world wars.[6] Although some reformers argued passionately that legislation singling out women for special protection and assistance had emancipative economic value for women, confirmed equalitarians vehemently disagreed.

Suffragists had made the independent woman citizen emblematic of women's achievement of equal political rights but had managed nevertheless to defer confronting the vast social and economic implications of legislating equality. The equal rights amendment forced such an engagement and thus stirred a host of organized women to begin to articulate the goals feminist citizens should and should not strive to accomplish for their sex. As the debate over the Mott amendment confirmed, former suffragists failed to reach unanimous agreement on a reform agenda. "The political rights of citizens are not properly dependent upon sex," concluded Florence Kelley, "but social and domestic relations and industrial relations are."[7] The NWP disagreed with the latter part of Kelley's statement—vehemently—but her words revealed why the issues of suffrage and nationality rights offered better opportunities for building consensus among female reformers than an equal rights amendment. Women's assumption of equal nationality rights was generally categorized as a political-rights issue. So defined, the campaign for women's nationality rights could keep the equal versus different debate, which was raging so forcefully on other fronts, partially at bay.

Prior to women's national enfranchisement, suffrage proponents could speak less self-consciously about "equality" between the sexes; but in the postsuffrage years, feminists' discussion of how to achieve

6. For more detailed coverage of the debate about an equal rights amendment between the NLWV, its cohorts in the WJCC, and the NWP, see Susan D. Becker, *Origins of the Equal Rights Amendment;* Christine A. Lunardini, *From Equal Suffrage to Equal Rights;* Cott, *The Grounding of Modern Feminism.*

7. Florence Kelley, "Shall Women Be Equal before the Law," *Nation* 114 (Apr. 12, 1922): 421.

such "equality" necessarily traveled beyond the neatly defined realm of political rights into some underexplored territory. As the outlines of the equality debate grew increasingly large and complex, so naturally did feminist discourse. Those women's organizations wedded to the idea that women as a group had special needs and interests that should be addressed through legislation fiercely resisted ideologues' sweeping and unqualified definition of—and pursuit of—gender equality. Although some feminists continued to propose that legislation must reflect that women were both equal to and distinct from men, equalitarian feminists condemned such a notion as a deadly contradiction.

In the face of fervent resistance to the equal rights amendment they set before Congress in 1923, the leaders of the NWP only grew more convinced than before that they were the true apostles of women's liberation. As the editors of the NWP's publication, *Equal Rights*, boasted: "The thing that marks the Woman's Party off from the other groups in the woman's movement in America is more subtle and more inflexible than any verbal credo. . . . It alone . . . holds beyond any possibility of compromise that women are the equals of men; it repudiates both privileges and disabilities based on sex in every sphere of human activity, and it possesses both a program of action designed to remove the remaining forms of the subjection of women, and the spirit to see the program through."[8]

At the height of the interwar debates over the nature and necessity of equality, major women's groups managed to maintain an undeclared alliance for pursuing women's nationality rights. The NWP and the WJCC's subcommittee on nationality lobbied steadfastly to abolish the same discriminatory clauses in the immigration and nationality laws. Despite this semblance of unity, the NLWV, the principal member of the WJCC subcommittee, later accused the NWP of disrupting the campaign for nationality rights by using that worthy reform effort to prop up their misguided quest for an equal rights amendment. The major piece of evidence supporting this accusation was the NWP's promotion in the 1930s of a global treaty banning sex discrimination in nationality laws and practices. This attempt to rechannel the rhetoric and rationale of equal nationality rights may have seemed inconsequential to neutral observers, but for the women involved in the heart of the campaign it was a critical moment. Comprehending the import of

8. "The Significance of the Woman's Party," *Equal Rights* 13 (Sept. 18, 1926): 252.

a treaty guaranteeing equal nationality rights, the NLWV broke openly with the equalitarians by condemning the treaty, refusing thereby to submit to a logic of reform that sprang from a feminist vision hostile to its own.

Interwar feminists had agreed that American women must assume "full citizenship rights" in order to function as independent American citizens. But what did this mean, even within the context of the nationality-rights campaign?

The movement for independent citizenship had offered a partial recess from the fatiguing internal struggles among organized women in the 1920s, but it was apparent by the 1930s that sustained cooperation among this broad base of reformers was possible only as long as the drives for an equal rights amendment and for legislation guaranteeing equal nationality rights remained separate. When the NWP proposed the ratification of a treaty for equal nationality rights, it deliberately broke through the boundaries between the two causes that the NLWV so desired to maintain.

In the years between the world wars women were still appealing for rather than commanding citizenship's replete rights, but gaining new political ground in 1920 created space for a thoughtful consideration by organized women of the concept of citizenship. The ongoing struggle to abolish marital expatriation and naturalization provided further incentives to shape a definition of citizenship relevant to the woman of the postsuffrage era. Some woman's rights advocates identified individualism and equal rights as the essentials of American citizenship. For other veterans of the suffrage campaign, however, citizenship remained defined as much by the service and sacrifices it demanded as by the privileges and rights it bestowed. The woman who answered the call to public service was truly to be the public's servant.

Judged by the standards of either of these groups, the immigrant woman who became an American simply by marrying an American was an anomaly, a woman citizen difficult to categorize or valorize. Equalitarian feminists challenged her existence not because they believed she necessarily lacked civic talents but because they questioned the invention and perpetuation of a dependent woman citizen. For feminists more likely than equalitarians to preach the virtues of Americanization, the practice of marital naturalization cheapened the cultural and political significance of naturalization and thus the value of American citizenship. Organizations like the NLWV expressed great confidence in the foreign-born woman's potential for "good citizenship" but argued that independent naturalization and assimilation were necessary avenues to the achievement of that state.

For the remainder of the 1920s Congress continued to focus on specific immigration reforms, but the 1930s saw a shift in attention to matters of nationality. Outside the United States, the Pan American Union's and League of Nation's developing interests in the question of women's nationality rights elevated this issue to a global concern. These international developments are the subject of the next chapter. Here the focus remains primarily on the domestic front, on the lingering problems created or aggravated by the immigration and naturalization laws framed in the 1920s, and on the voices of protest that pursued these policies across the threshold of a new decade.

The impact of the Cable Act on immigrant women—and the foreign-born wife of the American citizen, in particular—was an ongoing concern shared by the federal government and many of the women's organizations that had promoted the passage of the statute in 1922. As its earliest detractors had claimed, the Cable Act placed the country's policies on transnational marriages at odds with those honored by most countries, and by 1930 this situation had improved only slightly. Only Argentina, Chile, Colombia, Cuba, Panama, Paraguay, the Soviet Union, and Uruguay imposed no special restrictions on a woman citizen's marriage to an alien.[9] Consequently, most resident immigrant women who married Americans after the passage of the Cable Act became stateless on their wedding days and remained so until they earned a naturalization certificate.

During the course of the debates over the Cable bill, many lawmakers had predicted that the citizen's foreign-born wife would not seek citizenship on her own. This absence of initiative was, however, not apparent after the passage of the Cable Act, and even those women whom the government had assumed would be least inspired to seek naturalization because they were the least Americanized—the foreign wives of foreign citizens—also defied this prediction.

The Naturalization Bureau's annual statistical reports on female petitioners for naturalization in the 1920s did not indicate whether a woman was married to a noncitizen or whether she was foreign-born or a former citizen. However, under Cable Act rules, the former American wife of an alien and the foreign wife of a citizen did not have to

9. See Laura M. Berrien, "Nationality and International Relations," *Women Lawyers Journal* 19 (Fall 1931): 31–34.

file a declaration of intent. The Bureau's data on women filing declarations of intent after 1922 thus revealed the number of immigrant women seeking citizenship who were either single or married to noncitizens. The records show that the number of women submitting an official statement of their intention to become Americans more than doubled from the previous year of 1921, dropped significantly in 1930 and 1931, but then rose almost every year to reach 73,496 in 1939.[10] The dramatic increase in declarations immediately after passage of the Cable Act most likely represented the decision of thousands of married immigrant women to seek naturalization without the assistance or existence of an American husband.

Although the Cable Act's effect on immigrant women was profound, historians still know little of these women's responses to the impact of the law on their lives. Legislators, social workers, feminists, and government bureaucrats all freely expounded on the immigrant woman's needs and responsibilities, but the object of their investigation and speculation was often not present at those public forums to confirm or deny those conclusions. Too often the fact that she was foreign and feminized left the immigrant woman vulnerable to patronizing judgments regarding her political acumen and social skills. It is fortunate for her subjects and for us, then, that Sophonisba Breckinridge was the author of the principal study of the impact of the Cable Act on the foreign-born woman. Professor Breckinridge had already established her prominence in the field of social work education when she published her Cable Act study in 1931. She was also a cofounder of Chicago's Immigrants' Protective League, and her years of interaction with the foreign-born had nurtured a respectful attitude toward immigrant life and a sympathetic awareness of the challenges of adjusting to a new culture, It is not surprising, then, that Breckinridge recognized the importance of sampling foreign women's attitudes toward the Cable Act and the naturalization process in general. Her study, published as part of *Marriage and the Civic Rights of Women,* reflected well the convergence of Breckinridge's dual roles as social scientist and social reformer.

Breckinridge believed that most women could benefit from the opportunity to assume personal responsibility for their naturalization. Indeed, her interviewees assured her that this was true. But Breckinridge also wished to emphasize to the predominantly American readers of

10. Table 13 in U.S. Department of Commerce, Bureau of the Census, *Fifteenth Census of the United States: 1930. Population.* Vol. 2. (Washington, D.C.: G.P.O., 1933), 418.

her study that foreign women seeking citizenship faced significant new challenges in the post-Cable years. Many women did not possess the formal education required to pass the naturalization exam, she explained, and if these women arrived in the United States as adults, it was often difficult for them to overcome this disadvantage. Upon settling in the United States, Breckinridge observed, the immigrant woman moved "from conditions of poverty and hardship into conditions of domestic responsibility, with burdens of child-bearing, child-caring, and domestic management." Such a demanding domestic routine, she argued, gave the immigrant woman few chances to interact with the people of her adopted country. "While the man makes the contacts of his job, or his union, or his lodge, and the children make their contacts in the school, the wife and mother is without any similar opportunities."[11]

Breckinridge limited her pool of interviewees to married women of Polish ancestry who were living in the Chicago area, a sample that was small and relatively homogeneous but otherwise randomly selected from the petition files of the city's Naturalization Office. A small group of these women were former Americans who had lost their citizenship through marriage, but most of the women were foreign-born and seeking citizenship for the first time. Some in the group had successfully completed the naturalization process, while others had failed to qualify for naturalization. Despite the limitations of her method of sampling, Breckinridge's decision to let her subjects speak through her work provided a rare opportunity to hear the relatively unfiltered views of foreign-born women as they candidly reflected on the Cable Act's effect on their lives.

The eight women in the group who had retrieved U.S. citizenships lost by marriage applauded the passage of the Cable Act. Yet, predictably, they all questioned the government's insistence that they submit to naturalization proceedings. The Expatriation Act of 1907, they argued, had never altered their loyalties. Why couldn't the new law simply recognize that fact and pronounce them citizens once again? Nevertheless, these women believed the Cable Act had opened new doors to the immigrant woman by encouraging her to learn English and assert a personal allegiance to the United States. Perhaps, some suggested, by her example she could encourage her husband to seek citizenship. This

11. Sophonisba P. Breckinridge, *Marriage and the Civic Rights of Women. Separate Domicil and Independent Citizenship.* (Chicago: University of Chicago Press, 1931), 59.

cadre of women expressed the most emphatic and the most negative views of the Cable Act. Unlike the other women discussed below, these former expatriates viewed their reacquisition of citizenship as their due. Their criticisms of the Cable Act seemed to revolve around the fact that the law, by requiring them to become naturalized Americans, represented their reinstatement as citizens as a privilege bestowed at the discretion of the government rather than as their personal right. This distinction between birthright citizenship and naturalized citizenship also appeared more fully formed in the arguments presented by the female reformers lobbying for changes in the Cable Act.

The foreign-born women who had been naturalized independently also unanimously agreed that the citizenship process had bolstered their self-esteem and fostered greater interest in civic activities. Breckinridge reported that these women did not contest the notion that their naturalization was a privilege subject to whatever requirements the government might impose, and they expressed little, if any, opinion on the law that had opened the door to independent naturalization. The Cable Act was, as one woman explained casually, "just a law." But, then, this group represented the success stories—the immigrant women who had cleared the new legal hurdles and could proudly collect their naturalization certificates.[12]

These women's reasons for seeking naturalization varied, but foremost was the sobering realization that reentry into the United States was becoming more difficult and deportation more threatening. New immigration laws had magnified the disadvantages of alienage, making American citizenship appear more desirable, perhaps necessary. Another major incentive for individuals and families to pursue naturalization was the citizen's right to petition for immigrating relatives' admission. Becoming an American improved not only the individual's chances of staying in the United States but also the ability to effect reunions with family members seeking entry into the United States.

Some of the women interviewed were contributing the household's main or sole source of income because their husbands were physically unable to work. This reduction in income often left an immigrant family vulnerable to expulsion as public charges, but by becoming a United States citizen as a preventive measure, the wife could reduce the chances of the family's deportation. Women, like men, saw naturalization as a

12. See Breckinridge's chapter "Foreign-Born Women Who Have Succeeded," in *Marriage and the Civic Rights of Women*, 59–83.

means of adding a critical measure of stability to their family's future in the United States. Some of the interviewees remarked that becoming a citizen had also made it easier for them to buy homes or to open their own businesses.

Despite the procedural difficulties naturalization presented for many foreign-born, married women, naturalization statistics and Breckinridge's subjects challenged the prediction that the Cable Act would force a steep decline in the number of women seeking citizenship. In 1927, 549 married Polish women submitted petitions to the Naturalization Office in the Chicago. Under pre-Cable rules 174 of them could not have taken that step because they were married to aliens. The remaining 375 petitioners had naturalized husbands and, before the passage of the Cable Act, could have been automatically naturalized. Yet, these women had lost little time acquiring their own papers. Forty-one percent were naturalized within two years of their spouse's naturalization; 23 percent, between two and three years; and another 23 percent, between three and four years.[13]

Inevitably, without the guarantee of derivative naturalization, a smaller percentage of citizens' wives became Americans after 1922. Nevertheless, as the Chicago Naturalization Office's statistics revealed and the interviewed women suggested, regardless of a husband's nationality, married women had strong incentives to seek naturalization. Those who predicted that most married women would find the naturalization process too intimidating or inconvenient ignored the highly compelling reasons for achieving the protective status of citizen. The Cable Act changed the rules of naturalization, but it certainly did not reduced the advantages of acquiring citizenship. According to Breckinridge, the fundamental reality was this: "naturalization brings . . . security to the home."[14] This reality was infrequently acknowledged by the middle-class, native-born reformers who dominated the coalition for equal nationality rights and whose socioeconomic status offered them the luxury of viewing citizenship as a mandate for public service rather than a means of survival. While most of these reformers viewed naturalization as a critical stage in the foreign resident's assimilation, for many immigrant women the acquisition of citizenship serve much more basic human needs.

Several of the women Breckinridge interviewed aimed for citizen-

13. Ibid., 62.
14. Ibid., 82.

ship but fell short of the mark. The two major causes for failure, according to the official records, were the disqualification of one of their two required witnesses and "want of prosecution or ignorance." Most of these women felt frustrated but not defeated by their difficulties. Despite continued struggles with the English language and the fear of a second failure, a majority of these women said they intended to try again. They, too, expressed little discontent with the Cable Act, although some criticized the naturalization exam, which they thought asked few questions relevant to their lives as homemakers. The petitioners found the process a discomfiting experience but seemed to accept the necessity of submitting to some kind of civics test.[15]

Breckinridge noted that her subjects obviously possessed virtues traditionally esteemed by American society—traits evidenced best by their lives as devoted mothers. So why, she asked, did the naturalization examiner make no attempt to measure these qualities? Breckinridge suspected that the examinations carried a pronounced gender bias that caused the disqualification of many worthy female candidates. Although she did not dispute the need for maintaining some educational requirements for citizenship, Breckinridge wondered whether the standard tests "actually select on the basis of important community values."[16] Her comments framed a concern reiterated by generations of activist women.

Breckinridge also interviewed women who had never tried to take out first papers. Although problems with English seemed to be a major roadblock to naturalization, these women's economic circumstances did not distinguish them from those who had become Americans. Some of the women were struggling financially; some were not. Lack of time for concentrated study often explained their avoidance of the exam, but many had declined offers of help from friends and family in developing their language skills. All the women reported that hostility from family members was not a factor dissuading them from seeking naturalization. Although each woman offered different personal reasons for currently not seeking naturalization, a limited educational background and fears about the naturalization exam and interrogation seemed to be the most common concerns. Not surprisingly, friends' and family members' difficulties with the naturalization process added to these women's doubts

15. Ibid., 84–107.
16. Ibid., 60.

about their own chances of success.[17] Once again, however, the administration of the law rather than the implications of the law most disturbed these women.

Many of Breckinridge's subjects defied the stereotype of the retiring foreign woman who had to be coaxed out of her home to participate in the rites of citizenship. Many women exhibited the determination to overcome time, educational, or physical problems and become citizens on their own. The Cable Act had declared that naturalization would no longer be a wedding gift from the U.S. government, but most of the women interviewed recognized the advantages independent naturalization could bestow. The new law promised a resident woman increased control over her own destiny. Having an alien husband did not necessarily affect her ability to apply for citizenship, and she would have access to public assistance, which was available exclusively to citizens. Yet, Sophie Breckinridge recognized that lack of schooling, money, and time would always keep some women from approaching a naturalization court. In the end, her interviews could not erase her troubling conviction that "no friend of the foreign-born wife has urged independent citizenship."[18]

Congress, the Department of Labor, the federal courts, and influential women's organizations generally advocated, if they did not directly promote, a more stringent screening process than the one that was in place for naturalization candidates. At least one of those supporters, the NLWV, weathered some criticism for belittling the problems the Cable Act had created for married immigrant women. In response to an admonition from the National Council of Jewish Women, the editors of the League's *Woman Citizen* reassured the Council that it was not neglecting the unique problems of the foreign-born woman in the United States. Independent naturalization now meant citizens' foreign wives could be detained on arrival in the country, excluded, or even deported; but, argued the editors rather piously, "it has been felt that the greater good of the greater number should apply."[19]

17. Ibid., 108–117.
18. Ibid., 21.
19. "Where the Cable Law Pinches," WC 7 (Jan. 27, 1923): 15. The National Council of Jewish Women supported the Cable Act as members of the WJCC subcommittee but refused to endorse the equal rights amendment in 1922 as well as the Quota Act of 1921. In the early 1920s the Council was active in immigrant-aid work. Faith Rogow devotes a chapter to these efforts in *Gone to Another Meeting. The National Council of Jewish Women,*

At the same time, the *Woman Citizen* called for the intensification of Americanization efforts to hasten immigrant women's progression from foreign citizen to U.S. citizen. The NLWV remained keenly interested in establishing citizenship training programs for the foreign-born population. In order to demonstrate its ongoing commitment to aid the foreign-born woman, the organization's General Council approved the formation of a special committee for the study of immigrant problems in 1924. Frances Perkins chaired this committee, which boasted other distinguished members, including Julia Lathrop, Edith Abbott, Mary Guyton, and Josephine Roche. The NLWV also joined the throng of critics attacking the new immigration quota acts that divided alien and citizen families.[20] As for the implementation of the Cable Act, the NLWV did concede that "in enthusiasm for the principle [of independent citizenship], we should not overlook the possibility of softening the rigors that would lie in holding to the letter."[21]

The *Interpreter*, issued by the Foreign Language Information Service, carried optimistic reports on growing interest in woman's rights issues among immigrant women. One article reported anecdotally on a small-scale rebellion touched off by a "wife wanted" advertisement that had appeared in the Slovene press. The offending notice had advised divorced women not to bother to respond to the bachelor's notice for a wife. His warning elicited some rather indignant replies from women. "The letters," reported the *Interpreter* enthusiastically, "have been imbued with a strong sense of emancipation and equal rights."[22] Other articles in the journal announced the formation of new female organizations for political discourse and action, such as the Lithuanian Women's Citizenship Club of Baltimore or, in New York City, a female auxiliary to the Polish Democratic Club.[23] Americans commonly assumed that foreign-born women came to the United States with little or no political inclinations or experience. Thus, one of the standard gauges of a woman's progress toward Americanization was a demon-

---

1893–1993 (Tuscaloosa: University of Alabama Press, 1993), 130–166.

20. Minutes of League of Women Voters' Executive Committee meeting, Sept 12, 1929, *Papers of the League of Women Voters, 1918–1974*, pt. I, consulting editor Susan Ware (Frederick, Md.: University Publications of America, 1985), microfilm. These papers are cited hereafter as *NLWV I*.

21. "Where the Cable Law Pinches," 15.

22. "Among the Foreign Born: Equal Rights for Immigrant Women," *Interpreter* 2 (Apr. 1923): 13.

23. "Among the Foreign Born: Women Voters Organize," *Interpreter* 3 (May 1924): 12.

strated interest in public affairs. In publicizing bursts of political activism among foreign-born women, these observers of the foreign-born seemed eager to demonstrate that immigrant wives, a class of aliens believed to be highly resistant to assimilation, were growing increasingly responsive to American influences. Woman's rights organizations credited any political awakening of immigrant women to the Nineteenth Amendment, the Cable Act, and their citizenship-training programs.

The NWP never matched this intense desire to Americanize the immigrant. Throughout the interwar period and beyond, the Party remained more firmly focused on feminist issues than those organizations constituting the WJCC. But there is, perhaps, a further explanation for the Party's aloofness from assimilationist efforts. The leadership of the NWP never warmly embraced the nationalistic rhetoric that so often accompanied discussions about naturalization and assimilation during this era. That particular element of the dialogue simply did not contribute significantly to the Party's conceptualization of citizenship. The NWP's fundamental goal was the achievement of absolute legal equality between the sexes—a globalized objective that rendered the national seat of a woman's citizenship almost irrelevant. But the removal of both gender and national identity from the citizenship-rights equation was unpalatable to most other women's organizations in the loose reform coalition. For them, the fact that women were seeking the rights, privileges, as well as responsibilities assigned to the U.S. citizen was crucial.

The advent of the 1930s seemed to trigger a burst of Cable Act reforms. The relationship between the WJCC subcommittee and the NWP was growing shakier, but progress toward the goal of independent citizenship proceeded rather smoothly nevertheless. The House Committee on Immigration and Naturalization had remained open to entertaining amendments to the Cable Act, and John Cable, who had returned to Congress after a short hiatus, set to work refining his original handiwork. Cable introduced a new bill in February of 1930 to repeal the ineligible-spouse disqualification for naturalization as well as the presumptive loss of citizenship for residence abroad.[24]

---

24. H.R. 9405 and H.R. 10208, 71st Cong., 2d sess. (1930), latter rewritten as H.R. 10960. The House Committee held a hearing to discuss H.R. 10208 in which representatives from member organizations of the WJCC participated. The NWP did not appear but later sent written endorsement of H.R. 10960. Hearings before the House Com-

The bill promised changes in both the Johnson-Reed and Cable Acts. One section altered the Cable Act by removing many of the requirements for repatriation. A marital expatriate still had to apply for citizenship, but the process was shorter and simpler. She would appear before a naturalization examiner, prove she was a marital expatriate eligible for citizenship under current naturalization law, and then take an oath of allegiance. Not all women could benefit from these changes however. The government's determination to avoid supporting anyone's claim to dual citizenship limited the beneficiaries of these provisions to former Americans who were married to men eligible for naturalization and who had not themselves assumed another nationality by affirmative act.

The amending bill also offered to further ease the difficulties the nonresident woman encountered with the immigration laws by granting her nonquota immigrant status if she had lost her U.S. citizenship through marriage to an alien, marriage to an alien and residence in a foreign country, or her husband's denationalization or denaturalization. Another section of the amending bill explicitly repealed the expatriation provision in Section 3 of the Cable Act, which provided for the loss of citizenship for residence abroad. However, this bill did not furnish automatic repatriation to women who had already lost their citizenship because they married aliens and lived abroad.[25]

Acting Secretary of Labor Robe Carl White informed a Senate member of the Committee on Immigration that his Department did not oppose repealing Section 3 of the Cable Act, but he offered some reasons why Labor believed this action would have some undesirable results. Two categories of native-born women then fell under the pre-

mittee on Immigration and Naturalization, *Amendment to the Women's Citizenship Act of 1922*, 71st Cong., 2d sess., Mar. 6, 1930. At this time the WJCC's Follow Up Committee watched Cable Act amending bills. The Subcommittee on Amendments to the Cable Act, which was part of this standing committee, included the NLWV (its Gladys Harrison chaired the group), National Women's Trade Union League, American Association of University Women, American Home Economics Association, and National Federation of Business and Professional Women. By the following year the National Council of Jewish Women and the YWCA had also joined the subcommittee. "Minutes of the Meeting of the Women's Joint Congressional Committee, February 10, 1930," *WJCC*. See also "Cleaning Up the Cable Act," *Bulletin of the National League of Women Voters* (Feb. 1930): 1.

25. H.R. 10960. For text and analyses of this bill, see *Citizenship and Naturalization of Married Women*, 71st Cong., 2d sess., 1930, H. Rept. 1036 and S. Rept. 614.

sumptive expatriation rule. One group included women like Loretta Guignet—women who had grown up in the United States but had moved abroad as adults after marrying aliens. However, White was more concerned with the status of the other group: native-born women who had been removed to foreign countries during childhood and who now had foreign-born children. This group of women, whose size was difficult to estimate, would benefit from the repeal of Section 3.[26] If the amending bill became law, it would become much easier for these women to return to the United States and apply for citizenship. After reclaiming their original citizenship, resident women could then assist the admission of their foreign husbands and minor children as nonquota immigrants. The number of nonquota immigrants had already increased significantly, and the Labor Department was reluctant to sanction construction of yet another avenue for their entry.[27]

Despite the Department's reservations, the Cable reform bill survived a Senate vote. Gladys Harrison, who chaired the WJCC's subcommittee on amendments to the Cable Act, reported confidently that both houses of Congress were "thoroughly in favor" of the bill as it emerged

---

26. Ibid.

27. *CR* 72 (June 16, 1930), 10864. A large number of native Americans were living abroad. Between 1918 and 1929, over 435,000 natives were presumed to have left the United States permanently. Approximately 62,000 naturalized citizens had done the same. U.S. Department of Labor, *Annual Report of the Secretary of Labor* (1929), 15. As for the number of residents' petitions for alien relatives (nonquota or preference), the following statistics reveal the trend:

Fiscal Year Petitions Filed

1925	29,000 (est.)
1926	23,869 (est.)
1927	34,169
1928	38,460
1929	40,774
1930	36,703

Source: U.S. Department of Labor, Bureau of Immigration, *Annual Report of the Commissioner General of Immigration* (1929), 23, and (1930), 26.

Correspondingly, the number of wives and children of citizens admitted increased significantly. The number of wives jumped from a little over 4,000 in fiscal 1925 to 13,625 in 1928. The number of children admitted annually increased from 3,046 to 12,075. In 1930, 15,848 citizens' wives were admitted and 15,398 of their children. In contrast, only 859 alien husbands of American citizens gained entry. U.S. Department of Labor, Bureau of Immigration, *Annual Report of the Commissioner General of Immigration* (1930), 60–62.

from the House.[28] The intensive involvement of women's organizations, which Cable correctly insisted was critical to the survival of the bill, did corral votes. As Senator Royal Copeland observed, "I do not suppose there is a Senator here who has not been approached by several good women who are very much interested in the passage of this bill."[29] President Herbert Hoover signed it into law on July 3, 1930.[30]

The same day Hoover gave the nod to another bill that protected women racially eligible for naturalization and married to native-born veterans of World War I from exclusion under Section 3 of the Immigration Act of 1917.[31] These two new laws assisted separated couples and brought American women a few steps closer to enjoying equal nationality rights. Nonetheless, the remaining forms of legal discrimination against women and their families were consequential. Mothers still could not transfer their American citizenship to their "legitimate" children, and in 1930 the federal government appeared still unprepared to consider correcting that inequity. As for the clause in the Cable Act barring the naturalization or repatriation of women married to aliens ineligible for citizenship, the House Committee on Immigration and Naturalization remained divided over its repeal.[32]

Unlike the WJCC's subcommittees, the NWP had grown increasingly impatient with the pace of progress and by the early 1930s its leaders were pressing for a blanket bill covering equal nationality rights. The WJCC, State Department, and Bureau of Naturalization, however, did not share the NWP's enthusiasm for this remedy. Even Representative Cable declined to ally with the NWP in this endeavor, believing instead that a woman should still have to return to the United States to retrieve her lost citizenship. The NWP realized the high risks of proceeding without the approval of some of its main Congressional supporters and decided to delay its demand for a blanket bill to accommodate his reservations.[33] In turn, Cable introduced three bills to amend the Cable Act in one session of the Seventy-first Congress.

28. "Minutes of the Women's Joint Congressional Committee, June 2, 1930," *WJCC.*

29. *CR* 72 (June 27, 1930), 11884.

30. Act of July 3, 1930, 46 Stat. at 854.

31. Act of July 3, 1930, 46 Stat. 849. This law had an interesting provenance, as noted in Chapter 4. The law's provisions permitted the admission of Anna Ulrich, wife the American millionaire John Ulrich.

32. "Minutes of the Women's Joint Congressional Committee, January 5, 1931," *WJCC.*

33. The NWP would have accepted a special repatriation process for women who lost their citizenship by marriage—if it consisted only of taking a loyalty oath. The NWP

The WJCC's subcommittee on amendments to the Cable Act sent a letter to all members of the House urging support of Cable's initiative, a move that boosted the proposals' chances of surviving.[34] Within two months, the House and Senate had resolved their differences over a reform bill. Signed by the President on March 3, 1931, the new law finally removed the barriers to citizenship or repatriation plaguing women married to aliens ineligible for citizenship and women living in foreign countries.[35]

A combination of external pressures and internal incidents contributed to the Seventy-first Congress's willingness finally to abandon the controversial policies on foreign residence and spousal ineligibility for naturalization. Certainly the most significant factor was unrelenting lobbying by the country's most influential women's organizations. The act that amended the Cable and Johnson-Reed Acts had claimed an impressive group of major supporters: the NLWV, NWP, National Federation of Business and Professional Women, American Association of University Women, American Home Economics Association, National Council of Jewish Women, YWCA, General Federation of Women's Clubs, Woman's Christian Temperance Union, National Women's Trade Union League, as well as the Immigrants' Protective League and the American Federation of Labor.

---

wanted John Cable to introduce a bill erasing all restrictions standing between a woman expatriated by marriage and repatriation. The congressman refused. Copy of unsigned letter to Alice Paul, Dec. 15, 1930, *NWPP*. Cable presented his views in "The Citizenship of American Women," *Atlantic Monthly* 145 (May 1930): 649–653.

34. The WJCC subcommittee was preparing to part ways with the NWP in the nationality-rights campaign. Tension was building between feminists as the equalitarians made clear their intention to lobby for a blanket nationality bill and treaty. Some of the members of the WJCC subcommittee wanted to hold off endorsing further changes in the Cable Act until the group had time to discuss blanket equalization of nationality laws. "Minutes of the Women's Joint Congressional Committee, January 5, 1931," *WJCC*. The NWP needed the WJCC's support but realized it would now be increasingly difficult to secure. "We do not wish the other women's organizations to know about it but we have drafted all the nationality bills," confided Burnita Shelton Matthews to Jane Norman Smith. Letter of Feb. 24, 1931, *NWPP*.

35. Act of March 3, 1931, 46 Stat. 1511. Cable had introduced several bills before this session of the Seventy-first Congress: H.R. 14684, 14685, 16303, and 16975. This last bill gained the support of the NWP, NLWV, D. C. Woman's Bar Association, National Council of Jewish Women, National Federation of Business and Professional Women, National Association of Women Lawyers, and the General Federation of Women's Clubs. H.R. 16975 was added to the faster moving H.R. 10672 in February and passed the Senate in this form. Both houses accepted it, and the bill was signed by Hoover just before Congress adjourned. The conference report is reprinted in *CR* 74 (Mar. 3, 1931), 6905 and 7153.

The WJCC subcommittee's leadership in the movement and its cautious strategy to effect reform were critical factors leading to this phase of the campaign. It is doubtful that the nationality-rights crusade would have fared as well in the early 1930s if the NWP had dominated the scene during the 1920s. The WJCC's faith in the powers of persuasion and education had served the nationality-rights crusade well during that first post-Cable decade. Although legislators were willing to cooperate with women's organizations on nationality issues, they seemed stubbornly unwilling to tackle more than a small handful of problems at a time. The WJCC was willing to be patient. Even the restless leaders of the NWP saw the wisdom of playing by the movement's established rules if it wished to work successfully with Congress during this decade. In the 1930s, however, the pace of reform quickened as the NWP became a more confident and dominant player in the campaign.

Another strategic factor that bolstered prospects for reform was organized women's profitable campaign to keep legislators (and their constituents) informed about the consequences of the Cable Act and the immigration acts. An unfortunate but propitious incident involving one of Congress's newer members, Ruth Bryan Owen, contributed significantly to this program of education. Representative Owen had been denationalized for her marriage to a British officer but then recovered her U.S. citizenship through naturalization in 1925. After Owen's election campaign, her defeated opponent challenged her eligibility to serve, arguing that she had not met the residence requirement for the office following her repatriation. Owen, who was an advocate of equal nationality rights, gathered strong support from her Congressional colleagues and survived the investigation.[36]

Members of Congress were also aware that women's nationality rights had become the object of global attention—an awareness that probably improved legislators' concentration on the debate at home. Several other countries were wrestling with similar nationality issues, and the League of Nations was exploring the feasibility of creating international rules governing the nationality of married women.[37] In-

36. For one account of the Owen incident and its implications, see John L. Cable, "The Demand of Women for Equal Citizenship," *New York Times,* 13 Apr. 1930, sect. 11.

37. The Hague Conference on the Codification of International Law, held in the spring

deed, the passage of the Cable Act amending bills in 1930 and 1931 was, in part, a Congressional response to a League of Nations convention on nationality drafted in 1930.

Despite the substantial victories for women represented by the Acts of July 3, 1930, and March 3, 1931, the country's immigration and naturalization laws and practices still disadvantaged women in transnational marriages and their families. As noted earlier, American women could not transfer their nationality to their children. And if they had alien spouses, their husbands still did not automatically receive the quota breaks enjoyed by immigrating women married to citizens or resident aliens.

The remainder of this chapter tells the stories of a diverse collection of women whose predicaments all served as reminders to nationality-rights reformers that their business was still unfinished in the 1930s. As different as these women's worlds were in many respects, their lives were all wrenchingly disrupted by their marriages to foreign citizens. Some

---

of 1930, is discussed in the next chapter. Globally, women's nationality rights varied at that time, as the lists below indicate.

Equality between Sexes in Regard
to Effect of Marriage on Nationality

Argentina	Panama
Chile	Paraguay
Colombia	Soviet Union
Cuba	Uruguay

Equality between Spouses in Regard
to Changing Nationality after Marriage

Argentina	Paraguay
Brazil	Soviet Union
Chile	Uruguay
Guatemala	

Equality between Parents in Ability
to Transfer Nationality to Children at Birth

Argentina	Panama
Chile	Paraguay
Colombia	Peru
Soviet Union	Dominican Republic
Ecuador	Turkey
Nicaragua	Uruguay
Venezuela	

Men and women had full equal nationality rights in Argentina, Chile, Paraguay, the Soviet Union, and Uruguay.

of the women had lost their citizenship because of these marriages; others had not. Yet all encountered some of the legal difficulties hazarded by any American woman who, as some of their contemporaries put it, had the "bad taste" to marry a foreigner.

Lillian Larch had lost her birthright citizenship when she married a Canadian in 1917. Three years later she moved to Canada with her husband and American-born daughter. In 1926 the Larches, now a family of six, returned to the United States on visitors' visas. By 1930, Larch's husband was in a Detroit hospital, where doctors declared him "feeble-minded." (It is not clear why he was admitted to the hospital initially.) The city's Department of Public Welfare notified immigration officials that the family was on relief, thus prompting deportation proceedings to begin against them, with the exception of the one American-born child. Before the deportation orders were carried out, Lillian Larch's husband died. Under these circumstances Lillian Larch could most likely not have applied for naturalization under the Cable Act because she had entered the United States as a visitor not as an immigrant. Furthermore, as her sympathizers pointed out, her inability to read had probably kept her ignorant of her legal options.

The public's interest in the circumstances of the Larch family's deportation soon extended beyond the Detroit area. Immigration officials had given the family only one day to prepare for their departure to Ontario, where the destitute Larches had no friends or relatives. According to newspaper reports, the family had only the $1.50 the mother had received from the sale of a stove. But the most disturbing public revelation about the incident was the fact that Lillian Larch was an American-born woman. Larch was certainly not the first or only marital expatriate deported from the United States, but her case captured the attention of the NWP, which not only investigated the government's treatment of the family but avidly publicized the deportation.[38] The

38. Emma Goldman was probably the most famous marital expatriate deported from the United States, even though she was not a native born citizen. The *Detroit News* carried articles on the Larch case, of course, but those in the *New York Times* and *Washington Post* reached a larger audience. See, for example: "Larch Expulsion Backed," *New York Times,* 3 May 1931; "Women Score Deportation of American-Born Widow," *Washington Post,* 2 May 1931; "Larch Deportation Held Unavoidable," *Washington Post,* 3 May 1931; and "Deportation Hit as 'Inexcusable,' " *Washington Post,* 4 May 1931. For more details on Larch's condition after deportation, see telegram from Harry Shirley, chairman of the Charity Department in Wallaceburg, Ontario, to the NWP, Apr. 29, 1931, *NWPP;* letter from Muna Lee to Mrs. Rilla Nelson, chair of the Michigan Branch of NWP, May 1, 1931, *NWPP.*

Washington Post and *New York Times* printed NWP member and benefactor Anna Kelton Wiley's vehement condemnation of the deportation. The expulsion, she declared, was a "burning indictment of the inequalities remaining in our nationality law."[39]

As the NWP had intended, publicizing the case boosted interest in reforming the Cable Act. "The Lillian Larsh [*sic*] deportation case has pleased the newspapers as no other story has succeeded in doing for the past several months," reported a delighted Muna Lee, NWP's director of national activities. "It had all the popular elements, beside being [a] grand Woman's Party argument."[40]

At this point the reader might entertain the suspicion that the NWP's motives for generating this publicity were more selfish than humanitarian, but members of the NWP did appeal to Albert Johnson of the House Committee on Immigration and Naturalization to assist Lillian Larch's return. Johnson already knew about the case (of course), and he was reluctant to support the Larches. The country already had "too many of that kind now," Johnson told Anne Rotter of the NWP, but he did consent to call Theodore Risley in the Labor Department to see what might be done to ease Larch's difficulties. Risley, however, responded that the situation had probably progressed too far to be resolved.[41] A special act of Congress might be necessary to readmit the family because the Copeland-Jenkins Act of 1928 barred the reentry of deportees. And there were other barriers to Lillian Larch's recovery of her American residence and citizenship. The Larches, along with thousands of other immigrants, had the misfortune to become public charges when the United States was suffering a severe economic crisis. Furthermore, although immigrants from Canada were not subject to a quota count, they did have to pass a literacy test. As a married woman, Larch had not been required to submit to the test when she returned to the United States for the first time; as a single woman she lost that exemption. The marriage that had robbed her of her citizenship had later protected her from exclusion from the country as an illiterate, but it would ultimately clear the way for her final deportation. As a widow Larch was bereft of her husband, her citizenship, and her country. Her experience was in many ways a testament to the dual nature of marital

---

39. "Protests Deporting Canadian's Widow. Mrs. Wiley of National Woman's Party Seeks to Aid American-Born Woman," *New York Times,* 2 May 1931.

40. Letter of Muna Lee to Florence Bayard Hilles, May 16, 1931, *NWPP.*

41. Transcript of interview with Albert Johnson, dated May 13, 1931, *NWPP.*

dependency—a status that could simultaneously convey security against and vulnerability to the laws of expatriation and immigration.

Newspaper reports on Lillian Larch's condition offered the portrait of a woman who had lost the stamina and the will to challenge her deportation. She barely communicated with anyone, including those who wished to help her. As a frustrated official in Ontario told the *Washington Post*, "We are doing all we can for her but she seems to be unmoved by her predicament. She is even reluctant to give us information on which we may act. She appears not to care where she is sent."[42] The Larches' difficulties provoked a small surge of public sympathy at a time when many people feared that economic ruin could force their descent into the same numbing state of helplessness that now apparently gripped Lillian Larch. In the end Larch and her family were not welcomed back by the U.S. government. Despite the attention her situation attracted, she remained throughout the ordeal a lonely and enigmatic figure whose apparent passivity in the face of legal discrimination only added to the tragedy in her difficult life. Her pathetic story may have "pleased the newspapers" at the time, but this voiceless woman was soon forgotten by a public surrounded by too many other scenes of personal hardship.

Other individuals, strengthened by the advantages of collective protest, were able to defend themselves more successfully against the government's infringement of their Constitutional rights and privileges as American citizens. The Citizen Wives Organization (CWO) had a brief and productive life, one sustained by a single objective. The Citizen Wives were not drawn into the nationality-rights campaign by predilections for political activism. Their reasons for challenging sex discrimination in the immigration laws were, they would say, far more personal. They were Americans whose foreign husbands had been denied entry into the United States by the State Department.

The women of the CWO launched their well-organized protest at a time when Congress was preoccupied with the consequences of the economic depression. With a large number of American men out of work, the CWO's pleas for the admission of their foreign husbands were unlikely to meet with sympathetic consideration. One of the government's responses to the crisis had been a forced reduction in the number of noncitizens dependent on public relief. To this end, the Bureau of

42. "Larch Deportation Held Unavoidable."

Immigration had adopted more aggressive deportation strategies than it had used in the past, and, as illustrated by the Larch case, the Bureau swiftly exercised its authority to deport aliens who had become public charges within five years of their arrival in the United States.

Despite some calls for its suspension, the government did not halt immigration during these years of high unemployment, but the number of foreigners arriving plummeted when job opportunities in the United States dwindled. Roughly 241,700 aliens entered the United States in 1930; by 1932 that number had dipped sharply to 35,576. Immigration dropped to a level the country had not seen for a century. U.S. consulates had begun screening potential immigrants more meticulously than before in order to decrease the number of incoming aliens, and the classification of potential immigrants as aliens "likely to become public charges" (l.p.c.) reduced the number of foreigners admitted.[43] Indeed, this method of barring aliens was employed with such vigor that the practice generated some criticism within the federal government.

The escalation of l.p.c. exclusions can be linked to President Hoover's executive order of September 1930, calling for a reduction in immigration during the economic crisis. In the summer of 1931, all diplomatic and consular officers received the following statement regarding the admission of "old-seed" immigrants: "It would seem in the case of an alien wife or minor child who is coming to join her husband or parent employed in this country there is a natural inference that the alien would not be likely to become a p.c., since the husband or parent ordinarily could be expected to take steps to prevent the member of his immediate family from becoming a charge upon the public."[44]

In the case of wives seeking their alien husbands' admission, consulates were to demand evidence from the wife that the family's income would not evaporate "by reason of any temporary disability."[45] Following Hoover's suggestion, the Visa Division advised exercising some leniency toward citizens' relatives, but the distinction it had made be-

---

43. U.S. Department of Labor, Bureau of Immigration, *Annual Report of the Commissioner General of Immigration* (1932), 186.

44. Circular letter to all diplomatic and consular officers, June 24, 1931, Visa Division Files, U.S. Department of State, RG 59, National Archives, 150.062 Public Charge/219. (These papers will hereafter be cited as *VD*.)

45. Ibid.

tween cases involving alien wives and husbands was not overlooked by its agents.

The evidence indicates, however, that both men and women encountered difficulties convincing officials that their petitioning spouse would not become a public charge. Many consular officers had responded overzealously to Hoover's primary directive, prompting the consul general in Montreal to report with alarm that some were "refusing thousands of applicants who are not in fact in any degree liable ever to require public assistance." He cautioned against the repercussions of such draconian measures. "The Department may not . . . realize vividly how far-fetched, not to say irrational, this interpretation [of the l p.c. clause] appears in the eyes of intelligent persons in Canada and elsewhere," he warned.[46] Meanwhile, at least one legislator, from New York, lodged a similar grievance against the exploitation of the l.p.c. clause. "If a man had $25 or $50 in his pocket and a good pair of eyes and a good heart [in 1917], he was not [a] public charge." Now, he complained, "if you have $30,000 they can discriminate against you and label you p.c."[47]

Fanny Sunshine-Cypin, the president of the CWO, could personally confirm the congressman's charges. In 1931 the federal government had informed her that her Polish husband could not join her permanently in the United States because he was l.p.c. The law left Sunshine-Cypin with two disagreeable options: abandon her American citizenship to live in Poland with her husband or remain separated from him indefinitely. Sunshine-Cypin rejected both choices, believing that she deserved a more satisfactory solution to her dilemma as a citizen and resident of the United States. Hoping to establish contact with other Americans whose husbands had been denied visas, Sunshine-Cypin placed an advertisement in a major New York City newspaper describing her situation. In a short time, over three hundred citizens separated from their husbands by the immigration laws and policies answered her invitation.[48] The women quickly established themselves in an office pro-

46. Letter from Henry W. Goforth, consul general in Montreal, Dec. 17, 1930, VD, 150.062 Public Charge/74.

47. Samuel Dickstein, congressman from New York, in record of Hearings before the House Committee on Immigration and Naturalization, *To Exempt from the Quota Husbands of American Citizen Wives and to Limit the Presumption That Certain Alien Relatives May Become Public Charges,* 72d Cong., 1st sess., Jan. 14, 1932, 24.

48. There is a partial list of husbands of members of the CWO in *VD,* 150.062 Public Charge/291. The number of cases submitted by the CWO exceeded four hundred. See

vided by the Hebrew Immigrant Aid and Sheltering Society in New York City.

The State Department's investigation of 165 members of the CWO revealed that the majority had married in or before 1930 and shared Jewish and Polish ancestries. Most of the wives had met their spouses for the first time on a visit to Poland or had returned to that country temporarily intending to marry childhood acquaintances. Most of their husbands lived in Poland, but a good number resided in Cuba, probably because Cuba was a nonquota country. U.S. consulate officials had assured the affianced couples that the men could join their citizen wives in the United States within six months, but President Hoover's Depression-induced executive order to limit immigration abruptly altered that timetable.

Most of the future members of the CWO had received notice shortly after marrying that their husbands were l.p.c. and thus ineligible for visas at that time.[49] The Visa Division told some of the women that the withheld visas might be granted if they could prove possession of at least $2,000 in savings. Yet, when several of the women supplied the requested evidence, skeptical officials stalled for time in order to complete their investigation of what one wag in the Department dubbed the "lovelorn Jewish wives."[50]

State Department officials suspected that individuals and organizations interested in getting Jews into the country had lent the women the required funds. In support of that theory, the American consul in Havana reported that most of the thirty-eight cases he investigated revealed sham marriages, the product of an importation network designed to get Russian and Polish aliens, particularly Jews, into the United States.[51] Reports from the consul general in Warsaw also fos-

letter of A. Dana Hodgdon, chief of the Visa Division, to Abby Scott Baker, May 22, 1931, *VD*, 150.062 Public Charge/176.

49. Letter of Mollie Stafman-Kolinsky, treasurer of the CWO, to Secretary of State Henry Stimson, Feb.. 14, 1931, *VD*, 150.062 Public Charge/107. See President, "Second Annual Message to Congress," *CR* 74 (Dec. 2, 1930), 36, in which Hoover stated that, "under conditions of current unemployment, it is obvious that persons coming to the United States seeking work would likely become either a direct or indirect public charge. . . . Officers issuing visas to immigrants have been . . . instructed to refuse visas to applicants likely to fall into this class."

50. Letter of A. R. Burr, special agent in charge of New York Division, Department of State, to R. C. Bannerman, chief of special agents, Nov. 20, 1931, *VD*, 150.062 Public Charge/314-½. This file also contains various newspaper clippings on the cases.

51. Letter to Consul General F.T.F. Dumont, undated (May 1931), *VD*, 150.062 Public Charge/196. According to the consul in Havana, in the cases he investigated, the husbands

tered suspicions. His investigation of ten women's savings accounts revealed that most were held by the same two banks. The women had deposited their funds between the closing months of 1930 and the spring of 1931 in large round amounts such as $500, $1,000, and $1,500—figures that suggested they were donations rather than savings from wages.[52]

When questioned about their resources, some of the women explained that they received the money either as repayment for a debt or as a wedding gift. Ruth Bell-Bielski, then president of the CWO, balked at such inquiries and sent an indignant reply to the State Department. Noting its skill at asking, but not answering, questions, Bell-Bielski informed the Department that it was "no concern of the consul or any other government official where the money . . . has come from."[53] As a CWO member, her circumstances were not unique. The twenty-seven year old Bell-Bielski was a naturalized American who had returned to Poland in 1930 to marry a man whom she had known in her childhood. The American consul in Warsaw had assured her that her future husband, a farmer, could leave Poland for the United States within six months of their marriage. Bell-Bielski returned home, only to discover that her husband would not be permitted to join her because the Visa Division had classified him as l.p.c. Meanwhile, her husband had become unemployed. Believing he was leaving for the United States shortly, he had not contracted for another year's work.[54]

The women had wearied of serving as a "shuttlecock to be batted about from pillar to post," Bell-Bielski announced, but Assistant Secretary of State Wilbur Carr still resisted the CWO's demands. "If we yield to these people's importunities, we might as well say goodbye to

---

had modest jobs, could speak little English, and had been trying to get visas for years. The majority of the petitioning wives were naturalized Americans, residents of the United States for many years, and employed. The members of the CWO, with a few exceptions, were wage earners. The most common occupations of the women were needleworker and factory worker. A small number were domestics, four owned their own businesses, and one was a doctor. For a breakdown of the women's place of birth, residence, date of marriage, occupation, income, savings, and nationality of husbands, see House Hearings, Dec. 18, 1931, continued Jan. 14, 19, 28, 1932, *To Exempt from the Quota Husbands of American Citizen Wives.*.

52. Memo to J. Klahr Huddle, consul general in Warsaw from vice consul Elbridge Durbrow, *VD*, 150.062 Public Charge/300. The cases investigated included Fanny Sunshine-Cypin's and Ruth Bell-Bielski's, two presidents of the CWO.

53. Letter of Bell-Bielski, July 28, 1931, *VD*, 150.062 Public Charge/246.

54. House Hearings, Dec. 18, 1931, *To Exempt from the Quota Husbands of American Citizen Wives*, 2–4.

the policy which the President inaugurated last year, which is in the interests of the people of this country.," he protested. A colleague agreed but cautioned the chief of the Visa Division that the State Department "must be careful not to give rise to any thought that these people are being unfairly treated."[55]

The Visa Division remained outwardly obdurate, convinced that some kind of plot had produced the CWO marriages. In turn, the CWO continued to deny all charges of deception and accused the State Department of sex discrimination and the destruction of American women's families. Some of the women probably did receive financial assistance from relatives, other individuals, or organizations, but this was not an uncommon practice among immigrants. Consuls continued to speculate about the legitimacy of the women's marriages, but their reports to the Visa Division did not offer sufficient proof that the marriages were fraudulent.

In the end, the CWO members' faith in the power of their political voice finally shattered the stalemate between the wives and the Visa Division. Hoping to coerce the State Department into negotiations, the women actively sought sympathetic forums in which to broadcast their stories. Meanwhile, the press and other citizens were informing President Hoover that his immigration-restriction order was afflicting American citizens, not just aliens. Emphasizing this problem, the CWO drafted the following petition and delivered it to the President: "We the undersigned CITIZENS of the UNITED STATES of AMERICA, believing in the principle of the Sanctity of Family Life, respectfully petition the PRESIDENT of the UNITED STATES and the HOUSES of CONGRESS to REDRESS the INJUSTICE DONE to AMERICAN WOMEN, whose Husbands, being abroad, are being denied visas entitling them (the husbands) to enter this country as First Preference Quota in accordance with the provision of the Immigration Law."[56]

55. Letter of Wilbur Carr to William Castle, July 31, 1931, *VD*, 150.062 Public Charge/256; memo from Castle to Hodgdon, July 29, 1931, *VD*, 150.062 Public Charge/246-½. Carr told Castle to tell the women that there was no point in further interviews with State officials. Instructions to consuls were confidential and the Department still was unwilling to make any guarantees about the husbands' visas. The CWO continued to write and visit the Visa Division, although the women were again told that the information they requested could not be released. Memo for files, dated Oct. 20, 1931, *VD*, 150.062 Public Charge/296-½.

56. Copy of petition sent to President Hoover, dated June 11, 1931, Records of the United HIAS Service, HIAS-HICEM I Series Xb, RG 245.4, Yivo Institute for Jewish Research, New York, New York (hereafter cited as *YIVO*).

Rabbinical and women's organizations, as well as members of Congress (including Samuel Dickstein, chairman of the House Immigration and Naturalization Committee), sent similar pleas for relief to Hoover. Correspondence between the CWO, State Department, and other interested parties suggests that Jewish organizations in the United States were actively involved in the efforts to settle the CWO cases. The Hebrew Immigrant Aid Society of New York had assisted in the execution of 50 percent of the visa petitions for the husbands in Cuba.[57]

The executive director of the Federation of Polish Jews in America appealed to Secretary of State Henry Stimson on the couples' behalf, explaining that many of the men had sold their businesses or relinquished their jobs in anticipation of emigration. The National Council of Jewish Women was naturally concerned, as was the Union of Orthodox Jewish Congregations in America and the Social Justice Committee of the Central Conference of American Rabbis.[58] The NLWV and the NWP also added their voices in support of the women's cause. Abby Scott Baker of the NWP and Elizabeth Eastman of the WJCC accompanied a CWO contingent to the White House to urge support for legislation permitting citizens' husbands to enter the country as freely as citizens' wives. Almost every member of Congress from the state of New York scheduled a similar visit with the President.[59]

It was an opportune time for the CWO to place pressure on the Visa Division. The State Department could ill afford any incident that might further fuel public discontent with its consuls' actions. Despite the State

57. Memo to Consul General Dumont, *VD*, 150.062 Public Charge/196.

58. The *Jewish Daily Bulletin* carried several articles on the CWO. See, for example, "Stranded Husbands of Americans to Appeal to Hoover for Aid in Securing Visas" (Oct. 29, 1931); "Rabbis Ask Hoover to Admit Husbands of American Wives (Nov. 8, 1931); "State Department Rules Marriage to American Does Not Insure Visa" (Nov. 23, 1931). *YIVO* contains several letters from individuals and organizations written to government officials on the CWO's behalf. See also letter of Herbert S. Goldstein, president of the Union of Orthodox Jewish Congregations of America, to Senator Royal Copeland, May 29, 1931, *VD*, 150.062 Public Charge/197; Rabbi Edward L. Israel, chairman of the Central Conference of American Rabbis, Social Justice Commission, in Baltimore, to Senator Phillips Lee Goldsborough, June 3, 1931, *VD*, 150.062 Public Charge/206; Z. Tygel, executive director of the Federation of Polish Jews in America, to Secretary Stimson, Nov. 2, 1931, *VD*, 150.062 Public Charge/302; National Council of Jewish Women to Hodgdon, Nov. 17, 1931, *VD*, 150.062 Public Charge/313; Union of Orthodox Rabbis of the U.S. and Canada to State Department, Oct. 5, 1931, *VD*, 150.062 Public Charge/297; Belle Sherwin, president of the NLWV, to Hodgdon, Dec. 10, 1931, *VD*, 150.062 Public Charge/331.

59. Letter of Representative James Fitzpatrick to Rabbi Bril, June 19, 1931, *YIVO*. "U.S. Law Barring Alien Husbands Is Attacked," *Washington Post*, 14 May 1931.

Department's firm opposition to the measure, Congress was then drafting legislation to trim these officials' authority, and the House Committee on Immigration and Naturalization was holding hearings to determine whether the consuls had, as critics asserted, become "laws unto themselves."[60] Consuls enjoyed even greater autonomy than Immigration Bureau officials, whose decisions could be reversed by their Department's boards of review, the Secretary of Labor, or the courts. No law guaranteed the visa applicant the power to appeal a consul's negative decision.

State's Visa Division hoped the Labor Department would stand as its ally through the hearings, but Labor preferred to distance itself from the consul investigation and tend to its own political woes. A report issued by President Hoover's Commission on Law Observance and Enforcement in the spring of 1931 had severely criticized the administration's stringent l.p.c. policy. Reuben Oppenheimer, the author of the majority report, concluded that the Labor Department mistakenly assumed that the rising number of expulsions was "sufficient evidence of the soundness of the entire deportation system." Oppenheimer cited the widespread and unpopular effects of the l.p.c. policy on families and advised overhauling the administrative structure.[61] Both the Labor and State Departments realized that such openly critical reports on the conduct of their officials could only deal further injury to the President's plummeting popularity.

Members of the State Department voiced their fears that immigra-

---

60. Quoting Congressman Emmanuel Celler of New York, who announced that consuls had placed American women and their families "within a sort of immigration Chinese wall." House Hearings, Jan. 14, 1932, *To Exempt from the Quota Husbands of American Citizen Wives*, 26. Emma Wold of the NWP advised Ruth Bell-Bielski to emphasize consuls' conduct and considerable autonomy at the House hearing. Letter, Oct. 24, 1931, *YIVO*. For proposed legislation, see Hearings before the House Committee on Immigration and Naturalization, *Review of the Action of Consular Officers in Refusing Immigration Visas*, 72d Cong., 1st sess., Mar. 16, 1932; *Appeal in Certain Refusals of Immigration Visas*, 72d Cong., 1st sess., 1932, H. Rept. 1193; and the minority report, *Review of Action of Consular Officers in Refusing Immigration Visas*, H. Rept. 1193, pt. 2.

61. U.S. National Commission on Law Observance and Enforcement, Reuben Oppenheimer, "The Administration of the Deportation Laws of the United States," in *Report on the Deportation Laws of the United States*, Commission Report 5 (Washington, D.C.: G.P.O., 1931). Another report issued in 1934, this one by the Immigration and Naturalization Service, revealed embarrassing facts about the administration of the naturalization laws. U.S. Department of Labor, Immigration and Naturalization Service, D. W. MacCormick, *Naturalization Requirements Concerning Race, Education, Residence, Good Moral Character, and Attachment to the Constitution*, Lecture 8, Mar. 26, 1934.

tion policy was fast becoming "a football of partisan politics." It was a development the CWO was able to use to its advantage.[62] Weary of beseeching an obdurate executive department, the CWO members had realized the profitability of sharing their grievances against the beleaguered Visa Division with a partisan audience in Congress. In January 1932, members of the CWO, supported by New York congressmen, the NWP, the NLWV, and the Foreign Language Information Service, testified before the House Committee on Immigration and Naturalization on behalf of the husbands' admissions. The Committee members appeared generally sympathetic to the women's plight, the most hostile being the sharp-tongued Arthur M. Free of California, who badgered witnesses he suspected of "bootlegging" men into the country.[63]

Realizing that the women once casually dismissed as a group of "lovelorn Jewish wives" had now secured an opportunity to seriously embarrass the Visa Division before the House Committee, the State Department resignedly moved to expedite the CWO cases.[64] One year after the House hearing, out of the 172 cases monitored by the government, 119 of the "l.p.c." husbands had received visas.[65]

Legislation then before Congress promised to provide further assistance to some of the husbands. Earlier that year both houses of Congress had drafted bills granting nonquota status to any citizen's husband otherwise qualified to enter as an immigrant. The Senate amended this bill, which then went to conference. Samuel Dickstein, one of the legislators who had been a strong advocate of the CWO's cause, was frustrated by the Senate conferees' insistence on imposing deadlines on the nonquota entry of citizens' husbands, and complained that his opponents had "got busy over in the Senate [and] told all kinds of bugaboo stories." Now people believed that if this bill passed, "the gates of

62. Hodgdon to Carr, Nov. 5, 1932, *VD,* 150.062 Public Charge/470-½. The State Department had kept up to date on Congressman Dickstein's visit to Poland to investigate charges of abuses of authority by consuls blocking the emigration of Polish Jews. See "Dickstein Assails Cruelties in Operation of Alien Laws," *New York American,* 4 Nov. 1932.

63. House Hearings, Dec. 18, 1931, *To Exempt from the Quota Husbands of American Citizen Wives,* 1.

64. Ibid., 38. See also "Examination of Alien Relatives," circular letter to diplomatic and consular officers, Apr. 12, 1932, *VD,* 150.062 Public Charge/399.

65. For a partial checklist of the status of the CWO members' husbands in 1933, noting whether they received visas and, if not, the grounds for refusal, see *VD,* 150.062 Public Charge/291.

the United States would be thrown open to all the world."[66] In the final stages of negotiation the conferees agreed to retain some time restrictions. The privilege would apply only to men who had married Americans before July 1, 1932; all other foreign husbands with American wives remained preference immigrants.[67]

The CWO, not a group of seasoned female reformers, had orchestrated the passage of this amending law, and the incident testified to the sense of entitlement and power citizenship could convey to the immigrant woman. Yet, as the CWO members and many other women in transnational marriages knew, the biases embedded in the country's nationality and immigration policies could still expose married women to some of the law's harshest effects. American-born Rebecca Shelley, who became an alien when she married a German only weeks before the passage of the Cable Act, faced this stark reality on her long road back to citizenship. Courts' denials of repatriation to marital expatriates after 1922 were usually linked to circumstances of race or domicile, but Shelley's ineligibility for naturalization fell into the doctrinal category.

Shelley was born into a family that counted among its ancestors one Abraham Shelley, a Mennonite who had helped found a colony for religious refugees in William Penn's Pennsylvania. In 1915 Shelley resigned her position as a high school teacher to participate in the Women's International Congress held at The Hague. Inspired by her encounters with Jane Addams and other events at The Hague, Shelley embraced fully the pacifist ideals that would shape her future. Shelley went on to achieve some distinction as a tireless promoter of U.S. neutrality during World War I and as one of the major forces behind the much-publicized Ford Peace Expedition, but a nervous breakdown occurring shortly after the resumption of peace forced Shelley to assume a quieter lifestyle on a farm in Michigan, where she hoped to "build life anew upon the wreckage left by the World War."[68]

About a month and a half before the Cable Act went into effect, Shelley married Felix Rathmer, a German who had come to the United

66. *CR* 75 (July 7, 1932), 14825. For debate on the bill and conference report, see 14821–14828.

67. Act of July 11, 1932, 47 Stat. 656. As for citizens' immigrating wives, the conferees had considered but rejected placing similar restrictions on their admission.

68. A companion in reform during these years observed that "Rebecca had more fire and bull dog determination than I have ever seen wrapped up in one small person." Lella Secor Florence, "The Ford Peace Ship and After," in *We Did Not Fight. 1914–1918 Experiences of War Resisters,* ed. Julian Bell (London: Cobden-Sanderson, 1935), 101.

States before the war in order to escape further service in his country's navy. The couple had planned to marry later in the year, but their desire to take a wedding trip to Yellowstone National Park prompted them to marry in the summer. The decision proved costly, for if Rathmer and Shelley had not changed the date of their wedding, she would have been spared a thirteen-year ordeal to regain her citizenship.

For reasons that are not entirely clear, Shelley did not begin to pursue her repatriation earnestly until 1931. She had followed the appeal for citizenship of the well-known pacifist, feminist, and personal acquaintance Rosika Schwimmer.[69] At the conclusion of this highly publicized case, the U.S. Supreme Court had declared Schwimmer ineligible for naturalization because she had refused to agree to bear arms in defense of the country and Constitution. It was not routine procedure for naturalization courts to ask female petitioners whether they were "willing if necessary to take up arms in defense of this country," but the Women's Auxiliary of the American Legion had successfully requested that the question be put before Schwimmer.[70]

Although the facts of her case were not identical, Shelley knew the political mainspring of Schwimmer's defeat could also work against her repatriation. Nevertheless, Shelley ventured before a naturalization court two years later, personal appeal in hand, to challenge the laws that had stripped her of her legal identity as an American. "Before marriage I was a conscientious objector to war and exercised my right of free speech on the subject without molestation by the government," she told the court. "To bind me now, under the Cable Act to participate in war against my conscience, would be to deny me rights maintained and exercised before marriage, rights I would have exercised had I married after Sept. 22, 1922 and rights which the Cable Act guarantees."[71]

Shelley's defiant words highlighted some critical weaknesses in the Cable Act's repatriation policy. As she noted, native-born women did not enjoy "complete repatriation" under Cable Act rules but rather were invited back into the fold of citizenship as naturalized Americans. For Shelley, as for many other women, the distinction between naturalized

69. *United States v. Schwimmer*, 279 U.S. 644 (1929), overruled in 1946 by *Girouard v. United States*, 328 U.S. 61 (1946).
70. William H. Harbaugh, *Lawyer's Lawyer. The Life of John W. Davis* (reprint, Charlottesville: University of Virginia Press, 1990), 284–285.
71. Rebecca Shelley, "Statement to the Naturalization Court before presenting my Petition for Repatriation," copy enclosed with letter from Shelley to the NWP, June 12, 1931, *NWPP*.

and birth citizen was crucial. Shelley had satisfied the single requirement for native-born citizenship long ago, but, according to the federal government, an uncompromising pacifist could not meet the standards for naturalized citizenship.

As a resident woman shorn of her citizenship, Shelley might have fashioned her case into a strong post-Cable challenge to *Mackenzie v. Hare.* Despite the repeal of the rule that had denationalized Ethel Mackenzie, the Supreme Court decision upholding her expatriation remained untouched. The government's partial retreat from marital expatriation had not placed the constitutional legitimacy of legislative expatriation in question. By arguing that Congress had illegitimately robbed her of her citizenship without her consent, Shelley posed such a challenge, but her accompanying request for an exemption from the promise to bear arms required of naturalization applicants allowed the courts to avoid a confrontation of those grounds.

Before appearing in court, Shelley had sought assurance from the naturalization judge that she could claim such an exemption without prejudice. Initially, the judge, Blaine Hatch, concluded that since women were not required to serve in the military, he could administer the oath of allegiance to a female pacifist without violating her principles or the government's requirements for naturalization. However, when Shelley appeared in court to take that oath, the judge informed her that after consulting with a naturalization examiner, he could not proceed with her naturalization unless she answered the question "Will you take up arms?" affirmatively. Hatch respected her moral scruples, but nevertheless felt bound to withhold the certificate of citizenship when she refused to give the required response. "The gun," wrote a crestfallen Shelley after the hearing, was "the measuring-stick of my love of country."[72] Two years later Shelley submitted a new application for repatriation in Hatch's court. It was dismissed. She filed a third time in June of 1933 and received a court hearing early in 1936.

Meanwhile, Shelley's case had drawn support from different quarters. The proponents of equal nationality rights believed that Shelley's dilemma highlighted the unreasonableness of requiring marital expatriates to recoup their citizenship through naturalization. American pacifists hoped the case would undermine the integrity of *Schwimmer* and

72. Undated typed document, Rebecca Shelley Papers, Michigan Historical Collections, Bentley Library, University of Michigan, Ann Arbor, box 7, folder 1. (Papers cited hereafter as *RS.*)

other judicial decisions that infringed on pacifists' freedom of conscience.[73] Although it appears that the American Civil Liberties Union (ACLU) was interested in her case, a gradual breakdown in relations between Shelley and the ACLU commenced rather early in her quest for citizenship; but interest in preserving unfettered individual expressions of conscience prompted the formation of the Rebecca Shelley Repatriation Committee of One Hundred in 1932, a group boasting a membership roster that included the names of Jane Addams, Franz Boas, Alice Stone Blackwell and Catharine Waugh McCulloch of the League of Women Voters, Sophonisba Breckinridge, John Dewey, Sinclair Lewis, H. L. Mencken, Reinhold Niebuhr, Doris Stevens and Inez Haynes Irwin of the NWP, W. E. B. DuBois, Horace Kallen, William Allen White, and Dorothy Canfield Fisher.[74] Emily Greene Balch became chair of the Shelley Repatriation Committee in 1937.

But the Committee could not duplicate the success of the CWO. The CWO, arguing for family unity, had represented itself as a voice for traditional American values. In contrast, Shelley's political orientation was unpopular in an era when many Americans still viewed pacifists through distorted and red-tinted lenses. Although Shelley's appeals emphasized the discrimination she faced as a woman, she preferred to represent her case foremost as one of conscience.[75] Her contention that she had not pledged to obey her husband at her wedding ceremony and thus had not consented to expatriation was unlikely to receive attentive consideration from the court anyway; the same was true of her argument that the ratification of the Nineteenth Amendment had nullified Section 3 of the Expatriation Act of 1907. Shelley also declined to emphasize the fact that as a woman she was exempt from any military

---

73. See *Bland v. United States*, 42 F.2d 842 (1930), *United States v. Bland*, 283 U.S. 636 (1931); *Macintosh v. United States*, 42 F.2d 845 (1930), *United States v. Macintosh*, 283 U.S. 605 (1931). These two Supreme Court opinions upheld district court decisions denying naturalization to two conscientious objectors. The original judgments were reversed by the Circuit Court of Appeals but then affirmed by a badly divided Supreme Court. Shelley's situation was not distinguished from these cases, although she argued that because she was a former American, her case was one of repatriation rather than naturalization.

74. Shelley received further assistance from members of women's organizations. Dorothy Kenyon, a New York lawyer and member of the New York State League of Women Voters assisted Shelley with her second petition for repatriation. Besse Moton Garner, an attorney and member of the NWP also provided legal assistance.

75. The Shelley Repatriation Committee was interested in improving woman's rights, but its main objective was preserving liberty of conscience. Statement sent to Alice Paul, dated Mar. 11, 1932, NWPP.

obligation to participate in a war. No person, Shelley argued, should have to sacrifice conscience for citizenship.[76]

Shelley continued to argue that the Nineteenth Amendment had made her "a fully emancipated person" and thus granted her all the protections and privileges of a native-born male. If the courts continued to reject or ignore this argument (which they did), Shelley had a second defense: birthright citizenship ensured her against all obstacles to repatriation, except those also applicable to native-born men. In sum, Shelley claimed that she should not be treated as an alien for whom U.S. citizenship was an earned privilege but rather as a native for whom citizenship was a matter of natural right. The naturalization court, she averred, had erred when it required her to provide any evidence beyond her birth in the United States.[77]

Shelley was a conscientious objector and a native-born citizen when she married in 1922, and she believed that the Nineteenth Amendment and the Cable Act entitled her to recover in full and without interference her premarital status as citizen and pacifist.[78] The federal government could not exact more from her in exchange for repatriation than it required from her when she was a citizen. "My American citizenship is my birthright," she declared, "and I will embrace it as soon as legal bars are removed. But I do not surrender a hair's breadth of the freedom that was mine on the day of my marriage. . . . I exercised liberty even during the World War, and must not renounce it under the pressure of the reactionary forces it spawned."[79]

Shelley also challenged the court's disregard of Commissioner of Immigration and Naturalization D. W. MacCormack's recommendation to grant her petition.[80] MacCormack had concluded that Shelley's

76. Ruth Shipley, chief of the Passport Division, informed Shelley that the State Department allowed citizens requesting passports to take a "modified" affirmation of loyalty, provided such a modification did not compromise the purpose of the oath, which was swearing one's allegiance to the United States. Letter from Shipley, Sept. 26, 1932, box 7, "Correspondence, July-Dec., 1932," RS.

77. Shelley also noted that at the time of her marriage she was a citizen of Michigan, a state that provided a constitutional exemption from military service for conscientious objectors.

78. See Brief for Petitioner, submitted Jan. 31, 1936, to the District Court for the Eastern District of Michigan, Southern Division. Copy in box 7, "Papers, 1936," RS.

79. Brief on Behalf of Petitioner-Appellant, *Shelley v. Jordan*, 106 F.2d 1016 (1939), Appeal from the District Court of Eastern District of Michigan to Circuit Court of Appeals for Sixth Circuit, February Term, 1938, 51.

80. In 1933, the federal government consolidated the Bureaus of Immigration and

former status as an American-born citizen, her inopportune decision to marry just weeks before the passage of the Cable Act, and the absence of a military-service requirement for females were all factors favoring her repatriation. The judge's disregard of this recommendation, she charged, "amounted to usurpation by the Court of both the executive and the legislative function of government."[81]

In the wake of Shelley's defeat in the courts the Detroit Meeting of the Religious Society of Friends sent a letter to Secretary Frances Perkins requesting clarification of the Labor Department's views in this case. The Department solicitor responded assuringly that his Department had been following the case "with interest" and supported eliminating the requirement to promise to bear arms.[82] Encouraged by this information and Commissioner MacCormack's endorsement of her credentials for citizenship, Shelley appealed the decision. She reiterated her arguments about the liberating force of the Nineteenth Amendment and the Cable Act's intent to return the marital expatriate to her premarital citizenship status, and she challenged the constitutional validity of a naturalization requirement that compelled individuals to violate their religious beliefs in order to obtain citizenship.

The Circuit Court of Appeals for the Sixth Circuit, however, refused to overturn the lower court's decision, and a year later Shelley's suit was in the federal district court for the District of Columbia. When she lost that case in April of 1940, she appealed the decision and sustained yet another defeat.[83] This time, the court relied on its interpretation of a recent amendment to a 1936 statute that declared that a marital expatriate who had remained in the United States after her pre-Cable marriage was, upon repatriation, "a citizen of the United States to the same extent as though her marriage to said alien had taken place on or after September 22, 1922."[84] Shelley had lobbied for the new law and hoped

---

Naturalization, creating the Immigration and Naturalization Service. Executive Order 6166, June 10, 1933, sect. 14.

81. Objections to Court's Findings of Fact and Conclusions of Law, filed Oct. 18, 1937, in U.S. District Court, Eastern District of Michigan. Copy in box 7, folder 1, *RS*.

82. Letter from Alexander H. McDowell to Secretary Frances Perkins, Jan. 17, 1938; letter from Gerard D. Reilly, solicitor, to McDowell, Jan. 31, 1938. Both in Box 7, folder 1, *RS*.

83. *Shelley v. United States*, 120 F.2d 734 (1941). See also *In re Davies*, 53 F. Supp. 426 (1944). Apparently a woman could regain status as an American before taking the oath but could not necessarily then claim the rights and privileges of citizenship.

84. Act of July 2, 1940, 54 Stat. 715, amending Act of June 25, 1936, 49 Stat. 1917. For a follow-up on the interpretation of the 1940 statute, consult U.S. Department of Justice, "In the Matter of P——," *Administrative Decisions under Immigration & Nationality*

it would help her achieve repatriation, but the modified statute still required women to take an oath of allegiance in order to seal their claim to the rights of citizenship.[85] The court denying Shelley's latest appeal cited the language of the 1940 statute to support its decision.[86]

Over the course of the five years preceding this decision, Shelley had gradually seen her control over her life slipping away on other fronts. There is evidence that her husband did not share her devotion to her crusade, which placed considerable stress on an already troubled marriage. She had sold her business to get money for her husband's, but Rathmer's electrical shop never flourished, and Shelley was often the sole but struggling contributor to the household's income. Her repeated efforts to get her writings published met with limited success.[87] Shelley probably persisted with her legal battle because of rather than despite these trials. Although she met with successive defeats, her crusade provided her life with an engrossing purpose. In the midst of personal tribulation, Shelley drew comfort from the conviction that she was waging a moral campaign of transcendent significance.

Shelley's unyielding commitment to freedom of conscience, however, often inhibited her ability to take advantage of proffered assistance. In 1931, she had courted NWP support, assuring the organization that she wanted her case to be "by, of, and for women solely." Shortly after offering to surrender her case to the NWP's direction, however, she confided to an acquaintance that she suspected the NWP leaders were "ultra militant."[88] Shelley could not have been pleased by Burnita Shelton Matthews's comments about her litigation. The NWP's leaders had limited faith in the federal courts as instruments of feminist reform. Shelley's best bet, Matthews advised, was to support an amendment to the Cable Act rather than pursue a judicial remedy.[89]

Shelley's exchanges with ACLU lawyers over legal strategies also

---

Laws, vol. 1 (Washington, D.C.: G.P.O., 1947), 127–136. The original 1936 statute, modified by the above law, applied only to women who were no longer married to aliens.

85. The law provided that "no such woman shall have or claim any rights as a citizen of the United States until she shall have duly taken the oath of allegiance as prescribed in section 4 of the Act approved June 29, 1906 (34 Stat. 596)."

86. The U.S. Supreme Court refused to review her case, agreeing with the argument of Solicitor General Francis J. Biddle that Congress had not changed the law to assist Shelley.

87. Letter dated April 3, 1936, box 7, "Correspondence, 1934," RS.

88. Letter to Marion Paton Terpenning, June 14, 1931, box 7, "Correspondence, 1931," RS.

89. Letter from Matthews, July 5, 1931, box 7, "Correspondence, 1931," RS.

ended unsatisfactorily. She tried to convince Walter Nelson that she could easily distinguish her case from *Mackenzie v. Hare* (which looked "as antiquated as a yoke of oxen beside Ford's latest model") because that decision predated the ratification of the Nineteenth Amendment. Nelson tersely dismissed this argument, which Shelley cherished as one of her more brilliant, by responding that the Amendment had, after all, really only granted suffrage privileges.[90] And Roger Baldwin's prediction that the courts would refuse to heed the distinction she had made between the native-born marital expatriate seeking repatriation and the foreign-born woman seeking naturalization did not please Shelley either. She subsequently declared her frustration and annoyance with the New York office of the ACLU, citing its "entirely negative attitude" toward her case.[91]

By the next year, Shelley's faith in others' ability to share her vision had also begun to falter. She had initially believed her cause could unite the defenders of pacifism, conscience, and feminism into a formidable reform alliance, but that dream was never realized. Rather, Shelley found the responses to her impassioned invitations to join her crusade far from inspirational. Both Baldwin and Dorothy Kenyon, a member of the NLWV and the ACLU, both advised her to abandon her conscience arguments and to focus on the Cable Act's naturalization requirement for native-born expatriates.[92] Shelley, however, refused to sideline her claim to freedom of thought. The decision was admirable but costly. The NWP remained convinced of the futility of a litigious challenge to the Cable Act. Thus, when commenting on the NWP's bill to assist women such as Lillian Larch, Shelley gently reminded the Party not to slight the worthiness of her cause even if disapproving of her methods. "If you give relief to the beggars and Mary Magdalenes," she wrote, "don't forget the heretics."[93]

90. Letter from Shelley, July 5, 1931; letter from Walter Nelson, July 10, 1931. Both in box 7, "Correspondence, 1931," *RS*.

91. Letter from Roger Baldwin to Shelley, Jan. 19, 1932; letter from Shelley to Women's International League for Peace and Freedom, Jan. 13, 1932; both in box 7, "Correspondence, Jan.-June, 1932," *RS*. See also letter from Frances Witherspoon to Shelley, Nov. 16, 1932, box 7, "Correspondence, Jan.-June, 1932," *RS*, commiserating with her frustration with the ACLU and Baldwin.

92. Letter from Kenyon, Feb. 17, 1932, box 7, "Correspondence, Jan.-June, 1932," *RS*. Kenyon would later acquire the unfortunate distinction of being the first person tagged as a suspected Communist by Senator Joseph McCarthy.

93. Letter to Burnita Shelton Matthews, Feb. 22, 1932, box 7, "Correspondence Jan.-June, 1932," *RS*.

NLWV assistance was also elusive. Its president, Belle Sherwin, received an invitation to join the Shelley Repatriation Committee but declined, explaining that she had discovered that the public assumed that any cause she personally endorsed then carried the League's imprimatur. In this case the national organization had "never discussed for its program the principles involved in Miss Shelley's case, nor has any state League so far as I am aware."[94] Sherwin was apologetic but firmly refused to get involved in Shelley's crusade. Her response seems somewhat disingenuous however. Shelley was challenging the Cable Act's repatriation plan in the court, while the NLWV was pursuing the same by lobbying Congress; but Sherwin knew that championing conscientious objectors did not fit comfortably into the League's current reform agenda nor could it draw solid support from the organization's members. Moreover, League leaders were wary of such open association with the peace movement after their organization had suffered through some vicious red-baiting in the 1920s because of members' pacifist activities.

The Shelley Repatriation Committee was also unable to secure the assistance of Carrie Chapman Catt, who had orchestrated the League's disassociation from the Women's International League for Peace and Freedom during those years.[95] Catt, no stranger to the peace movement, brusquely told the head of the Shelley Repatriation Committee that she would not become a member "since I have never seen Miss Shelley and know nothing about her except what you tell me."[96]

Shelley slowly realized that her crusade would not be the magnet that would draw together pacifists and feminists. The leaders of these groups, she surmised, preferred to pursue independent agendas. As a disheartened Shelley reported to Jane Addams, her case appeared to fall "between two stools." "The left wing feminists say, it furnishes another argument for an equal rights amendment. While such a good pacifist as Dr. [Charles Clayton] Morrison would use the case as proof positive that his alien pacifist bill must be accepted."[97] Too few persons inter-

94. Copy of letter from Sherwin to Emily Balch, Jan. 5, 1933, box 7, "Correspondence, July-Dec., 1932," RS.

95. In 1925 the NLWV had distanced itself from the Women's International League for Peace and Freedom and joined another peace coalition founded by Carrie Chapman Catt. On the activities of and attacks against individual pacifists and organizations during these years, see Cott, *The Grounding of Modern Feminism*, 243–267.

96. Letter to W. W. Denton, April 20, 1933, box 7, "Correspondence, Apr., 1933," RS.

97. Letter from Shelley to Jane Addams, Nov. 1, 1932, box 7, "Correspondence, July-Dec., 1932," RS.

ested in her case shared Shelley's desire to close the distance between those two perspectives.

In 1944, Shelley's crusade for citizenship and conscience concluded successfully, but not because the repatriation laws had been altered in her favor. In fact in 1940, Congress had codified the country's nationality laws, and the resulting Nationality Act of 1940 unraveled some of the work of the earlier 1940 statute by requiring women like Shelley to do more than take an oath of allegiance to recoup their American citizenship. While those women who were no longer the spouses of noncitizens took an oath of allegiance to the United States to regain their citizenship, women still married to foreigners had to submit a petition for citizenship and a certificate stating that they had appeared before a naturalization examiner. They were also not exempt from taking the standard oath of loyalty.

According to the new nationality law, upon successful completion of the process, marital expatriates recovered "the same citizenship status as that which existed immediately prior to its loss."[98] Although this provision suggested that native-born women would now be recognized as birth citizens upon repatriation, it made the required "naturalization" of these women an even more illogical practice than it had been. But the law, despite its flaws, did not complicate Shelley's case further. In 1944 she was finally permitted to take the oath of allegiance with the understanding that her pledge to defend the country did not include a promise to bear arms.[99] What the government had refused to grant this pacifist in peacetime, it had bestowed during war.

Shelley recovered her American citizenship ten years after the U.S. government entered into an international agreement to end discrimination based on sex in the country's nationality law and practices. One could argue that the federal government never fully honored that commitment because it never turned the clock back to restore American citizenship to the thousands of women expatriated by marriage after the passage of the Expatriation Act of 1907. If Congress had consented to such a decisive repudiation of past policy, Shelley would have been spared her protracted and costly legal battle. But at a time when dual

98. See sect. 317(a) and (b), 54 Stat. at 1146–1147 (1940).
99. The oath prescribed by the Nationality Act of 1940 appears in sect. 335(b), 54 Stat. at 1157. It requires the naturalization petitioner to take the pledge "without any mental reservation or purpose of evasion."

citizens were viewed as hazardous to the health of the nation, the government continued to treat these women as persons of ambiguous loyalties. For Shelley, it was not only the marriage to a German that marked her as a person of divided allegiances but also her conscience. Shelley's devotion to the promotion of peace never abated, and she spent her final years troubled by the destruction of the Vietnam War. She wore mourning black for the duration of the conflict and sold the family farm to finance a trip that enabled her to take her pleas for peace in Southeast Asia to the rest of the world.

Shelley's long journey back to citizenship had often been a lonesome trek, but it was a significant one in the history of women's nationality rights. Her repatriation was, as she had devoutly believed, an affirmation of the rights of conscientious objectors. Shelley's defense had revolved on important Constitutional axes. She had challenged the legitimacy of a policy that permitted Congress to expatriate native-born citizens without their express consent. It was a bid for due process and consensual citizenship posed decades earlier by the pre-Cable case of *Mackenzie v. Hare,* then the principal Supreme Court decision on legislative expatriation.[100] Shelley was ultimately successful in her bid for repatriation, but her case did not dislodge *Mackenzie* from its throne. The standard of consent in expatriation cases remained troublingly ambiguous.

The dilemmas of Lillian Larch, Rebecca Shelley, and the CWO each highlighted a different aspect of dependent citizenship's cruel legacy. The suffrage movement had trained its veterans to define citizenship predominantly in terms of political rights and patriotic obligations, but the stories of the women related here served to remind female reformers of the equally vital civil and social rights of citizenship. Undoubtedly,

100. As for the question of Constitutional validation of legislative expatriation, the Supreme Court's words in *Mackenzie v. Hare* did not face a strong challenge until 1958, when the Court divided sharply on the expatriation issue in a series of cases. *Perez v. Brownell,* 356 U.S. 44 (1958); *Trop v. Dulles,* 356 U.S. 86 (1958); *Kennedy v. Mendoza-Martinez,* 372 U.S. 144 (1963). Quoting from the dissenting opinion in *Perez:* "Under our form of government, as established by the Constitution, the citizenship of the lawfully naturalized and the native-born cannot be taken from them," 66. Chief Justice Earl Warren's dissenting opinion also offered a historical summary of marital expatriation in questioning the current legitimacy of *Mackenzie v. Hare.* For discussions of expatriation generated by these decisions, see John P. Roche, "The Expatriation Cases: 'Breathes There the Man with Soul So Dead . . . ?' " *Supreme Court Review* (1963): 325–356; Irving Appleman, "The Supreme Court on Expatriation: An Historical Review," *Federal Bar Journal* 23 (Fall 1963): 351–373; Charles Gordon, "The Citizen and the State: Power of Congress to Expatriate American Citizens," *Georgetown Law Journal* 53 (Winter 1965): 315–364.

these cases also reaffirmed nationality-rights reformers' confidence in the expediency of pursuing legislative rather than judicial reform. Even Shelley, who had to appeal to the courts for her citizenship, finally achieved repatriation through the intervention of Labor Department officials, not federal judges. Furthermore, Shelley's struggle served as another disheartening reminder that litigation could be lengthy, costly, and fruitless and that the other party in such cases, the federal government, was usually prepared to pursue an appeal.

The CWO did accomplish its objective without a court battle, but the resulting Immigration Act of July 11, 1932, did not alleviate the disparities of privilege between American women and men with noncitizen spouses. Strictly retrospective in its effect, the law simply shifted the burden of discrimination onto those couples who married after the statute's passage. This chronic failing of piecemeal legislation finally prompted the introduction of a more dramatic solution to sex discrimination in the country's nationality laws—an international treaty that would destroy all remaining distinctions between women's and men's nationality rights.

In the 1930s, full citizenship for American women remained a vision, not a reality, but the issue of married women's nationality rights at home or abroad was no longer a neglected one. In the Pan American Union and the League of Nations, it would become a subject of recurrent discussion. The heightened attention to married women's nationality rights abroad gave the NWP a new audience for its ideas and set the stage for the unveiling of its proposed blanket treaty. But the Party's ambitions in this direction hastened the deterioration of the accord between the two organizational camps working to achieve women's equal nationality rights in the United States.

CHAPTER 6

Nationality Rights in International Perspective

The Cable Act had become part of an expanding intercontinental chain of nationality laws that, link by link, widened the boundaries of women's political autonomy. Between 1918 and 1929, eighteen nations enacted statutory protections against a married woman's involuntary loss of citizenship. In addition to the United States, the U.S.S.R, Belgium, Estonia, Norway, Rumania, Sweden, Denmark, Iceland, Guatemala, Finland, France, Turkey, Yugoslavia, Albania, China, Cuba, and Persia granted some of their female citizens the right to maintain independent nationalities after marriage. By 1930, rough estimates indicated that about half of the world's women could maintain a separate nationality after marriage. These strides by women toward independent citizenship notwithstanding, only four nations made no distinctions based on sex in their nationality laws.[1]

The interwar years marked an important transitional period for women's nationality rights globally; during this time some countries retained marital naturalization and expatriation, while many others decided to modify or abolish these practices. Some traditionalists among international law experts blamed woman's rights groups for disarranging the world's nationality laws, but the criticism was misdirected. Uniformity in nationality law had never been a global reality, and all parties interested in nationality reform, including feminists, agreed on the pressing need to reduce international conflicts of law.

---

1. The four countries were Argentina, Chile, Paraguay, and Uruguay. The Soviet Union was added in 1930. See Berrien, "Nationality and International Relations."

The transformations in expatriation and naturalization practices occurring in the two decades following World War I precipitated a rise in the number of cases of dual citizenship and statelessness among women globally; in the United States, the enactment of the Cable Act marked the onset of this trend. The United States no longer automatically naturalized the wives of citizens after 1922, but many of these women's countries continued to denationalize female citizens for marrying aliens. The Cable Act did provide some assistance to women rendered stateless by marriage to Americans by limiting the naturalization residency requirement for foreign wives of citizens to one year rather than the standard five.

At the same time, the gradual U.S. abandonment of marital expatriation in the 1920s and 1930s created a new class of dual nationals. Some American women married to foreigners were able to retain their U.S. citizenship and acquire a husband's nationality if his country automatically naturalized citizens' alien wives. The U.S. government, however, wishing to eradicate the option of dual citizenship, managed to limit married women's ability to acquire two nationalities by refusing to repatriate nonresident women married to aliens or marital expatriates who had acquired another nationality by some means other than marriage to an alien.[2]

The State Department, a vocal critic of dual citizenship in the interwar years, viewed its proliferation as a highly unwelcome result of the increasing lack of uniformity in nations' governance of expatriation, naturalization, and birth citizenship. Consequently, the Department declined to endorse Congressional bills in the 1920s that could increase the incidence of dual citizenship among American women, advocating instead the retention of existing practices or the creation of new rules that safeguarded against the assumption of dual nationalities by women, men, and children.

In its campaign to arrest dual citizenship, the State Department employed the same argument it had used to justify denaturalizing absentee citizens, emphasizing the significance of domicile as a determinant of nationality. Predictably, State Department officials had supported the original Cable Act clause that ensured the expatriation of nonresident American women married to aliens and resisted subsequent efforts to liberalize some of the rules governing the citizenship of women living abroad and their foreign-born children.

2. Sect. 317(a) and (b), 54 Stat. 1137 (1940).

It is apparent from the several changes in the laws of nationality in the 1930s that Congress was diverting some of the energy it had devoted to immigration policy in the 1920s to longstanding problems relating to the assumption and loss of citizenship. One obvious factor contributing to a heightened interest in a comprehensive reevaluation of the country's naturalization and expatriation laws was the debate over American women's nationality rights. Women's halting but forward movement toward independent citizenship had complicated rather than enhanced the government's ability to regulate the size of the citizen population living abroad. As the threat of expatriation had diminished for married American women with noncitizen spouses, their chances of retaining American citizenship or plural citizenships had increased.

The League of Nations responded to the growing global interest in nationality issues by organizing The Hague Conference on the Codification of International Law. The conference, held in the spring of 1930, would fall short of reaching admittedly overly ambitious goals. Nevertheless, the conference was a pivotal event in the history of women's nationality rights. It provided an international forum for the discussion of the global problems of maritally induced expatriation, statelessness, and dual citizenship, and its proceedings challenged the U.S. government to define and defend its position on women's nationality rights—an exercise that eventually yielded further progressive amendments to the Cable Act and related nationality statutes. The conference also fostered the coalescence of an international feminist movement for independent citizenship.

The first half of the 1930s yielded some significant advances in women's nationality rights, but, ironically, the pursuit of the most momentous of these achievements cleaved the organizational alliance for independent citizenship into two antagonistic factions. This chapter chronicles these developments—the intensifying debate over women's nationality rights internationally as well as the impact of that agitation for multinational reform on U.S. policies and on the women's organizations involved in those reforms.

Marital expatriation had been targeted for extinction by international women's organizations before the League of Nations addressed the problem in 1924.[3] During World War I American women married

---

3. Although the International Woman Suffrage Alliance launched its work on women's nationality in 1920, the International Council of Women had begun to investigate the situation in 1905. The Women's International League for Peace and Freedom also focused

to citizens of the Central Powers had been declared enemy aliens by marriage, and women in many other belligerent nations had suffered similarly for their marriages to aliens. The wartime exile of some women for foreign marriages and the sequestration of their property prompted the International Woman Suffrage Alliance (IWSA) to seek ways to prevent a repetition of these injustices. Resolving that married women should enjoy all the freedom granted to men to retain or alter their nationality, the IWSA established a committee to examine the status of married women's nationality rights. By 1923 the organization had issued a set of international rules designed to preserve a woman's premarital nationality as well as affirm her right to consent independently to expatriation. The IWSA guidelines, reproduced below, constituted the first organizational attempt to propose an international cure for the dismal state of married women's nationality rights:

A. Effect of Marriage. The nationality of a woman shall not be changed by reason only of marriage, or a change during marriage in the nationality of her husband.
B. Retention of Change. The right of a woman to retain her nationality or to change it by naturalization, denationalization or denaturalization shall not be denied or abridged because she is a married woman.
C. Absence of Consent. The nationality of a married woman shall not be changed without her consent except under conditions which would cause a change in the nationality of a man without his consent.[4]

The NLWV was the only U.S. member of the IWSA in 1923, even though the NWP was more global in its vision and focus than the League. After announcing its ambition to pursue legal equality for women throughout the world, the NWP sought recognition and support from the IWSA, but its membership in the Alliance was doomed by the schism that had developed between it and the opponents of the equal rights amendment. Protective legislation and the emerging prospect of an equal rights treaty for women had already become points of

---

on women's nationality rights after World War I. See Chrystal MacMillan, "Nationality of Married Women: Present Tendencies," *Journal of Comparative Legislation and International Law*, 3d ser., 7 (Nov. 1925): 143; Crystal Eastman, "Suffragists Ten Years After," *New Republic* 35 (June 27, 1923): 118–119.

4. In 1920, the IWSA Congress resolved "that a married woman should have the same right to retain or change her nationality as a man." International Woman Suffrage Alliance, *Programme of Women's Rights Adopted at the Eighth Congress* (Geneva, 1920). IWSA's 1923 guidelines are reprinted in Hill, "Citizenship of Married Women," 734.

friction among international women's organizations. When the NWP applied for membership in the IWSA in 1926, vehement protests by the NLWV and Mary Anderson of the U.S. Department of Labor's Women's Bureau scotched the applicant's chances of participating in the Alliance.[5]

Although denied a voice in the IWSA, the NWP managed to establish an important international base of operation and influence. In 1923, the Pan American Union's Fifth International Conference of American States had recommended that member countries not only investigate the status of its female citizens but consider repealing civil legislation discriminating against them.[6] At that time, a number of American republics had either outstripped the United States in abolishing marital expatriation or had never adopted the policy. Believing American governments had thus proven themselves more receptive than European governments to rights for women in this regard, the NWP dispatched Doris Stevens, Jane Norman Smith, Muna Lee, and Mrs. Valentine Winter to Havana in 1928 to buttonhole delegates at the sixth Pan American Union conference. The specific favor the women sought was the conferees' consideration of an equal rights treaty consisting of this simple but revolutionary pledge: "The contracting states agree that upon the ratification of this treaty, men and women shall have equal rights throughout the territory subject to their respective jurisdictions."[7] Like its domestic version, the NWP's equal rights amendment, this sweeping mandate for parity did not receive an enthusiastic reception from all woman's rights organizations.

The pro-treaty women at the Pan American Union conference were also determined to promote themselves, having informally resolved to challenge the tradition that left women with no direct or official voice in most international organizations. The women did manage to make some progress on this occasion. Doris Stevens, who quickly established

5. Becker, *Origins of the Equal Rights Amendment*, 166–170. Cornelia S. Parker, "feminists and Feminists: They Join Battle in Paris on the Issue of Protective Laws," *Survey* 56 (Aug. 1, 1926): 502–504.

6. James Brown Scott, "Inter-American Commission of Women," *American Journal of International Law* 24 (1930): 758; *Verbatim Record of the Plenary Sessions of the Fifth International Conference of American States,* vol. 1 (Santiago, Chile: Imprente Universitaria, 1923), 289.

7. "Lobby Reports," *DS*, 76–246, folder 314. Folder 312 contains Stevens's speech before the delegates on the equal rights treaty. For a more detailed treatment of the evolution of the treaty and opposition to it, consult Becker, *Origins of the Equal Rights Amendment,* 161–195.

herself at the forefront of the international nationality-rights campaign, was allowed to attend the first plenary session of the conference—but only as an observer. Shortly before the meeting convened, Stevens noticed that a woman had walked onto the floor and seated herself unobtrusively at the long table beneath the rostrum. Stevens's delight at the woman's entrance quickly turned to disappointment when she realized that the woman was a stenographer, not a delegate. "I reflected at the moment," she recalled with some bitterness, "that this was an accurate symbol of the international position of women in the Americas."[8]

Stevens, Smith, and Lee, as well as feminists from Cuba and the Dominican Republic, received invitations to participate in an open hearing before the delegates, and, according to Stevens, their appearance marked women's first opportunity to defend their interests at the plenary session of a diplomatic conference. The newcomers reported that they generally found most of the delegations attentive and sympathetic to the need to reduce the incidence of marital expatriation, but the U.S. representatives were comparatively noncommittal. Stevens thought Secretary of State Charles Evans Hughes patronizing and reported that although he appeared "courteous and gracious," the Secretary "treated us more or less like little children."[9]

Hughes had already received a flood of chain telegrams encouraging him to support the equal rights treaty, but when asked whether he favored an international solution to wives' dependent citizenship, the Secretary replied evasively that the United States did not want to "put anything over on the Latin-American countries." The women then reminded him that Guatemala and Costa Rica had already proposed such a treaty or convention. Pressed for a more decisive response, Hughes said he did not want an international agreement on the matter. "You have equal rights in the United States," he added impatiently.[10]

Hughes did not object so pointedly to the women's two other requests: a Pan American commission to study the status of women and a statement from the Union's conference advocating the nonpolitical appointment of female delegates to international conferences. Before the close of the conference, the conferees did unanimously adopt a reso-

8. *DS,* 76–246, folder 316. Stevens was the author of *Jailed for Freedom,* in which she recounted NWP members' arrest and imprisonment during the suffrage campaign.

9. *DS,* 76–246, folders 313, 314.

10. *DS,* 76–246, folder 313.

lution establishing the Inter-American Commission of Women. This exclusively female commission, created to collect data on the civil and political status of women in the Americas, would subsequently play a vital role in the campaign for equal nationality rights.[11]

Each of the twenty-one American states had a representative in the Inter-American Commission. The Governing Board of the Pan American Union appointed the first seven members, and these women in turn selected the remaining fourteen representatives. The Governing Board asked Doris Stevens to chair the new commission. A decade later the circumstances of her appointment to the Commission would stand at the center of a controversy between the NWP and Franklin D. Roosevelt's administration, but until Stevens's removal over a decade later the NWP was able to capitalize on its influence within the Inter-American Commission and sustain a high profile abroad.

The Inter-American Commission had five years to produce its report on women's nationality rights for the Pan American conference, but the chair of the Commission quickly sought avenues for more immediate dissemination of her reform plan. She was soon in Europe circulating preliminary proposals on nationality reform among other women's organizations. Stevens wanted her Commission's work on woman's citizenship rights to gain increased exposure—a goal she pursued with particular vigor after the League of Nations announced plans to hold an international codification conference in 1929 or 1930. Other women's organizations in the cause of nationality rights also grasped the potential significance of this particular world conference. The growing interest in the problems of marital expatriation and dual citizenship made nationality a likely candidate for codification.

The formation of the League of Nations and the Permanent Court of International Justice had renewed interest in devising an international code of law. The United States was not a member of the League of Nations, but by the mid-1920s the idea of a world court had amassed considerable support in the United States—at least in theory. Americans seemed to favor the formation of such a judicial body, and the platforms of their two major political parties endorsed it; but a two-thirds vote

---

11. Resolution of the Sixth Conference of American States, Havana, Feb. 18, 1928. The resolution is reprinted in James Brown Scott's *The International Conference of American States, 1889–1928* (New York: Oxford University Press, 1931), 408. Doris Stevens described women's activities at the Sixth Pan American Conference in "International Feminism Is Born," *Time and Tide* (Apr. 13, 1928): 354–355. See also Muna Lee, "Woman's Place in the Sun," *Independent Woman* 7 (Oct. 1928): 435–436, 475.

of the Senate proved difficult to muster, and the debate over U.S. membership in the World Court dragged on for several years.[12]

As for an international code of law, those who applauded the idea in theory also acknowledged that the process of drafting such a code was a formidable undertaking. Experts could readily identify problems relating to citizenship rights. The difficult task was convincing nations to discard some time-honored practices for the sake of global uniformity. Despite pessimistic predictions, the League of Nations sent questionnaires to member and nonmember nations to survey levels of interest in seven proposed subjects for codification. Three of these candidates for codification made it onto the agenda at The Hague Conference on the Codification of International Law; nationality was one of them.[13]

At the very least, The Hague conference in March of 1930 promised organized women an unprecedented opportunity to tender their views on nationality rights; at best, the international gathering could produce a nationality convention endorsing women's liberation from marital expatriation. Yet, some institutional barriers promised to hamper women's visibility at the conference. Their official participation in such assemblies was still limited because they were sparsely represented in international law organizations. Despite women's intense involvement in nationality-rights reform, convincing the U.S. government that some of these reformers had the credentials to serve as full-fledged delegates to the codification conference proved difficult.

Personally aware of the disadvantages of having an unofficial status at such legal conferences, Stevens campaigned determinedly for the appointment of female delegates. Invited to speak at a gathering of the

12. The NLWV was a strong proponent of U.S. membership in both the League of Nations and the World Court. Hans Wehberg considered the prospects for such a world court in *The Problem of an International Court of Justice* (Oxford: Clarendon Press for the Carnegie Endowment for International Peace, 1917). See also Manley O. Hudson, *The Permanent Court of International Justice and the Question of American Participation* (Cambridge, Mass.: Harvard University Press, 1925). For a critical account of U.S. temporizing over Court membership, see Denna Frank Fleming, *The United States and the World Court, 1920–1966,* rev. ed. (New York: Russell and Russell, 1968).

13. League of Nations, *Progressive Codification of International Law. Resolutions of Eighth Assembly, Sept. 27, 1927,* A.133.1927.V (1927). For nations' responses to questionnaires, see League of Nations, *Conference for the Codification of International Law, Bases of Discussion,* supp. to vol. 1: *Nationality,* C.73.M.38.1929.V (1929). The answers led the Preparatory Committee to conclude that "the replies submitted do not make it possible to hope for a general agreement establishing either the rule that marriage does not affect the wife's nationality or the rule that the wife takes by marriage [the] nationality of the husband" (94).

International Union of Societies for the League of Nations, she emphasized the importance of women's inclusion in international discussions of women's citizenship rights. "It is . . . our nationality that is at stake," she reminded her audience, " . . . and it would seem peculiarly within our domain to assist in codifying international law on this point."[14] Stevens's efforts to generate additional support for female participants were not very productive. The League of Nations Assembly did adopt a resolution submitted by Stevens advising countries that positions within the League should be open equally to men and women, but when the codification conference convened in the spring of 1930, female delegates constituted only a small minority of delegates.[15]

Some women's organizations prepared for the codification conference by undertaking independent comparative studies of nationality law. The Inter-American Commission was already gathering data to present to the next Conference of American States as well as The Hague Codification Conference. The International Alliance of Women (renamed the International Alliance of Women for Suffrage and Equal Citizenship) had submitted its 1923 convention on nationality to the League of Nation's Committee of Experts for the Progressive Codification of International Law; but the draft nationality convention unveiled by the League of Nations did not follow the Alliance's guidelines. The proposed convention ignored the legislative trend in several countries that granted women increased control over their nationality. The Alliance was disheartened further by the contents of a report submitted by the head of the League's Codification Committee that suggested that the issue of married women's nationality rights posed such a challenge to international regulation that its discussion would be an obstacle to codification efforts.[16]

After the League of Nations released its draft proposal, forty scholars and jurists gathered at Harvard Law School to design international conventions on the three subjects slated for discussion at the codifica-

---

14. Excerpt from Stevens's speech at a banquet for League delegates sponsored by the International Union of Societies for the League of Nations, Sept. 17, 1928, *DS*, 76–246, folder 308.

15. League of Nations, *Official Journal. Special Supplement No. 64. Records of the Ninth Session of the Assembly, Plenary Meetings* (1928), 143.

16. League of Nations, Committee of Experts for the Progressive Codification of International Law, Subcommittee on Nationality, *Report Submitted by M. Rundstein and Approved by M. De Magalhaes,* dated Oct. 8, 1925, C.43.M.18.1926.V (1926). Undated copy of the IWSA's letter to the League's Codification Committee, [June 1926], *NWPP.*

tion conference. The all-male gathering included the foremost experts on international law in the United States.[17] The Inter-American Commission of Women subsequently assembled some experts to draft a nationality convention for submission at the codification conference. This group included Alice Paul, Emma Wold, Burnita Shelton Matthews, Margaret Lambie, and Doris Stevens (all members of the NWP), as well as three members of the aforementioned Harvard Research Committee: James Brown Scott, the president of the American Institute of Law, who served as chairperson; Henry Hazard, who was an assistant solicitor in the State Department; and William Dennis, a former legal adviser to the State Department and then a professor of international law at American University. This Inter-American Commission roundtable considered the merits of the three circulating sets of draft conventions on married women's nationality and rejected all of them as too conservative.

The Inter-American Commission's advisory group then voted to draft an alternative agreement. The resulting treaty proposal, which bore the distinctive imprint of the NWP, provided that "the contracting parties agree that from the going into effect of this treaty, there shall be no distinction based on sex in their laws and practice relating to nationality."[18] The Inter-American Commission unanimously adopted the proposal, and the Executive Council of the American Institute of International Law also registered its approval. By then The Hague conference was merely a month away.[19]

17. The Harvard Research Committee was particularly impressive: Richard Flournoy, Jr. (who served as reporter), Clement Bouvé, James Garner, Henry Hazard, Manley O. Hudson, Charles Cheney Hyde, Philip Jessup, Arthur Kuhn, Jesse Reeves, George Wickersham, and Lester Woolsey attended. Their study was published in *American Journal of International Law*, supp., 23 (Apr. 1929). Apparently Wickersham was fiercely critical of the Cable Act at the Committee meetings. Indeed, Scott believed Wickersham's vehemence won the women's camp some converts. Papers of Jane Norman Smith, Schlesinger Library, Radcliffe College, Cambridge, Mass. (hereafter referred to as *JNS*), A-116, folder 125.

18. *DS*, 76–246, folders 323, 325; "Report of Work Done from April 1928 to April 1929 by the Inter American Commission of Women," [Apr. 1929], 5–6, *NWPP*. Although Charles Cheney Hyde did not participate in this roundtable, he would later support the treaty. Hyde was well known as a conservative jurist, and his decision after The Hague conference to endorse the NWP nationality treaty greatly satisfied Stevens and her colleagues. See Charles Cheney Hyde, "Aspects of Marriage between Persons of Differing Nationalities," *American Journal of International Law* 24 (1930): 742–745.

19. The American Institute also adopted a resolution recommending that the next Pan American Congress draft a convention embodying the ideal of equal nationality rights. For Stevens's report on the Commission's first meeting, see *DS*, 76–246, folder 325; also,

The acquisition of Scott as an Inter-American Commission ally was an important triumph for reformers working for equal nationality rights. As Stevens reminded Alva Belmont, Scott's stellar international reputation could boost the stature of the women's cause in some key circles. "Miss Paul thinks we have never made a more valuable friend," confided Stevens.[20] Indeed, Alice Paul would never have reason to doubt her enthusiasm over the acquisition of this advocate of the cause. Scott had valuable connections in several important international organizations and would ensure Stevens's and Paul's memberships in the American Society of International Law. He also quickly developed into one of the most influential and committed spokespersons for women's nationality rights.[21]

When Scott asked whether the League of Women Voters should also be included in their plans for presenting the women's case at the conference, Stevens advised against offering the invitation. "I pointed out," she wrote, "that they did not do Pan American work as we did, that they did not confine themselves to feminist work as we did."[22] Stevens had hinted loudly that the women's alliance for equal nationality rights had fractured along familiar lines. Although the NWP and the NLWV professed to hold the same high degree of commitment to nationality reform for women, they could no longer agree on the means of achieving their objective. In the final months leading to the codification conference, the NLWV and the NWP had both pressured the Hoover administration for guarantees that it would not support a discriminatory

pamphlet in *DS*, A-104, vol. 2, *Sixth International American Conference Addresses. Inter-American Commission of Women Assembled in the University of Habana, Feb. 17 to Feb. 24, 1930* (Havana, 1930).

20. Letter of Doris Stevens to Alva Belmont, Mar. 17, 1929, *NWPP*.

21. Scott's reputation as an international lawyer was well-established by this date. He was instrumental in the creation of the American Society of International Law in 1906 and later served as its president. He was also a founder and the first president of the American Institute of International Law. Scott maintained an affiliation with the Institute of International Law and the Carnegie Endowment for International Peace. He was an active lecturer and the author of several published works, including *Observations on Nationality with Especial Reference to The Hague Convention of April 12th, 1930* (New York: Oxford University Press, 1931).

22. Letter of Stevens to Belmont, Mar. 17, 1929, *NWPP*. The Nationality Committee of the Inter-American Commission was heavily stocked with members of the NWP. Alice Paul chaired the Commission, and six out of nine members were from the continental United States (Paul, Laura Berrien, Emma Wold, Maud Younger, Maud Bradbury, and Elizabeth Selden Rogers). The three other members of the Commission were from Chile, Cuba, and Puerto Rico.

nationality convention. One hundred women attending the NWP's annual convention descended on the White House three months before the international meeting in the Netherlands to request an audience with the President and Secretary of State Henry Stimson. They received a polite hearing but no promises.[23]

The codification conference marked a major fork in the road for women's nationality rights globally; it could lead to either a stunning victory or a dead end. Yet, in the months before the conference convened many advocates of woman's rights tried to remain very (if not overly) optimistic about what the conference might reasonably accomplish. Some observers hailed the international conference as a forum for the general promotion of woman's rights. Belle Sherwin, president of the NLWV, went so far as to declare that "the place of women in modern society" could be settled at The Hague. So inspired by the conference's possibilities, Sherwin sent a formal statement to the State Department urging the appointment of women to the U.S. delegation.[24]

Resistance to the inclusion of women in the delegation, however, was a reminder that the conference might have a conservative cast. Women's groups promoting equal nationality rights in the United States had gained the attention of Congress but had made a fainter impression in the male-dominated field of international politics. It was possible that the practice of derivative citizenship would not only survive the codification conference but be reaffirmed. Some women's organizations involved in nationality-rights reform contemplated another possible conference outcome they found hardly less distressing: the recognition of the Inter-American Commission's proposed equal-nationality treaty. Although the International Alliance of Women opposed this treaty and continued to stand behind its convention of 1923, Stevens promised to be an aggressive promoter of her Commission's proposal at The Hague.

Both sides in the treaty debate thus wanted to secure representation in the U.S. delegation, but Manley O. Hudson, appointed technical adviser for the United States at the conference, had made it clear that

---

23. Ruby A. Black, "Officials Hear Pleas for Equal Nationality," *Equal Rights* 15 (Dec. 21, 1929): 363–364. A copy of Emma Wold's address to President Hoover is in *NWPP,* dated Dec. 9, 1929. "We are giving all our time, energy and money right now to the work for nationality," Mabel Vernon reported to Margaret Whittemore a few months before the Codification Conference. Undated letter of Vernon to Whittemore, [Jan. 1930], *NWPP.*

24. Press release dated Dec. 3, 1929, *NLWV I.*

he did not want women to be officially part of the delegation. The NLWV nevertheless asked him to set aside his reservations and consider Sophonisba Breckinridge and Dorothy Straus as additions to his circle of advisers.[25] The NWP made a strong, although less unified, effort to secure a member's appointment to the U.S. delegation.[26] In the end, neither organization secured a delegatory position for one of their members. Only one woman, Ruth B. Shipley of the U.S. Passport Division, was part of the U.S. contingent. Wold went to The Hague, but as a technical advisor to the U.S. plenipotentiaries. In addition to Stevens and Wold, the NWP had in attendance Florence Bayard Hilles, Ella Riegel, Margaret Whittemore, and Mary Caroline Taylor; the Party sent them to the Netherlands with instructions to secure a hearing before the Nationality Committee. The NLWV commissioned its former president Maud Wood Park and Mrs. Pittman Potter to report on the month-long event.[27]

The NWP's and the NLWV's intentions for the conference were clear, but the U.S. State Department's plans were far more covert in order to minimize preconference commitments and confrontations. In 1926, the previous Secretary of State, Frank Kellogg, had informed the secretary general of the League of Nations that the United States believed there was "no real necessity for the regulation of these subjects [regarding nationality] by international agreement."[28] A change of administration had not altered this cautious appraisal of the value of international agreements on nationality. Four years later the State Department still thought it doubtful that any international convention would emerge from the deliberations in the Netherlands and preferred not to sign one if it did. Nevertheless, Secretary of State Stimson en-

25. League of Women Voters, Meeting of the Executive Committee, Jan. 23, 1929, *NLWV I*. Breckinridge was then serving as chair of the NLWV's Committee on the Legal Status of Women, and Straus was the organization's representative to the International Alliance of Women's Committees on the Nationality of Married Women.

26. NWP members disagreed over whether to suggest Emma Wold, Jane Norman Smith, or Doris Stevens. The papers of Doris Stevens, Jane Norman Smith, Sue Shelton White, and Alma Lutz at the Schlesinger Library, Radcliffe College, Cambridge, Mass., contain correspondence regarding this debate. *DS*, 76–246, folder 163; *JNS*, A-116, folder 75; papers of Sue Shelton White, A-74, box 3, folder 36 (papers hereafter referred to as *SSW*); papers of Alma Lutz, MC-182, box 1, folder 1 (papers hereafter referred to as *AL*).

27. League of Women Voters, Board of Director's meeting, Dec. 12, 1929, *NLWV I*.

28. Letter of Frank Kellogg reprinted in *For. Rel.*, vol. 1 (1926), 555–556. Apparently Joseph Cotton told Stevens that the delegation was to stand against any codification agreement at that time. Letter of Stevens to Belmont, Mar. 6, 1930, *DS*, 76–246, folder 278; letter of Vernon to Belmont, Mar. 6, 1930, *NWPP*.

couraged President Hoover to send representatives to the conference because the three subjects slated for codification were issues of vital concern to the United States.

Stimson was committed to attend the London Naval Conference when the codification conference convened, so Assistant Secretary Joseph Cotton served as Acting Secretary and primary director of the delegates' actions. Before the U.S. delegation left for the Netherlands, Cotton informed the delegation's chairperson, David Hunter Miller, that the United States was "in no sense to approve the Harvard drafts as a whole or to approve the League bases as a whole."[29] This instruction was mostly precautionary; Cotton actually doubted that there would be a convention to sign by the end of the conference. Two weeks into the month-long conference Miller informed Cotton that his forecast seemed accurate; there appeared to be "almost no chance" of agreement on the nationality issue.[30]

At The Hague the delegates discussed the complications created by statelessness and dual allegiances and tried to draft a nationality convention that would reduce the kinds of conflicts over citizenship and personal property that were aggravated by the global patchwork of nationality laws.[31] Governments and legal experts in the twentieth century were concerned with the rise in jurisdictional conflicts attributable to several factors, including the simple fact that the world's population had become increasingly mobile. As the U.S. State Department had noted with growing concern, Americans were traveling, working, settling, and marrying abroad in significant numbers. As more people traveled beyond their country's borders, an increasing number of children were born outside their parents' country or countries. These children could obtain two citizenships at birth if their father's country followed the rule of *jus sanguinis* (right by blood) and the nation in which the birth occurred adhered to the rule of *jus soli* (right by place). The situation only promised to grow more common and complex if more coun-

29. Letter of Cotton to David Hunter Miller, dated Feb. 27, 1930, reprinted in *For. Rel.*, vol. 1 (1930), 208.

30. Telegram from Miller, dated Mar. 24, 1930, ibid., 210.

31. Lawrence, *Disabilities of American Women Married Abroad*, 68–99, contains an appendix listing U.S. agreements with other nations regulating nationality. Also consult Flournoy and Hudson, *A Collection of Nationality Laws*, 645–710, for a list of bipartite and multipartite treaties on nationality; and Waldo Emerson Waltz, *The Nationality of Married Women. A Study of Domestic Policies and International Legislation*, Illinois Studies in the Social Sciences 22 (Urbana: University of Illinois Press, 1937), 59–118.

tries extended to mothers the right to transfer citizenship to their foreign-born children.[32]

At The Hague, while the advocates of women's nationality rights continued to denounce the discriminatory articles in the draft convention submitted by the League's Codification Committee, the U.S. State Department voiced its disappointment with several key provisions of the convention—specifically, the rules on expatriation. At the conference, the U.S. delegation's pronouncements relating to expatriation and plural citizenship emphasized the relationship between women's nationality rights and both of these issues. For the members of the U.S. delegation, a married woman's ability to hold an independent nationality and her ability to convey citizenship to her children were subsets of larger policy concerns.[33]

Although the U.S. delegation wished to focus on the issue of multiple citizenships, its members refrained from any blatant criticism of "hyphenated" Americans that could offend an international audience. Rather, the delegates spoke ardently of the citizen's right to expatriation—to sever ties to one country and to swear exclusive allegiance to another. Instead of representing expatriation as a power "inherent in national sovereignty" as the U.S. Supreme Court had done in *Mackenzie v. Hare,* the delegates described expatriation as a liberty exercised and controlled by the individual rather than the government.[34] Not surprisingly, Flournoy and Miller did not advert to the discontent back home with their government's interpretation of "voluntary" expatriation.

32. In 1930, seven countries granted a mother and a father equal power to change the nationality of their minor children: Argentina, Brazil, Chile, Guatemala, Paraguay, Uruguay, and the Soviet Union.

33. Shabtai Rosenne, ed., *League of Nations. Conference for the Codification of International Law* [*1930*], vol. 3 (Dobbs Ferry, N.Y.: Oceana, 1975), contains some of these discussions. See also League of Nations, *Acts of the Conference for the Codification of International Law, Mar. 13–Apr. 12, 1930,* vol. 1 and vol. 2, C.351.M.145.1930.V and C.351(a).M.145(a).1930.V (1930): Charles Cheney Hyde, *International Law: Chiefly as Interpreted and Applied by the United States,* vol. 2, 2d rev. ed. (Boston: Little, Brown, 1947), 1131–1143. For a useful and detailed summary of U.S. policy on dual nationality, see Greene Haywood Hackworth, *Digest of International Law,* vol. 3 (Washington, D.C..: G.P.O., 1942), 352–377.

34. At one point Flournoy did briefly refer to the U.S. practice of revoking the naturalization papers of a citizen who left the country, but his words were as dispassionate as the text of the law. A citizen might be left stateless by this rule, he admitted, but that hardship could only befall the undeserving individual "who has not carried out his part of the contract . . . in regard to naturalisation." "There is no reason why he should not be left stateless," concluded Flournoy. Rosenne, *League of Nations,* 1051.

Until the closing days of the conference, the U.S. delegation seemed unresponsive to feminists' exhortations to speak out forcefully for independent citizenship for the world's women. "Our delegates apparently have no intention of doing anything in regard to nationality," concluded an exasperated Ella Riegel.[35] Back home, Alice Paul was canvassing Senators tirelessly, trying to gather assurances from a critical third that they would oppose a world code that perpetuated women's subordinate citizenship. Paul managed to boost some flagging spirits with her frequent cables to colleagues in the Netherlands describing the strong support the women's cause still sustained in the United States.[36]

The force of the "feminine lobby," as Cotton called it, proved more effective in the United States than at the conference. At The Hague, even limited recognition of women's voices had not been granted easily. The International Council of Women and the International Alliance of Women had sent a joint memorandum to the conference, which was presented before the assembly of delegates on March 13; two days later a deputation of representatives from the two women's organizations were able to meet with the Bureau of the Conference. Emphasizing their twenty-five-year commitment to nationality-law reform, the representatives insisted on being given an opportunity to speak before the assembly on behalf of women. "Even a criminal is not refused a legal defender," said Louise van Eeghen of the International Council.[37] But the actions of the unofficial female delegations had antagonized the presiding officer of the codification conference, Theodorus Heemskerk, and jeopardized the reformers' chances of observing the Nationality Committee's meetings.

Claiming that groups of women were harassing the delegates, Heemskerk barred the alleged offenders from the grounds of the Peace Palace. The women simply regrouped and resumed their protests outside the palace gates. Such tenaciousness annoyed Heemskerk, who angrily informed the press that the women "came not merely as strangers,

---

35. Letter of Ella Riegel to Vernon, Mar. 15, 1930, NWPP.

36. Ruby A. Black, "United States Refuses to Accept Unequal Code," Equal Rights 16 (Apr. 19, 1930): 83–85. Several cablegrams are in Doris Stevens's papers at the Schlesinger Library.

37. "Joint Deputation of the International Council of Women and of the International Alliance of Women for Suffrage and Equal Citizenship on the Nationality of Married Women, Supported by Other International and National Bodies. Verbatim Report of a Meeting with the Bureau of the Conference, Held at The Hague on Saturday, March 15th, 1930," reprinted in Rosenne, League of Nations, 1196–1201.

but with the hostile intention of frustrating the work of the conference."[38] To the delight of the publicity-seeking protesters, news reporters pursued their story, hoping to enliven their coverage of what in
many respects seemed to be a rather dull international event.

Before the conference concluded, officials did yield some time to a
handful of the women who had been milling around impatiently outside the Peace Palace. Doris Stevens of the Inter-American Commission and four other women representing the International Alliance of
Women, the International Council of Women, the NWP, and the National Council of Chilean Women spoke at a meeting of the Nationality
Committee. The chairperson of the committee, M. Politis of Greece,
did not fail to remind them, however, that their invitation to speak was
"merely an act of courtesy on our part. . . . The decisions which we shall
make will not depend upon the hearings of the ladies."[39] Stevens then
chided the delegates for slighting the cause of equal nationality rights.
"We were told," she related, "that you had already taken up your attitude . . . and that we could not alter it." "We cannot go on waiting,"
she added defiantly.

Yet, women were forced to wait. Despite the bold efforts of Stevens
and many others, female reformers' opinions gained limited circulation
within the Peace Palace. Frustrated by the marginal role women had
again been compelled to play, Stevens reminded the distinguished male
delegates that they should be self-conscious rather than smug about the
power they wielded. It was, after all, "a mere accident that we were born
women and that you were born men."[40]

The convention that emerged at the conclusion of the sessions on
nationality was incompatible with U.S. policies on expatriation, and the
country's delegation voted against it. But the U.S. government's refusal
to support the convention was not based solely on conflicts with the
Cable Act. Dual citizenship and expatriation were ripe subjects for codification, but they were also sensitive political issues. Many Americans
accepted as axiomatic that a country, in order to remain strong, had to
command its citizens' undivided allegiance. Anxieties about heavy foreign immigration into the United States had cast a shadow of doubt

38. Press release sent to the *Christian Science Monitor*, dated Apr. 9, 1930, copy in *DS*,
A-104. See "U.S. Women Lose Equality Fight at Hague Law Parley," *Christian Science
Monitor*, 11 Apr. 1930.

39. "The Hague—Dr. Wold's Account," *Equal Rights* 16 (Aug. 2, 1930), 204.

40. Rosenne, *League of Nations*, 1063.

over those American citizens who had begun life possessing another nationality. Many native-born Americans expressed Flournoy's fear that the United States would inevitably face a severe crisis of identity and strength if the country could not command the undivided loyalty of its growing population of naturalized citizens. Yet, for the supporters of women's nationality rights, The Hague convention's greatest failing was the absence of any guarantee that citizen women would receive the nationality rights enjoyed by their male counterparts.[41]

The draft convention disappointed all advocates of equal nationality rights and appalled equalitarian feminists, who continued to exhort the U.S. delegation to speak out forcefully for independent citizenship for women and an international agreement that truly honored that goal. When Stevens stood before the full complement of delegates to condemn the arguments that had disarmed her cause, she once again tried to slake her anger by shaming her audience. "Equality will not bring uniformity," she conceded. "It will merely introduce into nationality laws justice to women."[42]

About a week before the close of the conference, Miller told Cotton that he, Hackworth, Shipley, and Risley wanted to vote against the entire convention. The United States would have to sign it with so many reservations that it seemed pointless to enter into the agreement.[43] Activity on the other end of the line of communication was also making accession to the convention a less prudent gesture. "Because of considerable criticism going on here by a certain group of women, I should prefer that there be no signing of conventions at all at The Hague," the Acting Secretary explained.[44]

The position of United States had remained uncertain until the final moments of the conference, but the significance of its decision did not. "American feminists here regard the vote to be taken tonight on their

41. The convention did limit the applicability of marital expatriation however. To protect against statelessness, a woman would not lose her citizenship upon marriage unless she also acquired her husband's citizenship. The full text of the "Convention Concerning Certain Questions Relating to the Conflict of Nationality Laws," is reprinted in Manley O. Hudson, ed., *International Legislation. A Collection of the Texts of Multipartite International Instruments of General Interest,* vol. 5 (Washington, D.C.: Carnegie Endowment for International Peace, 1936), 359–374.
42. Speech of Stevens before the First Committee [on Nationality]. Doris Stevens, "Doris Stevens' Plea for Equality," *Equal Rights* 16 (May 10, 1930): 109.
43. Telegram from Miller, Apr. 5, 1930, *For. Rel.,* vol. 1 (1930), 212. Flournoy was the only dissenter.
44. Telegram from Cotton to Miller, Apr. 9, 1930, ibid., 218.

nationality rights as the most important crisis in the fight for their worldwide emancipation," Stevens had reported on the closing day of the conference.[45] Throughout the sessions, the chairperson of the Inter-American Commission had been forced to remain apprehensive about her country's posture on woman's rights. Miller had never allayed her fears that the U.S. delegation might approve the convention, although organized women's demands reportedly had begun to have an effect back in the United States.

The day the plenary session was to vote on the nationality convention, Cotton had informed Miller that the influence of the "organized feminine lobby" at home had not abated. Indeed, the women had convinced both Congressional Foreign Affairs Committees to recommend that the United States decline to sign the nationality convention.[46] Two hours before the vote at the Peace Palace, representatives from the National Association of Women Lawyers and the NWP appeared at the White House to urge President Hoover once again to reject the convention. John Cable and James Brown Scott arrived on the same mission.[47] Meanwhile, Elizabeth Selden Rogers and a cadre of Republican women headed for the office of the Acting Secretary of State. "We want to launch the world code on an Equal Rights basis," she had announced to Cotton. The United States "has the power to put this over," and its women, she warned, "will not be satisfied until you do it."[48]

Back in the Netherlands, Stevens was observing the tense moments preceding the final vote on the nationality convention. It was late in the evening, in the closing hours of a conference that had produced only one codification convention, and, as Stevens recalled, as Miller rose to announce the U.S. position, "all eyes turned to the little knot of women in the high, far-away balcony." "Spontaneous applause came from these women," followed by "a sharp rap from the presiding officers gavel. . . . From then on the festive air gave way to one of almost solemn melancholy."[49] The U.S. delegation cast the only dissenting vote against the convention. Although defeated at The Hague, American feminists had held the home ground.

The U.S. delegation's reasons for disputing the convention were not

45. *DS*, A-104, vol. 34.

46. Telegram from Cotton to Miller, Apr. 10, 1930, *For. Rel.*, vol. 1(1930), 220.

47. "Women Lawyers Ask Equality in Nationality," *Equal Rights* 16 (Apr. 12, 1930): 76–77.

48. Ibid.

49. Text of speech given at NWP Headquarters, May 18, 1930, *DS*, A-104, vol. 30.

restricted to opposing the document's rules on married women's citizenship, although feminists argued that this flaw was sufficient to justify its rejection. The State Department had been predisposed not to sign an international agreement on nationality, and the convention's incompatibility with the Cable Act and other domestic statutes provided reasonable grounds for rejecting it. The United States could have signed the convention with reservations, as did many nations, but in the final hours critical efforts by women's organizations had made that option problematic. Although the U.S. action was generally applauded at home, some within the conference delegation did not support the rejection of the convention. Flournoy believed a vote for the flawed convention was preferable to flat rejection. Hudson, an adviser to the U.S. delegation, thought the State Department had cravenly succumbed to feminist lobbyists. The U.S. action, observed Hudson, suggested that the government "is more intent upon mollifying a section of its own public opinion than upon grappling with the very real problems which exist today and which the convention is designed to solve."[50]

American feminists were gratified temporarily by their delegates' action and by the State Department's subsequent pronouncement that the United States did not sign the convention because it was not in accord with two "principles" that were "firmly embedded in our law"— namely, expatriation and married women's nationality rights.[51] Although it appeared that many European countries would generally support ratification of the convention, equalitarian feminists hoped to find a stronghold of opposition within the American republics. The Americas had not been represented well enough at the codification conference to form a distinct core of dissent, but evidence of such solidarity did emerge at the Pan American Union conference in 1933.

The Hague conference would further stir rather than settle the debate over married women's nationality rights. Despite the strong vote for the nationality convention, many nations had voted for it with res-

---

50. Manley O. Hudson, "The Hague Convention of 1930 and the Nationality of Women," *American Journal of International Law* 27 (Jan. 1933): 122. Scott expressed his disappointment with the nationality convention in "Unprogressive Codification of Nationality at The Hague," *Women Lawyers' Journal* 18 (Apr.-Oct. 1930): 4–5, 38–43. The *Congressional Digest* devoted a volume to articles on the codification conference. See "Equal Nationality Rights for Women," *Congressional Digest* 9 (Nov. 1930), 257–288.

51. Statement by Assistant Secretary of State Joseph Cotton, Apr. 14, 1930, in U.S. Department of State, *State Dept. Press Releases, Jan. 4–June 28, 1930* (Washington, D.C.: G.P.O., 1930), 175–176.

ervations. The limited accomplishments of the codification conference suggested once again to many observers that a world code was perhaps an admirable but unachievable goal. Even the convention's preamble acknowledged that the economic and social conditions in many countries had made it impossible to find a "uniform solution" to the problems of statelessness and dual citizenship.[52]

Alva Belmont of the NWP offered praise for the U.S. stand against "the old world subjection of women." As for the Europeans, she dismissed their actions as a desperate attempt to preserve male power. "These men have lost their slaves. They have lost their serfs. They have lost their dominion over the working class. They still think they can dominate women. It terrifies them to think that in the future women mean to govern themselves," Belmont pronounced.[53] Undoubtedly, Congress imagined that the "Old World" was observing as it debated the latest Cable Act reform bill. Animated by events at the codification conference, the intense lobbying by women's organizations, as well as a surge of home support for the rejection of the convention, Congress passed the Nationality Act of July 3, 1930.[54] As noted earlier, this amending statute repealed the provision in Section 3 of the Cable Act expatriating women for maintaining a foreign husband and domicile.

The subsequent revocation of the ineligible-alien clause in the Cable Act also was hastened by the codification conference. As the House Committee noted in its report on the bill, despite the fact that the United States had repeatedly endorsed independent citizenship at a major policy conference, "there is no other country in the world which deprives its women nationals of their citizenship for the sole reason that they marry aliens ineligible for naturalization." In the afterglow of U.S. performance at The Hague, this practice had become acutely embarrassing to the federal government, which would abolish it the following year.[55]

52. League of Nations, *Convention Concerning Certain Questions Relating to the Conflict of Nationality Laws,* C.224.M.III.1930.V (1930). Text of the Final Act of the conference is in League of Nations, *Conference for the Codification of International Law. Final Act of the Conference for the Codification of International Law.* C.228.M.115.1930.V (1930).
53. Statement of Belmont delivered in Paris, Apr. 24, 1930, copy in *DS,* A-104, vol. 34. See also Mrs. O.H.P. Belmont, "Are Women Really Citizens? A Question Every Country Must Soon Answer. . . . ," *Good Housekeeping* 93 (Sept. 1931): 99.
54. 46 Stat. at 854 (1930).
55. Act of Mar. 3, 1931, 46 Stat. 1511. *Citizenship and Naturalization of Married Women,* 71st Cong., 3d sess., 1931, H. Rept. 2693, 3. The reform was supported by the NLWV, NWP, National Association of Women Lawyers, National Council of Jewish Women,

The repeal of the clause expatriating women for foreign residence demonstrated the power of American women's united voices. Women who had married and left the United States after its enactment could now retain their American citizenship by following certain administrative procedures. Congress, overriding the State Department's advice, had responded to American women's demands for a citizenship they could transport safely beyond the borders of the United States.[56] The U.S. citizenship of women expatriated before the passage of the law, however, was not automatically restored by the 1930 amendment. Once again Congress stopped short of repudiating and redressing past discrimination by guaranteeing a full reversal of its effects.

Equalitarian feminists' disappointment with the results of The Hague conference did not diminish their commitment to a world convention on nationality rights. The Inter-American Commission, Equal Rights International, and the Women's International League for Peace and Freedom remained firm proponents of this treaty solution. But some key players in the independent-citizenship crusade continued to withhold their support for an equal-nationality treaty. The International Alliance of Women and the International Council of Women preferred to advocate alterations to The Hague convention consonant with the guidelines elaborated by the Alliance in 1923.[57]

Disagreements among women's organizations over nationality-reform strategies had begun to brew before 1930; but the disputes had remained relatively subdued in spite of the politically charged atmosphere created by the introduction of the equal rights amendment.

General Federation of Women's Clubs, Woman's Bar Association of the District of Columbia, and National Federation of Business and Professional Women's Clubs.

56. The House of Representatives affirmed its commitment to women's nationality rights by passing a joint resolution introduced by Hamilton Fish of the Foreign Affairs Committee; the resolution stated that "it is hereby declared to be the policy of the United States of America that there should be absolute equality for both sexes in nationality, and that in the treaties, laws, and practice of the United States relating to nationality there should be no distinction based on sex." House Joint Resolution 331, 71st Cong., 2d sess. See *Relative to The Hague Conference on the Codification of International Law, and a Declaration of Policy for Both Sexes in Nationality,* 71st Cong., 2d sess., 1930, H. Rept. 1504; and *CR* 72 (May 21, 1930), 9314–9323.

57. Equal Rights International had formed to organize support for the equal rights treaty. Paula F. Pfeffer notes the rising influence of feminists from the United States in international organizations during these years. " 'A Whisper in the Assembly of Nations.' United States' Participation in the International Movement for Women's Rights from the League of Nations to the United Nations," *Women's Studies International Forum* 8, no. 5 (1985): 459–471.

Women's groups laboring for nationality rights seemed to have tacitly agreed to support one another's immigration and nationality bills (or at least to refrain from voicing disapproval publicly) and to avoid presenting competing bills during the same session of Congress. This arrangement had operated successfully throughout most of the 1920s, in part because the NWP felt compelled by Congressional intransigence to adopt the WJCC's gradualist strategies. Into the late 1920s, the NWP and WJCC could still present the impression of a united front in their crusade for independent citizenship; by the end of 1930, however, the introduction of the equal-nationality treaty had made any guise of such cooperation, particularly between the NLWV and the NWP, impossible to sustain.

Although the NLWV was deeply displeased with the authors of the equal-nationality treaty, it never repudiated the treaty's explicit intention, which was the abolition of sex discrimination in U.S. nationality laws. Nevertheless, the NLWV's leaders were too distracted by the obvious textual similarities between the nationality treaty and the proposed equal rights amendment to assess the merits of the nationality treaty independently. From the NLWV's perspective, the idea of a nationality treaty had to be arrested because it could serve as the means to a larger and destructive end: the abolition of all laws based on sex. Once equalitarian feminists unveiled the equal-nationality treaty, the NLWV's leaders were no longer able to discern even a faint ideological line between the NWP's commitment to equal nationality rights and its advocacy of an equal rights amendment. Indeed, the NWP had never drawn one.

The debate over the equal-nationality treaty was not directly tied to the disputes over protective labor legislation for women, which mired efforts to secure an equal rights amendment, but the NLWV's leaders were convinced that any blanket agreement embodying such an absolute definition of equality could ultimately threaten the status of special legislation for women. The League's national leaders feared that U.S. acceptance of the nationality treaty could be the toppling domino that would eventually touch off the ratifications of the equal rights amendment and its companion treaty. Although this prediction was unrealized, the prospect seemed genuine enough in 1930 to force a split in the women's coalition for nationality rights.

The International Council of Women and the International Alliance of Women reckoned candidly that the nationality treaty was "an ideal standard" but one that was presently "quite impossible." Although this unpublicized statement was not a clear renunciation of the treaty itself, the report also contained less diplomatic language describing equalitarians' "abstract declarations of principle."[58] The NWP's promotion of the equal-nationality treaty had contributed to its already unflattering image in some reform circles as a small congregation of ideologues who ignored economic and social—if not biological—realities in their selfish pursuit of "equality."

The fate of the women's alliance for nationality rights in the 1930s, however, revealed that the nationality treaty's proponents did not have a corner on stubbornness or myopia. The NLWV still continued to oppose the nationality treaty openly, even though the decision to fight against international recognition of the treaty placed the League in an awkward situation. League leaders had to explain their decision to renounce a treaty that promised to secure a series of reforms they had supported. Belle Sherwin, president of the NLWV, alluded to this dilemma when she made the somewhat cryptic announcement to members of the organization that "at a carefully chosen time the 'somewhat isolated and not-so-simple situation' in which the League of Women Voters finds itself will be explained to the State Department."[59] The League may have been forced to defend its position publicly sooner than it desired. The House Committee on Immigration and Naturalization scheduled a hearing in December 1930, to discuss a bill that carried now familiar language: "there shall be no distinction based on sex in the law and practice relating to nationality."[60]

58. Typed report of a joint conference of the International Council of Women and the International Alliance of Women, marked "incomplete and confidential," 16–17, folder 764, *MWPWRC.*

59. League of Women Voters, Executive Committee Meeting, Sept. 16, 1931, *NLWV I.*

60. H. of Rep., Hearings before the House Committee on Immigration and Naturalization, *Amendment to the Women's Citizenship Act of 1922, and for Other Purposes,* 71st Cong., 3d sess., Dec. 17, 1930, Jan. 23, 1931. There is considerable evidence that the NLWV was beginning to scale down its involvement in the nationality campaign after The Hague conference. The League appeared to retreat from participation in what had now clearly become an international movement with unpredictable repercussions. League leaders insisted, correctly, that there was still work to be done amending the Cable Act, and they concentrated on this objective. A month after the codification conference, the League designated reforming the nationality laws its "first minor legislative responsibility" and announced the next year that amendments to the Cable Act "will receive such support as circumstances will permit." League of Women Voters, Post-Convention Meeting of the General Council, May. 3, 1930, *NLWV I;* Letter of NLWV Executive Secretary Beatrice Marsh to Secretary of the WJCC Alice L. Edwards, *WJCC,* Dec. 21, 1931. See also Dorothy Straus's article emphasizing women's need to concentrate on reforming the laws of their

While the NLWV pondered how it might maneuver out of the corner into which it had unwillingly been driven, the League of Nations reopened its consideration of women's nationality rights.[61] To confirm its commitment to this investigation, the League of Nations had established a Women's Consultative Committee on Nationality composed of two representatives from each of the following international organizations: the International Council of Women, Women's International League for Peace and Freedom, Inter-American Commission of Women, Equal Rights International, World Union of Women for International Concord, All-Asian Conference of Women, International Alliance of Women for Suffrage and Equal Citizenship, and the International Federation of University Women. The NWP was able to secure a sure foothold within the Women's Consultative Committee through its involvement in the Inter-American Commission and Equal Rights International, and its strong influence in two of the others. The NWP's Paul, Stevens, and Whittemore all captured positions on the Commission. The antitreaty camp from the United States was not directly represented, although the International Alliance of Women contributed members to the Commission. The NLWV reportedly planned to publicize its dissenting view on the treaty—but only if "it should be necessary to counteract publicity heralded as the opinion of that of all American women."[62]

At its first meeting, the Women's Consultative Committee rejected The Hague nationality convention. Although the convention did not please anyone on the Committee, members' dissatisfaction with the general state of the nationality-rights debate varied in intensity. Equalitarians wanted to promote the equal-nationality treaty exclusively, while moderate members seemed appeased by the willingness of the League of Nations to reopen discussion of the nationality question. These differences in opinion appeared resolvable, but, according to some insiders' reports, the animosity and distrust fostered by past conflicts among the participating organizations began to complicate the Committee's task. Committee member Eugenie Meller of the Women's

---

own country. "Recognition Must Begin at Home," *League News: Bulletin of the National League of Women Voters* 5 (Dec. 1931): 1, 4.

61. Further support for international discussion came from the governing board of the American Institute of International Law (now with a woman member, Doris Stevens), which recommended that the Pan American Union approve both the equal-nationality and equal rights treaties.

62. Minutes of a Meeting of the WJCC, Dec. 7, 1931, *WJCC*.

International League for Peace and Freedom confirmed that rivalries had erupted within the Committee. "Personal antagonism," she admitted, "has dimmed objective reasoning."[63] The first report submitted by the Consultative Committee to the secretary general of the League of Nations, on July 16, 1931, bore little evidence of any serious division within the advisory body. The Committee urged the Assembly of the League of Nations to move quickly toward reconsideration of The Hague nationality convention and "to submit to the Governments for ratification a new Convention founded on the principle of equality between men and women with regard to nationality."[64] And the fact that some countries still seemed unprepared to accept such a revised convention was "not a reason for compromise with regard to the principle of equality."[65]

Representatives from the eight women's organizations signed the report, although the International Alliance of Women and the International Federation of University Women added that they signed "on the understanding that the equality asked for includes the right of a married woman to her independent nationality and that the nationality of a woman shall not be changed by reason only of marriage or a change during marriage in the nationality of her husband." This clarification seemed rather pointless—except as an excuse to insert the language of the International Alliance's 1923 nationality rights resolution into the record. The International Federation of University Women also gave notice that it took no stand on a child's derivation of citizenship from the mother, a reform endorsed elsewhere in the report.[66]

The Committee report left room for a later endorsement of an equal-nationality treaty, a maneuver that must have disturbed the NLWV. The League was also reminded of the consequences of its inability (or

63. According to Meller, Chrystal MacMillan, who represented the International Federation of University Women, and Margery Corbett Ashby of the International Alliance of Women were the major saboteurs. Copy of letter from Eugenie Meller to the Executive of the Women's International League for Peace and Freedom, May 28, 1933, NWPP.

64. League of Nations, *Nationality of Women. Report by the Secretary General,* A.19.1931.V (1931). (The Consultative Committee's statement begins on p. 7 as an "Annex" to the secretary general's report.) The response of the First Committee to the report is in League of Nations, *Nationality of Women,* A.84.1931.V (1931). For comments on the Committee report, see Rheta Childe Dorr, "Let Women Settle It," *Independent Woman* 10 (Nov. 1931): 483; Phyllis Lovell, "Women Seek Full Right to Citizenship," *Christian Science Monitor,* 14 Aug. 1931.

65. League of Nations, *Nationality of Women. Report by the Secretary General,* 8.

66. Ibid., 11.

unwillingness) to adjust to spiraling international developments as adroitly or as enthusiastically as the NWP and was left only with the consolation that it could still compete for control of the national scene. Not surprisingly, then, NLWV leaders chose to convey their response to the Consultative Committee's report through familiar domestic channels by seeking reassurances from the State Department that the Hoover administration would not endorse an equal-rights treaty.

When the Consultative Committee's report appeared, The Hague convention on nationality had still failed to receive broad and unreserved support. Sixty-six countries had been invited to sign, but almost two years after the codification conference only thirty-seven had done so (seven with reservations).[67] When the League Assembly met in 1932, it voted for a continuation of the Consultative Committee's work but turned down a resolution calling for revisions in The Hague convention. Instead, the Assembly urged member nations to ratify the convention quickly. Appealing to wavering countries, the Assembly defended the convention's provisions, admitting that it may have been a tentative step toward codification but that it was nonetheless an important one. Describing the convention pragmatically as a reflection of "the degree of progress which can at present be obtained by way of general international agreement," the Assembly also assured doubters that its ratification would not inhibit any nation that wished to endorse the principle of equality of the sexes.[68] So, although the Women's Consultative Committee had been asked to resume its task, its key recommendation had been rejected by the League Assembly—a reminder to the Committee that its work was strictly advisory.

Deeply concerned about the League Assembly's latest action, the NWP requested a hearing before the U.S. Senate Foreign Relations Committee to discuss the world code generally and, more specifically, to encourage the government to maintain its stance against the nation-

67. When the Consultative Committee submitted its first report, the following countries had signed the convention: Australia, Austria, Belgium, Canada, Chile, China, Colombia, Cuba, Czechoslovakia, Free City of Danzig, Denmark, Egypt, Estonia, France, Germany, Great Britain and Northern Ireland, Greece, Hungary, Iceland, India, Irish Free State, Italy, Japan, Latvia, Luxembourg, Mexico, The Netherlands, Norway, Peru, Poland, Portugal, Salvador, Spain, Sweden, Switzerland, Union of South Africa, Uruguay, and Yugoslavia. Only Monaco and Norway had ratified. The convention could not go into force until ten countries had deposited their ratifications or accessions with the League of Nations.

68. "Resolution of the Assembly," *Monthly Summary of the League of Nations* 12 (1932): 308–309.

ality convention.[69] "However admirable the League [of Nations] may be in other respects, it has no understanding of the movement for the freedom of women which is so strong in our country," warned the NWP.[70] Meanwhile, Alice Paul had remained in Geneva and was using Equal Rights International's headquarters as a base from which to observe the actions of the League Assembly. Although the subject of women's nationality was on the next session's agenda, Paul reported that League officials remained firmly set against allowing women before the Assembly to voice their objections to The Hague convention. The Assembly's continued promotion of that convention stoked Paul's fear that the eventual acceptance of the convention by one key country could set off a run of ratifications. The countervailing presence of the reformers, however, remained strong despite the women's exclusion from the institutional deliberations. "The handful of women who agitated almost unnoticed [in 1930], has grown to an army which goes on record as the largest ever recruited by women on any single political or juridical question," boasted one participant.[71]

Back in the United States, these ranks had been depleted temporarily of key players on the domestic front. Wold's departure from NWP headquarters and Paul's and Stevens's foreign-based activities for the equal-nationality treaty had left the NWP bereft of some of its most experienced leaders in the home campaign. Stevens's concern that the pace of reform at home had slackened, however, was hardly confirmed: bills to amend the Cable Act still received serious consideration by the House Committee on Immigration and Naturalization; the President had signed the Nationality Act of July 3, 1930; and John Cable was willing to sponsor additional reform bills (although he did refuse to back the NWP's equal-nationality bill). Furthermore, most of the members of the Senate Foreign Relations Committee had already voiced their dissatisfaction with The Hague convention and agreed to meet with the NWP in the spring of 1932.

At this hearing before the Senate Committee the NWP reiterated its request that the United States withhold support for the World Court

69. In its memorandum to Secretary of State Stimson the NWP also urged the federal government to declare that the United States would not enter the World Court if its code of law contained inequalities based on sex. Undated letter from the Committee on International Relations of the NWP to Stimson, [1932], *NWPP.*.

70. Ibid. See also copy of letter from Alice Paul to Mrs. (Anna Kelton) Harvey Wiley, from Geneva, Mar. 18, 1932, *NWPP.*

71. Phyllis Lovell, "Nationality at Geneva," typed article in *DS,* A-104, vol. 36.

if that body's decisions would be governed by a world code "based on the theory of the inferiority of women and the superiority of men."[72] Yet, this wariness was not shared by all the women's organizations involved in the nationality-rights movement. The NLWV, now clearly emerging as the fiercest critic of the NWP's international agenda, conveyed its disapproval of the NWP's views on World Court membership to the Senate Foreign Relations Committee's chairperson, William Borah. But, judging from Stevens's account of their appearance before the Senate Committee, the NWP's perspective gained more than just a respectful hearing in that forum: "We returned to headquarters . . . jubilant over one of the most successful hearings we have ever had in all our history. For the first time our opponents were given rough treatment at the hands of the members of Congress on the Committee."[73]

The Hague Codification Conference of 1930 had not produced a convention satisfactory to woman's rights groups involved in nationality-law reform, but it had revealed the potential of a global nationality-rights movement. And four years later it would become apparent that U.S. action at The Hague in 1930 had created expectations about that country's leadership in the cause of women's nationality rights—expectations the federal government could not diplomatically ignore.

In 1930, whether to purge U.S. nationality laws of all remaining distinctions based on sex was still a question tied to the government's attitude toward the foreign-born, although nationality-rights reformers were trying to cordon off the issue of women's nationality rights from the so-called immigrant question. The federal government, however, could never fully accept the feminist argument that the expatriation of women for foreign marriages was strictly a woman's rights issue because the granting of equal nationality rights to American women required changes in the law that could undermine the existing system of immigration and naturalization control. Allowing an American woman to retain her citizenship regardless of her domicile or the nationality of her spouse, providing for the nonquota admission of the alien spouse

72. Copy of statement by Burnita Shelton Matthews before U.S. Senate Foreign Relations Committee, May 7, 1932, *NWPP*. Minutes of the meeting of the National Council of the NWP, Mar. 23, 1932, and Apr. 17, 1932, *AL*, MC-182, box 1, folder 4. The NWP believed its views on the World Court would never receive consideration without a preparatory hearing before the Senate Committee. Hearing before the Senate Committee on Foreign Relations, *World Court*, 72d Cong., 1st sess., Apr. 6, May 7, 1932. Letter of protest from Belle Sherwin of the NLWV is printed on p. 40.
73. Letter from Stevens to Belmont, May 18, 1932, *DS*, 76–246, folder 281.

or child of an American woman, offering derivative naturalization to children of a citizen mother—these proposed innovations in the nationality and immigration laws all promised to produce increases in the absentee citizen population and in the number of nonquota immigrants entering the United States.

In the 1910s, media hyping of the titled American heiress had roused Congress's negative reactions to independent citizenship. In the 1920s, the response had thrived on affairs of greater weight, such as the preservation of family unity, the assimilation and naturalization of the immigrant mother, and the changing nature of women's citizenship. By the 1930s the advocates of reform faced opposition constructed from even more durable concerns. It was during the course of this decade that the debate over nationality rights between organized women and the State Department finally became publicly discernible. The State Department's responsibilities in the administration of the country's immigration and nationality laws had expanded over the course of the 1920s. Although the Labor Department remained the executive body most involved in the 1920s' debates over immigration policy, when the discussion turned more intently to expatriation and citizen absenteeism in the following decade, the State Department assumed the higher profile.

The Labor Department monitored naturalized Americans living in the United States, but the State Department focused its attention on those who left. One of the State Department's primary concerns was the long-term removal of citizen children to foreign countries. Government officials tracked the exodus of Americans of all ages from the United States, the majority of whom were presumed to be naturalized citizens, women with foreign husbands, or children with noncitizen or naturalized parents. The Office of the Commissioner General of Immigration reported that the number of emigrating Americans had actually diminished in the 1920s, peaking in 1922 at 79,198, dropping dramatically the next year to 36,260, and then falling to 20,739 by 1930.[74]

74. U.S. citizens permanently departed, for years ending June 30:

1918	56,998	1925	25,429
1919	39,543	1926	28,182
1920	64,564	1927	22,786
1921	71,391	1928	21,432
1922	79,198	1929	23,443
1923	36,260	1930	20,739
1924	29,661	1931	19,993

Source: Table 80 in U.S. Department of Labor, Bureau of Immigration, *Annual Report of the Commissioner General of Immigration* (1931), 215.

However, as the State Department reported in 1933—the year reformers were lobbying most vigorously for bills providing American citizenship to children born abroad to American women—the cumulative number of Americans living permanently in foreign countries had reached 420,459.[75]

While the country continued to absorb a significant annual infusion of new foreign-born residents, a much smaller but still substantial number of citizens left the United States permanently each year—a fact underemphasized by historians but not by the State Department during the interwar years. Children born in the United States contributed heavily to the volume of that exodus of citizens. In fiscal year 1932, for example, the Bureau of Immigration reported that 32,668 native-born Americans had permanently departed from the United States; 25,117 of these citizens were children under sixteen years of age.[76] Some of these young Americans who left the country with their parents at an early age inevitably would remain abroad and marry foreign citizens, but the State Department was equally concerned about the fact that the foreign-born children of this generation would also be considered Ameri-

---

75. The *estimated* 420,459 citizens living abroad permanently as of Jan. 1933 were scattered in this pattern:

South America	11,174
Mexico, Central America	18,337
West Indies, Bermuda	21,098
Canada, Newfoundland	246,101
Europe	93,789*
Africa	3,603
Asia	24,773
Fiji Islands, Society Islands	166
Australia, New Zealand	1,418

*Highest concentration in Italy (21,642) and France (19,466). No other European countries exceeded 10,000.
Source: "Americans Living Abroad," U.S. Department of State Press Release, No. 209, 1933, (Sept. 26, 1933), 186–89.

76. Table 22 in U.S. Department of Labor, Bureau of Immigration, *Annual Report of the Commissioner General of Immigration* (1932), 81.

According to 1920 federal census statistics, 88.7 out of 1,000 white children born in the United States in 1920 had a native-born mother and foreign father; 138.9 out of 1,000 had native-born fathers and foreign-born mothers. In 1930, data revealed that 71.7 out of 1,000 white children born in the United States had a native-born mother and foreign-born father; 216.5 out of 1,000 had a native-born father and foreign-born mother. Table 106 in U.S. Department of Commerce, Bureau of the Census, *Immigrants and Their Children*, 234; Table K in U.S. Department of Commerce, Bureau of the Census, *Birth, Stillbirth, and Infant Mortality Statistics for . . . 1930* (Washington, D.C.: G.P.O., 1934), 10.

can citizens because their parents were native-born and former residents.[77]

While the State Department made diplomatic comments about the political status and loyalties of the woman married to an alien, it contemplated her foreign-born child with undisguised alarm. In 1930, nationality law still did not allow minors to secure citizenship derivatively through an American mother. Providing derivative citizenship through either parent, a reform equalitarian feminists demanded, promised to increase the size of the citizen population living in foreign territories.[78] It also guaranteed a rise in the number of citizens holding multiple nationalities. From the State Department's perspective, both developments were dangerous.

The State Department's efforts to limit derivative citizenship for minors placed it at odds with equalitarian feminists, who expressed no sympathy for the administration's complaints that equal-nationality bills would promote the growth of another generation of American "aliens" and dual nationals. But as U.S. delegate Ruth Shipley told The Hague Committee on Nationality, women's and children's nationality rights were inseparable, not independent, "problems." "They are one," she explained. "We could not separate them if we would and, so far as my Government is concerned, we would not if we could."[79]

The State Department argued repeatedly that extending derivative citizenship rights to the child of an American woman or allowing a woman to maintain her citizenship while living permanently abroad

---

77. In the midst of the controversy over the equal-nationality treaty, the *Chicago Daily Tribune* carried a story about a family facing imminent deportation; the story illustrated the kind of situation that then worried the State Department. The parents had lived in the United States for eight years and had two native-born sons. Once deported, the parents would not be able to return to the United States as immigrants, which reduced their young children's chances of returning to their native United States before reaching majority. Nevertheless, the children of these American sons would be able to claim U.S. citizenship under the law then in effect. Virginia Gardner, "Mother Begs U.S. to Let Family Stay in Country," *Chicago Daily Tribune,* 28 Dec. 1933.

78. Sect. 1993, Revised Statutes of the U.S. (1878), read: "All children heretofore born or hereafter born out of the limits and jurisdiction of the United States, whose fathers were or may be at the time of their birth citizens thereof are declared to be citizens of the United States; but the rights of citizenship shall not descend to children whose fathers never resided in the United States." This provision was a reenactment of the Nationality Acts of April 14, 1802, 2 Stat. 153, and of February 10, 1855, 10 Stat. 604.

79. Shipley's speech was reprinted in David Hunter Miller, "The Hague Codification Conference," *American Journal of International Law* 24 (1930): 681–682.

would exacerbate existing problems. It is not surprising, then, that the State Department positioned itself as feminists' most influential opponent in the final years of the battle for women's nationality rights. In its warnings to Congress regarding the NWP's equal-nationality bills, State Department officials often criticized provisions offering women either the right to retain their American citizenship despite foreign marriages and domiciles or the power to transfer their citizenship to their children.

Following the amendments to the Cable Act in 1930 and 1931, few distinctions still remained between citizen men's and women's nationality rights and their alien spouses' access to naturalization, but those distinctions were significant ones. The law still withheld a simplified naturalization procedure from the resident alien husband of a citizen, and the children of married American women still derived their nationalities from their father or their place of birth. Women's nationality bills introduced in the years following the 1930 codification conference did address mothers' rights, but as noted above the State Department consistently objected to provisions allowing for the conveyance of American citizenship from citizen mother to her foreign-born child.

During the first session of the Seventy-second Congress, the House Committee on Immigration and Naturalization received one of the NWP's sponsored proposals directed toward that end.[80] When the House Committee on Immigration and Naturalization called a hearing on the bill early in 1932, members of the NWP dominated the field of testimony. Burnita Shelton Matthews was the official NWP representative, but she was flanked by colleagues Laura M. Berrien, Rebekah Greathouse, and Emma Wold, who appeared as spokespersons for the National Association of Women Lawyers, the Lawyer's Council of the NWP, and the Woman's Bar Association of the District of Columbia, respectively. James Brown Scott, president of the American Institute of International Law, also attended as an advocate of the bill.[81]

80. H.R. 5489, 72d Cong., 1st sess. (1932). See also *Provide Equality in Matters of Citizenship between American Men and American Women and to Clarify Status of Their Children*, 73d Cong., 1st sess., 1933, H. Rpt. 131. This bill would have altered portions of several major nationality laws.

81. Hearings before the House Committee on Immigration and Naturalization, *Relating to Naturalization and Citizenship Status of Certain Children of Mothers Who Are Citi-*

Scott emphasized the critical role the United States would assume in taking this bold step toward completing the equalization of nationality rights between the sexes, but everyone present did not share his enthusiasm. Committee member Mell G. Underwood objected to Section 5's abolition of all distinctions between women and men and trotted out the old argument that would not die—that "a woman is so much more emotional that she has to have the safeguards instead of removing them."[82] Belle Sherwin of the NLWV did not attend, but her letter of warning, which was introduced at the hearing, described Section 5 as a "blanket action" that would create "utter confusion" within the judicial system. Reform, advised the president of the NLWV with characteristic prudence, should proceed one measured step at a time.[83] However, Elsie Hill Redding, who claimed affiliation with both the NWP and the NLWV and who was present at the hearing, intimated that not all members of the League shared Sherwin's view.[84]

Raymond Crist, the Labor Department's commissioner of naturalization, also proposed eliminating Section 5. He had other concerns and suggested that if women were given the opportunity to bring their children into the country as citizens, they could file fraudulent petitions for the admission of minors who were not their children (a practice his Bureau believed was widely employed by the Chinese).[85] Burnita Shelton Matthews was surprised and annoyed by Crist's unfavorable assessment of the bill; he had earlier voiced his support for women's nationality rights. A few days later Matthews sent a rejoinder to Crist's complaints to the chair of the House Committee, Samuel Dickstein. Crist had suggested that the bill infringed on existing rights, but Matthews thought his point was misleading. Rights and policies would simply be applied equally to both sexes, she argued. Furthermore, Labor officials (including Crist) had long urged the establishment of a uniform rule of naturalization. The NWP's bill could advance that goal.

Matthews then digressed from the subject of nationality to address the still volatile issue of protective legislation; she assured Dickstein that "the Woman's Party has no objection to protective labor legislation

zens of the United States, and Relating to the Removal of Certain Distinctions in Matters of Nationality, 72d Cong., 1st sess., Jan. 7, 1932.

82. Ibid., 13.
83. Ibid., 19. Sherwin letter dated Jan. 7, 1932.
84. Ibid., 26–27.
85. Ibid., 27–29.

based on the nature of the work and has never advocated the repeal of any such legislation." Matthews's statement was a response to a letter from the American Federation of Labor, which had supported some past Cable Act amendments but now coupled its denunciation of this equalization bill with claims that its authors were attempting to repeal all protective legislation for women. Matthews accused the American Federation of Labor of "wander[ing] away from the bill under consideration" and unreasonably linking nationality rights for American women with the issue of special legislation.[86]

If Section 5 had been removed from the equalization bill, the NLWV might have felt obliged to support it. However, the NLWV's official position on children's nationality rights was still—and was probably intentionally—vague at this time. Maud Wood Park had reportedly told the U.S. Hague delegation that she personally thought the mother should have equal control over her children's nationality, but the League had not voted on the issue. Although the International Alliance of Women for Suffrage and Equal Citizenship registered approval of the NWP bill, the NLWV continued to withhold it. Yet, as Wold had observed rather wistfully, the support of the League "would undoubtedly be most helpful, perhaps even essential."[87] In the end the equalization bill went before the House Committee with the endorsement of the NWP, some local associations of female attorneys, the National Association of Women Lawyers, and the American Institute for International Law.

The convictions that drove the NWP's campaign for this equalization bill still fueled the organization's promotion of an equal rights amendment. Yet, the NWP did not want that fact to prompt antiamendment forces to withhold support for this equalization bill. That unwelcome response was, however, an inevitable one, and the association between the NWP's equalization bill and its more controversial endeavor to secure an equal rights amendment not only forced a split within the women's organizations supporting nationality rights but also left their Congressional allies divided. Cable informed Burnita Shelton Matthews that the equalization bill would never survive as written. Committee members disliked the citizenship provision for "illegitimate" children as well as Section 5, he reported; and those members who opposed an equal rights amendment were also

86. Matthews to Dickstein, letter dated Jan. 30, 1932, *NWPP.*
87. Letter from Wold to Mrs. Harvey Wiley, Nov. 28, 1931, *NWPP.*

opposing this nationality bill.[88] The NLWV's disassociation from the bill, the House Committee's unreassuring response, and the American Federation of Labor objections to its provisions all suggested strongly that the NWP's advocacy of the equal rights amendment and purported hostility toward special legislation for the female wage earner had alienated some key allies in the cause of independent citizenship.

The bill never made it to the statute books, but NWP's leaders could rarely be reproached as irresolute. A year later a similar bill was before the House Committee on Immigration and Naturalization. It was 1933, and the country had a Democratic president after a succession of Republicans. The Seventy-second Congress had been evenly divided between Republicans and Democrats in both Houses, but when the Seventy-third convened, sixty Democratic Senators sat with thirty-five Republicans, and House Democrats held a 310 to 117 majority over the Republicans (who had lost Cable in the Democratic sweep of 1932). When the House Committee on Immigration and Naturalization called its hearing on this new nationality bill, Cordell Hull had been Secretary of State for less than a month, but his Department immediately demonstrated that it planned to assume an active advisory role on nationality reform.

Secretary Hull wrote to House committee chairman Dickstein, informing him that the State Department maintained a skeptical posture on customized nationality bills that altered the rules on citizenship and expatriation.[89] Hull referred to a previous letter from Assistant Secretary Wilbur Carr to Dickstein that expressed the State Department's concern over the effects of such a bill. In this correspondence Carr had outlined the Department's reservations about legislation that fostered incidents of multiple nationality and absentee citizenship. Reinterpreting the rule of *jus sanguinis* to include a mother's right to determine her children's nationality would, warned Carr, "probably be more far-

88. Burnita Shelton Matthews to Alice Paul, letter dated Jan. 23, 1932, *NWPP*. Representative Cable thought the bill might fare better if it originated in the Senate. See Muna Lee to Alice Paul, letter dated May 16, 1932, *NWPP*.

89. Letter from Hull to Dickstein, dated Mar. 27, 1933, reprinted in Hearings before the House Committee on Immigration and Naturalization, *Relating to Naturalization and Citizenship Status of Children Whose Mothers Are Citizens of the United States and Relating to the Removal of Certain Inequalities in Matters of Nationality,* 73d Cong., 1st sess., Mar. 28, 1933, 8.

reaching than might be at first supposed." And, he added, it was "hardly necessary to say" that when an American woman married an alien man and moved abroad "the national character of that country is likely to be stamped upon the children, so that from the standpoint of the United States they are essentially alien in character." If the American mother had left the United States as a child, her foreign-born children (also Americans under the proposed bill) would have little if any opportunity to become familiar with their country's customs and values. The Department's main objection to this bill was its implicit promotion and protection of absentee "alien" Americans who, to compound their undesirability in the eyes of the government, might also be dual nationals. Carr complained that the proposed bill threatened to revive old problems by creating a class of citizens who were aliens in every respect but legally; in closing, he strongly suggested that Congress defer action on the issue of children's nationality until the completion of a comprehensive investigation of the nationality laws.[90] Secretary of State Hull repeated this advice and referred to developing plans to draft a U.S. code of nationality that would establish parity between the sexes.

This correspondence from the State Department to the chairperson of the House Committee on Immigration and Naturalization did offer some support for the idea that an American mother should have some control over her children's citizenship, but the Department emphasized the need to postpone any discussion of this issue until President Roosevelt summoned his nationality-code committee. The NWP, however, declined to mothball its bill until the executive department drafted a code.

The NWP worried that the Roosevelt administration's decision to

90. Copies of Carr's letter to Dickstein, dated Feb. 10, 1933, appear in *NWPP* and the record of the House Hearing, Mar. 28, 1933, *Relating to Naturalization and Citizenship Status* . . . , 9–11.

  A deputation from the NLWV did speak with State Department officials to ascertain the administration's position on blanket agreements. Greene Hackworth, solicitor general, assured the women that the Department did not intend to support the equal rights treaty. Copy of memo to Belle Sherwin from B. H. Marsh, dated Jan. 2, 1932, folder 765, *MWPWRC*. See also letter of Under Secretary William Castle to Mrs. Valentine Mott Vickery, dated Feb. 3, 1932, *NWPP*, in which Castle expressed the standard view of the State Department that an equal rights treaty would "involve various internal and domestic affairs of the Federal Government" and thus "should not be made the subject of treaty engagements of the United States."

organize a committee on nationality would stall their reform plans indefinitely. An executive committee on nationality composed of the Secretaries of State and Labor and the Attorney General is "perfectly frightful for us" wrote the NWP's Anita Pollitzer.[91] NWP leaders were convinced that a nationality code drafted by such a committee would be more complicated and, from their perspective, less satisfactory than their equal-nationality bill. Furthermore, the NWP's allies in Congress would be forced to choose between the two reform options. The NWP continued to defy the State Department's request for a hiatus, hoping to push the equalization bill through Congress before the executive committee completed its work. Securing passage of the equalization bill would send a strong message not only to the U.S. President but also to other national leaders. The Pan American Union conference was approaching, and the NWP wanted to exact some indication from the federal government that it would support the Inter-American Commission of Women's equal-nationality treaty. The NWP's decision to continue to lobby for the equalization bill was a gamble. Congress might support the bill, but the President could still decline to sign it.

In preparation for the House hearing on the equalization bill the NWP and State Department both wrote to key members of Congress to promote their positions. Alice Paul believed that the proposal could survive if Representative Dickstein and Senator Copeland, a member of the Senate Committee on Immigration, worked faithfully for its passage. One nationality bill had passed on the eve of Roosevelt's inauguration, but the action had sparked little celebration at NWP headquarters. According to Elsie Hill, the bill had been "mangled" by a State Department determined to "put over their exclusionist policy on the back of our campaign for equality."[92] At the hearing on the equalization bill, the discussion among House Committee members indicated that they viewed the legislation before them as an immigration rather than a nationality bill. Some of the representatives from California and Texas found the bill's proposals particularly unacceptable. Charles Kramer of California asked Matthews how she would feel if her daughter had to sit next to Asian boys in school every day. "Don't you feel that we are increasing the probability of bringing in more of the Chinese and Japanese, and what have you, from those nations over there, by

91. Pollitzer to Rilla Nelson, letter dated Dec. 8, 1933, NWPP.
92. Elsie Hill to Muna Lee, letter dated Mar. 27, 1933, NWPP.

reason of this bill?" challenged Kramer.[93] And, according to Martin Dies of Texas, every Mexican child that became an American would eventually return to Mexico, marry a Mexican and create another generation of hyphenated Americans.[94] Matthews expressed sympathy with the men's fears, but urged them not to let their commitment to restrictive immigration interfere with their championship of equal nationality rights for women. However, this digression on the perils of immigration spent the patience of Edith Houghton Hooker of the NWP. "If this law has been good enough for you all these years . . . it should be made to apply to us," she declared tersely.[95]

The NWP leaders were relieved when the House Committee described the bill favorably as an amendment to the Cable Act of 1922 that could establish "complete equality" between American men and women and their children in matters of nationality.[96] The bill allowed for the replacement of all references to wives and husbands in the Cable Act with the generic term *spouse* and thus allowed an American woman's alien husband to follow the shorter naturalization timetable then available only to male citizens' wives.

Equalitarian feminists in the United States tried to keep the treaty question alive by continually placing equalization bills before Congress. Meanwhile, the League of Nations Assembly continued to promote ratification of The Hague convention on nationality. In December 1933, when the Pan American Union held its convention at Montevideo, the Inter-American Commission's equal-nationality treaty was on the agenda. Proponents of the treaty predicted that it would fare well in the hands of the Pan American Union for several reasons: the Inter-American Commission was the Union's creation; some member countries had already embraced the treaty's principle; the United States had rejected The Hague convention; and Guatemala, Peru, and Venezuela had requested reopening the question of women's nationality within the League of Nations.

The conference lasted throughout most of December, but even before it convened most of the participating countries had announced

---

93. House Hearing, Mar. 28, 1933, *Relating to Naturalization and Citizenship Status . . . , 37.*
94. Ibid., 41–42.
95. Ibid., 51–52.
96. H. Rept. 131, *Provide Equality in Matters of Citizenship . . . , 2.*

their intentions to sign the treaty granting equal nationality rights. The United States was not among that number. President Roosevelt had established an executive committee on nationality in April, and his administration reiterated its wish to avoid any further action on nationality matters until the committee submitted its recommendations.[97] According to Departmental instructions to the U.S. delegates, the relevant committees in both houses of Congress had agreed to suspend consideration of nationality legislation, and it would be considered an act of "bad faith" on the part of the Roosevelt administration if the U.S. delegates then signed a nationality convention.[98]

The State Department likewise repeated its position: it did not favor settling the question of women's nationality rights by an international agreement. It also proposed dismantling the group that had helped keep the conversation active, the Inter-American Commission of Women. "American representation on that body has not served to reflect the views of this Government and the major groups of women with respect to the status of women in industry and in various social relations," and if a resolution for the Commission's continuation came before the conferees, the delegation was to abstain from voting and claim that it was "without instructions."[99] After the Conference of American States was in progress, however, the Acting U.S. Secretary of State informed his delegates that they should announce that the United States no longer wished to be represented on the Commission.[100]

News of the State Department's plans soon reached the pro-treaty reformers, and a delegation from the National Association of Women Lawyers promptly materialized at the White House to voice its objections.[101] Other interested parties relayed their hope that the United States would reconsider its strategy and sign this convention on nationality. By the second week of the conference, newspapers reported that

97. Executive Order 6115, April 25, 1933. The Committee consisted of six members of the Labor Department (including the Secretary), six from the State Department (including the Secretary), and Attorney General Homer Cummings. For the details of their final report, read *Nationality Laws of the United States.*
98. "Instructions to Delegates," *For. Rel.,* vol. 4, 1933, 78.
99. Ibid., 84–85.
100. Telegram from William Phillips to Cordell Hull, chair of the delegation, dated Dec. 11, 1933, ibid., 174–175. For reaction to U.S. Ambassador Alexander Weddell's announcement at Montevideo that his government "wishes to disassociate itself from the work of the Inter-American Commission of Women," see Arthur Ruhl, "Feminists Clash with Conferees at Montevideo," *New York Herald Tribune,* 17 Dec. 1933.
101. Telegram from Phillips to Hull, dated Dec. 14, 1933, *For. Rel.* vol. 4 (1933), 187.

"feminine pressure" to sign the document had reached "unexpected proportions."[102] Meanwhile, Secretary Hull, who headed the conference delegation, had been deluged by cables from treaty supporters.

The Roosevelt administration was caught off guard by the intensely negative response to its policy of inaction, and its critics were not just the usual crop of equalitarian feminists. Among women's reform organizations, only the NLWV had openly supported the administration's decision to drag its feet. The nation's press questioned the government's apparent recoil from at least the spirit of its 1930 Hague declaration. The introduction of the equal-nationality treaty had provided the United States with an opportunity to follow up its principled statements at The Hague with more concrete action, but the government now appeared to shrink from that avowal of the importance of woman's rights. Moreover, although the U.S. delegation was serving as ambassador of Roosevelt's "good-neighbor" policy, it stood in stark opposition to a treaty most American republics had agreed to sign.

On December 20, as Florence Bayard Hilles gathered a NWP delegation to meet with the President, she received the news that Secretary Hull had announced he would support an equal-nationality agreement. The day before, Acting Secretary of State William Phillips had sent the President a letter outlining the State Department's objections to the treaty solution, but the President had apparently already succumbed to public pressure. That night Phillips sent a telegram to Hull instructing the Secretary to support the agreement: "The President asks me to say for your personal information that the representative women of all parties and factions here are greatly aroused and that while he appreciates the undesirability of the proposed general language, the broad purpose is good and the reservation allows us to handle details later. He is sure you will agree with this."[103]

A Republican administration had successfully avoided signing an international agreement on nationality at The Hague in 1930, and Roosevelt had planned to follow suit at Montevideo, but the circumstances confronting the U.S. delegation three years later were significantly different. This time, the United States seemed to be playing the

102. Kendall Foss, "Women Insist U.S. Sign Pact at Montevideo," *Washington Post*, 20 Dec. 1933.

103. Letter from Phillips to Roosevelt, dated Dec. 19, 1933, and telegram from Phillips to Hull, dated Dec. 19, 1933, *For. Rel.*, vol. 4 (1933), 197–198, 201. The standard reservation referenced in the telegram stated "that the agreement on the part of the United States is of course and of necessity subject to Congressional action."

hypocrite rather than the hero. And even after the President announced that the United States would support the convention, the newspapers refused to close the book on the controversy and kept discussion lively by speculating on the masterminds behind the initial decision to reject the treaty. The name of Eleanor Roosevelt, of course, cropped up in the buzz of Washington gossip. The First Lady's disagreements with the NWP were public knowledge, but she vehemently denied any involvement in the incident. The State Department had requested her advice, she admitted, but she had declined to offer it. Women's organizations fighting against the equal rights amendment and now against an equal-nationality treaty believed they had a powerful ally in Eleanor Roosevelt, and Dorothy Straus of the NLWV rushed to the defense of the First Lady. In 1933, Eleanor Roosevelt did not favor an equal rights amendment, and she was an advocate of protective labor legislation for women, but according to the *Washington Post,* Roosevelt was "known to favor equality in nationality."[104] Roosevelt, however, said she did not support a blanket treaty, and her cautionary comments on the wisdom of granting citizenship to American women's children settled abroad suggested that she was in agreement with the State Department (and perhaps the NLWV's leaders) on this particular point.[105]

In the midst of this flurry of discussion over the Pan American Union conference, Dorothy Straus announced that the NLWV consid-

---

104. Foss, "Women Insist U.S. Sign Pact at Montevideo." The NLWV had sent a cable to Secretary Hull expressing an identical view on sex discrimination in the nationality laws. Belle Sherwin informed the Secretary that the NLWV had "long and resolutely" supported the principle "that nationality should be determined without discrimination on the ground of sex." However, the League preferred an approach conducive to "progressive evaluation and adjustment of law" and believed action by individual governments best promoted this orderly process of reform. Copy of cable in untitled report, dated Nov. 4, 1933, submitted by Rebekah Greathouse to NWP, *NWPP.* The NLWV had declared the treaty to be a "mere expression of a purpose, . . . no more self-acting than the Kellogg-Briand pact." See "Foes Tell Views on Women's Pact," *New York Times,* 21 Dec. 1933.

105. See Genevieve Forbes Herrick, "Mrs. Roosevelt Denies Opposing Woman's Treaty," *Chicago Daily Tribune,* 27 Dec. 1933; Foss, "Women Insist U.S. Sign Pact at Montevideo"; "U.S. Move to Block a Feminism Treaty Laid to Strife Here," *New York Times,* 18 Dec. 1933; "Pact Action Denied by Mrs. Roosevelt," *New York Times,* 27 Dec. 1933.

In a press release on the nationality treaty, the NLWV had questioned whether the ability to transfer nationality to one's children could be called a "right." Press release from the NLWV relating to the equal-nationality treaty, *Papers of Belle Sherwin,* Schlesinger Library, Radcliffe College, Cambridge, Mass., microfilm (hereafter cited as *BS*), reel 2, vol. 6.

ered the treaty proposal "meaningless" and "ineffectual," but there was strong reason to suspect that the League actually feared the opposite was true. The League had fought against the treaty because it carried such symbolic significance. The League dreaded, and the NWP hoped, that the treaty's ratification would be catalytic, stimulating a wave of equalization legislation in the United States and across the globe. According to a jubilant Alice Paul, acceptance of the treaty would mark "the beginning of the final stage in women's long struggle for justice and freedom."[106] Although the State Department still believed it could not afford to accept the view that equal nationality rights could be negotiated as strictly a "woman's question," it now had to acknowledge that not only the women seeking those rights but the press and the American public were apparently willing to judge the issue's merits on these narrow terms.

The State Department's actions had generated a surge of media publicity that offered pro-treaty reformers an ideal opportunity to air their views before a sympathetic audience.[107] Newspapers reporting on the Montevideo conference also probed the rift between women's groups involved in nationality reform. "Behind these events is a conflict twenty years old between two apparently irreconcilable philosophies held by women's groups," concluded Mildred Adams of the *New York Times*.[108] The *Times* editors sent a stern warning to feminists, urging them to mend their fences and begin to work cooperatively. "Does it occur to rival women's camps that they had better get together before it is too late?" asked the *Times*. "While they are quarreling about ways and means, a considerable part of the world is turning its back on the whole subject. . . . As the Fascist comes into the parlor, woman is chased back into the kitchen. National Woman's Party and the League of Women Voters had better take care. The Colored Shirts will get them both if they don't watch out."[109]

When the Montevideo conference adjourned on December 26, the

106. Articles on the treaty frequently contained similar Paul quotes, but this particular comment comes from Kendall Foss's article, "U.S. to Sign Equality Pact for Women," *Washington Post*, 21 Dec. 1933.

107. "Equal Nationality Rights," editorial, *Washington Post*, 22 Dec. 1933.

108. Mildred Adams, "Again Controversy Arises over Equality for Women," *New York Times*, 24 Dec. 1933. See also "A Mystery at Montevideo," editorial, *New York Times*, 19 Dec. 1933.

109. "Topics of The Times," editorial, *New York Times*, 20 Dec. 1933.

equal-nationality treaty carried the signatures of delegates from the United States, Honduras, El Salvador, the Dominican Republic, Haiti, Argentina, Uruguay, Paraguay, Mexico, Panama, Bolivia, Guatemala, Brazil, Ecuador, Nicaragua, Colombia, Chile, Peru, and Cuba. The conferees had rejected a proposal from the executive committee of the American Institute of International Law for an equal rights convention but had adopted a resolution recommending that countries take steps toward ensuring "the maximum of equality between men and women in all matters pertaining to the possession, enjoyment, and exercise of civil and political rights."[110] The Inter-American Commission of Women survived the conference, as did its indomitable chairperson, Doris Stevens. Secretary Hull approached Stevens near the close of the conference and complimented his challenger on her triumphs. "If I ever get into difficulty, I'm coming to find you to get me out of it," he quipped.[111]

The Conference of American States adjourned while the Seventy-third Congress continued its deliberations on women's and children's nationality rights. The Roosevelt administration had ostensibly bowed to demands for a comprehensive remedy to sex discrimination in the country's nationality laws. Yet, to equalitarian feminists' chagrin, when the House Committee on Immigration and Naturalization called a hearing on the NWP's equalization bill, the Secretary of State and commissioner general of immigration renewed their opposition. The Secretary of State reminded the Committee that his Department still harbored "serious objections" to this kind of nationality bill and its impact on children's nationality.[112]

110. "Resolution on the Civil and Political Rights of Women." The resolution also expressed the desire that the presidency of the Inter-American Commission of Women rotate among its representatives between conferences, a change in practice that would disrupt Stevens's preeminent position within the Commission. Text of the resolutions and conventions of the Montevideo conference are included in U.S. Department of State, *Report of the Delegates of the United States of America to the Seventh International Conference of American States, Montevideo, Uruguay, December 3–26, 1933* (Wash., D. C.: G.P.O.: 1934). The Montevideo delegation included Cordell Hull; Alexander W. Weddell, ambassador to Argentina; J. Reuben Clark, former ambassador to Mexico; J. Butler Wright, minister in Uruguay; Spruille Braden; and Sophonisba Breckinridge, professor of social service administration at the University of Chicago. Breckinridge was one of three female plenipotentiaries whose official status at a Conference of the American States marked a breakthrough for women.

111. "Hull Praises Miss Stevens on Her Victory over Him," *New York Times*, 25 Dec. 1933.

112. It should be noted here that although the State Department had expressed interest

The chilly reception for their equal-nationality bill in the State and Labor Departments irritated NWP leaders, who felt that key supporters within the administration had apparently defected and joined the opposition. Raymond Crist of the Bureau of Naturalization earlier had assured the women he supported equal nationality rights, and at the beginning of her tenure Secretary of Labor Frances Perkins had also presented herself as sympathetic. Greene Hackworth, solicitor in the State Department, had reviewed the bill for the NWP and expressed no objections to its provisions—until now. To add a little intrigue to apparent betrayal, the NWP discovered that the State Department had requested a private hearing with the House Committee in order to persuade Committee members not to report out the NWP's bill.

The day the House opened its hearing on the bill Hull wrote to William B. Bankhead, chair of the House Rules Committee, and advised him to await the administration's report on nationality before proceeding with the women's nationality bill. "I feel sure that the ladies will find that the code which we will propose will contain a solution better in consonance with their objectives than that contained in the bill they are now advocating," he assured.[113] Three days later, Frances Perkins informed Bankhead she also hoped his Committee would delay acting on this bill until the President's Interdepartmental Commission on Nationality completed its report.[114] The administration realized, as did the NWP, that passage of the equalization bill would probably hasten Senate ratification of the equal-nationality treaty. If the House Committee followed Hull's and Perkins's advice, however, the bill would sit idle indefinitely.

The NLWV continued to cultivate its relationship with the Roosevelt administration and withhold support for the latest NWP bill. According to Mildred Palmer of the NWP, Dorothy Straus had actually urged other highly placed League members to support this legislation,

---

in a more restrictive application of the rule of *jus sanguinis,* the Department submitted a memo from one of its legal advisors roundly condemning a House amendment to the bill that required a child to live in the United States five years before reaching majority. Hearings before the House Committee on Immigration and Naturalization, *To Amend the Law Relative to Citizenship and Naturalization and for Other Purposes,* 73d Cong., 2d sess., Mar. 24, 1934, 3.

113. Copy of letter from Hull to William B. Bankhead, dated Mar. 24, 1934, *NWPP.*

114. Copy of letter from Frances Perkins to Bankhead, dated Mar. 27, 1934, *NWPP.* See also copy of letter, dated Mar. 10, 1934, from Congressman T. A. Jenkins to Helen Clegg Winters, informing her that the State and Labor Departments and the NLWV remained opposed to the bill, *JNS* A-116, folder 215.

"but with the exception of two or three friendly souls, there was no comment whatsoever."[115] In a press release condemning the nationality treaty, the League issued the following enigmatic statement on the subject of expanding children's access to citizenship through their mothers: "The League believes that the fundamental right which should be considered is the best interest of the child, and not necessarily discrimination against father or mother. Equal rights for men and women may mean exactly nothing as to the nationality of their children."[116] By characterizing the derivative naturalization of minor children as strictly a child's and not a parental right, the League had managed to find a way to distinguish its nationality-rights agenda from the NWP's without appearing to compromise the goal of equal nationality rights for women. It was, however, an awkward and unconvincing effort. By the 1930s it was obvious that the nationality-rights movement was moving along a trajectory incompatible with the expectations and desires of the NLWV. The League clearly preferred to participate in a U.S.-focused effort and was equally bound by its faith in the virtues of gradual rather than seismic change. Yet, even though the debate over the treaty had begun to overrun the field the NLWV had once commanded, that organization's leaders were not willing to retire entirely and abandon their territory to the NWP. As an optimistic Alice Paul noted with relief after the House hearing on the NWP's bill, the League "did not appear for [the bill] . . . but they did not appear against it."[117] Indeed, some branches of the League had participated in the campaign for the bill, and to save face the NLWV conveyed its approval to Congress after the legislation passed.[118]

The NWP, which had established a more amicable relationship with

115. Mildred Palmer to Ruth Miller Sweet, letter dated May 2, 1934, *NWPP*.

116. Press release, NLWV, [1933], *BS*, vol. 6.

117. Copy of letter from Paul to Helen Clegg Winters, *JNS*, A-116, folder 215. The bill's avowed supporters (in addition to the NWP) included the General Federation of Women's Clubs, National Federation of Business and Professional Women's Clubs, National Association of Women Lawyers, National Council of Jewish Women, National Zonta Clubs, National Association of Women Physicians, National Association of Women Real Estate Operators, Women's International League for Peace and Freedom, National Soroptimists, and the Southern Women's National Democratic Association.

118. Other groups in the WJCC had endorsed the bill earlier. *Provide Equality in Matter of Citizenship between American Men and Women and to Clarify Status of Their Children*, 73d Cong., 2d sess., Mar. 1934, S. Rept. 865, 3. According to Stevens, when she visited Senator Pittman's office to thank him for his assistance with the treaty and bill, he showed her a memo from the NLWV received that day supporting the equalization bill but not the treaty. Letter of Stevens to Mildred Palmer, dated Aug. 3, 1934, *NWPP*.

the previous administration than with Roosevelt's, now complained about "Democratic opposition" to their nationality bill. The NWP's accusations of duplicitous actions on the part of the executive branch disturbed Secretaries Hull and Perkins, and probably the President. Both Secretaries disavowed any deliberate attempt to delay action on the bill or renege on promises to support women's nationality rights.[119] Their retreat helped clear the way for a vote on the NWP bill. When it finally reached President Roosevelt, he called a conference of advisors, which included the two sponsors of the bill, Dickstein and Copeland. After group deliberation, the President recommended some small changes in the bill's punctuation; Congress quickly complied, and the President signed the legislation on May 24, 1934—the same day the Senate ratified the equal-nationality treaty.[120] Under the new nationality law, the foreign-born child of an American woman or man assumed American citizenship at birth and maintained it, subject to certain prerequisites.[121] The new law also altered the Cable Act by extending to men the special rules for naturalization and renunciation of citizenship that since 1922 had been options available only to women in transnational marriages. It appeared that the "feminine lobby" had finally orchestrated a successful end to a splendid crusade. Women of the United States had achieved independent citizenship.

Immigration, naturalization, and expatriation policies had long defined both married women and minor children as dependents, making their citizenship and their future as residents of the United States subject to the independent actions of another family member. In the 1930s the rules governing women's and children's access to citizenship attracted great attention internationally, and although the U.S. State Department still preferred to drive these policy issues along close and par-

119. See copy of letter from Hull to Bankhead, dated Mar. 26, 1934, *NWPP*. Also, *Provide Equality in Matter of Citizenship . . .* , S. Rept. 865, 2; this report also includes a copy of a letter from Perkins to Bankhead, dated Mar. 27, 1934. See also letter from Alice Paul to Perkins, dated Mar. 26, 1934, *JNS,* A-116, folder 215.

120. Act of May 24, 1934, 48 Stat. 797. The next month the Act of June 27, 1934, 48 Stat. 1245, gave Puerto Rican women the option of repatriation if they had lost their status as American citizens prior to March 2, 1917, by marriage to an alien eligible for naturalization or by the husband's loss of U.S. citizenship. For discussion of the nationality treaty, see *CR* 78 (May 22, 1934), 9245, 9308–9309; *CR* 78 (May 24, 1934), 9489–9491.

121. The law altered the Expatriation Act of 1907, which allowed the child to assume citizenship immediately upon arrival in the United States. By 1934, a child born to a native or naturalized American had to live in the United States for at least five years before acquiring citizenship rights.

allel tracks, by early in the decade the nonresident married woman's and minor child's routes to citizenship had diverged. When the country's nationality law finally abandoned its automatic categorization of wives as adult dependents, the nation put to rest the notion that marriage constituted an act of elective expatriation.[122]

122. As more recent arguments about the status of native-born children of undocumented aliens have illustrated, the dependent status of minor children still leaves their claims to U.S. citizenship susceptible to debate.

For 1930s' cases relating to the citizenship status of minor children, see 36 Op. Atty. Gen. 535 (1932); *Perkins et al. v. Elg,* 307 U.S. 325 (1939). Only months before the *Elg* decision, the President's Interdepartmental Commission on Nationality had published its proposed nationality code. Its recommendations did not harmonize with the Court's subsequent opinion. *Nationality Laws of the United States,* 66. However, the nationality code finally enacted in 1940 did not strip American children of their citizenship because their parents chose a new nationality. Act of Aug. 16, 1940, 54 Stat. 1170.

Epilogue

May 24, 1934, was a triumphant day for equalitarian feminists in the United States. The President signed their equalization bill, the Senate ratified the equal-nationality treaty, and women could celebrate the successful culmination of their domestic struggle for equal nationality rights. The treaty marked U.S. abandonment of marital expatriation, although not the full erasure of its effects. Women who had lost their citizenship by marriage were not automatically reinstated as Americans, as Rebecca Shelley's tribulations demonstrated in striking detail. Sex discrimination would linger, its residual effects capable of affecting the citizenship of another generation.

The precedential status of *Mackenzie v. Hare* in the country's courts would also survive the abolition of marital expatriation.[1] The 1934 treaty left the legitimacy of government-initiated expatriation unchallenged. Also unsubdued was the political environment that stirred antagonism toward transnational marriages. Doubts about certain immigrant groups' willingness and capacity to assimilate and attendant

---

1. The Supreme Court took another serious look at legislative expatriation in *Perez v. Brownell,* 356 U.S. 44 (1958), and *Trop v. Dulles,* 356 U.S. 86 (1958). In these two cases the Supreme Court divided closely over Congress's authority to denationalize or denaturalize citizens. Four members of the Court believed Congress possessed no power to revoke citizenship and questioned the integrity of *Mackenzie v. Hare* as standing precedent. The Court confronted the same issue and overruled *Perez* in *Afroyim v. Rusk,* 387 U.S. 253 (1967). *Rogers v. Bellei,* 401 U.S. 815 (1971), appeared to be a retreat from *Afroyim,* but a more recent opinion was reaffirming. *Terrazas v. Vance,* 577 F.2d 7 (1978), 444 U.S. 252 (1980).

anxieties about the cultural and economic impact of immigration kept most restrictive immigration and naturalization laws firmly in place after 1934. Providing married men and women with a common set of standards for naturalization, expatriation, repatriation, and immigration marked the abandonment of one significant form of discrimination against individuals of foreign nationality or connections, but race, color, and national origin still remained weighty factors in an immigrant's attainment of permanent residency, citizenship, and social acceptance.[2]

The consummate goal of equalitarian feminists—the repudiation of The Hague convention and the global embrace of the equal-nationality treaty—also remained unrealized. American equalitarian feminists had managed to outmaneuver the critics of their blanket treaties in the United States. Yet, their opposition never conceded defeat but instead fought back with some success by urging the Roosevelt administration to break the NWP's hold on the Inter-American Commission of Women. Despite its recent achievements, the influence of the NWP within the federal government appeared to be ebbing, and the loss was particularly evident in its strained relations with the Roosevelt administration. The NWP was conspicuously and involuntarily absent from White House advisory meetings on women's issues. According to the *New York Times,* "Ever since the Roosevelt administration came in, the National League of Women Voters and the Consumers League have been numerously represented at all White House and other conferences on women' activities, relief, &c., to none of which any representative of the Woman's Party has ever been invited." The standard explanation for this partiality was the presence of Eleanor Roosevelt.[3]

On the international front, equalitarian feminists had not been able to break the stalemate with the League of Nations. The League Assembly continued to hear reports on the nationality rights of women, but five years after The Hague Conference its member nations remained deeply divided over the issue.[4] In the 1930s, most governments preferred

2. The Immigration and Nationality Act of June 27, 1952 (66 Stat. 163), abolished racial criteria for admission to the country and for naturalization. The Act of Oct. 3, 1965 (79 Stat. 911), marked the repeal of the national-origins system for selecting immigrants, which had been put in place by the Act of May 26, 1924.

3. "U.S. Move to Block a Feminism Treaty Laid to Strife Here," *New York Times,* 18 Dec. 1933.

4. League of Nations, *Nationality of Women,* A.61.1932.V (1932), and League of Nations, *Nationality and Status of Women,* A.19.1935.V (1935).

the League of Nations' Hague convention on nationality to the equal-nationality treaty, and the only consolation the NWP could draw from the situation was the absence of unified support for The Hague convention. The U.S.S.R., Chile, China, Cuba, Mexico, Norway, Sweden, Turkey, Uruguay, and the States of the Little Entente favored the principle of equality as expressed in the Montevideo treaty. Other League members supported the limited measure of equality extended by The Hague convention of 1930, while another group rejected the notion of independent citizenship for married women entirely as a threat to the family. The League of Nations Assembly adopted a resolution that acknowledged the landmark status of the Montevideo agreement, but members also reiterated the need to move quickly toward ratification of The Hague convention.[5] The Hague convention finally went into force in 1937, and the League acted no further on the question of married women's nationality rights. After World War II, that responsibility fell to the new United Nations.[6]

The League's Women's Consultative Committee on Nationality annually renewed its request to amend or delete those articles in The Hague convention that discriminated against women, and by 1935 its plea for women's nationality rights included an endorsement of the Montevideo equal rights treaty. Woman's rights organizations never reached consensus on the appropriateness of the treaty as a remedy for dependent citizenship, but the document sustained the support of several international women's groups. In addition to the League's Consultative Committee, the international women's organizations endorsing the equal rights treaty included the Inter-American Commission of Women (1933), International Soroptimists Clubs (1934), World Committee of Women Against War and Fascism (1934), Women's International League for Peace and Freedom (1934), International Alliance of

5. The League Council did hint at a willingness to move beyond the convention's parameters in the future, announcing that it would continue its investigation of international progress on women's nationality rights "in order to determine when such development has reached a point at which further concerted international action would be justified." See League of Nations, *Nationality of Women*, A.53.1935.V (1935). The Assembly adopted the resolution on Sept. 27, 1935.

6. The United Nations Convention on the Nationality of Married Women went into force on August, 11, 1958. For details on the drafting of the women's nationality convention, consult U.N. Commission on the Status of Women, *Nationality of Married Women (Report Submitted by the Secretary General)*, E/CN.6/254 (1954); U.N. Department of Economic and Social Affairs, *Convention on the Nationality of Married Women. Historical Background and Commentary*, E/CN.6/389 (1962).

Women for Suffrage and Equal Citizenship (1935), Equal Rights International (1934), International Council of Women (1935), All-Asian Conference of Women (1935), International Federation of University Women (1935), and the International Federation of Women Lawyers (1935).[7]

By the mid-1930s equalitarian feminists had reached the pinnacle of their power in the fight for equal nationality rights, but their domination of the Inter-American Commission of Women would soon face serious challenge. The Roosevelt administration's antagonism toward the Inter-American Commission subsided in 1938, but conciliation came at the NWP's expense. It was well known that equalitarian feminists, the supporters of the equal rights amendment, were not the favorites of the White House; and events at the 1938 Conference of American States in Lima, Peru, proved how far from favor the NWP had traveled. At this conference the U.S. delegation introduced one resolution proposing the reorganization of the Inter-American Commission and another endorsing protective legislation for women. The delegates averred that the U.S. government simply wanted to establish the Commission on an "official basis," which could be accomplished by having each government appoint its representative. The move was a clumsy but ultimately effective attempt to remove Doris Stevens from the Commission.[8] The delegation's other proposal supporting protective legislation was also a challenge to the present Commission's influence.

The first resolution received little support from other delegations, which objected to the insinuation that the Commission had not been operating as an official body of the Union. The Roosevelt administration nevertheless moved forward with its plan and appointed Mary Winslow of the Department of Labor's Women's Bureau as U.S. representative to the Commission. According to the U.S. State Depart-

7. National organizations in sixteen nations also favored the equal rights treaty as the optimal solution to sex discrimination. League of Nations, *Nationality and Status of Women* (1935).

8. "Bulletin of United States Delegations Proposed Resolution, Dec., 1938," copy in *DS*, 76–246, folder 373; "Memorandum Concerning the Creation and Organisation of the Inter-American Commission of Women from 1928 to 1938," ibid. The proposal appears in U.S. Department of State, *Report of the Delegation of the United States of America to the Eighth International Conference of American States. Lima, Peru. December 9–27, 1938* (Washington, D.C.: G.P.O., 1941), 205. See also U.S. Department of State, Cordell Hull, *Addresses and Statements by the Honorable Cordell Hull . . . in Connection with the Eighth Conference of American States* (Washington, D.C.: G.P.O., 1940).

ment, the Pan American Union rather than its government was responsible for Stevens's appointment as chair of the Commission, so she had never served as the official U.S. representative.[9]

The new appointee presented a striking contrast to Stevens. Winslow was a "protectionist" and thus an opponent of the equal rights amendment, and she had limited acquaintance with Latin American affairs. Eleanor Roosevelt had introduced Winslow as the Inter-American Commission of Women representative at one of her press conferences, and the gesture immediately fueled speculation about the First Lady's complicity in Stevens's removal. Roosevelt denied any involvement in the matter. Responding to the accusations of an NWP member printed in the *New York Times,* the First Lady avowed that she did not propose Winslow's appointment. "I happen to be connected with a group which does not believe as the National Woman's Party does. I think they have a good argument on an ideal basis and I have no quarrel with their advocating it. But we have to live in the world as it is." Roosevelt then added that she believed Latin American women were less prepared than women in the United States for an equal rights treaty.[10]

Secretary of Labor Perkins supported Winslow's appointment, as did Mary (Molly) Dewson. Indeed, both Perkins and Dewson had written to the State Department urging action against the Inter-American Commission in the form of a pro-protectionist statement and the removal of Stevens. After Stevens was unseated, an appreciative Dewson

9. Winslow had worked for the Department of Public Charities in New York City before her employment as an economic analyst for the Women's Bureau. At the time of her appointment she was an officer of the National Women's Trade Union League. The State Department explained it was complying with the resolution adopted by the Lima conferees on Dec. 22 instructing all countries not yet represented in the Inter-American Commission of Women to appoint a representative immediately. The resolution is printed in U.S. Department of State, *Report of the Delegation . . . to the Eighth International Conference of American States,* 130.

10. Quote taken from Bess Furman's typescript of Roosevelt's press conference, Feb. 27, 1939, as printed in Eleanor Roosevelt, *The White House Press Conferences of Eleanor Roosevelt,* ed. Maurine Beasley (New York: Garland, 1983), 94–95. See also copy of letter from Roosevelt to Una Winter, dated Feb. 28, 1939, *DS,* 76–246, folder 392A.

Eleanor Roosevelt's views on protective legislation and the equal rights amendment and treaty are examined in several essays in Joan Hoff-Wilson and Marjorie Lightman, eds., *Without Precedent. The Life and Career of Eleanor Roosevelt* (Bloomington: Indiana University Press, 1984). Lois Scharf's article, "ER and Feminism," 226–253, contains a brief discussion of Roosevelt's role in the Stevens affair and a more detailed analysis of her shifting views on an equal rights amendment. Also, Lois Scharf, *Eleanor Roosevelt: First Lady of American Liberalism* (Boston: Twayne, 1987).

assured Secretary of State Hull that "the women are immensely grateful for your appointment of Mary Winslow. The National Woman's Party may stew a little but thank Heavens they have lost, thanks to you, their strategic position." The NWP did cry foul and recruited a Congressional spokesperson to present their complaints. Senator Edward R. Burke of Nebraska agreed to introduce a resolution denouncing the action taken against Stevens.[11] Secretary Cordell Hull once again defended his Department's decision, this time in a lengthy letter to Key Pittman, chair of the Senate Foreign Relations Committee. The U.S. government, Hull argued, had never informed the Pan American Union or its Governing Board that Stevens was its designate. Furthermore, stressed Hull, the Inter-American Commission of Women was the creation of the Pan American Union but otherwise had "no direct relationship to the United States."[12] Winslow remained the U.S. representative to the Inter-American Commission of Women.

As the NWP's voice faded on the international scene, so did interest in an equal rights treaty. Yet, what the NWP had already achieved in the area of women's nationality rights represented its most significant victory in the postsuffrage years. One newspaper reporter observing the NWP in the 1930s declared that "it is no breach of confidence or courtesy to say that [the Woman's Party] . . . is actually, as well as figuratively, the small but stinging goad, the thorn in the flesh, the burr beneath the political saddle blanket. Its members glory in their position as the opposition force, the minute but mighty leaven that stirs up the otherwise inert mass."[13] The Party's participation in the struggle for equal nationality rights was a choice demonstration of its leaders' political talents. The NWP's entrance into the nationality-rights crusade in 1923 had given a noticeable boost to the movement's energy, and complacency never threatened to infect the cause after 1922. The NWP helped prod a sluggish federal government into episodic action, chal-

11. Copy of letter from Dewson to Hull, dated Feb. 15, 1939, in DS, 83-M93. Scharf, "ER and Feminism," 241–242, provides evidence that Dewson, Winslow, and Mary Anderson of the Women's Bureau (the latter an aggressive critic of the NWP) worked behind the scenes to destroy NWP influence within the Inter-American Commission of Women. Senator Burke's resolution was S. J. Res. 183, 76th Cong., 1st sess. (1939).

12. Letter of Hull to Key Pittman, Sept. 12, 1939, S. J. Res. 183, U.S. Senate, Files, RG 46, National Archives.

13. Mildred Adams, "Again Controversy Arises over Equality for Women," *New York Times*, 24 Dec.1933.

lenged gradualists' control over the pace of progress, and managed to transcend parochial concerns to combat derivative citizenship ably on an international scale. The NWP savored its successive achievements at home and abroad in the struggle for nationality rights and celebrated them as proof that the ultimate objective of legal equality for women was not only just but viable.

Organized women in the United States spent almost thirty years lobbying for the revision or repeal of nationality and immigration laws fashioned by the demands of a patriarchal society as well as its nativist element. Although the NWP and the WJCC subcommittee on nationality disagreed over the preferred pace of reform, their domestic political tactics had remained similar. As Michael McGerr has noted, even the NWP was less likely to "take to the streets" after 1920.[14] Although the nationality-rights coalition did work to educate the public on the injustices caused by marital expatriation, both the NWP and the WJCC placed almost exclusive faith in the effectiveness of their lobbying efforts. By the 1930s the participants in the independent-citizenship campaign had little reason to question that confidence. An intransigent Congress had once been the major obstacle in their course; now, the Senate, which had been more conservative than the House in its endorsements of nationality rights and immigration privileges for nonresidents, had ratified an equal-nationality treaty.

With the outstanding exception of *Mackenzie v. Hare*, supporters of equal nationality rights for women generally did not look to the courts to redress their grievances. Shelley's insistence on seeking a judicial resolution to her dilemma, for example, elicited a relatively lukewarm response from the NWP which preferred to pressure Congress more directly. In the 1920s and 1930s, judicial interpretation of the special applications of nationality and immigration laws to married women issued most often from cases involving the immigrant wives of U.S. citizens. Such cases, which could not serve as exhibitions of previous American women's struggles to recoup their citizenship, did not attract visible support from the majority of women's organizations involved in the independent-citizenship campaign.

Despite the fact that the nationality-rights campaign was unable to dispel the distrust among organized American women fostered by the

14. Michael McGerr, "Political Style and Women's Power, 1830–1930," *Journal of American History* 77 (Dec. 1990): 879–885.

conflict over the equal rights amendment, no other pre-World War II reform effort except woman suffrage rivaled it as a demonstration of the force of women's unified political strength brought to bear on the federal government. Conceived in the final years of the woman-suffrage movement, the nationality-reform movement bore a strong resemblance to the national struggle for the vote in membership and mindset. Woman suffragists had often claimed that their right to vote derived from their status as Americans, a supposition that acquired vivid nationalistic and sometimes nativistic undertones in the latter decades of the reform campaign. The sense of exceptionalism that persisted in the collective consciousness of Americans at times infused American women's appeals for the vote as well as for independent citizenship.

Much of the rhetoric promoting women's acquisition of these political rights celebrated American citizenship as a birthright of unparalleled value and distinction. Forced to demand the security of their American citizenship and its rights during years of abundant anti-immigrant sentiment, female reformers had found it highly profitable to represent the civic sensibilities of the citizen woman as singularly "American." Although woman suffragists never wholly abandoned their emphasis on equal rights based on personhood, they comprehended the benefits of fashioning an image of the American-born woman that would position her advantageously within a political culture that promoted a sense of solidarity and superiority among American-born men and women.

The fact that thousands of native-born married women began to lose their legal identities as Americans involuntarily after 1907 only magnified the need to secure public recognition of the American woman's value as a citizen. But some equalitarian feminists found such a nationalistic rendering less appealing than many of their allies in the movement for independent citizenship. For the leaders of the NWP, it could be a confining construction, one particularly inappropriate in the context of an international campaign for women's citizenship rights. The expansion of the general debate over women's nationality rights to international proportions provided the opportunity for some American feminists to break out of the narrowly nationalistic mind-set that had dominated the domestic campaign since its beginnings. The ensuing pursuit of an equal-nationality treaty represented equalitarian feminists' attempt to construct a conceptual base for independent citizenship that better served their vision of global equality for women, but the resulting skirmishes over the treaty at home and abroad left the nationality-rights movement in the United States shaken and divided.

In the 1920s the cause of equal nationality rights had accommodated both republican and liberal notions of citizenship, with their respective emphases on civic responsibility and individual rights; but the introduction of the equal-nationality treaty in 1930 threatened to destroy that visional balance, which was so critical to the reform movement's internal stability. Not only did the treaty provoke a resurgence of suspicion about the NWP's larger political objectives, it breached the rules of good citizenship as the NLWV and its closest allies understood them. Indeed, the promotions of the equal-nationality treaty, equal rights treaty, and equal rights amendment were all condemned as violations of an unwritten code of responsible citizenship.

Alexis de Tocqueville wrote that Americans "love change but they dread revolutions."[15] Tocqueville might have felt it necessary to qualify his observation if he had met some of the leaders of the NWP, but his assertion fairly described the political predilections of those reformers in the nationality-rights crusade who had great faith in the virtues of gradual reform and in the vices of revolutionary change. In the midst of the debate over the nationality treaty, Dorothy Straus of the NLWV felt compelled to warn that "sudden and violent advances have invariably been followed by repression." The reform-minded Eleanor Roosevelt had likewise counseled patience. "We must take the world as it is," she had admonished. Maud Wood Park's oft-quoted comment noting the NLWV's willingness "to go ahead slowly in order to go ahead steadily" described a strategy more than a philosophy of reform; but her accompanying statement, that the League had "not sought to lead a few women a long way quickly, but rather to lead many women a little way at a time," did convey something more profound, for not only women but the entire polity were the real objects of the League's carefully calibrated educational efforts.[16]

These and other statements by the antitreaty reformers in the nationality-rights campaign on the virtues of gradualism implied more

15. Alexis de Tocqueville, *Democracy in America*, vol. 2 (New York: Random House, Vintage Books, 1954), 270. Although Americans were his closest reference group, he was actually referring more generally to attitudes toward revolution in democratic societies.

16. The observation can also, of course, be interpreted as Park's view on the differences between the League and the NWP. Quote taken from dinner conference program for the NLWV held on April 29, 1927. Copy in *BS*, A-62, folder 23.

than just a disagreement over the instruments of women's advancement. For reform women possessing a strong communitarian outlook, the question at the heart of the treaty conflict was not really the treaty itself, which proposed to complete the work to which nationality-rights reformers were committed and which they had nearly achieved. Rather, it was the nontextual significances of the treaty that explained the intense opposition to it, at least within women's groups dedicated to independent citizenship. "We are not feminists primarily, we are citizens," Dorothy Straus had declared emphatically in an attempt to explain the NLWV's rejection of the treaty proposal.[17] It was a simple but profoundly revealing statement, one that distilled to its essential terms the larger conflict between the reformers' two camps.

Before the achievement of the vote and other political rights, a woman's value as citizen was traditionally defined almost exclusively not through a direct and public relation to the polity but indirectly through her relationship to family. The civic duties of cultivating moral sensibilities in the youngest generation of citizens and of "keeping the home fires burning" while men served their country as citizen-soldiers did give women a kind of adjunctive value as citizens. But as the Naturalization Act of 1855 and Expatriation Act of 1907 demonstrated so dramatically, molding the woman citizen from the cultural icons of nurturing mother and sacrificing wife still left her politically vulnerable. Nationality-rights reformers were thus keenly aware of the hazards of domesticating citizenship; but as they worked toward fashioning a model of good citizenship for the postsuffrage, post-Cable era, not all repudiated the belief that the citizen-mother played a distinctive role in the civic life of her community.[18]

Today, feminists are still contemplating how much women's en-

17. Quoted in William Henry Chafe, *The American Woman. Her Changing Social, Economic, and Political Roles, 1920–1970* (New York: Oxford University Press, 1972), 115.

18. More recently that discussion has been defined by a debate over the place of "maternalist thinking" in the practices and theorization of citizenship. See Jean Bethke Elshtain, *Public Man, Private Woman. Women in Social and Political Thought* (Princeton, N.J.: Princeton University Press, 1981), Sara Ruddick, "Maternal Thinking," *Feminist Studies* 6 (1980): 342–367; Mary G. Dietz, "Citizenship with a Feminist Face. The Problem with Maternal Thinking," *Political Theory* 13 (Feb. 1985): 19–37; Patricia Boling, "The Democratic Potential of Mothering," *Political Theory* 19 (Nov. 1991): 606–625; Carole Pateman, "Equality, Difference, Subordination: The Politics of Motherhood and Women's Citizenship," in *Beyond Equality and Difference. Citizenship, Feminist Politics and Female Subjectivity,* ed. Gisela Bock and Susan James (London and New York: Routledge, 1992), 17–31; Patrice DiQuinzio, "Feminist Theory and the Question of Citizenship: A Response to Dietz' Critique of Maternalism," *Women & Politics* 15 (1995): 23–42.

trance into the political arena has affected the practices of citizenship. The debate over the theoretical structuring of, and the relationship between, "public" and "private" life has grown increasingly complex as has the influence of feminism on the elements of citizenship. Interwar feminists' engagement with these matters was limited. The leaders of the nationality-rights crusade too often slighted issues of race and class in their discussions of the pursuit of "full citizenship for women" and were less than articulate about how feminist values might render a new paradigm of citizenship. Yet, until the 1980s, these observations could generally describe contemporary feminist writings. Those scholars now engaged in the formulation of a theory of feminist citizenship can perhaps best appreciate the exploratory offerings of this former generation of feminists and the pertinence of their struggles.[19]

The women of the nationality-rights crusade found themselves struggling to identify what Sara Evans has called upon feminist scholars to explore—a "feminist conception of public life."[20] For interwar feminists, the task was not a simple one because, for many, it meant a searching inquiry into the undisputed but thinly defined relationship between feminism and citizenship. For equalitarian feminists, there was no apparent tension between these concepts. American feminists were by definition good citizens because they promoted the ideals of equal rights and individualism associated with a liberal society. For those favoring a more communitarian than equalitarian vision, however, this resolution of the tension was problematical. The introduction of the equal-nationality treaty highlighted these differences among nationality-rights reformers.[21]

As long as all participants agreed that the purpose of the campaign for equal nationality rights was strictly the removal of sex discrimina-

19. For discussions of theoretical possibilities, see Mary G. Dietz, "Context Is All: Feminism and Theories of Citizenship," *Daedalus* 116 (Fall 1987): 1–24; Kathleen B. Jones, "Citizenship in a Woman-Friendly Polity," *Signs* 15 (Summer 1990): 781–812; Sylvia Walby, "Is Citizenship Gendered?" *Sociology* 28 (May 1994): 379–395.

20. Sara M. Evans, "Women's History and Political Theory: Toward a Feminist Approach to Public Life," in *Visible Women: New Essays on American Activism,* ed. Nancy A. Hewitt and Suzanne Lebsock (Urbana and Chicago: University of Illinois Press, 1993), 131.

21. Other scholars have explored the diversity of political traditions or cultures evident during the Progressive years and interwar years. Two analyses that I found particularly helpful on this subject were John D. Buenker, "Sovereign Individuals and Organic Networks: Political Cultures in Conflict during the Progressive Era," *American Quarterly* 40 (June 1988): 187–204, and Smith, " 'One United People,' " 229–293.

tion from the country's nationality laws, the sameness-versus-difference debate that so dominated interwar discussions of the wisdom or folly of an equal rights amendment was avoidable. Its achievement chiefly in the hands of native-born veterans of the suffrage campaign, independent citizenship was defined as a political entitlement and thus shared woman suffrage's emphasis on women's equal access to and participation in a political community. This was, however, a narrow representation of what citizenship was worth to women, as the petitions of the Citizen Wives Organization and Shelley's determined pleas for freedom of thought had demonstrated.

The intensity of the concern over an equal right amendment's impact on protective labor legislation suggested and women's participation in the administration of New Deal social welfare programs reinforced female reformers' movement away from a conceptualization of citizenship shaped by the long suffrage movement.[22] Suffrage and nationality-rights proponents had cultivated an understanding of and focus on what T. H. Marshall termed the rights of political citizenship, but by the end of the nationality-rights crusade it was apparent that a new dimension of citizenship was poised to gain greater prominence.[23]

The two world wars bracketed transformative years in Americans'

22. Wendy Sarvasy sees female reformers grappling with these issues as they sought to construct a feminist welfare state and to realize full citizenship for women. According to Sarvasy, "They assumed that a feminist welfare state with its guiding principle of gender equality would provide the context for the new women citizens and that the process of women becoming citizens would advance feminist welfare state development." "Beyond the Difference versus Equality Policy Debate: Postsuffrage Feminism, Citizenship, and the Quest for a Feminist Welfare State," *Signs* 17 (Winter 1992): 329.

23. Marshall provided this trifocal view of the "elements" of citizenship (T. H. Marshall, "Citizenship and Social Class," in T. H. Marshall and Tom Bottomore, *Citizenship and Social Class* [Concord, Mass.: Pluto Press, 1992], 8):

> The civil element is composed of the rights necessary for individual freedom—liberty of the person, freedom of speech, thought and faith, the right to own property and to conclude valid contracts, and the right to justice.... By the political element I mean the right to participate in the exercise of political power, as a member of a body invested with political power or as an elector of the members of such a body.... By the social element I mean the whole range from the right to a modicum of economic welfare and security to the right to share to the full in the social heritage and to live the life of a civilised being.

I have found Marshall's multidimensional description of citizenship useful but not his overly neat periodization of each element's "formative" stage, which, as several others have noted, obscures the disparate histories of various social groups' access to those enumerated rights. I would also broaden the definitions of each of these components of citizenship to include some recognition of service and obligation.

understanding of the elements of citizenship: the ratification of the Nineteenth Amendment left the invisible color line drawn around political rights untouched but nevertheless continued to carry both real and symbolic significance for many American women; the Supreme Court inaugurated the gradual process of nationalizing the liberty guarantees of the Bill of Rights; Congress passed a new citizenship law for American Indians; the federal government began its construction of a welfare system that would gradually alter the public's understanding of the government's obligations to its citizens; and American women secured the restoration of their independent claims to citizenship.Female activists had long been involved in the business of improving the law's protection of women as wives, mothers, and wage earners. And as federal and state programs to assist female-headed families with children increased in the interwar years, so did women activists' discussion of the importance of guaranteeing the social elements of citizenship before declaring that women had indeed achieved "full citizenship." Asserting women's claim on the new social rights of citizenship, however, first required securing women's grasp on that citizenship; the nationality-rights movement provided that security. The shift in female reformers' emphasis from political to social citizenship was significant because it brought the sameness-difference question directly to bear on their theoretical organization of citizenship. Whether feminists should advocate a "neutral" form of citizenship or assert women's unique contributions and needs as citizens was a question female activists had to grapple with then—and now.

Citizenship and feminism have both sustained multiple understandings. It is not surprising, then, that interwar feminists could not agree on one model of the feminist citizen. In the nationality-rights movement's final years, this disagreement and other conflicts threatened to obscure its goals, but its participants' shared commitments to political activism and belief in the value of membership in a national community continued to furnish a strong incentive to persevere in the work of women's citizenship rights. The nationality-rights crusade yielded evidence of a struggle of identity among organized women as they deliberated with new intentness on what it meant to be both a feminist and a citizen. The fact that activist women then proceeded to disagree on the answer to this fundamental question should be interpreted as a sign not of weakness but of strength—of female reformers' collective intellectual vitality. Indeed, the absence of such a debate would have been the true incriminating evidence, the proof of organized women's inability or reluctance to explore the tangled roots of their commitment to woman's rights. To judge these voices otherwise would not only slight the dialogic contributions of the first generation of postsuffrage feminists but the work of others who have faithfully cultivated and broadened this conversation. It remains, decades later, a discussion we are wise to sustain and enrich with the insights of our generations.

Bibliography

Archival Collections

Lutz, Alma. Papers. Schlesinger Library, Radcliffe College. Cambridge, Mass.

Park, Maud Wood. Papers. Women's Rights Collection, Schlesinger Library, Radcliffe College. Cambridge, Mass.

Roiter-Nyclich, Bella. Papers. Agudath Israel Archives. New York, New York.

Shelley, Rebecca. Papers. Michigan Historical Collections, Bentley Library, University of Michigan. Ann Arbor.

Sherwin, Belle. Papers. Schlesinger Library, Radcliffe College. Cambridge, Mass.

Smith, Jane Norman. Papers. Schlesinger Library, Radcliffe College. Cambridge, Mass.

Stevens, Doris. Papers. Schlesinger Library, Radcliffe College. Cambridge, Mass.

United HIAS Service. Records. HIAS-HICEM I Series Xb. Record Group 245.4. Yivo Institute for Jewish Research. New York, New York.

U.S. Department of Labor. Bureau of Immigration and Naturalization Files. Record Group 85. National Archives.

U.S. Department of Labor. Chief Clerk's Files. Record Group 174. National Archives.

U.S. Department of State. Visa Division Files. Record Group 59. National Archives Branch Depository, Suitland, Md.

U.S. Senate. Files. Record Group 46. National Archives.

White, Sue Shelton. Papers. Schlesinger Library, Radcliffe College. Cambridge, Mass.

Records on Microfilm

Papers of Belle Sherwin. Schlesinger Library, Radcliffe College. Cambridge, Mass.

Papers of Emily Greene Balch, 1875–1961. Swarthmore College Peace Collection. Wilmington, Del.: Scholarly Resources, 1988.

Papers of the League of Women Voters, 1918–1974, pt. I. Consulting editor Susan Ware. Frederick, Md.: University Publications of America, 1985.

Papers of the National Woman's Party, 1913–1972, ser. 1.. Glen Rock, N.J.: Microfilming Corporation of America, 1972.

Women's Joint Congressional Committee Records, 1920–1970. Washington, D.C.: Library of Congress, 1983.

Books, Pamphlets, and Essays in Books

Bar-Yaacov, Nissim. *Dual Nationality.* London: Stevens & Sons,1961.

Basch, Norma. *In the Eyes of the Law. Women, Marriage, and Property in Nineteenth-Century New York.* Ithaca, N.Y.: Cornell University Press, 1982.

Becker, Susan D. *The Origins of the Equal Rights Amendment: American Feminism between the Wars.* Westport, Conn.: Greenwood Press, 1981.

Beecher, Catharine. *Treatise on Domestic Economy for the Use of Young Ladies at Home and at School.* New York: Harper and Brothers, 1859.

Beiner, Ronald, ed. *Theorizing Citizenship.* Albany: State University of New York Press, 1995.

Blaine, James, J. W. Buel, John Clark Ridpath, and Benj. Butterworth. *Columbus and Columbia.* Philadelphia: Historical Publishing, 1892.

Bock, Gisela, and Susan James, eds. *Beyond Equality and Difference. Citizenship, Feminist Politics and Female Subjectivity.* London and New York: Routledge, 1992.

Borchard, Edwin. *The Diplomatic Protection of Citizens Abroad.* New York: Banks Law, 1927.

Boswell, Helen Varick. "Promoting Americanization." In *Americanization,* compiled and edited by Winthrop Talbot, revised and enlarged by Julia E. Johnsen, 297–301. New York: H. W. Wilson, 1920.

Boulding, Elise. "The Pacifist as Citizen." In *Pacifism and Citizenship. Can They Coexist?,* edited by Kenneth M. Jensen and Kimber M. Schraub, 5–14. Washington, D.C.: United States Institute of Peace, 1991.

Breckinridge, Sophonisba P. *Marriage and the Civic Rights of Women. Separate Domicil and Independent Citizenship.* Chicago: University of Chicago Press, 1931.

———. *Women in the Twentieth Century: A Study of Their Political, Social, and Economic Activities.* New York and London: McGraw-Hill, 1933.

Boyd, Mary Sumner. *The Woman Citizen: A General Handbook of Civics, with Special Consideration of Women's Citizenship.* New York: Frederick A. Stokes, 1918.

Burgess, Thomas. *Foreign-Born Americans and Their Children*. New York: Department of Missions and Church Extensions of the Episcopal Church, n. d.

Cable, John L. *Decisive Decisions of United States Citizenship*. Charlottesville, Va.: Michie, 1967.

Calavita, Kitty. *U.S. Immigration Law and the Control of Labor: 1820–1924*. London and Orlando, Fla.: Academic Press, 1984.

Catt, Carrie Chapman, and Nettie Rogers Shuler. *Woman Suffrage and Politics: The Inner Story of the Suffrage Movement*. New York: Scribner, 1926.

Chafe, William Henry. *The American Woman. Her Changing Social, Economic, and Political Roles, 1920–1970*. New York: Oxford University Press, 1972.

———. "Women's History and Political History: Some Thoughts on Progressivism and the New Deal." In *Visible Women. New Essays on American Activism*, edited by Nancy A Hewitt and Suzanne Lebsock, 101–118. Urbana: University of Illinois Press, 1993.

Chan, Sucheng. "The Exclusion of Chinese Women, 1870–1943." In *Entry Denied. Exclusion and the Chinese Community in America, 1882–1943*, edited by Sucheng Chan, 94–146. Philadelphia: Temple University Press, 1991.

Clark, Jane Perry. *Deportation of Aliens from the United States to Europe*. New York: Columbia University Press, 1931.

"Cleaning Up the Cable Act." *Bulletin of the National League of Women Voters*. February 1930.

Cole, William, and Florett Robinson, eds. *Women Are Wonderful. A History of Cartoons of a Hundred Years with America's Most Controversial Figure*. Cambridge, Mass.: Riverside Press, 1956.

Connelly, Mark Thomas. *The Response to Prostitution in the Progressive Era*. Chapel Hill: University of North Carolina Press, 1980.

Costin, Lela B. *Two Sisters for Social Justice: A Biography of Grace and Edith Abbott*. Urbana: University of Illinois Press, 1983.

Cott, Nancy F. *The Grounding of Modern Feminism*. New Haven, Conn.: Yale University Press, 1987.

Daniels, Roger. *Coming to America. A History of Immigration and Ethnicity in American Life*. New York: HarperCollins, 1990.

Dinnerstein, Leonard, and David M. Reimers. *Ethnic Americans. A History of Immigration and Assimilation*. New York: Dodd, Mead, 1975.

Drachsler, Julius. *Democracy and Assimilation: The Blending of Immigrant Heritages in America*. New York: Macmillan, 1920.

———. *Intermarriage in New York City. A Statistical Study of the Amalgamation of European Peoples*. Vol. 94 of *Studies in History, Economics and Public Law*. New York: Columbia University, 1921.

DuBois, Ellen Carol. *Feminism and Suffrage. The Emergence of an Independent Women's Movement in America, 1848–1869*. Ithaca, N.Y.: Cornell University Press, 1978.

Eastman, Allan J. "Australian Nationality Legislation: Nationality of Married Women." In *The British Year Book of International Law,* 179–181. London: Oxford University Press, 1937.

Elshtain, Jean Bethke. *Public Man, Private Woman. Women in Social and Political Thought.* Princeton, N.J.: Princeton University Press, 1981.

Evans, Sara. "Women's History and Political Theory: Toward a Feminist Approach to Public Life." In *Visible Women. New Essays on American Activism,* edited by Nancy A. Hewitt and Suzanne Lebsock, 119–139. Urbana and Chicago: University of Illinois Press, 1993.

Fleming, Denna Frank. *The United States and the World Court, 1920–1966.* Rev. ed. New York: Russell and Russell, 1968.

Flexner, Eleanor. *Century of Struggle: The Women's Rights Movement in the United States.* Rev. ed. Cambridge, Mass.: Belknap Press, 1975.

Florence, Lella Secor. "The Ford Peace Ship and After." In *We Did Not Fight. 1914–1918 Experiences of War Resisters,* edited by Julian Bell. London: Cobden-Sanderson, 1935.

Flournoy, Richard W., Jr., and Manley O. Hudson, eds. *A Collection of Nationality Laws of Various Countries as Contained in Constitutions, Statutes and Treaties.* New York: Oxford University Press, 1929.

Ford, Linda G. *Iron-Jawed Angels. The Suffrage Militancy of the National Woman's Party 1912–1920.* Lanham, Md.: University Press of America, 1991.

Gordon, Milton M. *Assimilation in American Life. The Role of Race, Religion, and National Origins.* New York: Oxford University Press, 1964.

Handlin, Oscar. *Race and Nationality in American Life.* Garden City, N.Y.: Doubleday, Anchor Books, 1957.

Harbaugh, William H. *Lawyer's Lawyer. The Life of John W. Davis.* New York: Oxford University Press, 1973. Reprint, Charlottesville: University of Virginia Press, 1990.

Hartmann, Edward George. *The Movement to Americanize the Immigrant.* New York: Columbia University Press, 1948.

Hathaway, Grace. *Fate Rides a Tortoise; A Biography of Ellen Spencer Mussey.* Philadelphia: John C. Winston, 1937.

Hazard, Henry B. "International Problems in Respect to Nationality by Naturalization and of Married Women." In *Proceedings of the American Society for International Law . . . April 22–24, 1926.* Washington, D.C., 1926.

Higham, John. *Strangers in the Land: Patterns of American Nativism, 1860–1925.* New York: Atheneum, 1963, 1971.

Hoff, Joan. *Law, Gender, and Injustice. A Legal History of U.S. Women.* New York: New York University Press, 1991.

Hoff-Wilson, Joan, and Marjorie Lightman, eds. *Without Precedent. The Life and Career of Eleanor Roosevelt.* Bloomington: Indiana University Press, 1984.

Hudson, Manley O. *International Legislation. A Collection of Texts of Multipartite International Instruments of General Interest.* Vol. 5. Washington, D.C.: Carnegie Endowment for International Peace, 1936.

———. *The Permanent Court of International Justice and the Question of*

American Participation. Cambridge, Mass.: Harvard University Press, 1925.

Hutchinson, E. P. *Immigrants and Their Children, 1850–1950.* Census Monograph Series. New York: Wiley, 1956.

———. *Legislative History of American Immigration Policy, 1798–1965.* Philadelphia: University of Pennsylvania Press, 1981.

Hyde, Charles Cheney. *International Law: Chiefly as Interpreted and Applied by the United States.* Vol. 2. 2d rev. ed. Boston: Little, Brown, 1947.

International Woman Suffrage Alliance. *Programme of Women's Rights Adopted at the Eighth Congress.* Geneva, 1920.

Irwin, Inez Haynes. *The Story of the Woman's Party.* New York: Harcourt, Brace, 1921.

James, Susan. "The Good-Enough Citizen: Female Citizenship and Independence." In *Beyond Equality and Difference. Citizenship, Feminist Politics and Female Subjectivity,* edited by Gisela Bock and Susan James, 48–65. London and New York: Routledge, 1992.

Johnson, Donald Bruce, comp. *National Party Platforms.* Vol. 1: *1840–1956.* Urbana: University of Illinois Press, 1978.

Kallen, Horace M. *Individualism. An American Way of Life.* New York: Liveright, 1933.

Kann, Mark E. "Individualism, Civic Virtue, and Gender in America." In *Studies in American Political Development. An Annual,* vol. 4, edited by Karen Orren and Stephen Skowronek, 46–81. New Haven, Conn..: Yale University Press, 1990.

Karst, Kenneth L. *Belonging to America. Equal Citizenship and the Constitution.* New Haven, Conn.: Yale University Press, 1989.

Kellor, Frances A. *Americanization of Women: A Discussion of an Emergency Created by Granting the Vote to Women in New York State.* New York, n.p., c. 1918.

Kerber, Linda. *Women of the Republic. Intellect and Ideology in Revolutionary America.* Chapel Hill: University of North Carolina Press for the Institute of Early American History and Culture, 1980.

Kettner, James. *The Development of American Citizenship, 1608–1870.* Chapel Hill: University of North Carolina Press, 1978.

Kraditor, Aileen S. *The Ideas of the Woman Suffrage Movement, 1890–1920.* New York: Columbia University Press, 1965; New York: Norton, 1981.

Krysto, Christina. "The Home Teachers." In *Americanization.* N.p.: General Federation of Women's Clubs, n.d.

Lawrence, William Beach. *Disabilities of American Women Abroad: Foreign Treaties of the United States in Conflict with State Laws Relative to the Transmission of Real Estate to Aliens.* New York: Baker, Voorhis, 1871.

League for the Protection of Immigrants. *Annual Report.* N.p., 1910–1911.

Lemons, J. Stanley. *The Woman Citizen. Social Feminism in the 1920s.* Urbana: University of Illinois Press, 1973.

Lissak, Rivka Shpak. *Pluralism & Progressives. Hull House and the New Immigrants, 1890–1919.* Chicago: University of Chicago Press, 1989.

Lunardini, Christine. *From Equal Suffrage to Equal Rights: Alice Paul and the National Woman's Party, 1913–1928*. New York: New York University Press, 1986.

Marshall, T. H., and Tom Bottomore. *Citizenship and Social Class*. Concord, Mass.: Pluto Press, 1992.

Maxson, Charles Hartshorn. *Citizenship*. New York: Oxford University Press, 1930.

Montgomery, Maureen. *"Gilded Prostitution": Status, Money, and Transatlantic Marriages, 1870–1914*. London and New York: Routledge, 1989.

Muncy, Robyn. *Creating a Female Dominion in American Reform, 1890–1935*. New York: Oxford University Press, 1991.

O'Neill, William L. *Everyone Was Brave: A History of Feminism in America*. Chicago: Quadrangle Press, 1974.

Park, Maud Wood. *Front Door Lobby*. Boston: Beacon Press, 1960.

——. *A Record of Four Years in the National League of Women Voters 1920–1924*. Cleveland: Acorn, [1924].

Pateman, Carole. *The Disorder of Women. Democracy, Feminism, and Political Theory*. Cambridge, U.K.: Polity Press, 1989.

——. "Equality, Difference, Subordination: The Politics of Motherhood and Women's Citizenship." In *Beyond Equality and Difference. Citizenship, Feminist Politics and Female Subjectivity*. Edited by Gisela Bock and Susan James, 17–31. London and New York: Routledge, 1992.

Phillips, Anne. "Citizenship and Feminist Theory." In *Citizenship*, edited by Geoff Andrews, 76–88. London: Lawrence & Wishart, 1991.

Proceedings of the American Society for International Law at Its Twentieth Annual Meeting Held . . . April 22–24, 1926. Washington, D.C., 1926.

Reeve, Tapping. *The Law of Baron and Femme*, 2d ed. Burlington, Vt.: Chauncey Goodrich, 1846.

Roberts, Peter. *The Problem of Americanization*. New York: Macmillan, 1920.

Roelofs, H. Mark. *The Tension of Citizenship. Private Man and Public Duty*. New York: Rinehart, 1957.

Rogow, Faith. *Gone to Another Meeting. The National Council of Jewish Women, 1893–1993*. Tuscaloosa: University of Alabama Press, 1993.

Roosevelt, Eleanor. *The White House Press Conferences of Eleanor Roosevelt*. Edited with an introduction by Maurine Beasley. New York: Garland, 1983.

Rosenne, Shabtai, ed. *League of Nations. Conference for the Codification of International Law [1930]*. Vol. 3. Dobbs Ferry, N.Y.: Oceana, 1975.

Salmon, Marylynne. *Women and the Law of Property in Early America*. Chapel Hill: University of North Carolina Press, 1986.

Scharf, Lois. *Eleanor Roosevelt: First Lady of American Liberalism*. Boston: Twayne, 1987.

——. "ER and Feminism." In *Without Precedent: The Life and Career of Eleanor Roosevelt*. Edited by Joan Hoff-Wilson and Marjorie Lightman, 226–253. Bloomington: Indiana University Press, 1984.

Schuck, Peter H., and Rogers M. Smith. *Citizenship without Consent. Illegal Aliens in the American Polity*. New Haven, Conn.: Yale University Press, 1985.

Schuster, Ernest J. "The Effect of Marriage on Nationality. In *Report of the*

Thirty-Second Conference of the International Law Association, 9–24. London, 1924.

Scott, James Brown. *The International Conference of American States, 1889– 1928.* New York: Oxford University Press, 1931.

———. *Observations on Nationality with Especial Reference to The Hague Convention of April 12th, 1930.* New York: Oxford University Press, 1931.

Seckler-Hudson, Catheryn. *Statelessness: With Special Reference to the United States: A Study in Nationality and Conflict of Laws.* Washington, D.C.: Digest Press, 1934.

Shklar, Judith N. *American Citizenship. The Quest for Inclusion.* Cambridge, Mass.: Harvard University Press, 1991.

Sinopoli, Richard C. *The Foundations of American Citizenship. Liberalism, the Constitution, and Civic Virtue.* New York: Oxford University Press, 1992.

Stanton, Elizabeth Cady, Susan B. Anthony, and Matilda Joslyn Gage. *The History of Woman Suffrage.* 6 vols. New York: Foster and Wells, 1881–1922.

Stevens, Doris. *Jailed for Freedom.* New York: Boni and Liveright, 1920.

Ten Years of Growth. The National League of Women Voters 1920–1930. N.p.: National League of Women Voters, May 1930.

Terborg-Penn, Rosalyn. "Discontented Black Feminists: Prelude and Postscript to the Passage of the Nineteenth Amendment." In *Decades of Discontent: The Women's Movement, 1920–1940,* edited by Lois Scharf and Joan M. Jensen, 261–278. Westport, Conn.: Greenwood Press, 1983.

Tocqueville, Alexis de. *Democracy in America.* Vol. 2. New York: Random House, Vintage Books, 1954.

Tsiang, I-Mien. *The Question of Expatriation in America Prior to 1907.* Johns Hopkins University Studies in Historical and Political Science, Series 60, 3. Baltimore: Johns Hopkins University Press, 1942.

Van Dyne, Frederick. *Citizenship of the United States.* Rochester, N.Y.: Lawyers' Cooperative, 1904.

Verbatim Record of the Plenary Sessions of the Fifth International Conference of American States. Vol. 1. Santiago, Chile: Imprente Universitaria, 1923.

Vogel, Ursula. "Is Citizenship Gender-Specific?" In *The Frontiers of Citizenship,* edited by Ursula Vogel and Michael Moran, 58–85. London: Macmillan, 1991.

Waltz, Waldo Emerson. *The Nationality of Married Women. A Study of Domestic Policies and International Legislation.* Illinois Studies in the Social Sciences 22. Urbana: University of Illinois Press, 1937.

Weatherford, Doris. *Foreign and Female. Immigrant Women in America, 1840–1930.* New York: Schocken Books, 1986.

Webster, Prentiss. *Law of Naturalization in the United States of America and Other Countries.* Boston: Little, Brown, 1895.

Wehberg, Hans. *The Problem of an International Court of Justice.* Oxford: Clarendon Press, for the Carnegie Endowment for International Peace, 1917.

Wise, John S. *A Treatise on American Citizenship.* Northport, N.Y.: Edward Thompson, 1906.

Woodward, Elizabeth A. *Educational Opportunities for Women from Other Lands.* Bulletin 718. Albany: University of the State of New York, 1920.
Young, Louise M. *In the Public Interest. The League of Women Voters, 1920–1970.* Westport, Conn.: Greenwood Press, 1989.

Journal and Periodical Articles

Abbott, Grace, and Frances Wetmore. "The Carrie Chapman Catt Citizenship Course: What Do We Mean by Americanization?" *Woman Citizen* 5 (September 4, 1920): 378–379, 384.
"Alice Paul Returns." *Equal Rights* 27 (April 1941): 31.
"Alien Wives and Alien Husbands." *Woman Citizen* 2 (December 22, 1917): 78.
"Aliens—Necessity of Residence for Naturalization by Marriage." *Harvard Law Review* 22 (May 1909): 532–533.
"Aliens—Status of Alien Wives of Citizens." *University of Pennsylvania Law Review* 74 (January 1926): 315.
Appleman, Irving. "The Supreme Court on Expatriation: An Historical Review." *Federal Bar Journal* 23 (Fall 1963): 351–373.
Aylsworth, Leon E. "The Passing of Alien Suffrage." *American Political Science Review* 25 (February 1931): 114–116.
Bagley, Grace H. "Americanization as War Service" and "Program of Suffrage Americanization Committee," *Woman Citizen* 1 (June 30, 1917): 84–87.
Baker, Paula. "The Domestication of Politics: Women and American Political Society, 1780-1920." *American Historical Review* 89 (June 1984): 620–647.
Bari, Valeska. "Citizens Who May Not Have Wives. Loyal Chinese Americans, Deprived by Law of an Elemental Human Right, Are Asking Us to End This Injustice." *Woman Citizen* 12 (December 1927): 20–21.
Bartlett, C. A. Hereshoff. "Women's Expatriation by Marriage." *Albany Law Journal* 70 (1908): 176–181.
Belmont, Mrs. O.H.P. "Are Women Really Citizens? A Question Every Country Must Soon Answer. . . . " *Good Housekeeping* 93 (September 1931): 99, 132, 135.
Berrien, Laura M. "Nationality and International Relations." *Women Lawyers Journal* 19 (Fall 1931): 31–34.
Bevis, Howard. "The Deportation of Aliens." *University of Pennsylvania Law Review* 68 (January 1920): 97–119.
Binney, Horace. "The Alienigenae of the United States." *American Law Register* 2 (February 1854): 193–210.
Black, Ruby A. "Officials Hear Pleas for Equal Nationality." *Equal Rights* 15 (December 21, 1929): 363–364.
———. "United States Refuses to Accept Unequal Code." *Equal Rights* 16 (April 19, 1930): 83–85.

Blackwell, Henry. "Italian Women in New York Tenements." *Woman's Journal*, July 23, 1904, 236.

Boling, Patricia. "The Democratic Potential of Mothering." *Political Theory* 19 (November 1991): 606–625.

Borchard, Edwin M. "The Citizenship of Native-Born Women Who Married Foreigners before March 2, 1907, and Acquired a Foreign Domicile." *American Journal of International Law* 29 (July 1935): 396–422.

———. "Decadence of the American Doctrine of Voluntary Expatriation." *American Journal of International Law* 25 (April 1931): 312–316.

Bouvé, Clement L. "The Immigration Act and Returning Resident Aliens." *University of Pennsylvania Law Review* 59 (March 1911): 359–372.

Boyd, Mary Sumner. "Have You Been Enfranchised Lately? Naturalization." *Woman Citizen* 2 (January 5, 1918): 114.

Buenker, John D. "Sovereign Individuals and Organic Networks: Political Cultures in Conflict during the Progressive Era." *American Quarterly* 40 (June 1988): 187–204.

Cable, John L. "The Citizenship of American Women." *Atlantic Monthly* 145 (May 1930): 649–653.

"Can the Wife and Daughter Vote?" Letter to the Editor. *Woman Citizen* 4 (April 24, 1920): 1167–1168.

Catt, Carrie Chapman. "The Nation Calls." *Woman Citizen* 3 (March 29, 1919): 917–921.

Catt, Carrie Chapman, and Jane Brooks. "The League of Women Voters." *Woman Citizen* 3 (May 3, 1919): 1044–1045.

"Chinese Wives of Citizens." *Georgetown Law Journal* 14 (January 1926): 202–206.

"Citizenship for Women." *Immigrants in America Review* 1 (September 1915): 12–13.

"Congress and Immigration." *Interpreter* 8 (February 1928): 3–8.

Crane, Lucius F. "The Nationality of Married Women." *Journal of Comparative Legislation and International Law*, 3d ser., 7 (1925): 53–60.

Das, Mary K. "A Woman without a Country." *Nation* 123 (August 4, 1926): 105–106.

Dietz, Mary G. "Citizenship with a Feminist Face: The Problem with Maternal Thinking." *Political Theory* 13 (February 1985): 19–37.

———. "Context Is All: Feminism and Theories of Citizenship." *Daedalus* 116 (Fall 1987): 1–24.

DiQuinzio, Patrice. "Feminist Theory and the Question of Citizenship: A Response to Dietz' Critique of Maternalism." *Women & Politics* 15 (1995): 23–42.

Dorr, Rheta Childe. "Let Women Settle It." *Independent Woman* 10 (November 1931): 483.

Eastman, Crystal. "Suffragists Ten Years After." *New Republic* 35 (June 27, 1923): 118–119.

Eckerson, Helen F. "Nonquota Immigration, Fiscal Years 1925–1944." *U.S. Immigration Naturalization Service Monthly Review* 3 (August 1945): 185–190.

"Equal Nationality Rights for Women." *Congressional Digest* 9 (November 1930): 257–288.

"Expatriation by Marriage." Editorial. *Virginia Law Register*, n.s., 1 (March 1916): 865–867.

Feeks, Dan. "Putting Mother in Her Right Place." *World Outlook* 4 (October 1918): 9–10.

Fields, Harold. "Shall We Naturalize Aliens Whose Wives Are Living Abroad?" *New American* 1 (August 1925): 1–8.

Flournoy, Richard W., Jr. "Measures for Revising Nationality Laws of the United States." *Federal Bar Journal* 2 (April 1934): 37–42, 62, 67.

———. "Naturalization and Expatriation." *Yale Law Journal* 31 (June 1922): 702–719, 848–868.

———. "The New Married Women's Citizenship Law." *Yale Law Journal* 33 (December 1923): 159–170.

Gordon, Charles. "The Citizen and the State: Power of Congress to Expatriate American Citizens." *Georgetown Law Journal* 53 (Winter 1965): 315–364.

Gundersen, Joan R. "Independence, Citizenship, and the American Revolution." *Signs* 13 (Autumn 1987): 59–77.

H.E.A. "Citizenship, Expatriation, Suffrage." *California Law Review* 4 (March 1916): 238–239.

Harrison, Gladys. "The Nationality of Married Women." *New York University Law Quarterly Review* 9 (June 1932): 445–462.

Hesse, Sigfried. "The Constitutional Status of the Lawfully Admitted Permanent Resident Alien: The Pre-1917 Cases." *Yale Law Journal* 68 (July 1959): 1578–1625.

Hill, Cyril D. "Citizenship of Married Women." *American Journal of International Law* 18 (October 1924): 720–736.

Hoinko, Marjorie P. "Naturalizing a Yankee. An American Woman Who Married an Alien before the Cable Act Became Law Measures the Red Tape That Restored Her Citizenship." *Woman's Journal*, April 1928, 13, 38.

Hover, Ernest J. "Citizenship of Women in the United States." *American Journal of International Law* 26 (October 1932): 700–719.

Hudson, Manley O. "The Hague Convention of 1930 and the Nationality of Women." *American Journal of International Law* 27 (January 1933): 117–122.

Hunt, Gaillard. "The New Citizenship Law." *North American Review* 185 (July 5, 1907): 530–539.

Hyde, Charles Cheney. "Aspects of Marriage between Persons of Differing Nationalities." *American Journal of International Law* 24 (October 1930): 742–745.

———. "The Non-Recognition and Expatriation of Naturalized American Citizens," pt. 2. *American Journal of International Law* 19 (October 1925): 742–744.

"I Am a Citizen, Too." *Life and Labor* 7 (May 1918): 95–96.

"Is the Quota More Sacred Than the Family?" *Interpreter* 6 (October 1927): 3–7.

Jacobs, M. W. "The Requisites of a Change of National Domicile." *American Law Review* 13 (January 1879): 261–279.

Jessup, Philip C. "Some Phases of the Administrative and Judicial Interpretation of the Immigration Act of 1924." *Yale Law Journal* 35 (April 1926): 705–724.

Jones, Kathleen B. "Citizenship in a Woman-Friendly Polity." *Signs* 15 (Summer 1990): 781–812.

Kelley, Florence. "Shall Women Be Equal before the Law." *Nation* 114 (April 12, 1922): 421.

Kerber, Linda K. "Women and Individualism in American History." *Massachusetts Review* 30 (Winter 1989): 589–609.

Lambie, Margaret. "Presumption of Cessation of Citizenship: Its Effect on International Claims." *American Journal of International Law* 24 (April 1930): 264–278.

———. "This Question of Nationality." *Independent Woman* 9 (May 1930): 199, 219, 222.

Lape, Esther. "Americanizing Our New Women Citizens." *Life and Labor* 7 (May 1918): 96–98, 104.

———. "Marriage and Citizenship." *Woman Citizen* 5 (July 2, 1921): 13.

Lee, Muna. "Woman's Place in the Sun." *Independent Woman* 7 (October 1928): 434–436, 475.

Levitt, Albert. "The Domicile of a Married Woman." *Central Law Journal* 91 (July 2–9, 1920): 4–14, 24–33.

"Loss of Citizenship by Marriage." *Iowa Law Bulletin* 2 (May 1916): 137–140.

MacMillan, Chrystal. "Nationality of Married Women: Present Tendencies." *Journal of Comparative Legislation and International Law,* 3d ser., 7 (November 1925): 142–154.

Maguire, John M. "Suffrage and Married Women's Nationality." *American Law Review* 54 (September-October 1920): 641–661.

Matthews, Burnita Shelton. "The Woman without a Country." *Equal Rights* 1 (May 26, 1923): 117–118.

McGerr, Michael. "Political Style and Women's Power, 1830–1930." *Journal of American History* 77 (December 1990): 864–885.

McGovney, D. O. "Race Discrimination in Naturalization." *Iowa Law Bulletin* 8 (March 1923): 129–161.

McWilliams, John Wesley. "Dual Nationality." *American Bar Association Journal* 6 (1920): 204–217.

Miller, David Hunter. "The Hague Codification Conference." *American Journal of International Law* 24 (October 1930): 674–693.

Mussey, Ellen Spencer. "International Marriages." *Daughters of the American Revolution Magazine* 54 (February, 1920): 92–93.

"Naturalization—Status of the Wife of a Naturalized Citizen." *Columbia Law Review* 9 (May 1909): 452.

"Naturalization of Women." *Century Law Journal* 3 (August 4, 1876): 506.

"The New Law." *Woman Citizen* 7 (October 7, 1922): 18.

Nielsen, Fred K. "Some Vexatious Questions Relating to Nationality." *Columbia Law Review* 20 (December 1920): 840–861.

Park, Alice L. "Women Naturalized by Marriage." *Woman's Journal,* July 15, 1911, 224.

Park, Maud Wood. "No Sex in Citizenship." *Woman Citizen* 6 (January 14, 1922): 15–16.

Parker, A. Warner. "The Ineligible to Citizenship Provisions of the Immigration Act of 1924." *American Journal of International Law* 19 (January 1925): 23–47.

———. "The Quota Provisions of the Immigration Act of 1924." *American Journal of International Law* 18 (October 1924): 737–754.

Parker, Cornelia S. "feminists and Feminists: They Join Battle in Paris on the Issue of Protective Laws." *Survey* 56 (August 1,1926): 502–505.

Peffer, George Anthony. "Forbidden Families: Emigration Experiences of Chinese Women under the Page Law, 1875–1882." *Journal of American Ethnic History* 6 (Fall 1986): 28–46.

Pfeffer, Paula F. " 'A Whisper in the Assembly of Nations.' United States' Participation in the International Movement for Women's Rights from the League of Nations to the United Nations." *Women's Studies International Forum* 8, no. 5 (1985): 459–471.

Poe, Elizabeth Ellicott. "America's Greatest Problem." *Daughters of the American Revolution Magazine* 54 (January 1920): 29–33.

"Privilege of Alien Enemies to Inherit under Treaty." *Yale Law Journal* 30 (December 1920): 176–180.

Reeves, Jesse S. "Nationality of Married Women." *American Journal of International Law* 17 (January 1923): 97–100.

"Resolution of the Assembly." *Monthly Summary of the League of Nations* 12 (1932): 308–309.

Richardson, Anna Steese. "The Good Citizenship Bureau." *Woman's Home Companion* 49 (September 1922): 28.

Roche, John P. "The Expatriation Cases: 'Breathes There the Man with Soul So Dead . . . ?' " *Supreme Court Review* (1963): 325–356.

———. "Loss of American Nationality: The Years of Confusion." *Western Political Quarterly* 4 (June 1951): 268–294.

Ruddick, Sara. "Maternal Thinking." *Feminist Studies* 6 (1980): 342–367.

Sapiro, Virginia. "Women, Citizenship, and Nationality: Immigration and Naturalization Policies in the United States." *Politics and Society* 13, no. 1 (1984): 1–26.

Sarvasy, Wendy. "Beyond the Difference versus Equality Policy Debate: Post-suffrage Feminism, Citizenship, and the Quest for a Feminist Welfare State." *Signs* 17 (Winter 1992): 329–362.

Scott, James Brown. "Inter-American Commission of Women." *American Journal of International Law* 24 (October 1930): 757–762.

———. "Unprogressive Codification of Nationality at The Hague." *Women Lawyers' Journal* 18 (April-October 1930): 4–5, 38–43.

Seller, Maxine. "The Education of the Immigrant Woman 1900–1935." *Journal of Urban History* 4 (May 1978): 307–330.

Sewell, Robert. "The Status of American Women Married Abroad." *American Law Review* 26 (May-June 1892): 358–370.

Sherry, Suzanna. "Civic Virtue and the Feminine Voice in Constitutional Adjudication." *Virginia Law Review* 72 (April 1986), 543–616.

"The Significance of the Woman's Party." *Equal Rights* 13 (September 18, 1926): 252.

Smith, Rogers M. " 'One United People': Second-Class Female Citizenship and the American Quest for Community." *Yale Journal of Law & the Humanities* 1 (May 1989): 229–293.

"Some Problems of Wives' Nationality." *Equal Rights* 12 (August 15, 1925): 214–215.

"Standard of Living." *Immigrants in America Review* 1 (March 1915): 45–55.

Stevens, Doris. "Doris Stevens' Plea for Equality." *Equal Rights* 16 (May 10, 1930): 108–109.

———. "International Feminism Is Born." *Time and Tide* (April 13, 1928): 354–355.

Straus, Dorothy. "Recognition Must Begin at Home." *League News: Bulletin of the National League of Women Voters* 5 (December 1931): 1, 4.

"Teaching English to Adult Women." *Survey* 42 (April 26, 1919): 156.

"The Hague—Dr. Wold's Account." *Equal Rights* 16 (August 2, 1930): 203–205.

"Victory for Independent Nationality of Married Women." *Independent Woman* 9 (October 1930): 429.

W.W.S. "Expatriation Resulting from Marriage to Alien Husband." *Michigan Law Review* 14 (January 1916): 233–235.

Walby, Sylvia. "Is Citizenship Gendered?" *Sociology* 28 (May 1994): 379–395.

Walton, Clifford S. "Status of a Wife in International Marriages." *American Law Review* 31 (November-December 1897): 870–875.

Whitehouse, Vira Boarman. "The Immigrant Woman and the Vote." *Immigrants in America Review* 1 (September 1915): 63–69.

"Where the Cable Law Pinches." *Woman Citizen* 7 (January 27, 1923): 15.

"Why Men Become Naturalized." *Interpreter* 8 (December 1929): 156–160.

"Why Worry?" *Woman Citizen* 2 (November 17, 1917): 470.

Wold, Emma. "American Women and the Immigration Law." *Equal Rights* 14 (March 26, 1927): 53.

———. "Hearings on Married Women's Citizenship." *Equal Rights* 13 (April 3, 1926): 62–63.

———. "A Woman Bereft of Country." *Equal Rights* 12 (August 15, 1925): 213–214.

"The Woman Citizen." *Life and Labor* 9 (May 1919): 115.

"Woman Loses Citizenship on Marriage to Alien." *Chicago Legal News* 46 (April 11, 1914): 285.

"Women and Citizenship." *Woman's Journal*, December 24, 1910, 247.

"Women Citizens at Work: The Next Campaign." *Woman Citizen* 6 (December 31, 1921): 18.

"Women Lawyers Ask Equality in Nationality." *Equal Rights* 16 (April 12, 1930): 76–77.

Woodward, Elizabeth A. "Language and Home Links." *Survey* 45 (February 12, 1921): 696–697.

Congressional Documents—United States

59th Cong., 1st sess., 1906. H. Doc. 847. *Compilation from the Records of the Bureau of Immigration of Facts Concerning the Enforcement of the Chinese-Exclusion Acts.*

59th Cong., 2d sess., 1906. H. Doc. 326. *Citizenship of the United States, Expatriation, and Protection Abroad.*

59th Cong., 2d sess., 1907. H. Rept. 6431. *Expatriation of American Citizens and Their Protection Abroad.*

61st Cong., 2d sess., 1910. S. Doc. 196. Dillingham Commission. *Importing Women for Immoral Purposes.*

61st Cong., 2d sess., 1910. S. Doc. 357. *Treaties, Conventions, International Acts, Protocols, and Agreements between the United States of America and Other Powers, 1776–1909.* 2 vols.

61st Cong., 3d sess., 1911. S. Doc. 756. *Statistical Review of Immigration, 1819–1910.*

62d Cong., 1st sess., May 29, July 10 and 11, 1911. Hearings before the House Committee on Rules. *Hearings on House Resolution No. 166 Authorizing the Committee on Immigration and Naturalization to Investigate the Office of Immigration Commissioner at the Port of New York and Other Places.*

62d Cong., 2d sess., serial 2, March 13, 1912. Hearings before the House Committee on the Judiciary. *Woman Suffrage.*

62d Cong., 2d sess., April 17, 1912. Hearings before the House Committee on Foreign Affairs. *Relating to Expatriation of Citizens.*

63d Cong., 2d sess., 1913–1914. S. Doc. 451. *Comments of Labor Department on Bill to Regulate Immigration.*

63d Cong., 2d sess., 1914. H. Rept. 771. *Citizenship of American Women Married to Foreigners.*

65th Cong., 2d sess., December 13, 1917. Hearings before the House Committee on Immigration and Naturalization. *Relative to Citizenship of American Women Married to Foreigners.*

65th Cong., 2d sess., 1918. H. Rept. 285. *To Amend Section 4067, Revised Statutes.*

65th Cong., 2d sess., April 26, 1918. Hearings before the House Committee on the Judiciary. *Limiting Right to Vote to Citizens of the United States.*

66th Cong., 1st sess., October 16, 1919. Hearings before the House Committee on Immigration and Naturalization. *Proposed Changes in Naturalization Laws: Education and Americanization,* pt. 6.

66th Cong., 2d sess., 1920. H. Rept. 846. *Naturalization and Citizenship.*

66th Cong., 2d sess., 1920. H. Rept. 1089. Committee on Interstate and Foreign Commerce. *To Amend Trading with the Enemy Act.*

66th Cong., 2d sess., January 29, February 3, 1920. Hearings before the House Committee on Immigration and Naturalization. *Readmission of Augusta Louise De Haven-Alten to the Status and Privileges of a Citizen of the United States.*

66th Cong., 2d sess., February 28, 1920. Hearings before the House Committee on Immigration and Naturalization. *Proposed Changes in Naturalization Laws.*

66th Cong., 3d sess., 1921. H. Rept. 1185. *Naturalization and Citizenship.*

67th Cong., 1st sess., May 26, 1921. Hearings before the House Committee on Immigration and Naturalization. *Naturalization.*

67th Cong., 1st sess., October 19–22, November 22, 1921. Hearings before the House Committee on Immigration and Naturalization. *Progress and Processes of Naturalization.*

67th Cong., 2d sess., 1922. H. Rept. 710. *Restriction of Immigration.*

67th Cong., 2d sess., 1922. H. Rept. 1110. *Naturalization and Citizenship of Married Women.*

67th Cong., 2d sess., 1922. Unpublished S. Doc. 3. *Citizenship and Naturalization of Married Women. Letter from the Secretary of State to the Chairman of the Committee on Immigration Transmitting Views Relative to the Curtis Bill, and Other Memoranda Bearing on the Curtis and Cable Bills.*

67th Cong., 2d sess., June 8, 1922. Hearings before the House Committee on Immigration and Naturalization. *Naturalization and Citizenship of Married Women.*

67th Cong., 4th sess., 1923. H. Rept. 1621. *Admission of Certain Refugees from Near Eastern Countries and Restriction of Immigration into the United States, Including Revision of the Quota Act.*

68th Cong., 1st sess., 1924. H. Rept. 350. *Restriction of Immigration, with Minority Report.*

68th Cong., 1st sess., 1924. H. Rept. 688. *Immigration of Aliens.*

68th Cong., 1st sess., 1924. H. Rept. 716. *Immigration of Aliens to the United States.*

69th Cong., 1st sess., 1926. H. Rept. 659. *Granting Non-Quota Status to American-Born Women Married to Aliens Prior to the Passage of the Cable Act.*

69th Cong., 1st sess., January 7, 1926. Hearings before the House Committee on Immigration and Naturalization. *Admission of Certain Relatives.*

69th Cong., 1st sess., January 26, 1926. Hearings before the House Committee on Immigration and Naturalization. *Immigration of Relatives of Citizens.*

69th Cong., 1st sess., February 16, 1926. Hearings before the House Committee on Immigration and Naturalization. *Admission of Wives of American Citizens of Oriental Ancestry.*

69th Cong., 1st sess., March 18, 1926. Hearings before the Senate Committee on Immigration. *Admission of Certain Relatives.*

69th Cong., 1st sess., March 23, 1926. Hearings before the House Committee on Immigration and Naturalization. *Immigration and Citizenship of American-Born Women Married to Aliens.*

69th Cong., 1st sess., March 24, 1926. Hearings before a subcommittee of the Senate Committee on Immigration. *Naturalization and Citizenship of Married Women.*

69th Cong., 2d sess., December 9, 1926. Hearings before the Senate Committee on Immigration. *Ratification and Confirmation of Naturalization of Certain Persons of the Hindu Race*, pt. 1.

70th Cong., 1st sess., 1928. H. Rept. 1317. *Relating to the Immigration of Certain Relatives of United States Citizens and Aliens Lawfully Admitted to the United States.*

70th Cong., 1st sess., 1928. H. Rept. 1918. Conference Report. *Grant a Preference to Wives and Minor Children Declarants in the Issuance of Immigration Visas.*

71st Cong., 2d sess., 1930. S. Rept. 442 and H. Rept. 1697. *Amending Cable Act to Permit the Wife of a Native-Born American Citizen and World War Veteran to Join Her Husband in the United States.*

71st Cong., 2d sess., 1930. S. Rept. 556. *Admission of Chinese Wives of Certain American Citizens.*

71st Cong., 2d sess., 1930. S. Rept. 614. *Citizenship and Naturalization of Married Women.*

71st Cong., 2d sess., 1930. H. Rept. 1036. *Citizenship and Naturalization of Married Women.*

71st Cong., 2d sess., 1930. H. Rept. 1504. *Relative to The Hague Conference on the Codification of International Law, and a Declaration of Policy for Both Sexes in Nationality.*

71st Cong., 2d sess., 1930. H. Rept. 1565. *To Admit to the United States Chinese Wives of Certain American Citizens.*

71st Cong., 2d sess., March 6, 1930. Hearings before the House Committee on Immigration and Naturalization. *Amendment to the Women's Citizenship Act of 1922.*

71st Cong., 3d sess., December 17, 1930, January 23, 1931. Hearings before the House Committee on Immigration and Naturalization. *Amendment to the Women's Citizenship Act of 1922, and for Other Purposes.*

71st Cong., 3d sess., 1931. H. Rept. 2693. *Citizenship and Naturalization of Married Women.*

72d Cong., 1st sess., 1932. H. Rept. 1193. *Appeal in Certain Refusals of Immigration Visas.*

72d Cong., 1st sess., 1932. H. Rept. 1193, pt. 2. *Review of Action of Consular Officers in Refusing Immigration Visas.*

72d Cong., 1st sess., 1932. H. Rept. 1753. *Exempt from Quota Husbands of American Citizens.*

72d Cong., 1st sess., December 18, 1931, January 14, 19, 28, 1932. Hearings before the House Committee on Immigration and Naturalization. *To Exempt from the Quota Husbands of American Citizen Wives and to Limit the Presumption That Certain Alien Relatives May Become Public Charges.*

72d Cong., 1st sess., January 7, 1932. Hearings before the House Committee on Immigration and Naturalization. *Relating to Naturalization and Citizenship Status of Certain Children of Mothers Who Are Citizens of the United States, and Relating to the Removal of Certain Distinctions in Matters of Nationality.*

72d Cong., 1st sess., March 16, 1932. Hearings before the House Committee on Immigration and Naturalization. *Review of the Action of Consular Officers in Refusing Immigration Visas.*

72d Cong., 1st sess., April 6, May 7, 1932. Hearings before the Senate Committee on Foreign Relations. *World Court.*

73d Cong., 1st sess., 1933. H. Rept. 131. *Provide Equality in Matters of Citizenship between American Men and American Women and to Clarify Status of Their Children.*

73d Cong., 1st sess., March 28, 1933. Hearings before the House Committee on Immigration and Naturalization. *Relating to Naturalization and Citizenship Status of Children Whose Mothers Are Citizens of the United States and Relating to the Removal of Certain Inequalities in Matters of Nationality.*

73d Cong., 2d sess., March 1934. S. Rept. 865. *Provide Equality in Matter of Citizenship between American Men and Women and to Clarify Status of Their Children.*

73d Cong., 2d sess., March 24, 1934. Hearings before the House Committee on Immigration and Naturalization. *To Amend the Law Relative to Citizenship and Naturalization and for Other Purposes.*

Congressional Record. Washington, D.C. 1906–1934.

Other U.S. Government Publications

Hackworth, Greene Haywood. *Digest of International Law.* Vol. 3. Washington, D.C.: G.P.O., 1942.

Moore, John Bassett. *A Digest of International Law.* Vol. 3. Washington, D.C.: G.P.O., 1906.

———. *History and Digest of the International Arbitrations to Which the United States Has Been a Party.* Vol. 3. Washington, D.C.: G.P.O., 1898.

Nationality Laws of the United States. Message from the President of the United States Transmitting a Report Proposing a Revision and Codification of the Nationality Law of the United States. Pt. 1: *Proposed Code with Explanatory Comments.* Washington, D.C.: G.P.O., 1939.

U.S. Department of Commerce. Bureau of the Census. *Birth, Stillbirth, and Infant Mortality Statistics for . . . 1930.* Washington, D.C.: G.P.O., 1934.

———. *Fifteenth Census of the United States: 1930.* Population. Vol. 2. Washington, D.C.: G.P.O., 1933.

———. Niles Carpenter. *Immigrants and Their Children, 1920. A Study Based on Census Statistics Relative to the Foreign Born and the Native White of Foreign or Mixed Parentage.* Census Monograph 7. Washington, D.C.: G.P.O., 1927.

U.S. Department of Commerce and Labor. *Annual Report of the Department of Commerce and Labor.* Washington, D.C.: G.P.O., 1906–1912.

U.S. Department of Justice. *Administrative Decisions under Immigration & Nationality Laws.* Vol. 1. Washington, D.C.: G.P.O., 1947.

U.S. Department of Labor. *Annual Report of the Secretary of Labor.* Washington, D.C.: G.P.O., 1912–1932.

U.S. Department of Labor. Bureau of Immigration. *Annual Report of the Commissioner General of Immigration.* Washington, D.C.: G.P.O., 1922–1932.

U.S. Department of Labor. Immigration and Naturalization Service. *Visa Petitions.* Lecture 5. March 13, 1934.

——. D. W. MacCormick. *Naturalization Requirements Concerning Race, Education, Residence, Good Moral Character, and Attachment to the Constitutions.* Lecture 8. March 26, 1934.

——. Leigh L. Nettleton. *Loss of Citizenship (Expatriation) and Presumptive Loss of Citizenship.* Lecture 27. December 17, 1924.

U.S. Department of State. *Admission of Aliens into the United States.* Washington, D.C.: G.P.O., September 30, 1925.

——. *Papers Relating to the Foreign Relations of the United States* [title varies]. 1861–1934.

——. *Report of the Delegates of the United States of America to the Seventh International Conference of American States. Montevideo, Uruguay, December 3–26, 1933.* Washington, D.C.: G.P.O., 1934.

——. *Report of the Delegation of the United States of America to the Eighth International Conference of American States. Lima, Peru. December 9–27, 1938.* Washington, D.C.: G.P.O., 1941.

——. *State Dept. Press Releases, Jan. 4–June 28, 1930.* Washington, D.C.: G.P.O., 1930.

——. Cordell Hull. *Addresses and Statements by the Honorable Cordell Hull . . . in Connection with the Eighth Conference of American States.* Washington, D.C.: G.P.O., 1940.

U.S. Department of the Interior, Bureau of Education, Americanization Division. "Connecticut's Plans for Women." *Americanization Bulletin* (October 1, 1919).

U.S. National Commission on Law Observance and Enforcement. Reuben Oppenheimer. "The Administration of the Deportation Laws of the United States." In *Report on the Deportation Laws of the United States,* Commission Report 5. Washington, D.C.: G.P.O., 1931.

League of Nations and United Nations Publications

League of Nations. *Acts of the Conference for the Codification of International Law, Mar. 13–Apr. 12, 1930.* Vol. 1: *Plenary Meetings.* C.351.M.145.1930.V. 1930.

——. *Acts of the Conference for the Codification of International Law, Mar. 13–Apr. 12, 1930.* Vol. 2: *Meetings of the Committees.* C.351(a).M.145(a).1930.V. 1930.

——. *Conference for the Codification of International Law. Bases of Discussion.* Supp. to Vol. 1: *Nationality.* C.73.M.38.1929.V. 1929.

————. *Conference for the Codification of International Law. Final Act of the Conference for the Codification of International Law.* C.228.M.115.1930.V. 1930.

————. *Convention Concerning Certain Questions Relating to the Conflict of Nationality Laws.* C.224.M.111.1930.V. 1930.

————. *Nationality and Status of Women.* A.19.1935.V. 1935.

————. *Nationality of Women. Report by the Secretary General.* A.19.1931.V. 1931.

————. *Nationality of Women.* A.84.1931.V. 1931.

————. *Nationality of Women.* A.61.1932.V. 1932.

————. *Nationality of Women.* A.53.1935.V. 1935.

————. *Official Journal. Special Supplement No. 64. Records of the Ninth Session of the Assembly, Plenary Meetings.* 1928.

————. Progressive Codification of International Law. Resolutions of Eighth Assembly, Sept. 27, 1927. A.133.1927.V. 1927.

————. Committee of Experts for the Progressive Codification of International Law, Subcommittee on Nationality. *Report Submitted by M. Rundstein and Approved by M. De Megalhaes.* October 8, 1925. C.43.M.18.1926.V. 1926.

U.N. Commission on the Status of Women. *Nationality of Married Women (Report Submitted by the Secretary General).* Doc. E/CN.6/254. 1954.

U.N. Department of Economic and Social Affairs. *Convention on the Nationality of Married Women. Historical Background and Commentary.* Doc. E/CN.6/389. 1962.

U.S. Statutes

(1 Stat. 103), Act of March 26, 1790.

(1 Stat. 414), Act of January 29, 1795.

(2 Stat. 153), Act of April 14, 1802.

(10 Stat. 604), Act of February 10, 1855.

(15 Stat. 223), Act of July 27, 1868.

(16 Stat. 255), Act of July 14, 1870.

(18 Stat. 477), Act of March 3, 1875.

(22 Stat. 58), Act of May 6, 1882.

(23 Stat. 332), Act of February 26, 1885.

(24 Stat. 414), February 23, 1887.

(25 Stat. 392), Act of August 9, 1888.

(25 Stat. 476), Act of September 13, 1888.

(27 Stat. 25), Act of May 5, 1892.

(28 Stat. 7), Act of November 3, 1893.

(28 Stat. 390), Act of August 18, 1894.

(30 Stat. 1496), Act of May 18, 1898.

(32 Stat. 1213), Act of March 3, 1903.

(34 Stat. 596), Act of June 29, 1906.

(34 Stat. 898), Act of February 20, 1907.

(34 Stat. 1228), Act of March 2, 1907.
(36 Stat. 263), Act of March 26, 1910.
(36 Stat. 929), Act of February 24, 1911.
(37 Stat. 356), Act of August 22, 1912.
(39 Stat. 874), Act of February 5, 1917.
(39 Stat. 951), Act of March 2, 1917.
(40 Stat. 885), Act of July 9, 1918.
(41 Stat. 981), Act of June 5, 1920.
(42 Stat. 5), Act of May 19, 1921.
(42 Stat. 1021), Act of September 22, 1922.
(43 Stat. 153), Act of May 26, 1924.
(44 Stat. 654), Act of May 26, 1926.
(44 Stat. 812), Act of July 3, 1926.
(45 Stat. 789), Act of May 28, 1928.
(45 Stat. 1009), Act of May 29, 1928.
(46 Stat. 581), Act of June 13, 1930.
(46 Stat. 849), Act of July 3, 1930.
(46 Stat. 1511), Act of March 3, 1931.
(47 Stat. 656), Act of July 11, 1932.
(48 Stat. 797), Act of May 24, 1934.
(48 Stat. 1245), Act of June 27, 1934.
(49 Stat. 1917), Act of June 25, 1936.
(54 Stat. 715), Act of July 2, 1940.
(54 Stat. 1137), Act of October 14, 1940.
(54 Stat. 1159), Act of January 13, 1941.
(54 Stat. 1170), Act of August 16, 1940.
(60 Stat. 975), Act of August 9, 1946.
(61 Stat. 401), Act of July 22, 1947.
(66 Stat. 163), Act of June 27, 1952.
(79 Stat. 911), Act of October 3, 1965.

Legal Cases

Afroyim v. Rusk, 387 U.S. 253 (1967).
Ainslie v. Martin, 9 Mass. 454 (1813).
Anderson v. Watt, 138 U.S. 694 (1891).
Banning v. Penrose, 255 F. 159 (1919).
Beck v. McGillis, 9 Barb. 35 (N.Y. 1850).
Bland v. United States, 42 F.2d 842 (1930).
Bradwell v. Illinois, 83 U.S. 130 (1873).
Broadis v. Broadis et al., 86 F. 951 (1898).
Burkett v. McCarty, 73 Ky. 758 (1866).
Burton v. Burton, 1 Keyes 359 (N.Y. 1864).
Campbell v. Gordon, 10 U.S. 176 (1810).
Chan Shee et al., Ex parte, 2 F.2d 995 (1924).

Chang Chan, Wong Hung Kay, Yee Sin Jung et al. v. Nagle, 268 U.S. 346 (1925).

Cheung Sum Shee et al. v. Nagle, 268 U.S. 336 (1925).

Cheung Sum Shee et al., Ex parte, 2 F.2d 995 (1924).

Chiu Shee, Ex parte, 1 F.2d 798 (1924).

Chung Fook v. White, 264 U.S. 443 (1924).

Chy Lung v. Freeman et al., 92 U.S. 275 (1875).

Comitis v. Parkerson et al., 56 F. 556 (1893).

Davies, In re, 53 F. Supp. 426 (1944).

Dorsey v. Brigham, 177 Ill. 250 (1898).

Dorto v. Clark, 300 F. 568 (1924).

Dred Scott v. Sandford, 19 How. 393 (U.S. 1857).

Findan, In re, 4 F. Supp. 189 (1933).

Fitzroy, In re, 4 F.2d 541 (1925).

(Ng) Fung Sing, Ex parte, 6 F.2d 670 (1925).

Girouard v. United States, 328 U.S. 61 (1946).

Gomez v. Nagle, 6 F.2d 520 (1925).

Goon Dip et al., Ex parte, 1 F.2d 811 (1924).

Gorelick et al., Ex parte, 296 F. 572 (1924).

Halsey v. Beer, 5 N.Y. Supp. 334 (1889).

Headman v. Rose et al., 63 Ga. 458 (1879).

Hopkins v. Fachant, 130 F. 839 (1904).

Hughes v. Techt, 188 N.Y. App. Div. 743 (1919).

Kane v. McCarthy, 63 N. C. 299 (1869).

Kaplan v. Tod, 267 U.S. 228 (1925).

Kaprielian, Ex parte, 188 F. 694 (1910).

Keller v. United States, 213 U.S. 138 (1909).

Kelly v. Owen et al., 74 U.S. 496 (1868).

Kennedy v. Mendoza-Martinez, 372 U.S. 144 (1963).

Keshishian et al., In re, 299 F. 804 (1924).

Krausmann, In re, 28 F.2d 1004 (1928).

Kwock Seu [sic] Lum, Ex parte, 287 F. 363 (1922).

Lazarus, In re, 24 F.2d 243 (1928).

Leong Shee, Ex parte, 275 F. 364 (1921).

Look Tin Sing, In re, 21 F. 905 (1884).

Low Wah Suey v. Backus, 225 U.S. 460 (1912).

Luhrs v. Eimer, 80 N.Y. 171 (1880).

Luria v. United States, 231 U.S. 9 (1913).

Lynch, In re, 31 F.2d 762 (1929).

Macintosh v. United States, 42 F.2d 845 (1930).

Mackenzie v. Hare, 165 Cal. 776 (1913). *Mackenzie v. Hare*, 239 U.S. 299 (1915).

Martorana, In re, 159 F. 1010 (1908).

Moore v. Tisdale, 5 B. Mon. 352 (Ky. 1845).

Nishimura Ekiu v. United States, 142 U.S. 651 (1891).

Page, In re, 12 F.2d 135 (1926).

Pequignot v. Detroit, 16 F. 211 (1883).

Perez v. Brownell, 356 U.S. 44 (1958).

Perkins et al. v. Elg, 307 U.S. 325 (1939).

Pezzi, In re, 29 F.2d 999 (1928).

Renner v. Muller, 57 How. Pr. 229 (N.Y. 1880).

Rogers v. Bellei, 401 U.S. 815 (1971).

Rojak v. Marshall, 34 F.2d 219 (1929).

Ruckgaber v. Moore, 104 F. 947 (1900).

Rustigian, In re, 165 F. 980 (1909).

Ryder et al. v. Bateman, 93 F. 16 (1898).

Shanks v. DuPont, 3 Peters 242 (U.S. 1830).

Shelley v. Jordan, 106 F.2d 1016 (1939).

Shelley v. United States, 120 F.2d 734 (1941).

Smith v. United States ex rel. Grisius, 58 F.2d 1 (1932).

Sutliff v. Forgey, 1 Cowen 89 (N.Y. 1821).

Takao Ozawa v. United States, 260 U.S. 178 (1922).

Takuji Yamashita v. Hinkle, 260 U.S. 199 (1922).

Talbot v. Jansen, 3 Dall. 133 (U.S. 1795).

Techt v. Hughes, 229 N.Y. 222 (1920).

Terrazas v. Vance, 577 F.2d 7 (1978) and 444 U.S. 252 (1980).

Tinker v. Colwell, 193 U.S. 473 (1904).

Trimbles v. Harrison et al., 1 B. Mon. 140 (Ky. 1840).

Trop v. Dulles, 356 U.S. 86 (1958).

Tsoi Sim v. United States, 116 F. 920 (1902).

United States v. Bland, 283 U.S. 636 (1931).

United States v. Cohen, 179 F. 834 (1910).

United States v. Dorto, 5 F.2d 596 (1925).

United States v. Eliasen, 11 F.2d 785 (1926).

United States v. Mrs. Gue Lim et al., 176 U.S. 459 (1900).

United States v. Humphrey, 29 F.2d 736 (1928).

United States v. Kellar, 13 F. 82 (1882).

United States v. Macintosh, 283 U.S. 605 (1931).

United States v. Martin, 10 F.2d 585 (1925).

United States v. Martorana, 171 F. 397 (1909).

United States v. Schwimmer, 279 U.S. 644 (1929).

United States v. Thind, 261 U.S. 204 (1923).

United States v. Wong Kim Ark, 169 U.S. 649 (1898).

United States ex rel. Anderson v. Howe, 231 F. 546 (1916).

United States ex rel. Bosny et al. v. Williams, 185 F. 599 (1911).

United States ex. rel. Gendering v. Williams, 173 F. 626 (1909)

United States ex rel. Nicola v. Williams, 173 F. 626 (1909).

United States ex rel. Sejnensky v. Tod, 285 F. 523 (1922).

United States ex rel. Ulrich v. Kellogg, 30 F.2d 984 (1929).

United States ex rel. Ulrich v. Stimson, 279 U.S. 868 (1929).

Wallenburg v. Missouri Pacific Railway Co., 159 F. 217 (1908).

Ware v. Wisner, 50 F. 310 (1883).

Whiting v. Stevens, 4 Conn. 44 (1821).

Windle, In re, 2 Edw. Ch. 585 (N.Y. 1836).
Wohlgemuth, In re, 35 F.2d 1007 (1929).
Wright, In re, 19 F. Supp. 224 (1937).
Zartarian v. Billings, 204 U.S. 170 (1907).
Zogbaum, Petition of, 32 F.2d 911 (1929).

Index

Abbott, Edith, 164
Abeldt-Fricker, Elisabeth, 27–28, 29
Absentee citizen population, 167n, 224–26, 224–25nn74–75
ACLU. *See* American Civil Liberties Union (ACLU)
Adams, Mildred, 237
Addams, Jane, 52n18, 183, 186, 191
African Americans, 17, 17n3, 135n58
Afroyim v. Rusk, 243n
Ainslie v. Martin, 66n49
Alien Enemy Act, 72n63
Alien Property Custodian, 68, 72n64, 78
All-Asian Conference of Women, 219, 246
American Association of University Women, 87, 89, 166n24, 169
American Civil Liberties Union (ACLU), 186, 189–90
American Federation of Labor, 169, 229, 230
American Home Economics Association, 166n24, 169
American Indians, 17n3, 255
American Institute of International Law, 204, 204n19, 205n21, 219n61, 227, 229, 238
American Legion Women's Auxiliary, 184
American Society for International Law, 106, 106n61, 139n70, 205

American University School of Law. *See* Washington College of Law
Americanization movement, 46–47, 50–56, 50n, 51n16, 52n18, 75, 82, 91–92, 94–96, 156, 164–65
Americans living abroad, 167n, 224–26, 224–25nn74–75. *See also* Expatriation
Americans married to foreign born. *See* Transnational marriages
Anderson, Mary, 199, 248n11
Anthony, Daniel R., 84
Anthony (Nineteenth) Amendment. *See* Nineteenth Amendment
Anthony bill, 84–85
Ashby, Margery Corbett, 220n63

Bacon, Robert, 137, 137n64
Bacon bill, 137n64
Baker, Abby Scott, 180
Balch, Emily Greene, 186
Baldwin, Roger, 190
Bankhead, William B., 239
Banning v. Penrose, 99n
Barrett, Kate Waller, 73
Beck v. McGillis, 19n
Beecher, Catharine, 52
Bell-Bielski, Ruth, 178
Belmont, Alva, 138, 148n94, 151, 205, 215
Bennet, William, 41
Berger, Victor, 121
Berrien, Laura M., 227

Compositor: J. Jarrett Engineering, Inc.
Text and Display: Galliard
Printer and Binder: Thomson-Shore, Inc.